The Altar of Love, Part II

By

Francis Santarose

Bulabu Publishing, LLC   New Mexico

The Altar of Love, Part II
By Francis Santarose

Copyright and trademark notice

This publication is owned and operated by Bulabu Publishing, LLC. Unless otherwise indicated, all materials in this publication, such as text, graphics, logos, images, photographs, are the copyrighted property of Bulabu Publishing, LLC. Bulabu Publishing, LLC, The Altar of Love II it's symbols and other marks, are trademarks of Bulabu Publishing, LLC. You may not modify, copy, reproduce, publish, transmit, distribute, or make other use of any of the materials obtained from this publication. You may utilize material from this publication for personal and non-commercial use only, provided that you keep intact all trademarks, copyright and other proprietary notices.

Release and indemnification

Points of view or opinions expressed in this book are those of the author and do not necessarily represent the positions or policies of any governing body. This publication is for informational purposes only and should not be used as a substitute for medical or other professional advice. If professional advice or other expert assistance is required, the services of a competent professional should be sought to address the particular circumstances.

Disclaimer

The views represented by Mr. Francis Santarose are for the purpose of providing useful information. The author makes no guarantee that by utilizing the information provided herein, one's healing is guaranteed, only that suggestive information can be accessed herein. This book is sold with the understanding that it is not meant to offer or replace medical advice. Bulabu Publishing, LLC makes no representation or warranties with respect to the accuracy or the completeness of the contents of this book, specifically disclaims any implied warranties of merchantability for any particular purpose, and shall in no event be liable for any loss of profit or any other commercial damages, including but not limited to, special, incidental, consequential, or other damages. The author encourages you to always consult with a professional regarding specific medical, health, and welfare.

Copyright © 2020 by Bulabu Publishing, LLC. All rights reserved worldwide.

Copyright © 2020 by Francis Santarose

All rights reserved

Published in The United States by Bulabu Publishing, LLC, New Mexico

Santarose, Francis

Includes Bible references

ISBN: 978-0-9815439-7-0

Printed in the United States of America

The Altar of Love, Part II

Table of Contents

Chapter 1 – Preface	8
Jesus Revealed	9
Justified	22
In Context	24
Walking without offense	28
Chapter 2 – Leg 1 – Identity	43
Father God	57
Trees in the Garden of Eden	63
Go home and don't look back	78
The little foxes	81
A believer's identity	87
By His stripes	89
Friend of God	99
God is Love	100
Spirit of Adoption	104
Questioning one's identity	114
Be transformed	116
Chapter 3 – Leg 2 - Righteousness	124
Righteousness delivers from death	125
Righteousness is the key	135

A heart to love	151
Sin	153
No longer a slave to sin	158
False conversions	161
Freedom from legalism	170
Righteousness & Grace	172
Obedience vs. Works	176
Repentance	191
Die to Self	194
Christian Martyrs	206
Chapter 4 – Leg 3 - Holy Spirit	**208**
Jesus, the homeowner and the devil	208
The Helper	210
Demon spirits	212
The Spirit of Truth	218
Zoe Life	228
Atheism	236
Receive the Holy Spirit	237
What are you asking for?	242
Another Advocate	257
Perfect Love	262
God has not given us a spirit of fear	267
Clothed with Power	270
Make disciples	276

5 Fold Ministry	277
Spirit of Grace & Truth	283
The Grace of God	283
The Truth	284
Self-Righteousness	286
Workers of Lawlessness	289
Tribulation	293
Our Weaponry	296
Old Testament Spirit vs. New Testament Spirit	303
Elisha receives a double portion of the Holy Spirit	306
We were made to house the Spirit of God	309
Kingdom Fruit	309
Take up Snakes	312
Good Gifts	314
Baptism of Fire	317
Chapter 5 – Leg 4 – Power & Authority	**321**
Power to do the Miraculous	323
Righteousness is superior to Power & Authority	327
Power & Authority has its place in the Kingdom	330
Fire from Heaven	333
Simon the Sorcerer	340
Power in the gifts of the Holy Spirit	344
"Ask and it shall be given..."	354
Miracles	354

Authority	358
Who do you resemble?	364
5 Things that hand over your authority	371
1. Do nothing	371
2. Practicing sin	374
3. Your words	378
4. Selfishness	381
5. Witchcraft of the heart	382
Authority misconceptions	385
After the cross	388
Parable of the growing seed	391
Prayer begins where Authority ends	393
Chapter 6 – All 4 Legs of the Altar	**397**
King Solomon	400
The Disciples	402
King David	405
How All 4 Legs of the Altar Fit Together	407
Chapter 7 – Transformation	**419**
Discipleship	420
Sin Conscious vs. Son Conscious	421
Treasures in Heaven	422
The Guilt of Sin or Apathy Towards It	435
About the Author	447

Altar of Love, Part II

Chapter 1

Preface

*...For **it is time for judgment to begin with the family of God**; and if it begins with us, **what will the outcome be for those who disobey the gospel of God?** ¹⁸And, <u>**"If it is hard for the righteous to be saved, what will become of the ungodly and the sinner?"**</u> ¹⁹So then, those who suffer according to God's will should entrust their souls to their faithful Creator **and continue to do good....***
1 Peter 4:18

Let me begin by saying, I love you and whether you agree or disagree with my revelation; I want absolutely nothing from you other than you standing next to me in the Kingdom. I wish only the best for each and every one of you.

As with the Altar of Love Part I, I am not looking to make anybody dependent upon me, but the One who died for each of us, Jesus. My mission here is for you to become the best son or daughter He created you to be, and He created you to be like Him. He made us in His image, and He came into His creation to restore that which was lost. Most people automatically assume that what was lost was our salvation, and that is true; however, Jesus came to restore so much more than just salvation.

Shortly thereafter, man no longer appeared as a creation in the image of God, instead, we took on the likeness of Satan to such an extent that we looked, talked, behaved and thought just like the devil. God's children no longer resembled His children, but looked like the wicked one who betrayed Him.

Along with losing his identity and his right-standing with God, Adam handed over his authority, the dominion that God had given Him. The legal right to rule and rein as Kings and Queens over the earth and everything in it was delivered to Satan on that fateful day. As we learned in the Altar of Love Part I, Satan used authority to rule the earth with an iron fist for the next 4000 years.

Jesus Revealed

I think it's important, when reading your Bible, whether in the Old Testament or New, that you look for Jesus to be revealed everywhere, even in the most obscure places and ways. Next, we should be looking for Jesus in our daily lives as well, not just in our Bibles. Finally, when we look in the mirror, we should see Jesus looking back at us.

> *So all of us who have had that veil removed can see and reflect the glory of the Lord. And the Lord—who is the Spirit—makes us more and more like Him as we are changed into His glorious image.* 2 Corinth 3:18

From what I have learned by helping set people free from demonical influence usually brought about by sin, the biggest hindrance for not being able to see and receive that they have been set free is that they don't like what they see when they look in the mirror. They have not come to terms with the fact that they have been set free as a result of their unbelief. I have done cases with dozens of mature Christians that still suffer from the bondage of low self-esteem brought about by the sin of their past and present, but the only reason it had any power over them whatsoever was their lack of identity. Furthermore, they've never even considered seeking righteousness and thus have never really had an encounter with the Holy Spirit, but if you read this and get a hold of what the Lord has shown me, you will never be intimidated, rejected or sense fear again. You will never be condemned, guilty or ashamed again, and neither will you be brought to a place of regret ever again.

> *Godly sorrow brings repentance that leads to salvation without regret, but worldly sorrow brings death.* 2 Corinthians 7:10

Our Father sees our potential, and He knows what we are capable of if we ever get out of our own way, submit to Him and allow Him to cohabitate with us. That is why He gives us until the day we die to judge us for our life's work. What about you; what do you see when you look in the mirror? Even if you are not where you want to be, do you see your own potential? Can you see past the faults to the awesome potential of God available to you? What about others, do you see the potential of an almighty God when you look at other people as well?

> *So, from now on we regard no one according to the flesh.* 2 Corinthians 5:16

What this means is that we are not supposed to look at and judge people by what we see, by their appearance or by their past or present behavior. We are required to look at and see and judge them according to their created value, and the way their Father sees them. This is an extremely mature way to think and behave and it requires a very mature believer to do so. It's remarkable, however, that even mature believers who can see others in this way, have a difficult time seeing themselves the way their Father sees them. They can judge others by the spirit, but they judge themselves by the flesh.

Jesus paid a very steep price to make us free from guilt, shame, condemnation and regret. He paid a price for us to never want to walk in willful sin. The price He paid on the cross was so valuable that, if understood, one should never want to sin and get away with it again. I know it sounds impossible, but I promise if you stay with me till the end of this book you will see that our Father not only wants you to walk without willful sin, He expects you too as well. Don't freak out, however, because your Father would never set you up for failure, with the expectation to walk righteously as He is righteous, He will provide you the power and ability through His Spirit to do just that. Assuming that His Spirit is the Spirit residing within you.

The gospel says that we can have freedom.

> *Therefore, whom the Son sets free, is free indeed.* John 8:36

It is not future tense; it does not say we will be free when we get to Heaven. Why? Because you don't need freedom then, you need it now. You need to be free from your past, your present, your sin and even yourself. Jesus came to give us abundant life, but the thief comes to kill, steel and destroy. Many of the false doctrine of men are given to them by the enemy to undermine the simplistic message of the Gospel and destroy the temple of the Lord, the Children of God.

When I got saved, my pastor never told me that I was bound or that I was the way I was because of something attached to me. He just kept telling me that I was free; free to seek the Kingdom of God and His righteousness so I could bask in the glory of His freedom. I believe that is the main reason why I am as grounded as I am, because I know who I am, whose I am and what I was created to be; a carbon copy of my Father as expressed by the life and Image of Jesus. He never told me that I was messed up because I was in the world for 30 years, he just kept telling me I was a child of my Father and I had the mind of Christ.

When my Father began using me for healing, He showed me the root cause of many of the sicknesses and illnesses that people suffer from. It was a process called the Altar of Love which begins by teaching a correct understanding of one's Identity as a Child of God, one's Authority as a Child of God, the critical importance of speaking life into every situation by the power of your words and the power of walking in Love. With that understanding, we then use our authority to chase off any demonic strongholds left behind. After dozens and dozens of cases, I have seen and witnessed hundreds of miracles and countless people set free.

And just when I thought I had it all figured out, the Father began showing me another side of His church, the unchurched believers, the mischurched believers and the deceived believers. Most notably those who have been misled by cunningly slick prosperity peddlers and the OSAS den of thieves. The unchurched believers are hungry orphans bound in denominationalism and learning nothing because it is the blind leading the blind. The mischurched are those who deny the promises and gifts of the Father because their leaders have no faith and are afraid to be exposed as frauds if they ever step out of the boat and attempt to believe. The deceived are the followers of the OSAS and the prosperity preachers. For those new to the saying, OSAS stands for Once Saved-Always Saved. It may very well be called the ministry of sin, because it basically teaches and believes that you can sin all you want and it is perfectly fine with God, because when you were 10, you said a sinner's prayer.

The originators of this false doctrine and most of those that are teaching it are no more than wolves in sheep clothing, and regardless of their intent, they have left the church in shambles. The Altar of Love part I was a process designed to remove the yoke and bondage brought about by a lifetime of willful sin so as to free believers to rightly become Children of God. After the completion of my book and several years of successful case studies, I began to feel the urge to go even deeper than ever before. That is when I awoke one morning and I heard an audible voice say, "Righteousness, study righteousness and teach it."

As the Father began showing me and teaching me about righteousness, I softly heard Him say, *"If my children had a proper understanding of their identity,*

of their son-ship and righteousness, there would be no need for an Altar of Love. My sheep have been misled; deceived by greedy pastors heaping up lie after lie. It's one false doctrine after another designed to make my sheep codependent upon these wolves in sheep's clothing for the sole purpose of filling their coffers with money and worldly possessions as well as bragging rights about who has the larger church. There are only a few preaching the simplicity of the gospel, the ministry of reconciliation and righteousness now. 2000 years after the cross, the church no longer looks like my sheep but like goats that belong to a different shepherd."

> *For certain men have crept in among you unnoticed—ungodly men, turning the grace of our God into a license for sin...* Jude 1:4

My first pastor, Jim Scalise was the worst kind of reprobate, dying in prison with 17 life sentences, he was miraculously healed and all charges against him dropped on a technicality. If you met him, however, you would have never know he had that past, because Jesus, by virtue and power of the Holy Spirit took Jim's entire personality, his worldly past and washed him in the blood, thereby removing all of it from him in an instant. Now I know it does not always work like that, sometimes it takes time, but I promise you this, that if you seek first the Kingdom of God and His Righteousness, He will perform the same kind of change in you.

I would best describe Jim as a child. He had childlike faith, in that, he just believed. He was a believing believer who believed his Father and he never compromised his belief. If he prayed for someone, he just believed it would happen, and it was my experience that pretty much everyone he prayed for received what they needed. It was the most remarkable thing to witness, and it never ceased to amaze me regardless of how many times it happened, and I dare say it was in the hundreds if not the thousands. And just how important is it to have childlike faith?

> *Jesus said, "I tell you the truth, unless you turn from your sins and become like little children, you will never get into the Kingdom of Heaven.* Matthew 18:3

We need to be childlike. A child trusts until they are taught not to trust or until they are deceived, but our Father will never deceive us, deception is always from the enemy; he comes to steal, kill and destroy, and he is the liar and the father of all lies. It is a superpower in and of itself to be young at heart, young in faith; not in maturity of age, but in our attitude of trust towards our Father. Just as a child believes his parents when they tell him a big fat man brought his bicycle down a 6 inch hole in the chimney, we are to believe that whatever we speak with our mouth and believe in our hearts, these things will come to pass.

Maturity does not come with the number of years you've been a Christian or how many Bible studies you have led. Maturity doesn't come just because you are an elder or on the board of directors of a ministry. Many board members are there because they have money and for no other reason. I'm not putting down being an elder or a board member, if you are one, congratulations. I'm also not saying if you are an elder that you are immature; if you are an elder or board member, that is awesome, God established such things for the proper function of the church, but those things do not make someone mature. Sometimes elders are chosen because nobody else volunteered. I am not against church leadership, but we cannot confuse a title with someone's walk with Jesus.

Maturity comes when you trust and believe every Word of God that you put inside you, the Word you actually walk out. Maturity comes when you are seasoned in righteousness and walk in love. For a Christian believer to function normally in the body of Christ, they must be rooted and grounded in love and their right standing with God. In the Old Testament it was what you had to do to be right with God, but now that Jesus has come, it's who you have become that makes you right with God. It's not what you do, it's who you be. You can't do anything to be righteous; righteousness is who you become if you are the righteousness of God the Father in Christ Jesus.

*God made Him who knew no sin to be sin on our behalf, so that in Him we **might become** the righteousness of God.*
2 Corinth 5:21

Might become – Strong's #1096 *gínomai* (ghin'-om-ahee)- to come into being, to become. I come into being, am born, become like. Properly, *transitioning* from one condition to another. It's **not** "to be," or *will be*, it is not future tense. It's present tense.

That's exactly what happened to my Pastor; he "became" like Jesus in a moment and walked as a little child in faith. But if you do not know what you *"might become,"* you will constantly try to *"do"* to *"be"* what you are unable to *"be"* by doing in your own power, but never receiving what He has done for you to empower you. You will try to *"do"* to please God and *"do"* to be approved, yet; thankfully we were not created to have to do anything in our own strength. "Doing to be" is not just a wrong way of thinking; it brings frustration and discouragement which leads to complaining, rebellion and all manner of ungodly thoughts and deeds. "Doing to be" is a works mentality and all of it will be burned up in the Day of Judgment.

If Christians try to *"do"* to *"be,"* they will try to **do** miracles to **be** noticed by men. They will do miracles to try to validate their right-standing with God, and the devil would love nothing more than for you to do things in order to prove who you are instead of just being who God has created you to be. Son-ship by adoption is the priority and the Spirit of Adoption has been afforded to all men who choose to be discipled by the Holy Spirit. To be adopted by the Father is an amazing offer, a once-in-a-lifetime privilege that you have the rest of your life to obtain. Do not postpone this offer though, because today is the day of salvation, and you never know when it is your time, so make a decision today, make it now, give your life to Jesus right now and submit to His authority, His rule forevermore. If you have already done so, but have allowed life to come in and dethrone Jesus as your priority, I urge you to recommit your life to Him now.

Our Father is a good, good Father. He is the best dad ever, and He knows exactly how to Father us, and He will too, as long as you seek His righteousness, His ways, His thoughts, His Son, His Kingdom and His Holy Spirit. God is love and the reality of the love of God is to know and be filled with the fullness of His love that is in Christ Jesus. It was the simplicity of the finished work of the cross that enabled even Peter to be set free from guilt for rejecting Jesus. It was transformation by way of the cross that saw Paul walk with boldness, not condemnation, even after murdering Steven. If you cannot see the simplicity that is in the Gospel of Christ as He reveals your new identity, then you should not move on from here until you do. To move ahead without a solid foundation in your identity and what Jesus accomplished on the cross to free you from, to move ahead without that understanding is to build your house on an unlevel foundation and the result is a crooked house. That house, your house will be fine as long as the weather is good, but as soon as a storm comes, it is destined to fall.

In this world you will have trouble. But take heart! I have overcome the world." John 16:33

If you do not see the simplicity of the gospel that enabled Peter and Paul to be free from guilt and shame, one day, when tragedy happens and things don't go as you hope, your lack of identity will expose your unbelief. Then you will do what most people do, you will blame God…they all do. They say, "He did it to me" or "He allowed it to happen," and offense will take root in your heart and the devil will have a field day with you and all that is precious to you. I venture to say that 95% of all people, Christians and non-Christians are angry with God in one way or another and all because they did not heed the #1 thing Jesus said to do, *"Seek ye first the Kingdom of God and His Righteousness."*

Jesus is the chief cornerstone and we are the righteousness of our Father in Him, because Jesus righteously walked out all 613 laws of Moses and all 10 Commandments. This Jesus who knew no sin became sin so that we might become righteousness. That is not to say that we had to do anything to become righteousness, all we have to do to obtain it is believe in what He did on our behalf and receive it. The only thing our Father expects from us, the only thing He wants from us is to believe, and in our believing, we submit and surrender all. Christians quote James 4:7 constantly, but this only proves the point that I'm always making about taking scripture out of context or leaving out parts that are difficult to understand or don't line up with their doctrine.

> ***Resist the devil,*** *and he will flee from you.* James 4:7

But look at the part they conveniently leave off because it doesn't fit their narrative.

> ***Submit yourselves to God.*** *Resist the devil, and he will flee from you.* James 4:7

Will you look at that, they conveniently leave off the *"submit to God"* part, but if you really want to do this correctly, read the entire section.

> ***Draw near to God*** *and He will draw near to you. Submit yourselves to God. Resist the devil, and he will flee from you.* ***Cleanse your hands, you sinner's, and purify your hearts, you double-minded....*** James 4:6

If you draw near to Him, He will draw near to you, if you seek Him, He will find you, and in doing so, if you submit to Him, His authority, His rule, His righteousness, He will empower you to resist the devil. Resistance is found in your submission. Not that He expects you to do it in your own strength; He knows you cannot. God watched for thousands of years as His children floundered in the Law of Moses, which is also known as the law of condemnation, trying desperately to do it in their own strength.

Righteousness will empower you with the ability to resist the devil which will make him flee from you because you will no longer be his slave to sin. Sin brings with it condemnation and condemnation brings separation from the Father. Not that He separates from you, no, your guilt, your shame will separate you from Him. Just as a friend avoids another friend due to guilt when he has borrowed money and cannot pay it back, likewise, do we avoid our Father when we walk in willful sin.

Submit – Strong's #5239 (hoop-ot-as'-so) To place or rank under, to subject, to obey. I place under, subject to, I submit to, I put myself into subjection.

Submit to God is implying a conscious choice, a willingness to give up your own wants, needs and desires. It's wanting what Gods wants for you, in place of what you want for you. It is another way of saying, "die to yourself" and let God be Lord of your life. James caps it all off by commanding them to stop sinning and purify their hearts, calling them double-minded.

Just as a proper understanding of your identity enables you to develop and grow into an accurate portrayal of your Father, a correct understanding of your authority enables you to recognize and realize that you were not created to run scared or afraid of the devil any more. James is accurately portraying how this plays out if you seek your Father and His righteousness. When you finally decide to seek Him, and if you are willing to submit and obey Him, the devil will flee from you. The last thing the devil wants is to pick a fight with a Child of God, who understands what it means to be a child, a Child of God in authority! Authority is a real-life superpower, your superpower, a superpower that the devil has been stealing from you, from all of us, even Christians for the last 2000 years.

Most Christians have no clue what authority really means. They've heard the word used in context with scripture, but they don't know how it works or where it fits in with their life. A few Christians understand what authority is, but they don't know how to use it. Still fewer realize they have it and know what it is, but they refuse to use it, because they were taught not to pick a fight with the devil out of fear of reprisal. Then there are those that know they have it, know how to use it but for some odd reason, they just choose not to. I don't know, maybe they're not trained to be warriors, maybe life has taken their focus off of all things Christian, or maybe they're just tired. Whatever the reason, authority unassumed is authority given away.

Because Jesus conquered death, hell and the grave, authority is now back in the hands of Gods children, so now the question is, do you know what it is and how to use it? You may have authority, but not knowing you have it, or not using it is worse than the Old Testament days, the 4000 years authority was legally in the hands of the devil by virtue of Adams sin.

If you are one of the few who knows how to use authority, the devil is in for a world of hurt, but as they say in Texas, "the devil ain't no fool," he's not going to stick around for the punishment, he will flee from you like a gazelle flees from a lion. I say this from experience of doing Altar of Love cases, the smart ones flee, because if they do not, they are in big trouble. Authority means that you are the sheriff, the judge, the jury and the executioner. You arrest them, you declare them guilty, you set the punishment and you command the punishment be carried out; so go ahead and get creative.

> *No weapon formed against you shall prosper, And every tongue which rises against you in judgment **You** shall condemn.* Isaiah 54:17

Notice who God says is the one with the authority to condemn the tongue that rises against you? It's you; if God had not given you authority, it would be Him who was condemning the tongue that rises against you, but He doesn't, He has given that power, that authority to you.

> *Truly I tell you, **whatever you bind** on earth **will be bound** in heaven, and **whatever you loose** on earth **will be loosed** in heaven.* Matthew 18:18

In my understanding of authority, I no longer fight the devil, I submit to God, command the devil and the devil flees because of my authority obtained by my submission. Submission to God is not just being "born again." Most people who are, or claim to be "born again," never submit to God, ever, and therefore, the devil will mess with that person continuously, until he breaks them. Even when they try to use their authority, the devil will return over and over because of their unwillingness to submit. Your submission to God is a character trait; it is paramount to resistance and the only thing that makes the devil flee in fear. Believers that try to assume authority without first submitting to God are still like a lion, but they are the lion that has been separated from the pride and are fighting a pack of hyenas all alone. They put up a valiant fight for awhile, but eventually, even with authority, they tire and give up the fight.

Being "born again" is essential, but its purpose is to unlock your potential and your potential is found in your Identity as a Child of God by submitting to Him and seeking His righteousness. All you have to do is Ask, Seek and Knock and it will be opened to you, but you have to want it bad enough to go after it, after Him with everything you have. What did you think Jesus meant when He said, *"Love the Lord God with **all** your heart, **all** you soul and **all** your mind?"* If,

> **The kingdom of God is** *not a matter of eating and drinking, but* **of righteousness, peace, and joy in the Holy Spirit.** Romans 14:17

And,

> *The kingdom of heaven is like treasure hidden in a field. When a man found it, he hid it again, and then in his joy went and sold all he had and bought that field.* Matthew 13:44

Then the contents of that treasure we are supposed to be looking for is righteousness, peace and joy in the Holy Ghost, but without a clear understanding of your identity and the importance of righteousness, you will constantly be looking into a rearview mirror revisiting things in the past that Jesus paid for and covered with His blood, things that God says are finished. It's equivalent to you sending $1000 per month to pay off a debt that Jesus already paid off for you, with an interest rate so high you can never pay it off. Then imagine that you've got several others just like it, maybe a dozen or so. If you are constantly looking back at something that's been finished, it's never going to be finished.

Routinely revisiting your past has another pitfall. If you let the devil know you don't believe you are forgiven of one thing, he will use everything else you thought you were forgiven of and cause you to question them as well. Suddenly, you will have all these things coming up that you initially thought you were free from and you will do altar call, after altar call, after altar call, yet you cannot understand why you're not happy, why you're totally stressed out, why you're not healed, why you're not set free. All because you were never taught a proper understanding of your identity, you were not taught the importance of righteousness, you were not filled with the Spirit of Grace and Truth and you never learned the power you had as a child in authority.

> *You priests have rejected me, and **my people are destroyed because they refuse to obey.** Now I'll reject you and forget your children, because you have forgotten my Law.* Hosea 4:6

Gods appointed priests (modern day pastors and preachers) have rejected the simplicity of the Gospel found in the cross, and because the people refused to submit and obey, God disciplines them as a loving parent disciplines a disobedient child. As He did in the Old Testament, God simply takes His hand of protection off His children so the enemy can have his way with them. It was a vicious cycle that Israel labored with until Jesus hung on a tree and cursed that curse. They struggled with the thought of God as their Father, choosing rather to see Him only as "God," because they never really grasped the concept of God as Abba or Daddy. Confusing, let me explain. God had children so He could live in them, but Adams sin literally pushed God away from him. God finds Abraham and chooses him to begin Fathering His children again, but on the day that God wanted to reunite with His children at the base of Mt. Sinai, they rejected Him, choosing Moses as their intermediary, but that is not how God wanted it.

God is a Father, and as a Father, He wants to have a relationship with His kids. That's perfectly understandable, but our Father is not just a regular Father, He is the God of all creation and He not only has the desire to live in us, He has the ability to so as well. He wants to live in us so He can walk through us, and talk through us and love through us, so together we can be Jesus everywhere we go to everyone we meet.

I won't be surprised if this message ruffles a few feathers. The modern church has no interest in this getting out, because when you are set free from yourself, you will be free from the codependent relationship church Pastors desire for you. In order for them to survive, they need you dependent on them. Where would they be without hundreds and even thousands of you filling their glamorous buildings every week always seeking but never finding the truth? And why, why is the truth never going to be found there, because the truth is hidden in righteousness, the righteousness they have no desire to teach. Since I began teaching on righteousness, I have seen my YouTube viewership drop from thousands to a few hundred. I've had people write hateful things to me all because I encourage them to walk in righteousness. However, *"blessed are those who are persecuted for righteousness sake."*

Christian counselors may be commendable, but only Jesus is the mighty Counselor who sets you free from you; the you that has been unable to escape the yoke of sin. If,

The Kingdom of God is not a matter of eating and drinking but of righteousness, peace and joy in the Holy Spirit. Romans 14:17

Then your joy comes from the peace that you have by knowing you have been made right with the Father by the blood of Jesus.

Therefore, since we have been justified by faith, we have peace with God through our Lord Jesus Christ. Romans 5:1

Justified

You have been justified, just as if you never sinned in your life, just as if you never missed the mark, not even one time. That is how your Father sees you now, so why can't we see ourselves that way? How come, when some believers look in the mirror, how come they don't see it that way? Because they don't believe, that's why. They're in unbelief and that's as simple as I can put it. Willful sin has kept the modern church in the bondage of condemnation, and they have no interest in you getting free.

Each and every one of us are supposed to be likeminded, the same faith, same hope, and same joy. One Father, one Lord Jesus, one Holy Spirit and all of us are supposed to think the same way, because we believe in the one who died to set us free.

You can be free from guilt, shame and condemnation, because you can be free of sin. Christians will tell you that it's not possible, but I'm here to tell you, it is. I'm not talking about a false sense of hope by way of the twisted hyper-grace of the OSAS doctrine. I'm saying you can be free of guilt because you can be free of the sin that has ensnared you; you can literally be free indeed. The Word says, "...*if Christ has made you free, you are free indeed,*" but if you are still in the same sin, how are you free? Because something's been missing, something in the way we have gone about this thing, something in the way we've been taught has been excluded and it's kept us on a marry-go-round of sin, guilt, shame, condemnation and repentance.

The purpose of this book is to examine the transformation Jesus underwent from the moment He was baptized and began His ministry. We will also look at Old Testament prophets and compare their anointing to that of Jesus to see what was missing. What was it that Jesus, Peter and Paul had that they did not have? As well, we look at all of the apostles to see how it was that they went from bumbling goofs to a virtual facsimile of Jesus...almost instantaneously. Then we will examine a principle, a very simple process that Jesus taught, and within it lays the map to the narrow path of eternal life and directions of how **not** to veer off.

But the one who perseveres to the end will be saved. Matthew 24:13

In Context

As in the verse above, so many of our Christian traditions, bedrocks of our beliefs are based upon scripture taken out-of-context or used to support other scripture also taken out of context in an attempt to make them fit a false narrative. They're building a house on sand, and when the trial comes and their house falls, they blame God and end up going back to the world. For those with an honest reverence of God and smart enough not to blame Him, they're still sitting among the shambles of a house destroyed by a storm, and their disillusionment of what they expected and hoped for in their pursuit of Jesus has sent them back to the world as well. Both foolishly latch onto the OSAS doctrine, like a drowning person might latch onto a rubber ducky in the middle of the ocean, in hopes that it is "the way," while they selfishly live their lives like it's "theirs" to live.

Looking at the verses just prior to the one above, we can determine who Jesus was speaking to and what He was warning them of. It's in Matthew 24 that the apostles have asked Jesus exactly how the end of days will play out.

> *"Tell us," they said, "when will these things happen, and what will be the sign of Your coming and of the end of the age?* Matthew 24:4

Jesus answered,

> **"See to it that no one deceives you.** Matthew 24:4

Deceives – Strong's #4105 planaó (plan-ah'-o) To cause to wander, to lead astray, to deceive.

If the road to salvation is the narrow path, Jesus sets up His answer to their question by warning them... no, He's warning us not to stray from the narrow path. Try to remember this exact point as you read on, because we will examine what the narrow path is later in this book, and you will be amazed when you see exactly who Jesus is talking to when He explains the wide and narrow paths.

Now we know beyond a shadow of a doubt that we are at the end of time, and if you are reading this book you've likely been awakened to that fact. God has either given you dreams or simply moved on your heart to come out of the world and make yourself ready for the wedding feast. He woke me up years ago with an amazing rapture dream that came out of nowhere.

Then He began moving on my heart to research and study it, followed by confirmation after confirmation after confirmation; each one more miraculous that the one before it. After awhile, you realize that you'd have to be delusional not to see what He is showing you. Now for those that may be reading this, and you don't know what time it is, may I suggest that you take some time to pray about it and ask your Father for confirmation, but don't be surprised when all hell breaks loose and don't be an ostrich and put your head in the sand when you get what you prayed for.

It's time to wake up, "this life," "your life" as a Christian is not "your life" to live "for you." The narrow path is narrow because it is a very difficult path to find, and only those who learn to die to themselves and live for the One who died for them will find it. This is not a cliché, I am speaking literally here, you need to examine your life and determine who and what you are living for, because your eternal life hangs in the balance. Don't think I am being overly dramatic here, I'm not; in fact, there are not words powerful enough for me to describe the urgency of the time and nature of the subject matter.

But I digress. Jesus then begins to describe how thing will play out. The first deception is,

> *For many will come in My name, claiming, 'I am the Christ,' and will deceive many....* Matthew 24:5

This has always been taught as false prophets claiming to be Jesus, but I remember the day God revealed the actual meaning to me as it came off the page in 3D. Jesus is not referring to false prophets claiming to be Jesus or "the Christ;"

when He says, *"Many will come in my name...."* He is referring to Christian preachers, preaching Christianity or more accurately, a demonic version thereof. Mark 16:17 Jesus says, *"In My name they will...,"* and because of that, Christian preachers are correctly taught to do and say everything "In the name of Jesus."

As Christians, we have no power or authority apart from His name. Therefore, when Jesus says, "*...For **many** will come **in My name**, claiming, 'I am the Christ,"*, He is referring to Christian Preachers, **many** Christian preachers, not just a few. The Greek word for many implies most of the preachers will be preaching a false Christian doctrine, "In the name of Jesus." They are not claiming to be Jesus, because when He says, "*...claiming, 'I am the Christ,"* they are not denying that Jesus is the Christ, but like so many other fake Christian doctrines, their doctrine is a lie from the pit of hell; based upon scripture taken "out of context" to spin a web of lies all designed to deceive almost all of the Christians.

You see, context is everything, and Jesus is not talking to the whole world here, He is talking specifically to His church and the great deception, the false doctrine that will lure **almost all** of the "wannabe" Christians away from the narrow path. Remember, Jesus said only a few find the narrow path, implying that most do not. From there, Jesus describes events leading to the end, followed by,

> *Then **they** will deliver you over to be persecuted and killed, and you will be hated by all nations on account of My name.* Matthew 24:9

Just exactly who is "they?" Who will deliver you over be persecuted? The Christian preachers that came "in the name of Jesus," claiming that Jesus was the Christ, but sent by the devil to deceive many, and by many, Jesus means almost all of the Christians will be deceived and delivered up by these cowards who will deliver up their sheep to save their own necks in the New World Order. Many of these pastors are card-carrying Masons and when it all goes down, after the rapture, and 99.99 % of the disillusioned so-called "Christians" are left behind because of unrighteousness; their pastors will hand over their flock by relinquishing all their information to the beast system to be rounded up and imprisoned. Everyone knows what will happen at that point so there is no reason for me to address it.

The point is this, we began this with a passage Jesus made regarding "the end," when He said, "*But the one who **perseveres to the end** will be saved;*" a verse used out of context to encourage believers to stay faithful to Jesus. When, in reality, it is a warning for us to stay faithful to the ministry of righteousness described by Paul in 2 Corinthians 3:9 and not to fall for the cunning deception of false prophets coming in the name of Jesus; most notably the OSAS and prosperity preachers. This is made further evident by the way Jesus describes the basis for the deception.

> *"...and many false prophets will arise and mislead many.*
> ***Because of the multiplication of wickedness,*** *the love of*
> *most will grow cold."* Matthew 24:11

If a tree is known by its fruit, this false doctrine that Jesus is referring to is known by its "multiplication of wickedness." Keep in mind, Jesus is not talking to the world, He's not talking to unbelievers; this is exactly what I mean when I say it's been taken out of context. We've wrongly associated this verse with Jesus speaking about or to unbelievers engaged in worldly wickedness but that could not be farther from the truth. He's talking to the church, His church, His baby sheep, and it has been infiltrated by false prophets, Masons claiming to be Christians and espousing a doctrine that condones a lifestyle of wickedness.

Wickedness, in the Strong's concordance, is described as sin, disobedience to the commandments, otherwise known as lawlessness. Jesus said, "*If you love Me,* **you will** *keep My commandments.*" He's talking about the OSAS doctrine of demons, a doctrine that teaches it's Ok to sin; it's natural, all have sinned, all will sin, sin all you want, by gosh, you're covered by grace. Then, over time, this false sense of grace morphs and gets so distorted that their lawlessness, their sin becomes so prevalent, so frequent, so pervasive it multiplies to a point where the church looks no different than the world, and in many cases, it's even worse.

Walking Without Offense

Since I began writing this book, God has moved on me to diligently make it my goal to walk free from offense in every situation, to every extent possible. I've been told that I'm deceived, or I'm in denial, but the truth is that righteousness has set me free from offense, people no longer offend me, because even if they behave wrong, I know it's not me they have a problem with, if it is people in the world, they're just groaning. If it is Christians, it's their lack of identity. Regardless, why would I allow what someone does not perceive, to affect what I now know and understand?

> *For we know that the whole creation has been groaning together in the pains of childbirth until now.* Romans 8:12

Man's spirit was created to be in relationship with Jesus so without that, people are just orphans groaning for a relationship with the only One who can provide what is missing in them. Orphans are people in the world who were created to be Children of God, but they have not come to the knowledge of it yet. Nothing but Jesus can fill the void within them, no spouse, no child, no job, no friend, not a beautiful house on the beach, nor wealth or fame, not any one thing or even all of them together can fill the hole in a heart that doesn't have Jesus. Happiness is fleeting for them, and the fear of death is ever present, because, what if they're wrong? Therefore, if they have a problem, they're problem is not with me, it's a lack of the One who died for them to be free. Knowing that one simple truth, how can anyone in their right mind take offense when people in the world act a fool towards them? Those poor souls, they're just groaning out of loneliness.

If it's a believer acting the fool towards you, they're orphans as well. They are children who do not know what it means to be a child; children who think and behave like orphans of the world. They are children with itchy ears being led astray by false Christian teachers who will tell them sin is OK, so they're excused. Fighting and arguing with them is futile, and it is not your job to get them saved, that is the job of the Holy Spirit and He is a much better evangelist than we can ever be. I know some people and situations are difficult, but the only thing you can do is love them and pray for them that God would reveal their true identity in Christ and let the Holy Spirit do His job.

There is a story that has floated around the Christian community regarding agnostics. Agnostics are those that don't necessarily believe, but they don't disbelieve either. They have that, "prove it to me" attitude. This story has been told as kind of a modern day parable, but the story actually came from a dream of an atheist who subsequently became a devout Christian. It is a true story.

In this dream a man saw a crowd of people standing in a field with a fence dividing them into two groups. A man came, whom he perceived was Jesus, and took only a handful of people who were on the right side of the fence. Just then, an evil man came that he knew could only be the Devil, and took a number of people too large to count from the left side of the fence. The man quickly jumped up on the fence to look around, but there was nobody left. That's when the Devil came back and told the man it was his time to come with him, but the man exclaimed, "I know I'm not ready to commit with Him (pointing to Jesus' side of the fence), but neither do I choose you. No-no, I'm sitting right here on the fence, that's what I choose." The Devil replied, "Oh, but you do belong to me, you see…I own the fence."

By not choosing Jesus, you get the devil by default. If you're still on the fence, if you're still not sure, may I recommend that you ask, seek & knock. For everyone who asks receives, everyone who seeks finds, and everyone who knocks it will be opened.

> "**Anyone who chooses** to be a friend of the world
> makes himself an enemy of God." James 4:4

The OSAS Christians are quite happy being in church and in sin at the same time. They are very comfortable thinking that they can have the best of both worlds;

they get to enjoy the lusts of the flesh and will one day enjoy the pleasures of heaven also ... or so they think!

However, the Bible makes it clear that we cannot be in sin and in Christ at the same time. We can't be a friend of God when we have one foot in this sinful world and one foot in Christ, like someone straddling a fence. It's all about context, so when you read this next verse, remind yourself that James was writing to believers, not "the world." And just notice how he begins the verse.

> **You adulterous people!** *Do you not know that friendship with the world is enmity with God? Therefore whoever wishes to be a friend of the world* **makes himself** *an enemy of God.* James 4:4

Have we become so delusional that we are under the impression that an enemy of God is saved? We are either saved or lost, there is no in between. Either Jesus is Lord of all or **not** Lord at all. Either Jesus is Lord keeping you from sin and preparing you for His wedding feast or the Devil is your lord, enticing you, encouraging you to enjoy the lustful pleasures of a sinful world before you are taken off to hell. We can't be in sin and in Christ at the same time. We need to be like Joshua who told the Israelites that they had a choice of serving the Lord God or the gods of this world and then he said,

> *"...choose this day whom you will serve, ... as for me and my household, we will serve the LORD"* Josh. 24:15

Now for you Christians who suffer with a multitude of issues, just know that Jesus died to cancel your lifetime subscription to issues. It's over, finished, the veil was torn, Jesus said, *"It is finished."* If you seek righteousness, Jesus will remove the veil that is still over your eyes, and cancel all your subscriptions.

> *And we all, with unveiled face, beholding the glory of the Lord, are being transformed into His image with ever-increasing glory...* 2 Corinth 3:18

He died that horrible death so that we could be, would be, transformed into the original image we were first created to be... like Him. Our Father put in motion a remarkable plan to get us back to the place we were in the garden, before Adam ever sinned against Him. Jesus was the last Adam, and His life giving Spirit paid for us to be restored to our original state. When Adam and Eve sinned, they tried to hide from God, but God sees everything. Surely you don't think that God doesn't see your sin, do you?

How much different would you behave if Jesus spent an entire day walking with you everywhere you went? What would you change? Would your speech change, would you soften the way you spoke to your family, your coworkers? Would you behave differently while driving, would you work harder, complain less or not at all? Will you continue to engage in fornication and tell Him, "It's OK, right, I'm in love?

Not just no, but hell no; you're not doing anything of the sort if Jesus is present, and do you want to know why? Because His law is written on your heart, and you know it's wrong, but you've been deceived into wickedness by the false hyper-grace doctrine of the OSAS, and lawlessness has multiplied to the point where you have made yourself an enemy of God and you don't even know it. Here's the thing, He is with you, every moment of every day, recording everything you do and say, every thought, and every emotion. God sits in the theatre of our soul watching everything we do like a movie; nothing is hidden from Him.

Sin caused Adam and Eve to hide from God and it will cause you to hide from God as well. If I could advise one thing only, it would be this; regardless of how horrible your behavior, repent daily, and ask your Father to give you wisdom and teach you righteousness. Ask to be filled with the Spirit of Grace and Truth. Humble yourself before Him and stay in the relationship, no matter what you have done. Never drift away; for He is a good, good Father and while He does not want you behaving like the world, His first desire is a relationship with you. He knows that over time, if you stay in a close relationship with Him, you will begin to transform. His seed will get in you and begin to grow, and when it does, that behavior that so easily ensnared you will become repulsive to you and you won't want to sin anymore and get away with it.

Sins main goal is to bring guilt and shame causing you to hide like Adam and Eve. Hiding brings separation in the relationship with the Father, and while He desperately wants to be in relationship with you, He is a gentleman, He will respect your decision to hide from Him. All the while He will be calling you, reaching out to you, beckoning you to come home to your first love, Him. Without Him, the sin will give birth to guilt and condemnation which will cause you to repeat it over and over without end until it has desensitized you and you become numb to it, never giving it another thought. Finally, sin destroys everything dear to you, everything and everyone you love, because sin is no respecter of persons, and it affects everyone close to it. Sin is an equal opportunity destroyer.

Sin has a remarkable way of making you think that you are actually in control while simultaneously making you feel like you can never get free from it, and you live this rollercoaster life of guilt, shame and condemnation engraved on your heart and on your conscience. You either become so numb that rebellion and wickedness become your new identity, or your guilt and shame cause your conscience to remain in a constant state of violation, but God says:

> *...the righteous are bold as a lion.* Proverbs 28:1

Just before that, however, it says:

> **The wicked flee when no one pursues**, but...*the righteous are bold as a lion.* Proverbs 28:1

To flee even when no one pursues implies a guilty conscience, the byproduct of sin absent relationship with the Father. Righteousness, however, gives you the confidence; the boldness to endure, to overcome sin, and to face any obstacle, any trial with complete assurance the Father has your back.

> *For the LORD will go before you, and the God of Israel will be your rear guard.* Isaiah 52:12

When righteousness is established, you know that you know you are never going to die. You are just going to be with Jesus, to die is gain, so I am never, ever, ever going to die, I am eternal. When I say yes to Jesus, no to the world, and submit to my Father to receive His righteousness, He is never going to change His mind about me, because He loves me. A million years from now, He's not going to say He regretted saving me.

> *"For who has known the mind of the Lord, so as to instruct Him?" But* **we have the mind of Christ**. 1 Corinth 2:16

This is viewed as heresy by more than a few Christians, but it is written and it was never available to the Old Testament saints. Living a condemnation free life was not available in the Old Testament. Moses was literally given, what was called by Paul as a ministry of condemnation engraved on stone, and it was considered glorious.

> *For if the ministry of condemnation was glorious, how much more glorious is* **the ministry of righteousness**! 2 Corinth 3:9

Now we have been given a ministry of righteousness so that we can literally have the mind of Christ, to know and do the will of the Father in every situation. A Word of knowledge, a prophesy, a miracle healing, an opportunity to minister the good news; we do not need to be looking for a place to minister...our entire life is a ministry. If, as the Word says, *"Christ in you, the hope of glory,"* and *"you have the mind of Christ,"* then you literally carry Jesus with you everywhere you go, all the time and with everyone you meet; every life you touch is an encounter with the King. There are no coincidences, no meeting is random or by chance, everyone you run into was planned before time began to get that person in a place for you, a "born again believer," walking in righteousness, and filled with the Holy Spirit to be a reflection of Jesus to them.

That never happened in the Old Testament, because of the torment they continually felt under the ministry of condemnation. If we have been given the ministry of righteousness, why are so many Christians still feeling stressed, burdened, sick, frustrated, angry, full of hatred, prone to rage, full of lust, greed and selfishness? The reason why they are they feeling so condemned, is because they never learned they are supposed to be walking in the ministry of righteousness. How can you walk in righteousness, the boldness, the confidence of a lion with the mind of Christ when you are walking in sin simultaneously? You cannot, and therein lays the great deception of the devil in this modern day and age of the ministry of prosperity and the OSAS. They have the same look and feel as the Law of Moses, the ministry of condemnation.

We have a new covenant, a better one than the one on stones, we have **the covenant of righteousness,** where our sins and our lawless deeds are not only forgiven, but God actually says, *"They are remembered no more."*

> ***"This is the covenant I will make with them*** *after those days, declares the Lord.* ***I will put My laws in their hearts*** *and inscribe them on their minds."* *¹⁷Then He adds:* ***"Their sins and lawless acts I will remember no more."*** Hebrews 10:16-17

He did not say that He would overlook sin for the time being and the two of you would revisit it later, no, He said, *"Their sin...I will remember no more."* We all say we know it, but do we really believe it if we are still in condemnation, guilt and shame? Obviously not, and why are we in condemnation, guilt and shame? Because we are still in willful sin; we never learned about or never submitted to the ministry of righteousness.

For those of you attempting to walk in righteousness, but finding it difficult to do so, if God doesn't remember your sins, but they still come to your remembrance, how are they getting there? Who is responsible for remembering something that God has forgotten? The devil remembers them, that's who! And he is a master at disguising himself in the voices of friends, relatives, Christian brothers and sisters as well as preachers. This message, the gospel of Jesus Christ is also called the Gospel of peace, but you cannot have peace unless you know you are right with God, and that is impossible unless you submit to the ministry of righteousness that Paul spoke of.

Without righteousness you will constantly be warring with your flesh, never realizing that the war has been settled. Willful sin and an un-renewed mind is at war with God, but when righteousness hits your soul it opens up your heart and enables you to see everything through the eyes and mind of Christ. Righteousness convicts your heart whenever you inadvertently sin, and conviction makes you go back and make it right with that person. Broad and wide is the road that leads to destruction and many go that way, but narrow and small is the road to salvation and only a few find it. News Flash! Jesus is not talking about atheists, Muslims, Buddhists or any number of other religions. He is talking to the body of Christ whose eye is not single, the body bound in the ministry of condemnation, because they never got a hold of righteousness.

In addressing the 7 churches of Revelation, 6 of whom He told to repent and come back to Him, to come back to their first love, Jesus. Why would you need to come back to someone unless you went astray from them in the first place? Let me encourage you to believe you are forgiven, believe you are loved, throw off the wisdom of the world, the ministry of selfishness found in the prosperity gospel, the OSAS doctrine of wickedness and when you do, when the ministry of righteousness hits your heart it will clean your conscience once and for all.

We've all heard of the phrase, "you have a guilty conscience," but the only thing that can wash away a guilty conscience is the blood of Jesus through the covenant of righteousness. The blood of Jesus was heavens answer to a guilty conscience and the ministry of righteousness is the vehicle used to get it to you. Do you understand the power that is in the blood of Jesus for it to wash away a guilty conscience?

> *On many past occasions and in many different ways, God spoke to our fathers through the prophets. ²But in these last days He has spoken to us by His Son...* Hebrews 1:1-2

The prophets of old spoke about the day when righteousness apart from the law was going to be imputed to us by the Holy Spirit and that day is here and available now, but as awesome as it was to them, the modern church has no interest in righteousness, because they're too busy trying to live their best life now and get rich doing it.

> *But now, apart from the law, the righteousness of God has been revealed, as attested by the Law and the Prophets.* Romans 3:21

Unfortunately, most people do not believe it is possible to live free from sin, guilt and condemnation, and they rail against this kind of teaching, but I promise you, it is real, it is possible, and it is for the body of Christ who desires righteousness and seek it out like a treasure. No, it is not a snap of the fingers and voila, you are suddenly righteous, but your Father needs for you to have the correct mindset, the proper motive and attitude towards this thing. You have to want righteousness so intensely that you are willing to seek it with all perseverance.

If you don't believe the blood is enough; if you believe that it is not finished, that it is to be continued, then you probably have a religious spirit convincing you to obtain salvation by works, and you will be in bondage and condemnation until you shake off those religious shoes. If that's you, if that religious shoe fits, kick it off.

Getting to God by works will never happen, because no flesh will glory in His presence. Jesus got up off His throne, gave up His divinity, took on the nature of a man and paid the highest price that has ever been paid for anything in the history of the world, and the currency He used was His blood. A covenant needed to be made between God and man in order to restore man's identity, his authority and his right-standing with God. The only way such a covenant would be lawful is if a sacrifice is made on our behalf, but not just any sacrifice will do; bulls and goats will not suffice, because this covenant is no longer going to be temporary, this covenant will be the final covenant; the one that stands for eternity. Therefore, in order for this covenant to be acceptable to God it had to be a man for a man, a pure, undefiled man. Thank God for Jesus, He paid the ultimate price and died to make a way for us.

Jesus did not fulfill the law as a God; He did it as a man in right relationship with God. I know Jesus was God, but he had to give up His divinity, submit Himself to the laws which govern the world system and walk out a life of pure, undefiled righteousness for the sacrifice to be sufficient; He had to do it as a man and not as God or it would not have met the standards necessary to free us from a sinful life destined to be separated from the Father. Jesus did it in righteousness, and by doing so He enabled us to do the same as He, as it is written, *we are the righteousness of God in Christ Jesus.*

Jesus was fully God, but He was also fully a man, and He laid aside His divinity, humbled Himself, became a bondservant and was tempted in all ways, even as we are.

> *For we do not have a high priest who is unable to sympathize with our weaknesses, but we have one who was tempted in every way that we are, yet was without sin.* Hebrews 4:15

There are many that will argue with the belief that Jesus was not here as God, and it is a difficult concept to grasp, but if Jesus was here as God and not a man the debt could never have been paid.

*Let no one say when he is tempted, "I am being tempted by God," for
God cannot be tempted with evil, and he himself tempts no one.*
James 1:13

The book of Hebrews says, *"Jesus was tempted in every way even as we are, yet without sin,"* but James says that God cannot be tempted, therefore Jesus walked without sin as a man and not as God. Furthermore, the requirements necessary to acquit us of our guilt would not have been met had Jesus died as God; it had to be a man for a man, not a God for a man. Jesus could have done what He did as God, but it would not have met the standards necessary for God to drop all the charges against us. Rather, Jesus did it as a man, in right relationship with God (in righteousness). Jesus gave up His divinity, came to the earth He created, humbled himself before His creation and walked out all 613 laws of Moses and the 10 commandments in order to be the perfect offering for our sin. He thus condemned sin in the flesh.

*For what the Law was powerless to do in that it was weakened by the
flesh, God did by sending His own Son in the likeness of sinful man, as an
offering for sin. He thus condemned sin in the flesh...* Romans 8:3

This plan of Gods was amazing and only Jesus was strong enough, righteous enough, faithful enough and courageous enough to walk it out. That is not blasphemy, it is in the Word. We could never have been in right relationship with God unless a man fulfilled His end of the contract and no other man was capable of such a task, but Jesus. So, why is all this important? Because, in understanding what Jesus did and how He did it, we begin to see the ministry of righteousness exposed, empowering us to do it as well. We are not ever going to be Jesus, but through righteousness, we are be being transformed into the likeness of Him day by day.

This thing that Jesus did for us cannot be taken from us once we get a full understanding of it. He paid the price for us, so now, *"to live is Christ and to die is gain."* But how would someone be able to die for the sake of the gospel of Jesus unless they truly understood and believed they were righteous and thus set free? Christians, as in the case of Peter, think that by sheer will alone, they would be able to die for their faith; that they would be able to endure being tied to a steak and burned without rejecting Christ, but they'd be wrong. Why, because sheer will alone wasn't enough to walk out the law, sheer will alone couldn't keep David from sin, sheer will alone couldn't keep Peter from denying Jesus and neither will it keep you from rejecting Him if the situation arose. For without the ministry of righteousness and power of the Holy Spirit from on high, we are no different than the disciples before the cross. Our flesh may be willing, but our spirit will be weak.

So, what made the disciples go from denying Jesus to boldly proclaiming His name without fear of being flogged, stoned, sawn in two and lit on fire as human torches to light up streets? What made them become as bold as lions and not deny Him anymore? That is the question; the question I had been asking, the question my Father put in my heart and then answered for me when He woke me up one morning and told me to study righteousness and begin writing.

When I consider the dysfunctional state of the church and witness her destruction at the hands of the OSAS doctrine and the prosperity gospel that is virtually mocking the ministry of righteousness with their hyper-grace, it almost makes me weep.

> *Greater love has no one than this, that he lay*
> *down his life for his friends.* John 15:13

That is what Jesus did for all of us, but he did not lay down His life and suffer like He did so we could continue to think like, act like and live like the devil. What were we thinking? He did it so we could be free from this sinful flesh that ensnares us like a prison. He did it so we could be in right relationship with the Father just as He was. He did it so we could be free of guilt, shame and condemnation. He did it so we could be like Him. He didn't do what He did so we could continue to wallow in sin like a pig in mud. What a sad day it would be if all we had in this life was a hollow Christian confession without ever getting transformed into the image of His righteousness. What a waist it would be to spend all our time and energy playing church, but never become a disciple of Jesus.

Jesus modeled life as a man in right relationship with God, but the church has been deceived and beaten down by unbelieving Christians and Masons planted as so called Pastors, elders and teachers to deceive the church into thinking that living righteously is impossible, obtainable by no man but Jesus. The truth of the matter is... that is a lie straight from the pit of hell.

The price that Jesus paid was sufficient to remove not just the sin but the stain of sin as well. That is, the blood of Jesus will remove anything the sin left behind, any blood diseases, any scars, any tracks, anything. It's not limited to just physical scars either, it is sufficient to remove unforgiveness, unworthiness, fear, resentment, bitterness, jealousy and the like. They are all stains left behind by a sinful past and the blood of Jesus is more than capable of washing us clean of every sin and stain thereof.

The blood of Jesus is powerful enough to take a prostitute and transform her into a virgin, and I am not just speaking symbolically here, but literally as well. If the power in the name and blood of Jesus is enough to repair a back, a torn rotator cuff, or an ACL, why would it not re-grow a hymen? It can, it will and it does; HIV gone, hepatitis gone, genital warts gone, all of it, whatever it is, gone. If you are willing to die to your old self and live for Jesus who died for you, then the old you is dead completely and all the residue of the dead man will be washed away with the death and burial of the old you followed by the resurrection of the new you.

The church desperately needs to stop dabbling in Christianity, people need to stop playing the part of a Christian, stop pretending you are saved, stop being deceived into believing that a certain amount of sin is acceptable, and become an actual disciple of Jesus. A disciple is sold out to the faith; it means that Jesus is your master, your Lord. It is one who makes no decision without consulting Him who saved them, and says nothing without considering the results. It is one who looks, acts, and thinks just like his Lord. It's a believer who no longer lives their life to please themselves but the One whom they now serve.

I'm not going to lie to you, this life of righteousness that Jesus modeled for us is unattainable unless you fully surrender; you cannot have one foot in the world and one in the Kingdom, you cannot serve two masters. Jesus displayed a life that is impossible to live while in condemnation and condemnation is impossible to escape as long as you walk in willful sin and excuse it with false grace. The doctrine of OSAS is designed to keep you in condemnation, removing you from grace and placing you back under the law which cannot save you. The ministry of righteousness, however, moves you out from under the law where the Spirit of Grace can come and reside within you.

We desperately need to stop playing church, surrender completely and receive the ministry of righteousness which will set us free from guilt, shame and condemnation. I am longing for a new generation to look in the mirror and finally see who they are and whose they are. I desire for you to know who your Father is, what He looks like, how He feels about all things and to know the Love of Christ that was poured out for you so that you no longer would be bound under the law of condemnation brought on by a doctrine that falsely tells you that a certain amount of sin is acceptable when you know, deep down in your heart it is not.

It is the goal of this book for you to know the will of the Father, and that will is for Him to have a relationship with His children by way of a covenant of righteousness through Jesus. If anyone decides to go into the ministry, that is awesome, but more than that, I want you to see your created value to the Father. He wants to have His children believe Him and trust Him; in so doing, Jesus receives the full reward for the suffering He endured. Anything less is unacceptable. What good is it for believers to go to bed every night feeling condemned? What good is it for Worship Leaders, Nursery Teachers, Youth Ministers, Deacons, and Pastors to wake up every day feeling guilty? What good is it for Jesus to suffer and die like He did, if we remain in the same sinful state and never transform into His likeness?

The Altar of Love, Part II
Chapter 2
Leg 1 - Identity
Son-ship, The Spirit of Adoption, Bride of Christ

The Lord God, the God of all creation, the God of Abraham, Isaac and Jacob was rarely referred to as "Father" in the Old Testament. When Jesus began referring to The Lord God as "Father," it was not only a new way to address the Lord God, but it was sacrilege to the Jews. It's just one more thing that Jesus did to anger them, but why? Why would referring to The Lord God as "Father" provoke such animosity in the Jewish leaders of the time?

> *You are the children of your father the devil, and you love to do the evil things he does.* John 8:44

Why, because after Adam and Even handed over their rightful authority in the Garden, the devil had spent the next 4000 years corrupting man's image of himself, his identity. Mankind went from looking like a Child of the Lord God to looking like a child of the devil. When Jesus comes on the scene and begins referring to the Lord God as "Father," the religious leaders freaked out, because, as Jesus said, they were children of their father, the devil, and they were filled with the spirit of the world; the devil's spirit and Satan realized that all his hard work, all the groundwork he had laid was now being exposed. If the orphans ever learned that they were actually children with a Father who loved them, it would undermine all his plans to rule on earth as God rules in Heaven.

> *...the kingdom of heaven suffers violence, and the violent take **it** by force.* Matthew 11:12

That is to say, "the Kingdom of Heaven suffers violence by the devil and his hoard of wicked demons, but the diligent, the dedicated, the faithful, the righteous, the former orphans who have been adopted as Children of God will now take **it** back by force and with authority as a result of their new relationship and love for the Father." **It** is obviously the "Kingdom of Heaven," and **It** is anywhere the Holy Spirit is residing. If then, the Holy Spirit resides within us, we are where the "Kingdom of Heaven" is; we are the "**It**" Jesus is referring to. God's children have been suffering violence from the enemy since the fall of man, but our Father wants to put His Kingdom Spirit, the Kingdom of God within us so we can take back everything the devil has stolen by violence; our identity, our authority and our salvation.

> *For indeed, the **Kingdom of God is within you**." Luke 17:21*

This Kingdom, the Kingdom of God is within you when you are filled with His Holy Spirit.

> *...And I will ask the Father, and He will give you another Advocate to be with you forever - the Spirit of truth. ...for He abides with you and will be in you. ¹⁸**I will not leave you as orphans;** I will come to you.*
> John 14:16-18

An orphan is everyone and anyone not filled with His Holy Spirit. Jesus said, "*...for He abides **with** you and will be **in** you*," because the Holy Spirit was not yet "In them," but would soon be "In them" when He fills them in the Upper Room at Pentecost. Until that day came, the Holy Spirit would be close to them like a faithful friend stays close in good times and bad.

In the Altar of Love part I, I explained in great detail, the reasons our Father had Jesus scourged like he did, yet I believe it is worth stating again. Isaiah 52 prophesied in great detail and with remarkable accuracy what would happen at Calvary on the cross over a thousand years before it occurred.

Cat – O' - Nine Tails

> *"His appearance was so disfigured beyond that of any human being and His form marred beyond human likeness."*
> Isaiah 52:14

Just one of the implements used to torture Jesus was known as the Cat-O'-Nine Tails in English. Romans inflicted scourging on slaves, prisoners and criminals condemned to death by crucifixion. Many times, the victim died before the scourging was finished due to the extreme torture and loss of blood. Victims veins were laid bare, and the inner muscles, sinews, even their entrails were exposed. Romans did NOT call theirs a Cat O' nine tails. They called it a flagrum. Ancient artifacts reveal that the British Cat O Nine Tails was like a toy in comparison to the Roman version. The Roman flagrum had 9 cords with heavy lead hooks at the end designed to wrap around the body and hook into the flesh, then they would violently pull them back to tear the flesh away in strips AKA stripes, creating maximum damage.

The Bible does not lie nor does it exaggerate so when it says, *"His appearance was so disfigured beyond that of any human being..."* it is saying that no man in the history of the world has ever been tortured like Jesus was; not before, nor after. And when it says, *"...and His form marred beyond human likeness,"* it is saying that the beating and torture Jesus endured, was so horrendous that He no longer looked like a human being on the cross. Anyone that has seen the movie, the Passion, can attest to the gruesome scene in the courtyard where Jesus was scourged. There were several times that I had to look away, it was that horrible, but the way the text is written, the movie wasn't even close to the actual event. Jesus must have looked like a piece of shredded meat while he hung on the cross.

But why, why would God allow His son to endure that kind of abuse? If Jesus was simply coming for our salvation, why would He have to be tortured like that? What did it have to do with salvation? Wasn't it enough for Him to just die for our sins? No, it wasn't, and the reason it wasn't, the reason Jesus did not look like a human anymore to us, is because we no longer looked like what God created us to be. We had so taken on the image and likeness of Satan that we no longer looked like His Children. Jesus took our devilish identity so He could give us His righteousness, it would be a fair and even exchange.

You see, forgiveness was just the avenue through which He could transfer our rightful heritage back to us, and if salvation was the only thing the cross had done for us, it would be a divine gift, but the cross accomplished so much more than just our salvation. It restored our position as children in the Kingdom by regaining the identity Satan had stolen from us in the Garden, the same Identity he's been hiding from us since the cross.

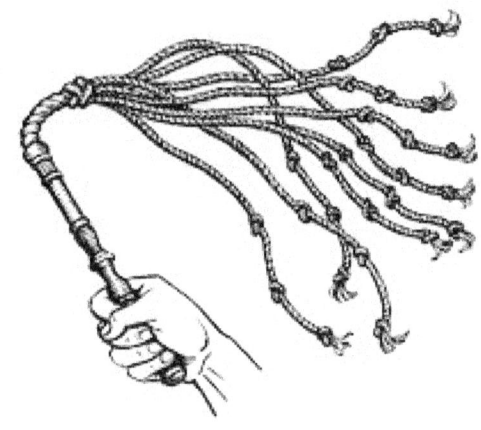

Instead of looking and behaving like children whose Father is the Lord God, the God of all creation, we behaved like orphans and looked like the race of scorpions that dwell alongside us. Displaying all the characteristics of an unwanted child, we are hateful because Satan is hateful, we are jealous because Satan is jealous, we are depressed because Satan is depressed, we feel condemnation because he is condemned, we murder because Satan was a murderer from the beginning, we are lustful because Satan is full of lust, we are rebellious because Satan was a rebel, we are rude, prideful and selfish because Satan is all those things and more. Every evil act, every wicked emotion, every depraved, despicable and selfish thought comes from the devil, and Satan has successfully projected his disgusting, vile nature upon the Children of God.

There was just one thing that Satan never expected, one thing he was not prepared for; that the God of all creation would allow His son to step down off the throne, become a man, and die as a sacrifice for us all. Jesus, by way of the cross, made a way for Satan's grotesque nature, the spirit of this world, to be replaced and exchanged with His Spirit, the Holy Spirit.

> Yet **it pleased** the LORD to bruise Him...Isaiah 53:10

It pleased the Lord to bruise Him? Why would it please our Father to allow His Son to be tortured in this way, and to that extent? Because, with every lash, with every strike of the flagrum, with every stripe it inflicted, it was paying for the total price of our identity. So far was our fall, that Jesus had to be beaten, flogged and tortured until God was satisfied that His disfigurement sufficiently equaled the disfigurement we had assumed. If Jesus was marred more than any man in history, if He was disfigured beyond the likeness of a human, and it was done to regain our identity as children; no words sufficiently describe, no matter how we try to explain it, how disgusting mankind had become and how awful we must have looked to the Father.

I have known all that for quite some time now, but for the first time, I saw it through different eyes, the eyes of Jesus. If it pleased our Father to shred Jesus so, you know it must have pleased Jesus to be tortured as well. What? Think about it, Jesus always said He only did what He saw the Father do and He only said what He heard the Father say. He and the Father were One, One in heart and mind, therefore if it pleased the Father to bruise Him; it must have pleased Jesus to be bruised as well. Therefore, Jesus would have taken every blow with joy for the redemption and restoration of the relationship and identity of His wayward children. Paul attests to this in the book of Hebrews.

> *Let us fix our eyes on Jesus, the author and perfecter of our faith*, **who for the joy set before Him endured the cross**, *scorning its shame, and sat down at the right hand of the throne of God.* Hebrews 12:2

Can you believe it? How amazing, how much love does it take to not only agree to take the punishment meant for another, but to do it with joy? It is almost unfathomable, but the more I consider it, the more I see it in the scripture, the more sense it makes to me, because it's so like Jesus to not only do that for us but to do it with joy. Isn't that awesome, isn't that just the most amazing thing ever? Yes, it is, and Jesus never expects us to do anything He has not done or isn't willing to do Himself.

> *I have been crucified with Christ. It is no longer I who live, but Christ who lives in me. And the life I now live in the flesh I live by faith in the Son of God, who loved me and gave himself for me.* Galatians 2:20

Paul was obviously speaking metaphorically when he says he was crucified with Christ, because the Holy Spirit had revealed the full truth of the purpose of the cross to him. We were scheduled for punishment, a punishment we well deserved, a punishment we were ill-equipped, unprepared and entirely unable to pay on our own. Our Father, the God of all creation has seen enough, and He is no longer satisfied with the temporary atonement of sin by the insufficient blood of bulls and goats. He's been planning this since the Garden of Eden, so Jesus leaves divinity, comes down off His throne to take our punishment, and all because He loved us so. The extent of the scourging and its seemingly excessive torture of the Lord was not overly heavy-handed at all, it was exactly what was required by the Father to save us from an eternity of separation from Him while restoring our identity and our authority so as to regain all that was lost by Adam in the Garden.

God never intended for us to just exist on the earth, He wanted His children to have dominion over His creation. What Father doesn't? We were created to dominate the earth and all that He created. He created us to rule the earth as He ruled in Heaven, but we rebelled, and in our rebellion, we began conforming into the image, the likeness of the most disgusting, vile, despicable, evil creature that has ever existed or will ever exist. We were guilty of treason, the verdict given, the punishment set, the sentence is death followed by an eternity of torture.

This case is different though, because the Judge is the Father of the convicted felon, so out of love for His children, He comes down from His throne, submits Himself to His own Law and takes the full brunt of the sentence they deserved. Every blow Jesus took was one less we would receive for our iniquity, and the punishment would continue until the Father determined that the debt was paid in full.

And for anyone who might doubt the biblical account of the trial, scourging and crucifixion of Jesus; I believe God waited until this time in history, because the Romans were the most advanced civilization to that date. The Roman system of government was very sophisticated; America's republic was birthed out of it, and they kept impeccable records of the entire event in which every word of the Bible surrounding the crucifixion of Jesus is factually proven. But you will never hear that on CNN, because it does not fit the evolution narrative that they attempt to deceive the world with.

This scourging that Jesus endured is way deeper than we have ever considered before. For without it, we never would have had the right to be called Children of God, nor could we have become the righteousness of our Father in Christ Jesus. Jesus took such a beating, because we had transgressed so far in our sin that the scourging and the cross were the only thing sufficient to save us, and for us to willingly sin in the face of the knowledge of this, is an insult to the Father and the Son in light of everything They unselfishly did to restore us to our rightful place as children and heirs to the throne.

One of the main reasons Satan tries so hard to hide this truth from us is the effect it would have on us. He knows that if you get a true revelation of the cross, what Jesus selflessly endured on your behalf, and why He did what He did; Satan knows it would change your outlook on everything, especially sin. Whenever you are tempted to do anything now, you are likely to be reminded of the sacrifice

Jesus made for you and the price your Father paid to set you free from sin. Those two alone will cause you to reconsider your behavior as well as your motives.

Only because Jesus humbled Himself and submitted to scourging and the cross, are we even eligible, now, to be holy as He is holy, and only if we are "in Christ."

> *For I am the LORD your God; consecrate yourselves*
> *therefore, and be holy, because I am holy.*
> Leviticus 11:44.

The scourging and the cross purchased us the right and the ability, by way of the Holy Spirit to take on all the characteristics of Jesus. As He is faithful, we can be faithful, as He is gentle, kind and considerate so can we be. We are encouraged and full of joy because He is. We now have the lawful right and the ability to take all His beautiful qualities and personality traits because He took away our disgusting image on the cross. Jesus exchanged our sin for His righteousness so we could be saved; obtaining righteousness for us, and transforming us from the likeness of demons to the appearance of Jesus in the eyes of the Father again. That was the full purpose of the cross and the very essence of who you are, if you are "in Him." That is your identity, the right and the ability to look like King Jesus through the express empowerment of the Holy Spirit, because of the torture He lovingly, joyfully endured to redeem you.

Every evil, angry, lustful, hateful, depressed, selfish, anxious, unforgiving and murderous characteristic of the Devil was paid for that day in the courtyard and on the cross by Jesus, so you could be a reflection of Him to a lost and dying world. That is why this life is not about you, your wants or your desires any longer, it's about the One who literally gave up His Throne, became a man and died a hideous death in your place. He did it so you could regain all that was lost in the Garden and look like Jesus to the Father again; not so you could continue in sin and keep looking like the devil. As Jesus loves and forgives unconditionally, so are you able, as He is compassionate, and full of grace and mercy, you can be as well. No longer do you have to look, think and behave like the enemy of your Father, but now you can literally become the likeness of the King.

> *God has highly exalted Jesus and given Him the name above all names, ¹⁰that at the name of Jesus every knee will bow, in heaven and on earth and under the earth, ¹¹and every tongue will confess that Jesus Christ is Lord,...* Philippians 2:9-11

Some people willingly, others reluctantly, but all will bow none the less!

Lastly, the cross gained you back more than just your salvation and your identity, it returned your authority. The one thing Satan never imagined he'd lose... authority; the legal right to rule and rein as Kings and Queens was stripped from him and made available to us again. The lawful right to exercise dominion over all the earth is now returned to its rightful owners, children of the living God. From the Garden until the cross, the most valuable thing Satan possessed was authority, and now it has been delivered back to us by way of Gods Spirit of Adoption. We are the true and rightful heirs of a loving Father, children that understand their identity. God desires for His children to know who they are and why they were created in the first place, so now they can step back into their rightful position of authority.

> *What is man that You are mindful of him, ⁵You made him a little lower than the angels; You crowned him with glory and honor. ⁶**You have placed everything under his feet.*** Psalm 8:4-6

To properly understand your identity is to fully comprehend who you are and what you were created for in the first place. You were not created to lust after the flesh and identify with the world. You were not created to think and act like vermin; you were created to rule and rein as a King, a Queen, a son or daughter of the living God. Because of the cross, the price has been paid for you to be free from the prison of sin. It is not as if Jesus just paid your bail so you could be temporarily free, only to be tried later; He paid the fine so you could be completely free, but free from what? Free from the bondage of sin so it would no longer enslaved you.

> *My little children, I am writing these things to you **so that you will not sin.*** 1 John 2:1

The cross paid for us to be free from sin so that we do not sin, not so we could sin and get away with it. The OSAS doctrine completely undermines the purpose of the stripes Jesus so gallantly endured by almost encouraging sin and excusing it, but Christians who do so, are virtually indistinguishable from people in the world, the children of the devil. Tell me, where's the identity in that? So then, did Jesus pay such a heavy price for us to look the same as we did before we come to the knowledge of the Truth? Heavens no! Why would He go through all that just so we could stay in the same pitiful, sinful state, looking like the very thing He came to rescue us from? It doesn't even make any sense when you consider it logically.

Any conversion that does not include transformation into His likeness is a false conversion. Because of the nature of sin, so many people have nearly destroyed everything they love in their life and they feel like they have hit rock bottom; but in so doing, many of them turn to God for deliverance. That is both good and bad, because on the one hand, they realize they have messed up their lives because of their own sinful behavior, but on the other hand, they have no intention of changing their behavior, they just want God to get them out of the mess they created. So, they run to Him, hoping He will fix all their problems, but that is not His passion for them. God is trying to get them to a place of submission where He can transform them into the image of Himself as exemplified by Jesus, so when God doesn't fix all their issues the way they want, they grow angry and bitter towards Him.

Christians are notorious for doing this; they're famous for becoming angry at God if He does not answer their prayers the way they want. Jewish people who still believe in the God of Abraham, Isaac and Jacob are much more mature regarding the nature of God because they have a much better understanding of the relationship as natural born children. Christians are adopted by the Spirit of Adoption, but they are never taught that, and therefore have a warped understanding of God; viewing Him more like Santa Clause or a Genie in a bottle.

Christians go to church, plead before the altar, pray a sinner's prayer and go right back to their sin. They call themselves Christians, but they have nothing to do with God except when they want something from Him or if they get in trouble again. They behave no different than they did before they confessed Christ, and the same people they surround themselves with, other children of the devil. Then they look down their noses at other people, as well as their precious Jewish brothers and sisters, thinking lowly of them for not believing the message of the cross, but why would any person, especially Jewish people want what Christians have when everything they say and do comes from a place of ignorance and selfishness?

Selfishness is the most common character trait of the world, yet Christians, as a result of the prosperity gospel, don't seem much different. And the devil…he is all over it with his OSAS mega churches and the tithing guilt trip they heap upon their poor, misguided, misinformed, deceived souls like an ambulance chasing attorney goes after an accident victim. If I could say just one thing to my Jewish brothers and sisters it would be this, "please forgive Christians and the way they behave, for they know not what they do." How offended faithful Jews must be when they witness Christians treating God like an errand boy and tarnish the image and reputation of the living God by their ignorance.

Just how many deceived, so-called Christians are there now? That question can be answered with a question; just how big and numerous are the mega churches nowadays? The prosperity pimps in these MEGA churches behave like idols and they have no interest in telling their idolaters that they are children of the Most High God. They want them...no, they need them right where they are, in a stupor, a constant state of sin leading to worldly sorrow, leading them back to church, leading them to tithe in hopes God will grant them a blessing because of the money they gave to a preacher who will only use it to buy a limo, a mansion and a new jet. If I didn't know the honest truth and reason for the cross, and if I had only an ounce of decency, I'd almost be ashamed of calling myself a Christian because of the shameful way most of them behave now.

These OSAS, ambulance chasing prosperity preachers have no desire for anyone to learn their identity, they've got them right where they want them, right where the Old World Church had people before Martin Luther let the cat out of the bag and exposed them for what they truly were, agents of the devil strategically placed there to keep people from learning who and what they were, children of the Living God, children in authority.

The identity of a Christian can be a difficult concept to grasp for many who were physically or emotionally abused by their parents or whoever raised them. However, one of the greatest benefits of understanding your identity as a Child of God and as an heir, is becoming aware that your past does not determine who you are now that you are "in Christ." Your childhood, your parents, your past mistakes, your race, your hair texture or skin color as well as any other negative or traumatic events that formed or shaped your personality and belief system; none of those things determine who you are now if you are a Child of God.

Satan simply used people in your past as a weapon against your self-image; people who had no understanding of their true identity, why they were created. Then, Satan holds you in bondage through unforgiveness, hate, anger and resentment towards them and God. But why would we allow anyone, believer or unbeliever, past or present, why would we allow people to who have no idea of their identity, to imprison us. 99.99% of the population, saved or not, have no idea what or who they were created to be, but you do now, and once we realize that they are just orphans groaning for that which is missing in their life, we move from being offended by them to loving them with pity and forgiveness. Believer or unbeliever, preacher or heathen, religious or not, if they are living in the world, living for worldly things, behaving like the world; just like the religious leaders in the days of Jesus, their father is the devil and they can only do what is in their nature, but you can break the cycle.

Make Jesus your Lord, die to yourself, receive the Spirit of Adoption, become a Child of God and make it your goal, your quest to walk in the likeness of Jesus everywhere you go. Your identity is and should always be based upon who your Heavenly Father is, what your Lord and Savior Jesus did for you on the cross, what They say about you and who They say you are. They define you now!

> *How precious to me are Your thoughts, O God, how vast is their sum!* [18]
> *If I were to count them, they would outnumber the grains of sand;*
> Psalm 139:18

Your Father has more thoughts towards you than the grains of sand in the world, and all of his thoughts for you are always good. Did you know that there are over 1.1 billion grains of sand in just one cubic foot of sand? So how many thoughts does our Father have about us? What if you got hold of only 10 of those thoughts daily and meditated upon them? Never, I repeat, never take anything that anyone say to you, about you to heart, unless it mimics what your Father says or thinks about you. You may not look like Jesus at the moment, but if you make it your goal to seek the Kingdom of God and His righteousness, He will begin transforming you into His image.

The first step is for you to want to be like Him and not the world any longer. He's not going to force Himself on you, and you have to want this thing more than you want the pleasures of the world. His Holy Spirit will handle the transformation process, but you have to supply the "want to" by asking, seeking and knocking.

The Devil is a liar and he's going to lie to you about you and everyone else you love for that matter. He will ridicule and put down those you love in an attempt to lower your opinion of them so he can destroy your relationship with them; his favorite strategy is to divide and conquer. It is imperative that you spend time in prayer as well as get the Word in you and find out what your Father says and thinks about you. That is what you dwell on, that is what you fashion your mind upon; becoming Jesus is now your number one goal in life, because you are A Child of God, an heir to the throne and the Bible says that you are seated in heavenly places with Christ Jesus, far above all principalities and powers. Far above means that you are higher in rank and therefore higher in authority than Satan and all his demon forces. You are higher in favor and honor; in a more modern vernacular some would say, "you da' man now!"

> *For it is Christ Jesus, the one having died, now rather having been raised up, who is seated at the right hand of God, and who is interceding on our behalf.* Romans 8:34

And,

> *And God raised us up with Christ and seated us with Him in the heavenly realms in Christ Jesus,* Ephesians 2:6

And that's right where the Father and Jesus want you to see yourself; seated right smack dab next to them, not over in the courtyard like a servant, but all snuggled up next to Jesus and the Father. This is where you belong now, because this is who you are when you choose to die to yourself and come out of the world; you are now a Child of God. No longer are you at enmity with God. The cross enables us to go from enemy of God, to Child of God, in an instant.

Whether you're male or female, you are referred to as a son in the Bible. If I can deal with being called "the bride of Christ," you women can deal with being called a son. Even when you mess up now, your Father is not looking at you thinking what a bone-headed move you just made or what a screw-up you are. No, as long as you sincerely set your heart to become like Him, He sees you the way He created you to be. He sees you through the eyes of a loving Father, rooting and cheering for you to see yourself the same way He sees you. You Father is not a vindictive God, and he doesn't just love. He is love, and He wants you to see yourself as beloved, because that is exactly what you are to Him now... beloved.

The only reason Christians continue in sin, the only reason they behave the way they do is because they never learned their true identity as Children of a loving Father. If believers are not properly instructed on the virtues, the rights, the responsibilities and privileges of being a Child of God, they will likely end up going back to the world; forgetting they were children, they begin living like orphans again because it's what they are familiar with.

Immediately after a heartfelt confession of Jesus as Lord is made by a soul in need of a savior, they are surrounded by what the Bible calls, "familiar spirits," whose only job is to lure them back to "the world," a world they are all too familiar with, a world they are comfortable with so they can be taken to the pit and used as food for a race of locusts in the not too distant future.

Jesus said, *"If you love me you will keep my commandments,"* but doesn't that also mean if you don't keep His commandments, you obviously don't love Him? And don't freak out, because the entire purpose of this book is to teach you how to walk without sin and love the Father with all your heart, all your soul and all your mind so you can reposition yourself as a Child of God, not an orphan. It's not about anything you do to become righteous, it's about denying yourself and becoming love so that, as a child, you literally become the righteousness of Him who died for you.

Father God

Only a handful of the Old Testament patriarchs had what could be construed as a father/son relationship with the Lord God, however, God refers to Himself as our Father, on several occasions, by referring to us has his children.

> *Then you shall say to Pharaoh, 'Thus says the LORD, Israel is my firstborn son,... Exodus 4:22*

This is the first time God speaks of Himself as a Father, by referring to the children of Israel as His firstborn son. After the fall of Adam, and for the next few hundred years, it seems as if the presence of the Father was no longer on earth; that is until Enoch comes on the scene.

> *Enoch walked with God, and then he was no more, because God had taken him away. Genesis 5:24*

By the time Enoch is taken away by God, the earth is almost completely corrupted by the Fallen Angels or the Runaways as they are referred to in the Book of Enoch. FYI, Jesus quotes from the book of Enoch and Peter references Enoch, therefore we should consider it as a source worthy of quoting as well. God put His plan for redemption and Son-ship into motion immediately after Adam and Eve are separated from Him by sin.

> *And I will put enmity between you and the woman, and between your seed and her seed. He will crush your head, and you will strike his heel." Genesis 3:15*

Here, God is prophesying that Satan will bruise the heal of Jesus at the cross, but Jesus will crush the head of the serpent upon His resurrection. And it will come by way of the Seed, the Holy Semen of God and the seed or egg of a woman. Satan counters Gods plan for redemption in corrupting the bloodline to Jesus by having the Fallen Angels mate with the daughters of Adam, and the offspring were Giants, also known as the Nephilim.

> *...the sons of God saw that the daughters of men were beautiful, and they took as wives whomever they chose. Genesis 6:2*

The Sons – Strong's #1121 - ben (be·nê) Used as son, male child and/or angels.

of God – Strong's #430 - elohim (el-o-heem') Angels, mostly used as angels, god with a little g, indicating it is not the Lord God, but a godlike one, a false god. Rarely is elohim used to describe the Lord God and almost always refers to Satan or the fallen angels.

The sons of the Lord God in this verse were the fallen angels that Satan deceived into thinking that they could leave their spiritual state, enter into a world system they were not created for and have licentious freedom with human women, a different race of beings. Eloheim is used when referring to the angels of the Lord God in the first 5 books of the Torah which were written by the Hand of God through Moses. There are a few times Old Testament prophets use the word Eloheim when referring to the Lord God, so context is imperative whenever the word eloheim is being used, because it is likely referring to Satan and/or his army of fallen angels. To the Lord God, the mixing of two different races of beings is a most despicable act, and would be comparable to a human having relations with an animal; it is disgusting to the Lord God.

The blood of a child is determined by the sperm of the father, therefore

Satan had the brilliant plan of corrupting the bloodline to Jesus with the semen of his followers so Jesus can never happen, but Satan probably never thought that God would flood the entire earth and kill off all the Giants.

GIANTS' SKELETONS FOUND.
Cave in Mexico Gives Up the Bones of an Ancient Race.
Special to The New York Times.

BOSTON, May 3.—Charles C. Clapp, who has recently returned from Mexico, where he has been in charge of Thomas W. Lawson's mining interests, has called the attention of Prof. Agassiz to a remarkable discovery made by him.

He found in Mexico a cave containing some 200 skeletons of men each above eight feet in height. The cave was evidently the burial place of a race of giants who antedated the Aztecs. Mr. Clapp arranged the bones of one of these skeletons and found the total length to be 8 feet 11 inches. The femur reached up to his thigh, and the molars were big enough to crack a cocoanut. The head measured eighteen inches from front to back.

The New York Times
Published: May 4, 1908
Copyright © The New York Times

There were giants on the earth in those days, and also afterward, when the sons of God came in to the daughters of men and they bore children to them. Those were the mighty men who were of old, men of renown. Genesis 6:4 When it says, *"in those days and also afterwards,"* it implies that there were giants before and after the flood. Before the flood, in the book of Enoch, the giants were described as being 300 cubits tall. A cubit was a form of measurement consisting of the length of a man's arm from the tip of his finger to his elbow and was generally about 15 to 18 inches in length. That would put the pre-flood giants at 450 feet tall and many skeleton remains unearthed from around the world would attest to that fact. In the picture top left, compare the size of the bones to the size of an excavator. In the picture to the immediate left, the giant skull itself is larger than the human. It is noteworthy that the angels were not interested in the daughters of Cain; the text states specifically that they *"came into,"* meaning *"had sex with,"* the daughters of Adam. The Greek translation for *"man"* in the verse is *"Adam."* The English translators probably chose to translate it from Adam to man, because of their conservative nature at the time.

As soon as any remains proving the existence of pre and post flood giants are found and reported, however the Luciferian run Smithsonian Institute swoops in and confiscates them, never to be seen again. Any reports are immediately scrubbed from the media, but there were thousands of news articles written in the 1800's regarding such findings. Many articles from around the world are archived in the historical microfiche data bases of independent local news agencies.

In Genesis it says that Eve was beguiled by the snake. The word Beguiled in the Strong's is ek and apatao; properly translated *"to seduce."* It is saying that Satan seduced Eve into a sexual encounter in the garden. When God enters the picture in Gen 3:17, He says to Adam, *"Because you have listened to your wife..."* The word for wife here is Ishashah, and the Strong's Definition of Ishashah is **"adulteress,"** so first it states that Satan seduced Eve, and then God calls her an adulteress. Why would God refer to Eve as an adulteress unless she had committed adultery, and with whom did she commit this adultery... Satan?

The Hebrew word for snake is Nachash – Snake, serpent, <u>shining like brass, shining one</u>. Many times, in Hebrew they substitute a verb for the noun, therefore instead of *"a snake,"* the intention of the word was, *"the shining one,"* which is why Paul said, *"Satan presents himself as an angel of light."*

1 John 3:12 is rendered *"from the evil one,"* while many other versions have

"of the evil one." Jewish interpreters took this to mean that Cain was literally the son of a serpentine being of light in the Garden of Eden. In Jewish legend, (Louis Ginzberg, The Legends of the Jews, Vol.1, Johns Hopkins University Press, 1998,

ISBN 0-8018-5890-9, p.105-9) "**The serpent from the Garden of Eden was the father to firstborn Cain."**

Genesis 4:1, upon conception of Cain, Eve declared that she had gotten a man with the lord (lord in the Hebrew - Jehovah). However, prior to Eve's declaration in this particular verse, the word Jehovah is **always** followed by the word *"Elohim,"* forming "Lord God".

Lord - Strong's # <u>433</u> (el-o-heem) - God, gods, goddess, godlike one, angels, demons, magistrates.

Eve's declaration marks a change in the way she addressed God. Instead of calling Him *"the Lord God,"* she simply says *"lord."* Why? She either profanes the name of God by referring to Him as a lesser god or she was actually referring to a different god, or as Strong's defines, a god with a little "g," an angel, demon, magistrate... Satan. Therefore, in order to differentiate Himself from Satan in Genesis, all references to the Lord God, the God of Abraham, Isaac and Jacob is *"Elohim Jehovah,"* or *"The Lord God,"* and all references to Satan are simply *"elohim."*

> *When Adam had lived one hundred and thirty years, he became the father of a son **in his own likeness**, according to **his image**, and named him Seth. Then the days of Adam after he became the father of Seth were eight hundred years, and he had other sons and daughters.* Genesis 5

Remember, God dictated the book of Genesis to Moses personally, so why would God specify that Adam had a son *"in his own likeness,"* unless there had been another son, not in his likeness? Also notice that it is stated twice, *"in his own likeness"* and *"according to his image."* We must also consider the genealogy of Cain and Abel. Given the usual preferential status assigned to firstborn sons, by all rights we should expect that Cain would be the first son listed instead of Seth in Adam's genealogy. This omission speaks volumes, because God is very specific on the accuracy of genealogies. Cain's genealogy is given separately, before Adam's, in chapter 4. This genealogy begins with Cain, naming neither Adam nor another before him. The apostle John acknowledged that Cain was Satan's son when he wrote,

> ...not as Cain, **who was of the evil one** and slew his brother, and for what reason did he slay him? Because his deeds were evil, and his brothers were righteous. 1 John 3:12

Trees in the Garden of Eden

What about Trees in the Garden of Eden? The "Tree" is a metaphor - There's a saying you may find familiar: "The apple doesn't fall far from **the tree**." It's an observation that a person is like their parent, usually their Dad. It is similar to the expression: "Like father, like son." Have you ever heard of a "Family Tree?" But how can we know that a tree is being used as a metaphor for genetic lineage without a biblical example?

> But I was like a gentle lamb led to the slaughter; And I did not know that they had devised plots against me, saying, **"Let us destroy the tree with its fruit**, And let him cut him off from the land of the living, That his name be remembered no more."
> Jeremiah 11:19

The tree is the man and his fruit is his offspring or the potential offspring of his loins, his genetic material. The fruit holds the seed and the seed is the semen.

> He will be like a tree firmly planted by streams of water, which yields its fruit in its season and its leaf does not wither; and in whatever he does, he prospers. Psalms 1:3

From these examples we understand that when we read in the Bible about trees and their fruit the reference is likely to be men or heavenly beings and their offspring, or their procreative ability. The best confirmation of this is in Ezekiel 31 which refers directly to the trees in Eden as the fallen angels;

> *...so that **all the trees** by the waters may not be exalted in their stature, nor set their top among the clouds, nor their **well-watered mighty ones** stand erect in their height. For **they have all been given over to death**, to the earth beneath, **among the sons of men**, with **those who go down to the pit.**"* Ezekiel 31:14-15

Since trees obviously don't go to pit of hell, God is clearly talking about a person or some other entity.

> *...I made the nations quake at the sound of **its** fall when I made **it** go down to Sheol with those who go down to the pit; **and all the well-watered trees of Eden**,* Ezekiel 31:16

Once again, if He isn't talking about a tree going to hell, who is the Lord God talking about? Whoever "**it**" was, "**it**" made a sound when "**it**" fell to the pit in Sheol (Hell).

> ***They*** *also went down with **it** to Sheol to those who were slain by the sword; and those who were **its** strength lived under **its** shade among the nations.* ¹⁸"***To which among the trees of Eden*** *are you thus equal in glory and greatness? Yet **you will be brought down** with* <u>**the trees of Eden**</u> *to the earth beneath; **you** will lie in the midst of the uncircumcised...!" declares the Lord GOD.* Ezekiel 31:17-18

Clearly, the trees in the Garden of Eden were Satan and the fallen angels.

> *When the woman saw that the tree* (Tree of Eden - Satan) *was good for food* (procreation), *and that it was a delight to the eyes* (Satan was the most beautiful of all the angels), *and that the tree was desirable to make one wise, she took from its fruit and ate;*

64

and she gave also to her husband with her, and he ate. Genesis 3:6

The Targum is the translation of the Hebrew Bible into Aramaic. Before the Christian era, Aramaic had in good part, replaced Hebrew as the vernacular of the Jews. The Targum is considered the oldest and most authentic of all translations from the original Hebrew. The following is taken from the Targum.

*...And the woman beheld Sammael, the angel of death, and was afraid; yet she knew that the tree was good to eat, and that it was medicine for the enlightenment of the eyes, and a desirable tree by means of which to understand. And she took of its fruit, and did eat; and she gave to her husband with her, and he did eat.... And Adam **knew** Hava his wife, **<u>who had desired the Angel</u>**; and she conceived, and bare Kain; and she said, **<u>I have acquired a man, from the Angel of the Lord.</u>** And she added to bear from her husband Adam his twin, even Habel.* Genesis 3 & 4

The word for Angel here is elohim. The text states that Eve desired *"elohim"* the Angel of the Lord, and admits that she conceived from the Angel and sought to add another from Adam. Is that even possible? Super fecundation is the fertilization of **two** or more ova from the same cycle by sperm from separate acts of sexual intercourse or two different men. So, yes it is!

"And Adam knew his wife Eve, who had desired the Angel; and she conceived, and bare Cain; and she said, I have acquired a man, the angel of the Lord ..." The *Targum Jonathan* to Genesis 4:1

And Adam *"knew"* his wife Eve. The word *"knew"* in the Hebrew always implies sexual relations, so Adam had sex with Eve after she desired and had sex with the angel of the Lord (Satan). The Jewish Rabbis taught that Satan was obsessed with

Eve upon seeing her, and considering how the Bible describes Satan as being the most beautiful of all Gods creations, he must have looked good to her as well.

> *...but of the fruit of the tree which is in the midst of the garden, God has said, 'You shall not eat it, nor shall you **touch it**, lest you die.' " Gen 3:3*

Touch – Strong's #5060 (naw-gah) to touch, i.e. Lay the hand upon. It was a euphemism of its time for "**to lie with a woman,**" or "**to have sexual relations with.**"

"Don't touch her" is a phrase that is still used to this day, implying that person ought not to have sex with her. The concept of Eve having sex with Satan first, then running to Adam to have sex with him so that she was impregnated by the sperm of 2 different men was likely horrifying to the ultra-conservative puritans at the time the Bible was being translated into English. As well, the Bible was the main textbook for educating children at the time so that may have had an impact on the wording chosen by the translators. They likely changed it to an apple to be more palatable for the reader. How do we know?

It has long been taught that the apple was the forbidden fruit of the garden, but there is no mention of an apple anywhere in the story. So, how did it get there, how was the apple known as the fruit that Eve ate? Man made it up, or more likely, Satan convinced man to tell it that way to hide his real intention. If it was common knowledge that the fallen angels were having sex with the daughters of Adam and we had the physical evidence of giant bones to prove it, which would vindicate the Bible completely and all but destroy the theory of evolution. Ever wonder why museums are full of dinosaur bones and not the bones of giants?

I have known all this for quite some time now, but what God showed me as I was researching this was that the forbidden fruit in the garden was sex for procreation not pleasure. Satan told Eve that if she ate the apple she would be like God, but this was always confusing to me, because it doesn't say in what way she would be like God except to know the difference between good and evil. But even that is symbolic at best, it's abstract, there's nothing tangible in that statement, nothing that would seriously entice Eve to go against God's command.

Except, what if Satan taught Eve about having children? What if Satan gave Eve the lesson of the birds and the bees, and what if Satan told Eve that she would be like God, in that, she could create life just like God? This would play on her emotions and her maternal instincts, but does the scripture support this theory?

> *...and Eve said, **I have acquired a man, from the Angel of the Lord.** And she added to bear from her husband Adam his twin, even Habel.* Genesis 4:1 Targum Jonathan

If it was sex in the garden, what was the motive behind the sex? Modern civilization thinks of sex mainly to be used for the feeling it brings, but that was not the reason for Eve. Eve was fascinated by the thought of being able to create new life, and that is evident by her words, *"I have acquired a man."* Eve was excited about being pregnant, so much so that she went straight to Adam to do it again. Sex was in the garden, but it wasn't for lust, it was for procreation. Eve wanted children, because Satan had convinced her that she would be like God; able to create new life.

If it was lust, she would have gone to Adam and talked about how awesome it feels, thereby seducing him with desire, but she does not. The scripture says that she went to add another child to her womb. Maybe she thought, "If one child was good, two would be twice as good!"

If what John said about Satan being the father of Cain is true, then Satan's DNA was already in Cain and his offspring, therefore Satan only needed to corrupt Adams bloodline which explains why the Scripture says,

> '*...the sons of God saw that the daughters of men (Adam) were beautiful, and they took as wives whomever they chose.*'
> Genesis 6:2.

The word for man is translated from the word (aw-dawm') or Adam, therefore, the fallen angels were only interested in the daughters of Adam, not the daughters of Cain. Sex was just a side benefit, corrupting the bloodline to Jesus was Satan's main priority, and he very nearly pulled it off.

> *There were giants on the earth in those days,* ***and also afterward****,* Gen 6:4

The purpose of the flood was to destroy everything that Satan was creating on the earth. Satan then deceived even more angels to mate with the daughters of Adam after the flood. There are many accounts of the children of Israel doing battle with giants after coming out of Egypt, up until the times of King David.

> *We saw Nephilim there, the giant descendants of Anak. We felt as small as grasshoppers, and that's how we must have looked to them."* Numbers 13:33

Just as the lifespan of man began to decrease from roughly 900 years to approximately 70 years after the flood, the size of the giants began to decrease with each passing generation as well. To cause the flood, God burst the water in the firmament above the earth, and brought up the water within the earth. By doing so, scientists conclude that the oxygen levels as well as the atmospheric pressure each decreased after the flood, causing the dramatic decrease in lifespan, and making it impossible for the giants to reach their enormous dimensions any longer. It also explains why we did not see dinosaurs after the flood as well.

Ever wonder why God strictly forbid the Jews to marry other races? It wasn't because God was prejudice; it was to keep the bloodline pure to Jesus. Satan's plan to corrupt the bloodline to Jesus has a secondary effect on the population of earth as well. The evil nature of Satan himself has been infused in the DNA of man and its ramifications are clearly evident as the growing population becomes exceedingly wicked. Mankind has begun taking on the very image of the devil, and the Fathers children begin looking more like His mortal enemy than Himself.

> *Then the LORD saw that the wickedness of man was great on the earth, and that **every intent of the thoughts of his heart was only evil continually**. Gen 6:5*

The nature of The Lord God is love; the book of Romans says that *the Kingdom of God is righteousness, peace and joy in the Holy Spirit and whoever serves Jesus in this way is pleasing to God and approved by men....* The Bible says, "... nothing comes out of a man's mouth except what is in his heart...," therefore, if every thought and intent of man's heart was "...*only evil continually*," then every word spoken by man must have been evil continually as well.

> *And the LORD regretted that He had made man on the earth, and it grieved Him in His heart. Genesis 6:6*

This verse used to trouble me because it didn't sound like the nature of a loving Father, which the Lord God is. The way it's translated, it sounds as if God wished He never had children, but Jesus said,

> *"So, if you sinful people know how to give good gifts to your children, how much more will your heavenly Father give the Holy spirit to those who ask him?"* Matthew 7:11

Compared to God, we are evil, so if we know how to love our children, how much more a loving Father God? Loving parents don't regret having children, even when they mess up; they pray for them and hope the best for them and do what is necessary to get them back on the right path. So, when I took a deeper look at this verse, the Hebrew word for regret is "naw-kham," but regret is not the best translation. The number one use of the word Nacham is "moved to pity." Which one sounds more like the nature of a loving Father: a) He's angry at us because of what Satan did to us, or b) He had pity on His children that were deceived by His enemy? If you had a 4 year old child and the 12 year old neighbor kid had deceived them into misbehaving, would you be angry with your child, or feel pity that they were lured into the behavior? The latter of course, but then there is this:

> So, the LORD said, "I will destroy man whom I have created from the face of the earth, both man and beast, creeping thing and birds of the air, for I am sorry that I have made them." Genesis 6:7

This verse would seem to disprove any theory of a loving Father and paints the picture of a vengeful God, but what if God was sorry about his creation for other reasons, deeper reasons. The book of Joshers mirrors Genesis exactly, but elaborates on this time period quite a bit more.

> ...and the sons of men (Fallen Angels) in those days took from the cattle of the earth, the beasts of the field and the fowls of the air, and **taught the mixture of animals** of one species with the other, **in order therewith to provoke the Lord**; and God saw the whole earth and it was corrupt, for all flesh (DNA) had corrupted its ways upon earth, all men and all animals. Jashers 4:18

God was angry, but not with His children, He was angry with the fallen angels who had corrupted His creation by perverting the DNA of both man and beast. "The mixture of animals" spoken of here is the splicing of DNA, it is genetic engineering, a virtual Jurassic Park on steroids. When the angels fell, they fell with all the knowledge of the universe. They had complete knowledge of all the sciences, chemistry, mechanics, biology, engineering and physics. They were experts at science and probably know much more that we have not even learned yet. If we can do it now, they could do it back then. They are the ones that taught it to people. If we can splice genes now, they could then, and the book of Joshers says just that.

The fallen angels had not only infused their DNA with the DNA of humans, but they also began mixing their DNA with that of the animals. Ever wonder why the dinosaurs were so big? If the DNA of a fallen angel would produce a 450 foot giant, what would mixing their DNA do to a lizard? And why were the dinosaurs not spared from the flood like all the other animals? Because God did not create them, Satan did. Just as God destroyed the offspring of the fallen angels, the giants, He also destroyed all the animals that they genetically recreated from their seed.

> *But Noah found favor in the eyes of the LORD.* Gen 6:8

Noah found favor in the sight of God because of his righteousness and because he was the last person on earth, along with his sons that had not been corrupted by the DNA of the fallen angels. But what about the different nationalities, where did they come from? Noah's wife and daughters-in-law held the genetic material of the other races and would pass down those genetic traits, but they had no determination of the bloodline, that comes only from the sperm of the father.

> *This is the account of Noah. Noah was a righteous man, blameless in his generation; Noah walked with God.* Gen 6:9

The phrase, *"Blameless in his generation"* has nothing whatsoever to do with Noah's goodness or his sin; it implies Noah's bloodline to Adam was pure, undefiled by the fallen angel's DNA. With the exception of Noah, the entire earth had been corrupted by the fallen angels and their demonic DNA. Wickedness is the inherent genetic quality in Satan's DNA and sin is the byproduct of it, but holiness is the genetic quality inherent in the DNA of our Father and righteousness is the fruit thereof.

> *Do not be conformed to this world, but be*
> *transformed by the renewing of your mind.*
> Romans 12:2

Upon the conversion of a Christian, the righteous blood of Jesus empowers the Spirit of Adoption to purify our DNA with righteousness, just as if we never sinned before. We then, become righteous and blameless in our generations, just like Noah, but we must renew our minds with the Word of God to remain in that state and walk out this new righteousness; otherwise we can be conformed back into the image of the world. To be transformed implies a change, but more specifically, it indicates a change from the inside out.

Being transformed by the renewing of your mind occurs when you begin reading Gods Word and the Holy Spirit begins teaching you, convicting you, correcting you and training you in righteousness. As this seed of righteousness grows, it begins to change you from within, so you see things from a different perspective; from Gods point of view, from a righteous standpoint.

To be conformed also implies a change, but it is a change from the outside-in. To be conformed to the world occurs when a believer who either never transforms his mind by reading the Word, or began the transformation process but stopped for any number of reasons. To be conformed back to the world is to be influenced by worldly things in an attempt to lure them back to their former selfish, sinful state. But God has given you "free will" to follow whom you will, therefore you are free to make Jesus your Lord and *"continue to the end"* or free to go back or be conformed back to the world you once knew.

Once you get washed in the blood of Jesus, once your DNA is purified by the blood of the lamb, it is imperative that you be transformed into the image of Jesus by renewing your mind with the Word of God. We were all infused with the wicked DNA of the devil and we were all born in and indoctrinated into his matrix world system, along with his selfish way of thinking and behaving. But if you are "in Christ," you have been set free from all that, as long as you choose to die to your selfish desires and seek the kingdom of God and His righteousness.

So, if the Son makes you free, you shall be free indeed. John 8:36

If that is you, you must relearn everything from Gods point of view. If everything you ever learned was from Satan's world system, it was from his wicked, sadistic point of view and being *"the father of all lies,"* you must throw out every concept, every position, every theory, every opinion and every hypothesis that you have ever formed regarding the world you live in and this life you lead and find out, search out, what your Heavenly Father feels and thinks about it.

You must determine in your heart that if your Father has a different view from yours regarding a subject or a matter, you are wrong, and He is right. You must immediately discard your demonically inspired thoughts and opinions and adopt your Fathers. Let me give you a simple example: Abortion is argued as a woman's right to her own body, but to God it's just plain murder, and according to the commandments, *"Thou shall not take an innocent life,"* is there anything more innocent than a baby? In America, we have many animal species that are protected on the endangered species list, so that if you were to kill one of them or even an egg in some cases, you can be severely fined and even go to jail. Yet we think nothing of aborting a human baby, and we don't see the hypocrisy. Why? Because this is Satan's domain, he is the god of this world system and he only comes to kill, steal and destroy; it's all he knows how to do.

Never let the thoughts and opinions of the world conform you or remold you back into their wicked, twisted, perverted way of thinking. Technology and advancement in culture does not persuade the Father to change His mind about anything. Right is right and wrong is wrong, and there is just no right way to do a wrong thing. By renewing your mind with the Word of God, He will teach you, convict you, correct you and train you to look, think and act like Jesus.

Jesus did not just die to get you into heaven, He died to get heaven into you, so you could look like Him to a lost and dying world. If Jesus' only goal was for us to get "saved," then we would have just vanished when we received the truth. But we didn't, and the reason we didn't just sky-up and go to heaven is because there was so much more to our lives than just getting out of here. If that was the main focus, why have children at all, God could have just fellowshipped with us while we were souls in heaven.

*"Before I formed you in the belly, **I knew you**.* Jeremiah 1:5

The biggest problem people have with God several years into their Christian walk is that things in their life have not changed. The things in your life will not change unless or until you do, and that only occurs when you renew your mind with His Word. Satan has successfully used the prosperity message to deceive Christians into thinking they will receive all kinds of blessings if they only tithe; and the more they tithe, the bigger the blessing. After they have given thousands and thousands of their hard earned dollars to a prosperity preaching pimp, who squanders it all on worldly things for himself, years later, when they are evicted from their home for failure to pay their mortgage, they get angry at God because He didn't hold up His end of the prosperity bargain. Then, because Satan has successfully coupled the false prosperity message with the Once Saved-Always Saved lie, these poor souls leave the church broken, bitter and angry at God, going back to their sinful worldly life thinking, "why bother being righteous, I'm saved by grace, my Father loves me no matter what."

Jesus didn't die such a brutal death to give you worldly things that only enhance the demonic image He's trying to rescue you from. He died so you could look like Him, but that won't happen as long as you lust after the things of the world. The Exodus of Egypt is a marvelous depiction of this process. Just as a drug addict must stop using drugs in order to overcome the addiction and cravings for it, Israel had to be removed from Egypt and the delicacies they had grown accustomed to so God could teach them how to rely on Him again. And so, it is with us, the prosperity message opposes the actual intent of the cross which is to purge the world out of us so He can live in us and we can live for Him.

You were made to become the likeness of Christ, but if you do not renew you mind by reading His Word and seek righteousness as the very first thing you do, you will be ruled by your feelings and circumstances instead of ruling over them. Maybe you have a boss that is horrible towards you and you are praying to be removed from your job. You want God to find you another job because this one is unbearable. They cuss like sailors, treat you disrespectfully, insult your intelligence, mock you repeatedly for taking a Christian stand and you just cannot take it any longer. You're praying to God to remove you, you're applying for different jobs all over the city, but there is no response and your situation is only getting worse, not better. By this time, you say that you're not mad at God; you're just frustrated with Him about it. But the truth is, you are angry with God, you're angry that He has not *"made a way of escape that you will be able to bare it."* Your particular situation may be different, but the concept is the same.

Most Christians treat God like He's a waitress at a diner, ordering Him around to better suit their life, because they have not yet learned that it's **not** all about them anymore. Apparently, they were never *"transformed by the renewing of their mind."* Most likely, they were never taught anything but blessings and prosperity and therefore never got the concept of "dying to themselves," so they could pick up their cross and follow Jesus. Until they do, their situation will not only **not** improve, but it will get worse. You see, Satan knows how aggravated we are when we mutter to ourselves, "Ugh, if my boss does that one more time!" Rest assured, he will, and it'll get worse and worse, until we realize why. Why did the Israelites go around the mountain for 40 years? Yea, you got it, because they complained.

We should not test Christ, as some of them did, and
were killed by snakes. 1 Corinthians 10:9-11

> *They willfully tested God by demanding the food they craved.* Psalm 78:18

> *And **do not complain**, as some of them did, and were killed by the destroying angel.* [11]*Now **these things happened to them as examples and** were written down **as warnings for us**...*1 Corinthians 10:9-11

Israel had not been out of Egypt very long, yet the recollection of the delicacies of Egypt induced them to despise the manna. And don't forget that Jesus said He was the manna, so in despising the manna, they were despising Jesus. In Exodus, 12:38, a mixed multitude of foreigners had accompanied them on their journey. They attached themselves to the redeemed Israeli nation because the influence of miracles and circumstances, but they were ignorant to the grace of God who had chosen Israel from among the nations. The presence and grace of the Lord God, who had promised Canaan to His people as their inheritance, meant nothing to these alien sojourners. All they wanted, all they hoped for was to better their own condition by attaching themselves to this obviously blessed nation. When they found that they had exchanged the indulgences and luxuries of Egypt for the toil and travail of the wilderness, albeit with the promise and provision of the Lord God for their every need, they almost immediately regretted the choice they made, and it was with them that the dissatisfaction and murmuring began.

> *Now **the mixed multitude that were among them** yielded to intense craving; so the children of Israel also wept again and said: "Who will give us meat to eat?"* Numbers 11:4

The murmuring and complaining of the foreigners among them influenced the Israelites to complain as well. God had transformed Israel from a slave to a free man, but the mixed multitude began conforming them back to their slave mentality.

> *Who shall give us flesh to eat? We remember the fish, which we did eat in Egypt freely; the cucumbers, and the melons, and the leeks, and the onions, and the garlic. But now our soul is dried away: there is nothing at all beside this manna, before our eyes.* Numbers 11:5-6

The harsh bondage Israel suffered in Egypt made them despise the fish and cucumbers and melons they had while they were there. The chains of their slavery pressed so heavily that they groaned continuously for Gods deliverance. Their groaning was heard and God delivered them; joy of their deliverance filled their hearts, and they sang the praises of their Deliverer, but soon afterwards they forgot the chains which made their food in Egypt bitter. More importantly, they forgot that which so filled their hearts with gladness, the grace of their Redeemer and the wonders of their redemption, when suddenly, all they remembered now was the fish and the cucumbers, the melons, the leeks, the onions and the garlic which they ate in Egypt freely!

It's easy to look at Israel here and wonder how they could possibly complain or even question God's motive towards them after all the miracles He performed in delivering them from slavery, but Paul warns Christians in 1 Corinthians 10 to be careful that they not fall into the same trap.

> *I do not want you to be unaware, brothers, that our forefathers were all under the cloud, and that they all passed through the sea. ⁵Nevertheless, God was not pleased with most of them, for they were struck down in the wilderness. ⁶<u>These things took place as examples to keep us from craving evil things as they did.</u> ⁷Do not be **idolaters**, as some of them were. ⁸We should not commit **sexual immorality**, as some of them did, and in one day twenty-three thousand of them died. ⁹We should not **test Christ**, as some of them did, and were killed by snakes. ¹⁰<u>And do not complain, as some of them did, and were killed by the destroying angel.</u> ¹¹Now **these things happened to them as examples** and were written down **<u>as warnings for us</u>**,*
> 1 Corinthians 10:1-11

The sad state of the modern Christian church proves that they have **not** heeded Paul's words of caution. Paul cleverly used Israel's exodus from Egypt as a warning to us, a type and shadow, a metaphor for the born again experience. Removing Israel from Egypt was the easy part of the Exodus, but removing Egypt from the heart of Israel was a task so difficult that out of several million, only Joshua and Caleb entered the Promised Land. Christians tend to look at this story and consider only the children of Israel, but let's not forget that there were two distinct groups of people coming out of Egypt. Egypt is a symbol of Satan's world system and most Christians are more likened to the mixed multitude that accompanied Israel than the children of Israel itself.

At least Israel new they were in covenant with God; if nothing else, they were very confident of that fact, something Christians have no clue of. Israel's perspective of the relationship with their Father had obviously gotten warped after 400 years of slavery, but deep down; they understood He would honor the covenant He made with them. The Children of Israel that were cursed to wander in the desert for 40 years is actually an accurate picture of the OSAS. They believe in God as a Father, but their warped version of the gospel has them so deceived that they cannot see the forest through the trees; grumbling, complaining, and unwilling to give up the delicacies, the lust of the world. The mixed multitude is more closely identified with the prosperity gospel, people who attach themselves to a move of God just for the blessing, the favor, the miracles and the power they experience by merely associating with the movement. Do not be deceived, God knows the motive of one's heart.

Go home and don't look back

It is time to come out of Egypt, out of the world and die to yourself by allowing God to purge Egypt out of you. Whether you are a new convert or a backslidden believer, it's time to wake up and see Egypt, see the world for what it truly is; the devils matrix designed to lure you back to it with its delicacies designed to deceive and kill you.

Touching our hearts in such a way as to cause us to see our sin and our need of a Savior is actually the easy part of what our Father must do with us and in us to get us home safely. Removing 20, 30, 40 even 50 years of "the world," from us and keeping us from returning to it is the difficult part. Why else would Jesus say the road to destruction is wide and **most** people go that way? Why did only 2 out of millions make it into the Promised Land, because, like most of us, their hearts, minds, and loyalties were still in Egypt.

Satan uses the lusts of the flesh and all manner of worldly pleasures to fill and deceive our hearts, desensitizing us with his wiles that bind us and lead us captive to his will. This is the reason Jesus said, upon conversion to "***seek first the Kingdom of God and His righteousness.***" The righteousness of God pours into our hearts like a flood making us sensitive to the slavery of sin in which Satan holds us, for without righteousness there is no escaping the quest for self-preservation. When righteousness comes in, selfishness dies and the world's pleasures cease to entice us, but it can only happen if and when you seek righteousness like one who seeks a treasure. Knowing your Father and acquiring His righteousness has to be the object of your desire, not the lusts of the world.

> *Jesus replied, "Truly, truly, I tell you, no one can see the kingdom of God unless he is born again."* John 3:3

The born again life is not about giving to receive, it is about dying, to give. He wants you to **die** to yourself, your wants and desires so you can **give** your life to Him, because He gave His life for you. We are adopted children of the Lord God and the blood of the slain lamb becomes our refuge from the death sentence which hung over us. The resurrection of Jesus assures us that the power of the Enemy is set aside forever; that he who had the power over death has no further claim on us. It proclaims, moreover, that God is for us, and enables us triumphantly to ask, *"Who then, can be against us?"* The joy of this establishes a place in our hearts which the world once held, and we gladly leave all to follow the pillar of cloud and fire across the desert to the Promised Land, regardless of how difficult the trek may be.

There are those who follow the Father to the end without ever so much as looking back. Caleb and Joshua were such in their day and serve as excellent examples for us. Paul too, who gave up everything for the faith, who not only counted all things but loss for the excellence of the knowledge of Christ when that knowledge was first revealed to him, but which enabled him thirty years later to say, "*I count it all as dung that I may win Christ.*" But oh, how uncommon is this kind of faithful, trusting attitude amongst modern believers? It still happens, but rarely, and mainly because the gospel has been hijacked by the OSAS & prosperity hucksters preaching your best life now.

Just as the complaining of the "mixed multitude" who accompanied Israel out of Egypt corrupted the identity of Gods children and negatively affected their attitude, likewise, does our mingling with prosperity driven believers, the OSAS as well as unbelievers corrupt our identity and affect our attitude. Without a solid foundation of one's identity as children of the living God, it is possible to fall prey to the wiles of the devil just as Israel did in the Exodus. This is the warning Paul speaks of.

Israel groaned under the heavy hand of slavery while eating delicacies in Egypt; God delivers them from their bondage only to have them groan again so that they could satisfy their flesh with foods that were once bitter to them by the bondage they previously groaned about. Likewise, people nowadays groan under the heavy hand of sin, trying desperately to make sense of where they fit in this lost and dying world. God delivers them from the sin that ensnares them through the blood of Jesus only to have them return to it like a dog returns to his vomit, and all because He didn't change their difficult life situation or give them their best life now like they were told.

I am the bread of life; he who comes to Me will not hunger, and he who believes in Me will never thirst. John 6:35

Just as Israel's lack of identity caused them to forget the harshness of Egypt's chains and the bitterness of her delicacies, a lack of identity on the part of a Christian will motivate them to seek after the things of the world instead of righteousness, and prevent their Father from doing what He has wanted to do from the beginning; to come and live inside them and transform them into the likeness of Jesus. Therefore, a lack of identity will result in a lack of transformation and cause the joy of their salvation to cease to satisfy their soul. A lack of identity is the number one reason why Christians backslide to the world they so joyfully left.

> *Moses said,* **He humbled you**, *causing you to hunger and then feeding you with manna, which neither you nor your fathers had known,* **to teach you** *that man does not live on bread alone but on every word that comes from the mouth of God.* Deuteronomy 8:3

Jesus is "The Word," He was the Manna in the wilderness, and when Israel eventually despised the worthless Manna, they literally began to despise Jesus. Similarly, a lack of identity will cause Christians to begin to despise the Word they once loved returning them to worldly compliance and fleshly indulgence. Our flesh still remembers the pleasures from which we were delivered, and while our hearts craved ardently for manna (Jesus, the Word) at first, only a proper understanding of our identity as a Child of God will prevent us from eventually despising it. You may recall a time when to feed on Christ was all you wanted. Your first thought in the morning, the last at night, and the only one in your heart all day, but as time passes and "life happens," Satan will remind you of the joys of the world and the delicacies of Egypt.

The Little Foxes

How is it possible for a person who was once on fire for Jesus, who tasted the good fruit of the Spirit and personally witnessed miracle after miracle, how is it possible for them to abandon the faith and return to the world? It's a slow desensitization that begins to dull a heart and mind as they compromise a little here and a little there until the tempting of Christ begins,

"Is there nothing at all but this manna before our eyes?" Numbers 11:6

"Is there nothing but the Bible to read, are there no movies worth watching, how boring life has become!" "Surely I can indulge in a few delicacies; just a little won't hurt me." "I miss my old friends." "I'll just hang out with my coworkers at happy hour to be social." "I don't need to drink so it'll be Ok." "I suppose just one drink won't hurt." "Nobody gets drunk on two."

That's just about the time we begin justifying our behavior with the Bible by quoting more scripture out of context, saying, *"All things are permissible,"* never stopping to consider the fact that Paul was using sarcasm by quoting their words back to them, thereby showing them the foolishness and hypocrisy of their line of thinking.

You say, "I am allowed to do anything," but (I say) not everything is good for you. You say, "I am allowed to do anything," but (I say) not everything is beneficial. 1 Corinthians 10:23

And you can be sure that Satan will be right there lying to you, saying, "You're right, they're just being religious; you're saved by grace now, all your sin is excused, past, present and future, so go ahead, indulge a little, you're not hurting anybody."

Catch for us the foxes, the little foxes that ruin the vineyards, for our vineyards are in bloom. Song of Solomon 2:15

"Foxes" is obviously a euphemism for sin and "little foxes" is a euphemism for little sins, or sins that don't seem like they should be classified as sin, because nobody is being harmed by them...or so you think. You are spoken of as a vine which produces fruit for everyone in your life to pick, to glean from. For most people we are the only representation of Jesus they will ever see.

We are instructed to shine as a light, a beacon of hope to a lost and dying world. But it's the little foxes that ruin the vine and spoil the fruit. It's the little sins, the seemingly insignificant things we allow in, that make us an ineffectual witness in our sphere of influence. It's the little foxes that cause the world to see us as hypocrites. It's the little foxes that begin our slow descent back to the world and tramples on the blood of Jesus and the stripes He endured to free us from our sin in the first place. Beware the little foxes; eventually they ruin the whole vine.

God doesn't change, and He is a Father raising children, so like a good Father who loves His children and disciplines them when necessary, God responds to us much the same way He responded to Israel in the desert and it's never pretty, but this thing He's trying to do in us is vital to make us ready for a life in the Kingdom of Heaven. Just as He wanted Israel to trust completely upon Him back then, He wants us to do the same now, therefore any lack of faith to count on His unfailing resources to meet our needs must be addressed just as direct disobedience or willful sin is addressed. Think of Jesus, He had to trust God completely on the cross to deliver Him from death, hell and the grave.

Moses sank under the burden of the complaining Israelites,"*Whence should I have flesh to give unto all this people? For they weep unto me, saying, Give us flesh that we may eat.*"

> *I cannot carry all these people by myself; it is too burdensome for me.* Numbers 11:14

In the children of Israel we begin to see the evil of the flesh longing after the indulgences of Egypt, while in Moses, we see the weakness of his flesh and its inability to bear the burdens of the children of Israel, because he was trying to do it in his own strength instead of casting it upon God and believing for His strength. How differently does the Lord deal with these two forms of failure?

The murmurings of the people are punished by the bestowment of that for which they lusted.

> *And say to the people, 'Consecrate yourselves for tomorrow, and you shall eat meat, for you have wept in the hearing of the LORD, saying, "Who will give us meat to eat? For it was better for us in Egypt." Therefore the LORD will give you meat, and you shall eat.* ¹⁹<u>*You will eat it not for one or two days, nor for five, ten or twenty days,*</u> ²⁰*but for a whole month,* **until it comes out of your nostrils and makes you nauseous**, *because you have rejected the LORD, who is among you, and have cried out before Him, saying,* **'Why did we ever leave Egypt?'"** Numbers 11:18

Complaining about the manna in favor of meat was a type and shadow of us complaining about living righteously in favor of worldly desires and delicacies. If Jesus was the manna, the bread of life, then Israel's rejection of the bread for meat was their way of rejecting Jesus for the delicacies of the world, and is a type and shadow of believers rejecting Jesus by walking in willful sin expecting grace to excuse it. And so it was, the lusting of meat by Israel was punished, and the unbelief of Moses reproved by the outstretched arm of God.

> *Now a wind went out from the LORD and drove quail in from the sea. It scattered them up to two cubits deep all around the camp, as far as a day's walk in any direction....* ³³*But while the meat was still between their teeth, before it was chewed, the LORD's anger burned against the people, and the LORD struck them with a severe plague.* Numbers 11:31-33

It is a fearful thing to fall into the hands of the living God. I know it sounds a bit harsh, but as a loving Father, God knows that in order for Him to get them ready for the Promised Land, He must put an end to Israel's orphan mentality. Murmuring and complaining is nothing more than a lack of identity, for them as well as for us now. They needed to learn how to trust Him to provide for them, and so do we; otherwise we will end up just like they did. As in the case with

Israel, God chastens us by giving us the very things we lust after until it makes us sick and we despise it, thereby wanting it no more. It is the absolute best way to remove our desire for it if we are not willing to submit and obey. Unless or until you begin to despise the sin which ensnares you, you will not be able to die to it.

In a similar fashion, our unbelief will receive the same reproof given to Moses when the Lord took some of the Spirit that was on him and gave it to seventy elders. God will either remove the Spirit which empowers the gift we have been given or remove us from our ministry altogether. Besides Moses saying he was not able to bear all this people alone, because it is too heavy for him, he also added,

> *"If this is how you intend to treat me, just go ahead and kill me. Do me a favor and spare me this misery!"* Numbers 11:15

So, the Lord relieved Moses of the burden which so oppressed him and God gave Moses what he asked for; Moses died before he entered the promised land. God will use extreme measures to teach us our identity, and like the Israelites, we too will go around the mountain until we learn that we are no longer orphans, but children of the living God. Our Father wants us to look like His children, children who walk like Jesus, talk like Jesus and think like Jesus.

Children who act, react and behave like His children should, and not like the orphans they used to be when they were in the world. If you want to come out of the wilderness, you must come to terms with this one simple truth; you are a child of the Living God, but in order to begin thinking and acting like it, you must die to your old way of thinking. It is time to cast off the orphan mentality, and pull up a chair at your Father's dinner table.

It's time Christians stop grumbling and complaining about their spouse, their kids, their job, their boss or their coworkers and begin enduring every temptation, test or trial with the same mind that Jesus endured the scourging; *"...with the joy that was set before Him."* Our good attitude in the face of a difficult situation may be the very thing that serves as an example to that one person who sees and notices our walk of love, and gives their heart to Jesus. The sooner we understand that we are no longer in Egypt and stop lusting after the decadence and delicacies of the world, the sooner we will learn to walk in righteousness and enter the promised land that Jesus died to get us into; a land of peace and unspeakable joy, a land without grumbling or complaining, a land without selfishness or unbelief.

> *...Is not God your Father, who created you, who made you and established you?* Deut. 32:6

In 1 Corinthians 10, Paul uses the Exodus from Egypt as an example for us to see God as our Father while seeing ourselves as children and not orphans any longer. The problem is, most of us were in the world so long it is a difficult concept for us to grasp and even more difficult to do; so difficult for Israel in fact, that only 2 out of millions entered into the Promised Land, and eerily similar to what Jesus says in Matthew 7.

> *Enter through the narrow gate. For wide is the gate and broad is the way that leads to destruction, and many enter through it.* ¹⁴*But small is the gate and narrow the way that leads to life, and only a few find it.*
> Matthew 7:13

God purged the Egyptian culture out of Israel by leading them around the same mountain for 40 years just as He uses grace to purge the world from us.

> *Listen, O heavens! Pay attention, earth! This is what the LORD says: "The children I raised and cared for have rebelled against me."* Isaiah 1:2

The purpose of grace is never to excuse your sin, it is an etching tool God uses to remove your desire for it. God's grace demands transformation, or it is not grace from Him at all. God's Grace is His tattoo of holiness upon your heart revealing His righteousness in your life.

> *Do not be conformed to this world, but be transformed by the renewing of your mind. Then you will be able to test and approve what is the good, pleasing, and perfect will of God.* Romans 12:2

The word conformed implies a change of behavior resulting from outside influences, but transformation implied a change brought about from the inner man, your heart and conscience. When the time came, God decided that He wanted to have a personal relationship with His children, so He sent Moses to tell them to gather at the base of Mt. Sinai. But when they witnessed the thunder and lightning and the mountain enveloped in smoke, they trembled in fear and stood at a distance.

> *"Speak to us yourself and we will listen," they said to Moses. "But do not let God speak to us, or we will die." Moses replied. "Do not be afraid, for God has come to test you, so that the fear of Him may be before you,* **to keep you from sinning**.*"...*Exodus 20:19-20

A Believer's Identity

Too many times I hear Christians talking about how they are sinner's and they're always going to sin, that's just the way it is. In essence, they are arguing for the fact that they're always going to fail. I'm not saying that I'm perfect here; I'm just saying that I'm not waiting and expecting to fail. I'm not following any life experience or any form of doctrine either, I'm following Jesus and He never sinned and tried to get away with it. Most Christians are still relating to and being conformed into the "old man" instead of perusing and being transformed into the "new man" that Jesus died for them to become; a man or woman of righteousness.

The Word says that if we live righteous conscious it'll begin to produce the fruit of holiness without us trying to be holy. If we can just believe that God sees us right in His sight, the effect of believing it produces righteousness in us without us trying to act righteous. Now that sounds a lot more like the actual definition of grace than an excuse of willful sin, and the best part is, God gets all the glory because it's not anything we did, but what He did and continues to do inside us as He transforms us.

You see, it didn't happen because we were some kind of super Christian. It happened because of the scourging and the cross and our desire "to know" and to "be known" by Him. A desire that grew out of the seed of righteousness that was planted in our hearts when we decided to seek righteousness instead of our best life now immediately after the Truth was revealed when we knocked on the door of the Kingdom of God.

The modern church studies fallen man and say's "this is who we are," but that couldn't be farther from the truth. We're supposed to be studying Jesus and saying, "This is who I am now." People will argue and debate with this line of reasoning, they will refer to some book they read or a former pastor that filled their head with all kinds of nonsense which he hypothesized while walking in sin and excusing it with false grace, but books and preachers are not our barometer, Jesus is. I want to challenge every lie you've ever been told by the blind guides, false preachers, the grace and prosperity peddlers, as well as the world and its ridiculous theories of human existence...

> *Once you were alienated from God and were hostile in your minds because of your evil deeds. ²²But now the Father has reconciled you by Christ's physical body through His death* **to present you holy,** *unblemished, and blameless in His presence,* **²³if indeed you continue in your faith**, *established and firm, not moved from the hope of the gospel you heard...Colossians 1:22*

This scripture should inspire hope in everyone who reads it, but the problem is that most believers have never read it, and the ones that have must simply be skimming over it, never comprehending its powerful implications. They've been told that they're always going to sin, that no matter how hard they try; failure is inevitable, that we're all just sinner's saved by grace. But that's not what the

Bible teaches; nowhere does it say that you are just a sinner saved by grace, but it does say, in various places and on multiple occasions to reckon yourself dead to sin.

By His Stripes

So many Christians quote Bible verses like cliché's, out of context and with no real understanding of their actual meaning or use. One such verse found in 1 Peter and is quoted by Christians as they pray for healing.

> *"By His stripes you are healed."* 1 Peter 2:24

But they never took the time to see what it is that puts them in position to receive the healing they are seeking after, or just exactly what kind of healing the verse is addressing. As you recall, we just spent time regarding the stripes on the body of Jesus inflicted by the flagrum or Cat-O-Nine Tails. Strips of flesh were ripped off His body by each strand of the flagrum which were about ½ an inch wide and 8 to 12 inches long or longer and looked like stripes from a distance. Peter quotes this prophesy written first by the prophet Isaiah more than 1000 years before the cross and well before the Romans even began using scourging and crucifixion as a means of torture.

Don't misunderstand me here, I am not saying this is not a verse we can use to sow like a seed for healing, because it is, but how many times is it used for its unintended purpose with no results? How many times do Christians pray for healing by the Stripes of Jesus only to see the sickness persist? All too often I suspect, and why, because nobody ever considers the deeper meaning of the context of the entire verse. Yea, that's right, the whole verse. You see, while you likely know and have quoted that verse on dozens, maybe hundreds of occasions, you probably didn't know it was the finale of a much more important point that Peter was trying to make.

> *He Himself bore our sins in His body on the tree,* **so that we might die to sin and live to righteousness**. *"By His stripes you are healed."* 1 Peter 2:24

Jesus took the stripes so we might die to sin and live in righteousness, not to heal us of the flu or an injury. This verse is not intended to be sown on behalf of physical healing, its intended purpose was for the healing of your soul; healing which is so desperately needed for the wounds which were afflicted upon us through our own sinful behavior. Now these types of wounds are mostly emotional and psychological but not always, sometimes they are physical as well. Christ bore our sin in His body by the stripes He took so that we could die to the nature of sin that holds us in bondage to it, thereby providing us the ability to live in righteousness. If the stripes of Jesus were intended to remove our desire for sin which ensnares us, then the stripes of Jesus also helps to restore our identity from orphans to children which was lost, due to a sinful nature.

The purpose of the scourging, the reason behind the stripes was to put to death our need, our desire, and our lust for sin so we could live righteously by His stripes. The more I consider the implications and the magnitude of this revelation, the deeper and wider it goes, because there is an added benefit to the stripes of Jesus, a secondary form of healing along with the healing of our soul. Yes, the stripes were given to remove the need and craving for sin, but they also remove the stain of sin, the byproduct of sin itself. Jesus took those stripes not only to heal our soul from the emotional scars left after years of sinful behavior, but it also heals us of the physical scars that sin has left behind.

By His stripes we are healed of the desire for sin so that we might become righteous as He is righteous. By His stripes the emotional wounds like condemnation, guilt and shame left behind after years of sin are also healed. By His stripes, physical wounds which remain from a life of sin are healed as well.

How many Christians are finding it difficult to forgive themselves for abusing and hurting the people they loved, and are now estranged from them because of years of drug or alcohol addiction? How many Christians who engaged in a life of promiscuity now have the stain of that sin as a daily reminder? A stain called HIV or Herpes or genital warts constantly reminding them of the sinful life they once lived. Former drug users with hepatitis, suicide survivors with cuts or scars from the sin they now regret.

These stains are used by the enemy as a constant reminder that they are just an old sinner saved by grace, and they'll likely never be free from it because they have the scars to prove it...but at least they're saved (sarcasm here). Only the devil could concoct such a ridiculous lie, feeding it to ignorant preachers to regurgitate, further heaping guilt and condemnation upon the heads of these tormented souls.

Just as the stripes of Jesus paid to have the desire for sin removed, it paid the price to cleanse us of the byproduct of a sinful life, washing us clean, just as if we had never engaged in that activity before. Our Father asked Jesus to take the stripes, because He does not want us sin conscious, that is, He does not want us walking around focused on the sin of our past, yet we are reminded of our past every time we notice the stain left behind by the past we are trying to leave behind. The devil will use these stains as a constant reminder of our past to make us sin conscious. Satan wants us focusing on sin, trying not to sin in our own power, because he knows it's impossible for us.

If the natural man had power over sin in his own strength, there would have been no need for the stripes or the cross. When we are sin conscious, we are focused on sin, trying not to sin, but failure is inevitable. Then, when we finally succumb to it, Satan is right there to condemn us, trying desperately to get us to concede to it saying, "I'm guess I'm just a sinner saved by grace."

Our Father does not want us sin conscious, He wants us Son conscious. He wants us focused on Jesus and the stripes He took to remove the desire for sin. He does not want us focused on who we used to be or the scars that our past left behind, because if our focus is on the Son and not the sin it will begin to transform us into His likeness, into His righteousness. That is why it pleased the Lord to bruise Him as it says in Isaiah 53, because by His stripes we are healed from the disease of sin so we might die to it and become righteous.

Altar of Love, Part II — *Ask, Seek & Knock*

> *Yet it pleased the LORD to bruise Him...Isaiah 53:10*

One of the most fascinating lessons in the Altar of Love part I was learning that past sin leaves a stain of sickness and disease by handing over one's authority to demonic spirits, which ushered in the affliction and all its symptoms. Confession and repentance transfer the authority back to the rightful heir so the spirit can be removed and the disease along with all its symptoms are removed as well. Sin is the root cause of almost every disease, but they were paid for by the stripes of Jesus so we could be cleansed of the desire for it, as well as the stain it left behind. Therefore, when sowing this verse like a seed by confessing it over yourself or another person in need, its intended purpose would be like this, "Father, by the Stripes of Jesus may any and all desire for the sin which resulted in this sickness be removed, as well as any stain it left behind, in the name of Jesus." This is confirmed by Jesus when He heals a man who had been an invalid for 38 years.

> *Afterward, Jesus found the man at the temple and said to him, "See, you have been made well.* **Stop sinning,** *or something worse may happen to you." John 5:6*

This is concrete evidence that sin hands our authority back to the enemy, enabling him to legally inflict us with sickness and disease. I find it interesting that Jesus told the man to stop sinning; present tense. Sin caused the problem in the first place, yet he hadn't learned his lesson after all that time for he was still bound by it. If the Children of God knew and understood that sickness and disease only have authority over them if and when they walk in willful, premeditated, habitual sin, would it cause them to run from it? Furthermore, if their desire for the sin which held them in bondage was miraculously removed by the stripes that Jesus endured, would they continue in it if they knew something worse may happen to them. On a different occasion this happened,

> *...and His disciples asked Him,* **"Rabbi, who sinned,** *this man or his parents, that he was born blind?"* John 9:2

The ancients all knew and understood that sin was a portal to sickness and disease and the very reason why Satan wants us focused on it, he wants us sin conscious. Yet, I would be no better than those who take the Bible out of context if I did not tell you the rest of the story.

> *Jesus answered, "Neither this man nor his parents sinned, but this happened so that the works of God would be displayed in him.*
> John 9:2

God is so vast, and He knows the end from the beginning; there are times that He will allow things to happen so that we are placed in a position for a miracle as a witness to those around us. It reminds me of a time I was dealing with an injury for almost a year, when finally, God miraculously healed it as a witness to an unbeliever who got saved because of what happened. Therefore, we should not look at someone who has been afflicted and automatically assume sin was the cause. We may never understand why things happen the way they do, but we need to learn to simply trust that our Father has our best interest at heart. God is a good Father, with really good fathering skills, and He loves you so much He allowed Jesus to be brutalized beyond recognition so that you might be made free from all the sin that holds you in bondage, not so you could continue in it, because like it or not,

> *For the wages of sin is death, but the gift of God is eternal life in Christ Jesus our Lord.* Romans 6:23

The gift of God is eternal salvation which is only made available by the stripes that Jesus endured with joy for the sole purpose of removing your desire to continue in sin. The payment received for unrepentant, willful sin leads to spiritual death, eternal separation from the Father.

So how do you know if the thing you are dealing with was brought about as a result of past sin or whether it has a deeper, more useful intended purpose? Ask, Seek & Knock; this is an excellent example of what Jesus was referring to when He said, *"Ask, and it shall be given…."* If it is sin, He will reveal the sin to you, so you can deal with it. If it was not a result of sin, He will bring about the intended purpose. You just need to be patient and wait in faith for Him to do His thing when the time has come.

While at work one evening, I received a call from my daughter who was crying hysterically. Apparently, she had accidentally filled her truck with diesel fuel instead of gasoline and it was DOA in a parking lot. After I calmed her down and assured her it was all going to be Ok, I grumbled within myself wondering why that was allowed to happen and how I was going to resolve it. The following day I prayed over the vehicle, hoping that God would turn the diesel into gas. I know what you're thinking, what a goof, right? But I figured, if God could use Jesus to turn water into wine, He could use me to turn diesel into gas. Needless to say, God did not turn the diesel into gas, but what He did do was nothing short of amazing. Not only was I able to easily find a traveling mechanic to fix it, but God miraculously healed 12 people throughout the entire day. Everywhere I went, He would speak to me and tell me what was afflicting this person or that person and every time I prayed for them, He healed them. Now I am talking about absolutely crazy miracles here, from schizophrenia to two different torn ACL's, 3 torn rotator cuffs, back injuries, neck injuries and more.

At one point in the evening, I went to Chili's for dinner on my way home from work and noticed the hostess had a big Band-Aid on her right index finger. I asked her about it as she walked me to my table, and she said she had just cut it in the back, that it was very deep and painful. I asked, and she allowed me to pray for her when she sat me down. Within 3 minutes I had waiters and waitresses and kitchen staff, cooks, and bus-boys coming to my table for prayer, because by the time she got back to the kitchen her cut was completely healed. The kitchen manager was freaking out because he personally witnessed her cut it, and the cut was completely gone, without even a scar. I'd share the story of the entire day, but it was so remarkable, it would take up an entire chapter alone. Suffice it to say; what I thought was the beginning of a miserable day, turned out to be the greatest day of miracles and blessing I have ever witnessed.

If we read our Bibles and listen to the message it's teaching, the theme is never to sin and get away with it, it's message is always to change us from who we were in the world into who He wants us to be in His Kingdom...the likeness of Him. That likeness, the likeness of our Father was revealed to us, by His Son, Jesus who was the express image of the Father. How many times did Jesus tell them that He only did what He saw the Father do? That He and the Father were one, and that if you saw Him, you saw the Father, because He was displaying the very nature of our Father to us by His life's example.

What makes Jesus so believable was the fact that He never, EVER, took credit for anything He did...EVER! False prophets always exalt themselves; the selfish antichrist spirit is always looking to glorify itself, because that's what and who Satan is...selfish. But not Jesus, He was very humble and sooooo sweet; He was always kind to everyone He met, even those outside the covenant. Jesus never failed to give credit to whom credit was due, His Father, and I find it remarkable that more of the religious leaders did not see His selflessness as proof of His divinity. The following verse is just one example, but Jesus says this very same thing about a dozen times throughout His ministry.

> *I can do nothing by Myself;... because I do not seek My own will, but the will of Him who sent Me.* John 5:30

The Jews were a slight bit prejudice, in that, they were forbidden to intermingle with the people of other nations and cultures unless absolutely necessary. Samaritans were considered as dogs to the Jews, but Jesus treated them, as well as everyone He encountered with love, regardless of their heritage, their state of sin, their job, or their gender. He would heal anyone who came to Him, even lepers who were supposed to be quarantined outside the towns. People wouldn't even go near someone with leprosy, let alone touch them, but Jesus did. He would touch them every time his Father led them to Him for healing.

The woman with the issue of blood was considered impure and therefore defiled, according to the Law of Moses, she was supposed to be separated from society until she was made pure, but that could not happen as long as the bleeding persisted, which it had for years and years. By faith, she breaks the Law, and goes to Jesus with the hope that by merely touching His robe she will be healed. Her subsequent healing defies the Law of Moses and angers the Jewish religious leaders in the process, but it only goes to show the heart of the Father is more concerned with loving His children than keeping the 613 laws of Moses.

Why? Because God does not just love, He is love. He loves His creation, and He wants to see all of us get saved and made whole through His Son Jesus, whom He sent to be the very reflection of Himself to His wayward children. People have no idea how much their Father loves them; they say, "If He loved me then why did He do this, or why did He allow that to happen?" None of that is even close to the truth, the fact is, if He does nothing more than what He did by scourging Jesus and putting Him on the cross, while we were all still sinner's, He's already done more than enough.

> *...when we were enemies of God, we were reconciled to Him through the death of His Son, Romans 5:10*

Most of us go around thinking that if God just changed the people around us, it would make everything in our world better, but that is the most selfish point of view anyone could ever have and exactly what the enemy wants you to think. If people are pushing your buttons, don't pray that God deal with them or change them, pray that God removes all your buttons.

Never let the misappropriations, the mistakes, the frustrations of people harden your heart towards them or God for that matter. I hear so many people say that they do not attend church any longer because they were hurt by the church or the pastor or such, but we can't afford to let what people do not see, affect what we do see. Many of the people that I speak with in public say they believe in God, but they are not attending church any longer because someone offended them. The rest are offended at God for not answering their prayers the way they expected.

They consider themselves Christian and say, "they believe," but they say it like they're asking a question rather than making a statement. They won't admit it, but they're not really sure what they believe any longer. The real question is not whether they believe God exists, that's a given for most of them, but whether they have a relationship with the Father or not. Jesus said, *"Go away, for **I never knew you**."* He didn't say go away you unbelievers, He said, *"Go away, because you didn't have a relationship with me."* And for you precious people who had a wonderful relationship with Jesus at one time, but life, work, divorce, or tragedy has caused a break in that relationship; the Bible says,

> *Because of the multiplication of wickedness, **the love of most** will grow cold.* Matthew 24:12

It does not say that they never knew love, these people were Christians and they understood the commandment of love, but something happened to them which made their love grow cold. It is also worth noting that when it says many, He means most. Most Christians will grow cold regarding the law of love and they will find themselves left behind. However,

> *...the one who perseveres to the end will be saved.* Matthew 24:13

This does not simply imply that they persevere as Christians, never denying God; it is saying that they did not allow their walk of love and righteousness to grow cold but persevered in the commandments to love God and people unconditionally as in the days of their conversion. Are we really so numb from life as to assume that God is OK with a "been there-done that, got the T-shirt," attitude towards Him? Was Christianity just a fad, a phase or an out of date fashion like bellbottom jeans of the 60's & 70's? In chapters 2 & 3 of Revelation, Jesus is pleading with His wayward church to come back home. I encourage you to read it… again and again if necessary and notice the loving tone in which He beckons those that once loved Him, but have since gone back to serve their former sinful lusts in the world.

> *But I have this against you: You have abandoned your first love.* Revelation 2:4

This is the great danger of the OSAS lie; their attitude is so arrogant they don't even have the decency, the moral wherewithal to feel a sense of remorse for the awful sin in which they engage. I've been writing a lot about how we need to stop letting condemnation keep us in bondage to a cycle of sin, but at least those people have enough sense to feel guilty in their sin, at least they have a heart. How deprave is the soul of the Christian living in willful, wanton sin, all the while thinking everything is hunky-dory between them and God. There's no need to repent for anything, they're saved by grace…not!

> *Therefore, keep in mind how far you have fallen. Repent and perform the deeds you did at first.* Revelation 2:5

The first step on the road to recovery for an addict is to admit they have a problem. Jesus is telling them to wake up and consider where they were and where they are now, so hopefully it will inspire them to repent from their sin and return to their former life of righteousness, but why?Why is repentance necessary for a Christian who has returned to the world like a dog to his vomit?

> *If we confess our sins, He is faithful and just to forgive us our sins and to cleanse us from all unrighteousness.* 1 John 1:9

Repentance is a gift given by our Father to cleanse us of unrighteousness. In my business I have customers that may remain members for years, and occasionally I would develop friendships with them. These are people I would see several times a week at work and even socially sometimes, so that the relationship was fairly well developed. Yet, if their child lost interest and discontinued their training so that I no longer saw those customers, the once close relationship would begin to fade. There have been times I ran into some of these people a decade or so later, and I can barely remember them. The situation is almost always awkward at best. That is what Jesus is saying. Knowing who He is and having an intimate relationship with Him are two entirely different things.

> *But now that you know God, **or rather are known by God**, how is it that you are turning back to those weak and worthless principles? Do you wish to be enslaved by them all over again?* Galatians 4:9

Our Father wants to know us intimately, the God of all creation wants a close personal relationship with you, He wants to adopt you as a son or daughter, to live in you so you can live for eternity in His Kingdom and dine at His table. Do you know Him, is the question that most people ask, but the real question to be asking is, does He know you? Do you spend time with Him, do you talk to Him, read His Word, ask for His advice and seek His righteousness? This thing our Father did by putting His Son on a cross was not so "we believe" so we "could receive," He did it so He could live in us, and "become love" through us, to a lost and hopeless people.

Don't ever let a bad experience deposit a rock of bitterness in your heart causing you to turn away from church fellowship. You are never supposed to go anywhere to be loved; you are called to become love to everyone who does not know love. If the place you are attending is devoid of love, don't leave it looking for love; fill that void of love, with love, by your presence. Unless you are being called to go, stay where He has planted you, and love.

Friend of God

> ..."*My Father. You were my friend in my youth.*" Jeremiah 3:4

We are so blessed and fortunate to have a Father that loves us so. Not only is He a wonderful Father, He also wants our friendship, but the only way to develop a friendship is through fellowship. The more time you spend with someone, the stronger the bond of friendship.

> *No longer do I call you servants, for a servant does not understand what his master is doing. But I have called you friends, because everything I have learned from My Father I have made known to you.* John 15:15

Children, in their immaturity rebel from their parents, but as they get older and mature, they draw closer to their parents and a friendship begins to develop. They come to realize that their parents have much more wisdom than they ever really knew, and they desire to glean from that wisdom. Speaking as a parent, one of the greatest joys in life is to develop a close friendship with your children through fellowship.

> *Greater love has no one than this, that someone lay down his life for his friends.* John 15:13

God is Love

To say that God loves is to belittle the point; God is the very essence of love, the definition of love. Even the Pharisees who hated Jesus marveled at the way He loved sinner's, lepers, whores, tax collectors, and even Roman soldiers; Jesus loved everyone, everywhere, all the time. He never turned anyone away...ever! Yet they lied about Him, plotted against him, and tried to set Him up with trick questions, and He knew the whole time because He knew their thoughts and what was in their heart. Finally, they bribed Judas with 30 pieces of silver to betray Him, had Him tortured beyond recognition, and ridiculed Him while He hung on the cross, but He still asks the Father to forgive them. How much love does that take? Jesus had every right to be offended but He was not, and because of that, neither should we be.

Harboring resentments from past experiences and relationships robs you of intimacy with the Father. It usually has little to no effect upon the one who offended you, making you the real victim, so that you're the only one suffering from it. You were not created to hold onto unforgiveness, anger and hatred towards people; your Father made you to have a relationship with Him so His unconditional love could flow through you into every person and situation you encounter. With a proper understanding of your identity, you learn that every injustice at the hands of another is nothing more than an opportunity for you to show them Jesus. Once you realize your true identity and Jesus gets hold of your heart, your entire life becomes a ministry; therefore, make it your mission to live to love. Call it your living to love ministry.

Instead of letting negative experiences produce negativity in us, let them be an example to us of how not to behave, and inspire us to fill the void of love that caused the problem in the first place, with the love of Jesus inside us.

Don't ever let sin against you produce sin in you.

If you say or feel like, "they started it" or "I wouldn't be in this position if they...," all you are doing is showing your selfish hand to the devil and giving him your authority to have power over you. They then, become your government, and the actual definition of government is to control the mind or mind control. We reason it by saying, "but I wouldn't be in this place if "blank" didn't happen," but the truth is, "blank" isn't your Lord...is it? Because it only makes sense for you to think like that if "blank" is lord over you, but if Jesus is your Lord, then the only response to that, as well as every situation is to reply with love not "blank."

When you hear others talk like this because of a similar situation they are experiencing, you can relate, but that doesn't make it truth and it won't set either of you free to talk about it, it only provides the enemy an opening or an opportunity to produce sin in both of you. We are never supposed to **talk about** our problem; we are instructed to **speak to** our problem like Jesus in the desert.

Altar of Love, Part II — Ask, Seek & Knock

> ***What** then **shall we say** in response **to** these things?*
> *If God is for us, who can be against us?* Romans 8:31

We need to be good stewards of our hearts with the time our Father gives us here, because most everything we think we are doing for the Lord will be burned up like twigs, everything except a selfless walk of love and righteousness. Your time here is really very short so make it count. If you knew you were going to die in one week, I assure you that you would not allow anything to upset you or disappoint you. You wouldn't be moping around all frustrated, losing your temper with people, especially those you love. You would be kind, gentle, supportive, encouraging, loyal, dependable, and faithful; you would walk in love. If you lived each day like it was your last you would most likely be fulfilling the commandment of love.

Protect your heart and your mind, as they are interconnected, because a clean conscience is just a reflection of a pure heart and mind.

> *Finally, brothers, whatever is true, whatever is honorable, whatever is right, whatever is pure, whatever is lovely, whatever is admirable, if anything is excellent or praiseworthy, think on these things.*
> Philippians 4:8

Therefore,

> *Be anxious for nothing, but in everything, by prayer and petition, with thanksgiving, present your requests to God. ⁷And the peace of God, which surpasses all understanding, will guard your hearts and your minds in Christ Jesus.* Philippians 4:6-7

Worry is toxic to your heart, as well as, your conscience, but time in the Word of God along with time in prayer is the detox that purifies them, and peace is the result. Sin violates your conscience, and shipwrecks your faith; if your conscience is violated it makes it nearly impossible to look upward and receive from Him when you are alone with Him. If, you can even get alone with Him at all, because a guilty conscience will cause division and separation as evidenced by Adam and Eve who were hiding from God due to their guilt and shame, but if your conscience is clear you have confidence before God.

> *Beloved, if our hearts do not condemn us, we have confidence before God.* 1 John 3:21

A lack of identity will prevent us from walking in righteousness. Using grace as an excuse to sin is cowardly rebellious and nothing more than a lack of one's identity. A lack of identity will allow the sin to violate our conscience, a lack of identity receives condemnation, and a lack of identity destroys our faith.

> *But he must ask in faith, without doubting, because he who doubts is like a wave of the sea, blown and tossed by the wind. ⁷That man should not expect to receive anything from the Lord. ⁸He is a double-minded man, unstable in all his ways.* James 1:6-8

A lack of identity causes us to look for and make excuses for our sin, which violates our conscience, creating a condemned heart within us, causing us to withdrawal from our Father, thus destroying our faith so that our prayers are not answered. This is a difficult hole to dig out of, a sad state of affairs, and it all began with a violated conscience due to sin that was excused by false grace. At this point, most people will grow cold in their love, and begin drifting back into the world trying desperately to ignore the Lord's loving tug at their heart to repent and come back to Him. And never forget the enemy is ever present, feeding you with thoughts of hopelessness saying, "What's the use, you try and try not to sin, but you just can't stop, so you might as well just give up. Who needs this anyway; it's nothing but a headache?"

However,

> *... if our hearts do not condemn us, we have confidence before God and whatever we ask we receive from him, because we keep his commandments and do what pleases him.* 1 John 3:21

Are you beginning to see the danger and the demonic footprint of the OSAS message? Its design is to separate us from the Father through a guilty conscience produced by sin. A guilty conscience is not a bad thing, on the contrary, the Holy Spirit can and will use it to convict your heart that the sin you so capriciously engage in is not acceptable to the Lord, **it is not Ok with Him and you know it**. Your guilty conscience is God's law of love written on your heart proving the OSAS doctrine is a lie from the pit of hell.

Therefore, your guilty conscience is evidence that your Father loves you and has His heart set on redeeming and delivering you from the bondage and cycle of sin that ensnares you. A redemption so pure it empowers you to die to sin so that it has dominion over you no more. The real danger is not that you have a guilty conscience, it's if you don't. **Woe** to any believer who has fallen for the OSAS doctrine of demons to such an extent that they willfully sin and it no longer affects their conscience...for great dread is the only outcome!

> **Let your conscience be your thermometer for sin and let Jesus be your barometer for righteousness.**

The Spirit of Adoption

> *For you did not receive a spirit of slavery that returns you to fear, but you received **the Spirit of Adoption**, by whom we cry, "Abba! Father!"*
> Romans 8:15

Think of the world prior to the 10 commandments as the lawless Wild West, survival of the fittest; an every man for himself world with no rules, winner take all. When God delivers the 10 commandments, the world now has a constitution, a law of the land, a code of ethics and morals to live by. It is true that much of our system of government was largely inspired by the Roman system, however the basis for all American laws come out of the 613 Mosaic laws and the 10 commandments. Traditions such as marriage, home ownership, business & commerce, laws, judges and courts all come from Gods laws to govern us and give us a sense of direction, a moral compass. One of these laws was adoption. God had very specific requirements for adoption, probably because He would later use it as an example of the type of relationship Jesus would ultimately reestablish through the scourging and the cross.

Adopted children had very specific rights and privileges that natural born children did not have. In those days, it was not uncommon for natural born children to be sold into slavery to pay off a debt, or purchase a field or a house and the child remained indebted to that person until the debt was paid in full; then they would be released and sent home to the natural parents. But Gods law forbids the selling of an adopted child as chattel. Jewish parents of unruly and rebellious children were financially responsible for their children's foolishness. Such children could actually be divorced by their parents. But not adopted children, they were children for life unless they chose to end the relationship.

In the New Testament, Israel is the natural born child and Christians are the adopted children. Never, ever look upon our Jewish brothers and sisters with anything but respect, for without them, we would never be. They are the olive tree and we have been grafted in.

Abba Father is a term of endearment; it simply means "Dear Daddy." Paul is confirming to the early Christians that the relationship has now changed from God and servants to Father and adopted son, and Jesus even goes so far as to call us "friend." Paul understood perfectly his identity because of the close, personal relationship he had with the Father, and he describes this new relationship as an adoption because he understood the significance and terms of adoption within the culture of his time. Paul contrasts the Fathers Spirit of Adoption with Satan's spirit of slavery, the world's spirit that we once possessed or should I say, once possessed us. When we were in the world, we were ruled by Satan's spirit and slaves to sin, but when we knock on the Kingdom door and we say yes to Jesus, our Father supplants the spirit of the world with His Spirit and we are converted from down to up, from darkness to light, from death to life, from the kingdom of the devil to the kingdom of God.

However, if we do not know the benefits of adoption, if we do not understand how adoption changes our future heritage, we will continue to act like orphans. If a poor beggar orphan boy is suddenly adopted by a loving generous man, but returns to the streets each day continuing to beg, he has not received the benefits of his adoption. He no longer needs to behave like that, but it's all he knows, so he returns to what is familiar. His new Daddy has a fabulous business and He would love nothing more than for His new son to submit to His authority, put away his criminal past, his street mentality and learn the family business. And just what is the family business? To go around finding other orphans who are tired of living like vagrant beggars and thieves on the streets and bring them into the Fathers family as well.

The Fathers heart is so big and full of love, He wants all the orphans that are through living a selfish self-centered life to come back home to Him. Whether they realize it or not yet, all orphans want a family with a Daddy who loves them unconditionally. It's actually a pretty sweet deal if you ask me. This is the picture of Christianity, and we are being offered this Spirit of Adoption so that we can get off the streets, into our Fathers house and cry out DADDY!

Imagine yourself as the unloved, unwanted orphan when unexpectedly, the sweetest, kindest, richest man in the city comes and adopts you. But you know, it's really much worse than that, you're not just an abandoned orphan, you're an orphan that has been bound in an orphanage right out of a horror movie. Each day you and the other orphans are abused by a ruthless, sadistic headmaster, held captive and without hope.

To make matters worse, you were born into your situation by a mother that was held captive before you, so it's all you know. You've never been free before, so you don't even know what freedom looks like, what freedom feels like. For you, no other kind of life exists. Suddenly, the compound is raided, you are freed from the slavery and adopted by a kindly, loving Father with an awesome family and exposed to a new life altogether; a life of love, peace and joy by a caring Daddy who adores you even in all your faults. A Father that only sees, hopes and believes the best in you.

When Paul says *"we did not receive a spirit of slavery,"* what is he referring to? What is a spirit of slavery, and what or whom were we in slavery to?

> *For when you were **slaves to sin**, you were free of obligation to righteousness.* Romans 6:20

When we were in the world, we were slaves to sin, we were powerless to its devices. Even if you were fortunate enough to be born into a Christian home where Christian morals and values are exemplified by your parents, you were still born into a slave system, and for 100% of us, it's all we knew. FYI, being born into a Christian home no more makes you a Christian than standing in your garage makes you a car. Being a Christian is a decision you make, not one your parents make for you, and it happens when the blinders are removed and you realize Jesus was tortured and killed so you could be adopted by a Father who loves you.

Most Christians are Christian in name only and continue to live in and behave like orphans. They think because they were raised in a Christian home and went to church every Sunday, they are saved. For other people not raised by Christians, their sin got them in such a difficult situation that they went to a church hoping for a get out of jail free card; expecting God to fix all their problems so they can continue in their sin. And why in the world would they think God will fix all their problems, where did they ever get such a crazy notion? From the prosperity pimps, that's where. They're foolishly taught if they tithe ten percent of their earnings to the church, that God will bless them by fixing all their money related troubles. This is not an indictment on tithing, but on the liars deceiving you regarding the truth of tithing so they can get rich. God is not interested in fixing your problems, He's trying to get you out of the world, so He can get the world out of you, then He can get His Holy Spirit into you, and you can look like Him.

Many people say the coveted "sinner's' prayer," but nothing changes because there is no desire to transform, they just want an escape from the mess they made of their lives so they can continue living like orphans. Even when we knew what we were doing was wrong, it's as if we couldn't resist doing it anyway, because we were slaves to sin, following our master the devil, and doing his bidding. Therefore, as a slave to sin, we were under no obligation to behave righteously.

> *For when you were **slaves to sin**, you were **free of obligation** to righteousness.* Romans 6:20

Being free from obligation to righteousness means we behaved however we wanted; because the motto of the devil is literally, "Do what thou wilt." It is written in the satanic Bible and it is the code of ethic of the world we live in. Do whatever makes you feel good, regardless of whether or not it hurts another, because it's all about you. You are under no obligation to do what is right when you are under the adoption of the world, so do as you please.

I knew a man whose wife of 25 years filed for divorce, saying she was tired of living in his shadow. He was a successful hair stylist and when they got married, she became an integral part of his business, but the business was founded by him on his reputation and the devil used that to harbor resentment in her towards him. As in all marriages, there were other difficulties I'm sure, but resentment and bitterness were the catalyst Satan used for divorce, so that she looked at him one day and said, "It's time for me to do me."

This is the spirit of slavery at work exploiting her lack of understanding of her identity in Christ, for if she knew who she was (her identity) in Christ and what she was created for (love & righteousness); she never would have made it all about her. It was a perfect example of the spirit of the world doing what it does best, using selfishness to destroy. It is the very opposite of the Kingdom of God where the Spirit of Adoption, the Spirit of Grace and Truth come in and remove all selfishness because it's not about you any longer. It's all about Jesus who saved you from you as well as an eternity of torture, torment and separation from a loving Father. It's taking the love that God extended to you through the crucifixion and becoming that same love to everyone you meet. It is the least selfish message the world has ever known and the devil hates it and everyone associated with it.

> *You, however, are controlled not by the flesh any longer, but by the Spirit, if the Spirit of God lives in you...* Romans 8:9

If you are a disciple of Christ, you will not be controlled by the flesh any longer, because you are motivated by the Spirit of Gods who lives in you now. If it's no longer about you now, the evidence of your conviction is clearly obvious, because you will not want to sin and get away with it any longer. The spirit of selfishness, the world's spirit no longer rules you, because you are an adopted child with your Father's DNA. The Spirit of Adoption lives inside you now, teaching you, convicting you, correcting you and training you not to sin and how to live in righteousness.

This is in direct contradiction to the OSAS doctrine of demons that tells Christians it's Ok to sin because they covered by grace. So, let's look at this logically, God hates sin...No, that's a huge understatement, sin is repulsive to God and He is going to judge the entire world for their sin according to the 10 Commandments. Yet, according to the OSAS doctrine, if Christians sin, it's perfectly fine with God because they said, "the prayer." Are we to assume that a righteous God will just allow His Children to live in debauchery, wallowing in willful sin, but judge the rest of the world for it?

Anyone who thinks that way is breaking the very first commandment, *"...You shall not make for yourself an idol of any kind....."* In the futility of their own mind, they have just created their own false god. An idol god who is approving of all their sin as long as they say a sinner's prayer, but punishes the rest of the world with eternal damnation for doing the very same things. Is that really what the OSAS are trying to get us to believe? God hates sin, He loathes it, sin can and will have no part of Him or His Kingdom and only the devil could concoct such a ridiculous doctrine as the OSAS hyper-grace lie, and we might as well throw in hyper-prosperity for that matter.

> *But if Christ is in you, your body is dead because of sin, yet your spirit is alive because of righteousness.* Romans 8:10

What Paul is saying here is that if you have the Spirit of God in you, you become dead to sin, that is, you no longer want to sin and excuse it with grace. If you are dead to something you no longer want anything to do with it. People in the world have a saying for people who have offended them, they say, "You are dead to me." It means they consider them as dead and they want nothing to do with them ever again. Well...where do you think that saying came from? It came from right here, it came from Romans 8:10 when Paul says that if Christ is in you, sin is now dead to you, so that you have no relationship with it any longer. You are dead to sin. Therefore, the OSAS follower that walks in willful sin and excuses it with grace obviously does not have the Spirit of God in them, because they are not dead to sin.

If we were to say it in a more modern vernacular it would sound like this, "look dude, if you are walking in willful sin, you are not dead to it so you obviously do not have the Spirit of Christ in you, and if you don't have the spirit of Christ, you're not saved like you think you are."

> *Therefore, brothers, **we have an obligation**, but it is not*
> *to the flesh, to live according to it.* Romans 8:12

This is a very good point that Paul is making. If we are in Christ, if we choose to give our allegiance to Jesus and become a disciple of His, **we have an obligation now**, whereas before, when we were in the world, Paul said we had no obligation to righteousness. However, now we do have an obligation, and it's not an obligation to sin and excuse it with grace. We are obligated to live righteously as He is righteous. An obligation is never a choice, it's a requirement, and it's expected of us now that we are "in Christ." But why, why is righteousness required of us now?

> *For if you live according to the flesh, you will die; but if by the*
> *Spirit you put to death the deeds of the body, you will live.*
> Romans 8:13

He's talking about spiritual death here, so Gods not messing around, whether you call yourself a Christian or not, He knows willful sin will harm us on earth, but it will also separate us from Him eternally as well.

> *For all who are led by the Spirit of God are sons of God.* Romans 8:14

It's really quite easy to tell if someone is a Christian by more than just name alone. If they actually have the Spirit of God within them, it will rule them, drive them, and motivate them all through their daily lives. For those who have the Spirit of God are led by the Spirit of God, so that those who are led by the Spirit of God, walk in love & righteousness and those who walk in love & righteousness are the sons of God.

> *Ask and it will be given to you; seek and you will*
> *find; knock and the door will be opened to you.*
> Matthew 7:7

We will be using this verse a lot in this book, because it is much deeper than we ever thought, and it is chock full of great information. For this chapter on Identity & Sonship, let's look at the part about knocking. Jesus always spoke in figures of speech and parables to hide the truth from Satan. In Corinthians, chapter 2, Paul writes, *"For had they known they never would have crucified the Lord of Glory."* Therefore, Jesus spoke in mysteries that require Holy Spirit discernment to understand, and this is one of those times.

Jesus is explaining a very important Kingdom principle and He hides it by reversing its order of importance. By placing Ask before Seek and Knock, it wisely conceals the actual meaning. We will get to Ask and Seek in subsequent chapters of this book, but for now we'll consider the part about knocking. So, what does it mean to knock?

Knock – Strong's #2925. Krouó (kroo'-o) I knock, to beat a door with a stick, **to gain admittance.**

Ok, Jesus is advising us to knock on a door, but what door are we supposed to knock on?

But seek first the kingdom of God... Matthew 6:33

Seek – Strong's #2212 zētéō (dzay-teh'-o) I seek, search for, desire, require, demand. To investigate, to search, "getting to the bottom of a matter."

Jesus tells us what door we should be knocking on in Matthew 6:33 when He says to seek the Kingdom of God. To seek the Kingdom of God is to knock on the door of the of God's Kingdom. In the Strong's concordance, to Knock is to gain entry; therefore, it is the quest for salvation. It's getting to the point in your life when you realize that the world is not really your friend, that there is something more, something better for you. It's realizing that you don't fit in, that something just isn't right with the world and you decide that you want to know that which you finally realize you know not. Furthermore, something inside you is telling you this is really important, it is a "need to know" urgency, and you need to know it now!

> *⁸For everyone who asks receives; he who seeks finds; and **to him who knocks, the door will be opened**. Matthew 7:7-8*

It's your ah-ha moment, the moment you realize you have been lied to your entire life and everything you thought was true, is not. If you knock on this door, He will open it and reveal to you the truth about Jesus. A truth that is hidden from the prideful, and the self-righteous that feel they have no need for God. This is where salvation begins, for you cannot enter the door of the Kingdom until you knock first and He opens.

> *... the whole world is under the power of the evil one.* 1 John 5:19

If we know that the Bible does not lie and it does not exaggerate, and the whole world is under the power and control of Satan, then you must assume that everything in the world comes from his point of view, his thoughts and opinions. This is Satan's world, and everyone in it is being lied to by him and they have no clue it's happening. Everything, from academia to the arts, from radio and TV to music and theatre, all sports, movies, pop culture and we cannot leave out politics. Everything is run by Satan, therefore every opinion, every thought, every decision you ever made came from a place he created, fed and manipulated. Therefore, everything you know is a lie and you need to relearn everything from Gods point of view, what He feels, how He thinks, and what He says about a matter and that is best accomplished by reading Gods word.

If you are not a Christian or if you are a Jew who does not read the Torah, and you are getting all your information from the world…you are being deceived. If you call yourself a Christian and you have stopped reading God's Word daily, you will be deceived eventually; maybe not today or tomorrow, but it's just a matter of time. The enemy is a cunning, crafty liar and he's been lying for 6000 years that we know of, so he's got a lot of practice at it. Imagine how good you'd be at something if you did it all day long, every day for 6000 years. Jesus called Satan the father of lies.

For Christians that have grown weary and stopped reading and praying, it is subtle at first, you won't notice it, it is a slow desensitization until you are numb to the things of God, but little by little you will begin to migrate back into the things of the world and as it happens you will begin to think like the world again. Once Satan has you thinking like him again, he's pretty much got you, because the flesh always follows the mind, so I highly advise you to stay out of the world as much as possible and into His Word as often as possible.

Questioning One's Identity

I say it all the time and it's worth repeating, the armor of God is not a prayer you pray to put on every morning, it is a lifestyle, it is your character, your very being. Think logically here, in what situation would you ever take off the helmet of salvation? The helmet of salvation is there to secure our identity; it's the one place the devil is constantly attacking us, through our mind by placing thoughts that would undermine our identity. The only way the devil can cause a believing Christian to stumble, one who knows who and what they are, the only way Satan can get them back into sin is to undermine their identity. It is true that Satan tempted Jesus in the desert, three times, and in three different ways; lust of the flesh, lust of the eyes and with the pride of life, but if you look deeper, the first two temptations went directly at His identity, saying, *"If you are the Son of God..."*

Satan places all kinds of warped thoughts in your mind to confuse or confound your identity with the goal of moving you away from righteousness, your right standing with God. He knows that once you become aware of Gods plan for salvation and choose to leave his domain of worldly, demonic living, he must keep you from righteousness and the best way to do that is to undermine your perception of who you are as a Child of God.

He will try and deceive you with his hyper grace doctrine, telling you that you're saved by grace because you said "the prayer," so there's no need to change anything, sin all you want now, God loves you just as you are. He will make you think you've done enough, that you've served your time, you've been a good soldier, now you can relax and enjoy a little sin. He will try and make you think you haven't done enough, that your Father is not pleased with you, heaping condemnation upon you, pushing you towards works trying to earn your Fathers approval. He wants to make you think that you're something special if you walk around doing miracles and exercising the gifts of God so that your faith is in the miracles or the gifts and not in your Lord.

If your faith is in any of the gifts of God, that gift will eventually become your identity. If that happens, you're only doing as good as the last miracle you saw happen. Satan may try to make you think that you're less than you are when you do not see the gifts of God flowing in you as in others. He wants to make you think you are greater than you are, so pride will puff you up and a seed of arrogance sprouts. He will tell you whatever it takes, anything that confuses, clouds, minimizes or completely disrupts your identity as a beloved, adopted Child of God in authority. Satan wants to make you offended, belittled, ashamed, embarrassed, humiliated, harassed, rejected, unappreciated, mocked, misused, abused, mistreated and misunderstood, and he loves using the most important, the most influential people in your life to do it; the people closest to you, people you love, respect, admire and trust.

He wants you to think, "every time I put myself out there for God and pray or try to be a blessing to someone, they hurt me." Jesus helped everyone He came in contact with, everyone, yet He wasn't anybody's doormat. If anybody ever had a reason to get offended, it would have been Jesus, but He never did. Even when they tried to take Him in the garden and Peter cut off the ear of the Roman soldier; Jesus didn't look down His nose at him and say, "Look at you now, see what you get, what you sow is what you reap." No, He simply healed his ear.

Do not concern yourself with the reactions of people, positive or negative, because it does not matter what they think about your quest for righteousness.

Never seek the appreciation, notoriety or gratification of any person, because people are fallible, they will eventually let you down and if your identity is not grounded in who you are as a Child of God, you will get hurt, offended, hardened or arrogant. Do not seek the respect or the accolades of people, but seek ye first the kingdom of God and his righteousness and all the things the world is searching for will be added to you.

Be Transformed

> ***Do not be conformed*** *to this world, but **be transformed** by the renewing of your mind. Then you will be able to test and approve what is the good, pleasing, and perfect will of God.* Romans 12:2

The phrase "do not be conformed" is a warning for us not to assume the identity of the world. Do not take on the likeness, the image of the people in the world, but rather assume the identity of Jesus. Paul is admonishing Christians to no longer identify with their old nature; the sinful nature that Jesus died to save us from. Most Christians, after their so-called conversion by way of a sinner's prayer of salvation, go through the rest of their life never coming to the full revelation of their new identity. Some of them begin to transform, but the enemy is right there to dethrone any hope of that with sin via the OSAS deception. It is a cunningly crafted demonic plan to deceive and desensitize us into identifying with a lost and dying world; the very world that Jesus suffered and died to deliver us from.

And I get it, nobody wants to be mocked, hated or thought of negatively. Who doesn't want to be liked, but Jesus said, *"If they hated me, they will hate you."*

> **If the world loves you, it's probably because you love it and that is where the danger lies.**

In my personal opinion, I believe that James says it best.

> *You adulterous people! Do not know that friendship with the world is enmity with God? Therefore whoever wishes to be a friend of the world **makes himself** an enemy of God.* James 4:4

First, James is talking to Christians here, which makes what he is saying alarming to say the least. He begins by calling them adulterous, but why, why would James call Christians adulterous people, because God views their friendship with the world as them committing adultery on Him. Adultery is not just you cheating on your spouse, adultery is also when you cozy up to the world and become its friend. Second, James destroys one of the foolish lies that the OSAS preachers deceive their masses with; that God loves them just as they are so there is no need for repentance once they say a "sinner's prayer." It is true, God does love them, but that's not the issue here, the issue is that they do not love God. By becoming friends with the world, **they make themselves** an enemy of God. They are alienating God, not the other way around.

THIS IS WAR! Never forget that God and the devil are at war and we are the commodity for which they battle. Throughout history, wars began with arguments and disputes over various things. Some wars were for gold, others for land, and some for strategic ports or precious minerals. More modern wars have been about oil or world domination, but whatever the reason there is always collateral damage. Innocent bystanders are killed or injured, and neutral parties forced to pick sides because they were drawn into the conflict by one reason or another. This is war, make no mistake about it, and we are smack dab in the middle of it. Like a bank robber uses hostages as leverage for his crime, Satan uses the Children of God as human shields for his crime. Whenever war begins, all the players must take sides, and neutrality is not an option. By rejecting Jesus or refusing to choose Him you will get the devil by default, that's easy to understand, but any friendship with the world also establishes your loyalty to it, Christian or not.

> *Therefore whoever wishes to be a friend of the world*
> ***makes himself an enemy of God.*** James 4:4

God does not reject you when you are friends with the world...YOU ARE REJECTING HIM! **You make yourself** His enemy. Walking in willful sin thinking you are saved by grace is no different than you becoming a traitor of your country and joining the enemy side. Adultery with the world is you committing treason on your Father. Who and what did you think Paul was referring to when he said, "Adulterers will not inherit the Kingdom of God."

> *Do you not know that the wicked will not inherit the kingdom of God? Do not be deceived: Neither the sexually immoral, nor idolaters,* ***nor adulterers,*** *nor men who submit to or perform homosexual acts,* ¹⁰*nor thieves, nor the greedy, nor drunkards, nor verbal abusers, nor swindlers, will inherit the kingdom of God.*
> 1 Corinthians 6:9-10

Paul was talking to Christians, about Christians when he made that statement as evidenced by the following verse.

> *Instead, you yourselves cheat and do wrong, even against your own brothers!* 1 Corinthians 6:8

Are we so depraved that we can read Paul's warning and automatically assume he's not talking to us Christians? Context is everything when reading God's Word. Christians foolishly assume Paul was talking to unbelievers here, and they take their misunderstanding of the Word and make a perverted doctrine out of it like God hates homosexuals. God does not hate homosexuals any more than you would hate your 3 year old who lied about taking a cookie while his hand is still in the jar. God loves His creation; He hates none of them. Paul is speaking directly to the church and homosexuals are listed along with the sexually immoral, idolaters, adulterers, thieves, the greedy, drunkards, verbal abusers, and swindlers, because all those behaviors were found to be in the church and Paul was cleaning house.

Therefore, when Paul instructs us not to be conformed to the likeness of the world in Romans 12, he is encouraging new believers to stay with the homeland, the kingdom they were born to be loyal to. At the same time, he is warning mature believers not to conform back into the world that Jesus saved them from in the first place. I suppose it would also include people who were raised in the church, not to leave the safety, the comfort, the peace and security of the church for a taste of the world.

Being conformed to the world literally means to take on the likeness, the image, the personality, the motives, the thoughts and actions of the world. Depression exists because Satan lives in a constant state of depression being alienated from a loving God. Worry exists because Satan is worried about his inevitable fate in the Lake of Fire. Hatred, murder, unforgiveness, lust greed and selfishness all exist because Satan suffers with them all. He is a cornucopia of anxieties and phobias, with a side helping of doubt, anger, resentment, bitterness and hatred.

There's an old saying, "misery loves company." Satan, being full of misery would love nothing more than for everyone to be as miserable as he is. Therefore, he projects all his trash on us, and because the church does not teach the identity of a Christian to new believers, Satan loves nothing more than to step in and father them in his vile and disgusting identity. And for any person that calls himself a Christian and has gone back to the world, but is without conviction…it's time to wake up and go home, the world is no place for you.

> Do not be conformed, **But be transformed**… Romans 12:2

The Greek word here for transformed is metamorphous… It's used to describe the process by which a caterpillar changes into a butterfly. Like the butterfly, true Children of God become a completely new species with new DNA. Thus, is the saying, "born again!" We are literally reborn as a new creation, with all new God DNA. Just as the caterpillar changes into a beautiful butterfly, we are supposed to change from the ugly, worldly nature of the devil into the beautiful, loving nature of Jesus.

The metamorphous of a caterpillar to a butterfly is the perfect representation of sinful, unredeemed man, bound to crawling on his belly, in the dust of the earth, suddenly being redeemed and transformed into a new man; one set free from certain death and given supernatural abilities to walk, talk, think and act like King Jesus.

> *For I am sure that neither death nor life, nor angels nor rulers, nor things present nor things to come, nor powers, neither height nor depth, nor anything else in all creation, will be able to separate us from the love of God that is in Christ Jesus our Lord.* Romans 8:38-39

At first glance, this list seems to cover just about everything, but there are two things this list does not mention...you and your past. If you do not come to the understanding of the redemptive blood of Jesus washing away all your sins, Satan will use your past to prevent you from growing in the knowledge of the butterfly you are supposed to be transforming into. You are the only one who can separate you from the love of God by becoming friends with the world that Jesus died to save you from and/or never letting go of your past.

> *...Do not be conformed to this world, but be transformed **by the renewing of your mind.*** Romans 12:2

By the renewing... Strong's #342 - a change of heart, a complete renovation, a change for the better "make fresh, new" achieved by God's power.

True conversion should be clearly obvious in true believers, because people who are sincere about leaving the world for team Jesus display a "change of heart." It does not make them perfect, but they are not who they used to be any longer.

They are visibly different now, and if they are not different it's a sure sign that they were not sincere about their conversion, they likely did not have a change of heart. As I have said before, sometimes people just need to escape from a difficult situation and this whole "Jesus thing," seems like a good way out. Occasionally these people will eventually get it if they stay in a Bible based church long enough and see what real conversion looks like.

This metamorphous we are supposed to be going through is accomplished by a renewing of our minds. A new mind that comes to the understanding that you no longer want to be a child of the world; you are defecting from Satan's army, crossing enemy lines and returning to your homeland to be adopted as a Child of God. As a child of the world, you thought like the world, it's how you were raised, it was your environment, your sphere of influence; it was all you knew. Repentance, in the truest sense of the word, means to change your thinking; stop thinking like the world and start thinking like your Father. The word is telling us to be transformed by the renewing of our mind. To do so we must cease thinking like the world, then we will cease behaving like the world. If we begin to think like our Father, we will begin to behave like Him as well.

Most Christians never get to this place, because they are not taught about their Identity as Children of God. Many pastors, preachers, and teachers don't teach it because they themselves do not know who they are as adopted children; and you can tell because they behave just like orphans too. Have you ever wondered why so many pastors, ministers and church leaders are caught in adultery and homosexual affairs, or why so many of them view other churches as competition instead of brothers in Christ?

Why on earth would they put their congregation in debt by building vainglorious sanctuaries or why do they feel the need to live in multimillion dollar mansions and guilt their followers into buying them not just planes but the most expensive leer jets in the world? It's because they don't know their Identity as children and have assumed the identity of the world, the selfish identity of Satan himself.

Personally, the worst offenders are the prosperity pimps, who, out of selfish ambition to acquire many things, grow large congregations, by peddling the Word of God for profit. What did Paul say about the prosperity gospel?

We are not like the many hucksters who peddle the Word for personal profit. We preach the word of God with sincerity... 2 Corinth 2:17

If baby Christians are not instructed in their new Identity as a Child of God, they will never renew their mind from the "old man" they used to be. By remaining in their "old mindset" they never transform into the likeness and image of Jesus. They are no different than a butterfly who does not know they are a butterfly, but continues to crawl on the ground like a caterpillar.

Likewise, if mature Christians do not continue in the word, they will forget their identity as Children of God, and revert back to their familiar place in the world. They are like a butterfly that hit his head and got amnesia; he doesn't remember what it was like being a butterfly, and goes back to crawling on the ground like a caterpillar. He may even look at himself in the mirror and know he's not the same as a caterpillar, but he's comfortable where he is. Within time, he'll forget all about his days of flying and snuggle in nicely to the filth and scum of the dust of the earth.

The Altar of Love, Part II

Chapter 3

Leg 2 – Righteousness

Wisdom of God, Fruit of the Spirit, Fruit of Righteousness, Love

Is the life you are living worth the price Jesus paid?

> *This is how we distinguish between the Children of God from the children of the devil; anyone who does not **practice** righteousness is not of God…*1 John 3:10

Righteousness is the perfect holiness of Christ. It is an essential attribute to the character of God; quite literally meaning "One who is right with God." Think of it as the polar opposite of sin. To commit sin is to go against God's design for our lives, therefore righteousness is the only living standard that is acceptable for us to stand before the Father and be counted as Holy. In 1 John 3:10 we are instructed to **practice** righteousness, but what does that look like? Speaking to His followers about the church, Jesus said,

> *Then I will tell them plainly, 'I never knew you; depart from Me, you who practice lawlessness!'* Matthew 7:23

A practitioner of lawlessness is a life of habitual sin; sin without remorse or without an attitude of repentance. But what Christian would practice sin and not feel a need to repent, who would do such a thing? The OSAS, that's who; they say, "I'm saved by grace, therefore I have no need to repent."

Jesus said, *"No one can see the Kingdom of God unless they are born of the Spirit of God,"* therefore true believers will have Gods Holy Spirit residing within them and the evidence of His Spirit is more than just avoiding sin, it is an attitude that detests the very thought of sin. True believers will hate sin and practice righteousness; *"... you will know them by their fruit."*

God views sin in His children like drugs and the addict. If your child was addicted to drugs, you don't hate your child, you hate the drugs. You see the evil in the drugs and how they are destroying your child. As a parent, you know the awesome potential of your child and you can see that potential slowly going down the drain; the drugs have made them a mere shell of the person they used to be, the person they were created to be, and the person you hoped they'd become. Unless something happens to stop the addiction, you know the end result is unthinkable. That is exactly how God feels about sin in our lives and why He sent Jesus to die, so that we **might become** righteousness and fulfill all we were created to do. The wages of sin is death, but:

> *In the path of righteousness is life, and in its pathway there is no death.* Proverbs 12:28

Habitual sin leads to spiritual death, but practicing righteousness leads to eternal life. The OSAS doctrine believes just the opposite; they view salvation as simply saying a sinner's prayer; much like obtaining a hunting license. If they hunt without a license, they are breaking the law, but if they get a hunting license, they can hunt all they want without recourse. They're just not looking at this subject logically; they're not seeing it from Gods point of view.

God hates sin to such a degree He is willing to let His own children choose eternal separation from Him for practicing it. He didn't send Jesus to die such a horrendous death so we could continue in sin; He died to free us from it. God's not looking for a way to excuse sin, He wants to remove it.

I used to think righteous living had more to do with behavioral modification than heart transformation. An outward appearance of holiness was what mattered to me, rather than Spirit-filled change. I thought that if I tried to stop losing my patience or tried to remember to walk in love, it meant I was practicing righteousness.

While those are good and righteous works, the more I began to understand my identity as a Child of God, the more I learned that I had it backwards. Righteousness actually produces those works, not the other way around.

> *...and having been freed from sin, you became **slaves of righteousness.** Romans 6:18*

Righteousness – Strong's # 1343 (dik-ah-yos-oo'-nay) ("the *approval* of God") It refers to what is deemed right by the Lord, after His examination, i.e. what is approved in His eyes; integrity, virtue, purity of heart, uprightness, correctness in, acting, feeling, and thinking.

When you hear the word "righteous," most people think, "morally right," and while this is correct, righteousness goes much deeper than that. Just as the armor of God found in Ephesians 6 is not a prayer you pray on each day, but a way of life:

1. **Righteousness is who you become (not just what you do).** It's not just your actions; it's what's in your heart.
2. **Righteousness is expressed in relationships.** It's not just morality; it's morality in relationship with God, brothers and sisters in Christ as well as people of the world. This is the very definition of the fruit of righteousness; living, exemplifying and walking out righteousness in relationship with God and people.

Righteousness Delivers from Death

> *Treasures gained by wickedness have no lasting value, but **righteousness delivers from death**. ³The LORD does not let the righteous go hungry, but He denies the craving of the wicked. Proverbs 10:2-3*

He's talking about spiritual death; the Lord will not let the righteous go hungry, because He knows their needs even before they ask and He provides all their needs according to His riches and glory in Christ Jesus. The opposite of righteousness is wickedness. Unrighteousness is immorality while in relationship with God and other people. Righteous believers wear a crown of blessings which provides fruit to those around them called the fruit of righteousness, while the wicked wear a muzzle of violence and produce pain, suffering and misery to those around them. The righteous leave behind them a wake of blessing in the memories of everyone who knew them, but the stench of the name, and reputation of the wicked rots like a corpse.

> *Ask and it will be given to you; seek and you will find; knock and the door will be opened to you. ⁸For everyone who **asks** receives; he who **seeks** finds; and to him who **knocks**, the door will be opened.*
> Matthew 7:7-8

What if Jesus was talking about something other than that which...on the surface... seems apparent? What if we've been taking this verse out of context to justify the getting of stuff, fulfilling our desires or acquiring worldly possessions? I'm not saying it is wrong to ask God for things... as long as we are in this world, we all have need of things, a job, a home, a car, food, etc., but what if that's not what Jesus is talking about when He says, "Ask, Seek, Knock."

If we take a closer look, we see that Jesus was not, in fact, speaking about needs or things whatsoever.

> *Therefore do not worry, saying, 'What shall we eat?' or 'What shall we drink?' or 'What shall we wear?' ³²For **the pagans strive after all these things,** and your Heavenly Father knows that you need them. ³³But **seek first the kingdom of God and His righteousness, and all these things will be added unto you.** Matthew 6:31-33*

According to Matthew 6:33, the thing we are to be seeking for in Matthew 7:7 is righteousness. Therefore, it could be read this way: *...seek righteousness and you will find it;...* **⁸For he who seeks righteousness shall find righteousness;** ...

"Seek First the kingdom of God and His righteousness"

Seek – Strong's #2212 zētéō (dzay-teh'-o) Properly, to investigate to reach a resolution; to search, "getting to the bottom of a matter."

*"Seek **First** the kingdom of God and His righteousness"*

First – Strong's #4412. Proton (pro'-ton) Order of importance. Before all else, at the beginning, chiefly, first of all.

Jesus is instructing us to seek out this thing called righteousness like a detective conducts an investigation, and we do not stop seeking until we get to the bottom of the matter. Seek "first" implies an order of importance; we are to conduct this investigation for righteousness as the very first thing we do once the door is opened, and the Truth about Jesus is revealed to our heart.

> *The desire of the righteous leads **only to good**, but the **hope** of the wicked brings wrath.* Proverbs 11:23

Good is the outcome for the one who desires righteousness, but wrath awaits the selfish in their wickedness. To seek righteousness is to seek the heart of the Father, for He is the embodiment of righteousness. In seeking righteousness, we learn to give up selfishness and our motives begin to change. I am no longer living a selfish, self-centered life, but the life I live, I live for Jesus. I am a bondservant, my life is not mine to do with what I please, but I live to do what pleases my Father who lives in me.

If my motive is to please my Father, then my desires change. I used to desire the things of the world, the lust of the flesh, the lust of the eyes and the want for worldly things, but now I seek righteousness and it has changed my desires so that I no longer crave selfish things in a vain attempt to satisfy selfishness, but the will of my Father.

If I seek righteousness I'm not going to leave my spouse if she begins to suffer from depression brought about by a lack of her identity; I fast and pray for her Father to open the eyes of her understanding so that she sees who she is and what she was created for. If my spouse leaves for whatever reason, righteousness does not make it all about me; righteousness prays for her to be restored back to her Father, because she is in danger, wandering helplessly in a world whose only motive is to destroy her. And let not your prayer be selfish either, righteousness is not about getting her back to me; it's about praying for the restoring of her relationship with her Father.

Righteousness will change your desires from being all about you, to being all about Him and the needs of His children, which only leads to good, because with righteousness, there is no other possible eternal outcome. For believer and unbeliever alike; wrath is the end of hope for those who selfishly desire the things of the world over righteousness. Yes, even for Christians; when our desires are not for righteousness sake, even our prayers are full of selfishness. If we are in selfishness our prayers are full of needs and wants, and the end result is never good. If I am praying for God to change my situation or change my spouse, it is a selfish attempt to move, remove, change or alter something that is making me uncomfortable. In doing so, I have made it all about me again, and if it is about me, I am the real problem, not my situation.

Every difficult situation you are exposed to is nothing more than an opportunity for you to shine in. A chance to show a lost and dying world what Jesus actually looks like as you display the fruit of righteousness. The witness of your behavior will carry much more weight with onlookers than the witness of your words.

Not long ago I awoke one morning with a verse going through my head:

> *You desire and do not have, so you murder. You covet and cannot obtain, so you fight and quarrel. You do not have, because you do not ask.* James 4:2

That sounds eerily similar to what Jesus was saying in Matthew 7:7-8. Is it possible that James is expounding upon Jesus' teaching regarding righteousness, giving us a deeper insight after having walked out this Christian life and taught it for several decades?

I have known for a long time that the verses and chapters were placed in the Bible by men, and most are so well done, but some are not correct. For instance, in the parable of the sower, Jesus is speaking of and describing how the Kingdom of God is like sowing seeds. The translators took it upon themselves to separate the teaching into sections that appear to be completely different subject matter, when it is not. It is all one continuous lesson of Kingdom principles and laws, using farming as a metaphor. Therefore, I wondered if the same thing had happened to the book of James. What I saw was amazing.

In chapter 3, verse 18, of the book of James he writes, *"And those who are peacemakers will plant seeds of peace and reap a harvest of righteousness."* But that section ends and it goes to chapter 4, which would make it appear as if it is a different subject matter altogether, but what if it's not? If we combine the last verse of chapter 3 and the beginning of chapter 4, it sounds exactly like what Jesus is saying in Matthew 7. Check it out.

> *And those who are peacemakers will plant seeds of peace and reap a harvest of righteousness.* James 3:18

> *What is causing the quarrels and fights among you?* James 4:1

First, how can we be sure that these two go together? James 3:18 is talking about peacemakers planting seeds of peace while James 4:1 is talking about the quarrels and fights that are among them. Remember, the verse numbers were placed there by men, so the actual manuscript would have no such numbers of delineation. Without the chapter separation, the text would have read like this: *Since you well know that the harvest of righteousness is reaped by those who are peacemakers planting seeds of peace, what is causing the quarrels and fights among you?*

It's as if James is saying, 'Y'all know you are supposed to be peacemakers planting seeds of peace, right? So why are you fighting, because if you are fighting, you're not walking in righteousness and you know how important righteousness was to the Lord Jesus.'

James, like all the disciples understood that we were instructed to seek after righteousness, not the things of this world, and now that we have established the connection between the two verses, let's examine the entire context of this section, and see what's really being taught.

If righteousness is the harvest of peacemakers who plant seeds of peace, then righteousness is the produce we reap from peacemaking. Therefore, the topic of discussion, or the subject-matter has to be righteousness, and if it is, what else is James saying about it? To determine that, let's not forget that James is speaking to believers.

> *This letter is from James, a slave of God and of the Lord Jesus Christ.* ***I am writing to the "twelve tribes,"*** <u>***Jewish***</u> <u>***believers***</u> *scattered abroad. Greetings!* James 1:1

Just look at what James has to deal with.

> *The quarrels and fights among you come from the evil desires at war within you. ²You want what you don't have, so you scheme and kill to get it. You are jealous of what others have, but you can't get it, so you fight and wage war to take it away from them.* James 4:1

This is exactly what happens when Christians deviate away from seeking the Kingdom of God and His righteousness and begin seeking after prosperity and the things of the world. It's as if Satan was doing to the church then, the exact same thing he's doing now with the false hyper-grace and prosperity deception. James continues,

> *"You want what you don't have, so you plot schemes to try and steal it away from them, but if you cannot do that, you murder them to get it. You are so jealous of what others have, but if you can't get it yourself, you start fights and wage war to take it away from them. Yet you don't have what you want because you don't ask God for it."* Personally, the next verse is just as damning, if not more so. *"³And when you finally do humble yourselves and ask God, you do not receive, because you ask with wrong motives, so that you may squander it on your lustful pleasures."* James 4:2-3

I cannot stress this enough, James was speaking to believers. If this is not an indictment on the prosperity message and the OSAS lie, and a dire warning to all Christians to run from their false teaching, I don't know what is. If they wanted what they didn't have, so they schemed and murdered to get it, they are coveting, selfish and murderous. They were so jealous it drove them to steal, and because their desire was for the things of the world and not for the righteousness of God, even when they did break down and go to God for his counsel, it was only to ask Him for more stuff so they could engage in more lustful pleasures.

In the book of Ecclesiastes King Solomon wrote, *"There is nothing new under the sun."* It might be 2000 years later, but we are dealing with the same deceiving spirits and doctrine of demons that James was dealing with. Jesus knew we would be tempted with the things of the world, so He gave us very specific instructions to keep us focused on the Truth of the narrow path.

> *Therefore, I tell you, **do not worry about your life**, what you will **eat or drink**; or about **your body, what you will wear. Is not life more than food** and the body more than clothes? ... For the Gentiles strive after all these things, and **your Heavenly Father knows that you need them.** But seek first the kingdom of God and his righteousness, and all these things will be added to you.* Matthew 6:26

The Jewish Christians were a mess, craving after the things of the world; killing, coveting, quarreling and fighting. In verse 4 James even calls them adulteresses because even though he was writing to men, they were considered the bride of Christ, yet they had abandoned Jesus, their bridegroom for lustful pleasures, shunned righteousness, went back to the world and played the harlot on their King.

> *And when He comes, He will convict the world in regard to sin and righteousness and judgment.* John 16:8

To convict the world of righteousness means that I stay in a place of right standing with God, therefore, when Satan uses someone to come against me, I know it's because they don't understand their identity, so I'm not offended by them. It doesn't matter who they are, what matters is that I'm not offended, because righteousness requires me to walk in love. This thing called righteousness is not just about our talk; it's about our walk, because a tree is known by its fruit. It cannot be attained by doing good works either, but by a willingness to submit to your Father and obey His commandment of love.

Being convicted of righteousness means I am fully aware of my actions when they might offend my right standing with God. I'm not condemned, I am convicted, therefore I seek with all of my heart, and all my mind, all day, every day the kingdom of God and His righteousness. If I do something, anything, even the smallest, seemingly insignificant thing that isn't right, conviction pricks my conscience and it urges me to repent immediately. This is a good thing, it is not condemnation, it is your very heart convicting you of righteousness, and it is imperative that you listen to and obey immediately this conviction of righteousness. It is grace at work; grace is **not** God excusing your sin, it is His etching tool instructing you, convicting you, correcting you, and training you how to walk in righteousness.

It is the righteousness of God that trains our senses to notice and determine when something we have done, something we are in the process of doing or something we are thinking about doing is right or not. Righteousness is the ability to perceive the difference between good and evil and to choose good because your conscience won't allow you to do anything that is contrary to His will, His way, His righteousness.

The world's definition of good is a far cry different from Gods. People go the entire day lying, cheating, manipulating, lusting and coveting, then give $3.00 to a homeless beggar and at the end of the day they think their good outweighed their bad, but that is not the way it works with God. That is the very definition of self-righteousness. You are not going to step on a scale which weighs your works and sins to find a balance. The Bible says, *"If you have transgressed one law, you have transgressed them all."*

Gods definition of good is perfect and only Jesus was able to obtain that level of goodness. Jesus walked out all 613 laws of Moses and the 10 commandments without missing even one of them. A 4 year old draws a picture that may actually be considered good for a child of that age, but it is nothing compared to a Rembrandt. Jesus said our goodness is like filthy rags compared to Gods standard of goodness.

> *Then a certain ruler asked Him, "Good Teacher, what must I do to inherit eternal life?"* Luke 18:18

Good – Strong's #18 agathós (ag-ath-os')– inherently (intrinsically) good; good whether it be seen to be so or not. Agathós describes God and what originates from God and is empowered by Him in one's life, through faith. **Only God is agathós.**

By calling Jesus agathos (good), this rich young ruler as he is described in Mark's gospel is acknowledging Jesus' righteousness, His godliness, and His divinity. In order to conclude that, he must have taken some time to observe Jesus; the way He acted and interacted with the people. Only God is agathos, therefore by calling Jesus agathos, he recognized that Jesus was who He says He was; the Son of almighty God Himself. This story disproves the OSAS theory entirely, because this man believed in his heart that Jesus was who He claims to be, God, and he speaks it with his mouth when he calls Jesus "Good Teacher." Jesus confirms the man's conclusion with a follow-up question.

> *And Jesus said to him, "Why do you call Me good? No one is good (agathós) except God alone.* Mark 10:18

Jesus knows the man's heart, therefore He doesn't even need to ask this question, but He does so for all those around them to witness, as well as for the record it will leave us to read and learn from. What Jesus says in response to the ruler's question is this: *"Only God is agathos (good), for no man can obtain that level of goodness but God, therefore by calling me Good (agathos), you are calling me God...right?"* Jesus is mildly impressed with this man's ability to recognize Him as God, so He lovingly takes him through a few of the 10 commandments to show him where he is lacking. The man claims to have kept all the commandments from his youth, so Jesus, knowing his heart, gets down to the real problem.

Jesus confirms that this man has done a commendable job keeping the commandments, probably not as perfectly as he thinks in all his self-righteousness, but he must have done a commendable job, because Mark writes, *"Looking at him, Jesus felt a love for him...."* Now, let's not forget what started this conversation, this man asked Jesus what he had to do to obtain eternal life. The OSAS would have you believe that the man was already saved by the fact that he acknowledged Jesus as God, however, His self-righteous attempt to keep the 10

77commandments is not sufficient, and neither is his confession and profession that Jesus is Lord by calling Him *"Good Teacher."* There was still *"One thing he lacked;"* there's a problem with his heart.

> *...Jesus felt a love for him and said, "One thing you lack: go and sell all you possess and give to the poor, and you will have treasure in heaven; and come, follow Me."* Mark 10:21

Prosperity seekers beware; we will stand before an Almighty God one day, the God of the universe whose definition of good is on an entirely different level than ours, and just like this rich young man, we will be judged not just on our confession and profession of Jesus as Lord, nor on our outward works of following the law, but we will be judged on the righteousness of our hearts as well. Are we really willing to give up the things of the world, are we ready to abandon all to follow Jesus, because that is exactly what He is asking us to do to be saved?

> *...But at these words he was saddened, and he went away grieving, for he was one who owned much property.* Mark 10:22

The rich young ruler's lust for wealth and his unwillingness to give up the things of the world for the Kingdom of God sealed his fate. This man was clearly not an atheist, but his inability to die to his selfish desires and SEEK FIRST THE KINGDOM OF GOD AND HIS RIGHTEOUSNES established his loyalty to Satan's world system! Let this serve as a warning for all you OSAS hopefuls and prosperity seekers.

Righteousness is the Key

> *All Scripture is inspired by God and profitable for teaching, for reproof, for correction, for training in righteousness; it's for training in **righteousness**.* 2 Timothy 3:16

ALL SCRIPTURE is for <u>teaching</u>, <u>reproof</u>, <u>correction</u> and <u>training</u> in **RIGHTEOUSNESS**! That's interesting, have you ever considered that before? All scripture, which is inspired by God, is profitable for teaching us what it means to be righteousness and how to walk in righteousness. All Scripture is for reproof, that is, it convicts our hearts of righteousness to go back and right a wrong we may have committed. All Scripture corrects us so that we stay in righteousness, and all Scripture is for practical on-the-job training of righteousness. No wonder why Jesus said, *"... seek ye first the Kingdom of God and His righteousness..."*

Therefore, Scripture teaches us what righteousness is all about. Scripture convicts our conscience every time we walk outside righteousness. It is constantly correcting our perception of righteousness, so we do the right thing in the moment and It trains us how to daily walk out this thing called righteousness. Really, scripture does all that?

> *In the beginning was the Word, and the Word was with God,*
> *and the Word was God. He was with God in the beginning.*
> John 1:1.

Obviously, it's referring to Jesus here, so it's basically saying: *In the beginning was the Word (Jesus), and Jesus was with God, and Jesus was God, in that He came from God. Jesus was with God in the beginning.* With that in mind, 2 Timothy 3:16 would also be saying: Because Jesus is the Word and the Word is Scripture, all Scripture is Jesus. Therefore, if all Scripture is Jesus, then Jesus is teaching us, convicting us, correcting us and training us to walk and talk and think and act righteously like Him.

No devil in hell, no person can take away your righteousness, your right standing with God. Only you can give it away by choosing to turn from righteousness and go back to the world. We are instructed to put on the breastplate of righteousness, why? Because righteousness, like a bullet proof vest, guards our heart. *"There is now, therefore no condemnation for those who walk in the Spirit,"* as long as you walk with the breastplate of righteousness on.

> *Beloved, if our hearts do not condemn us, we have confidence before God, ²²and **we will receive from Him whatever we ask**, (Why) because we keep His commandments and do **what is pleasing** in His sight.* 1 John 3:21-22

I have actually heard this verse used by the OSAS and prosperity peddlers to ask for stuff and increase the tithe. They taught, because you are righteous by grace whether you sin or not, you can ask for anything and get it. Then they'd cleverly attach some obscure tithing verse to it out of context so the people would use it to try to get things, and the pastor would use it to increase his coffers. Neither is true, however, because the thing we are supposed to be asking for is righteousness, not worldly stuff. It must be, otherwise John would be contradicting Jesus, and he's not. In fact, John begins this section with this:

> *By this the children of God are distinguished from the children of the devil: **Anyone who does not practice righteousness is not of God**, nor is anyone who does not love his brother.* 1 John 3:10

There's a "mic drop" moment! John's litmus test for distinguishing real Christians from children of the devil is those who practice righteousness and love... or not! When we die to ourselves and seek righteousness our hearts won't condemn us, instead we have an unwavering confidence and boldness before the Father, believing that we will receive the supernatural ability to walk in the righteousness we seek after. It's this supernatural, God infused ability that empowers us from the inside out to keep the 10 commandments and do what is pleasing in our Fathers sight. It is a constant pursuit of righteousness that enables us to walk by faith and not by sight.

> *And without faith it is impossible to please God...* Hebrews 11:6

Jesus said that the Father already knows what you need before you ask, so you don't even need to ask for any-**thing**. If you **seek first** the Kingdom of God and

His righteousness, He will provide all the things He knows you have need of, all the things the world is searching after. We seek righteousness and He supplies our needs. In order to do that, we need to move from selfishness and worldly desires to righteousness and love in everything we do. In our marriage, righteousness and love, on our job, righteousness and love, in relationship with friends and family, righteousness and love, in relationship with random people on the street, in a store, with whomever and wherever we are at the moment. We should think, act and react just like our Lord, in righteousness and love; especially in regards to the way we pray. If you change the focus of you prayer and stop praying for things or needs and begin praying for and asking for His righteousness, you will find that the things you have need of will just show up.

> *And my **God will supply all your needs** according to His glorious riches in Christ Jesus. Philippians 4:19*

And just how does God do that?

> *And **God is able to make all grace abound to you**, so that in all things, at all times; having all that you need, you will abound in every good work. 2 Corinthians 9:8*

Christian or not, if your goal is for riches and wealth out of a selfish heart, all your wants and desires will be bound up in the things of the world, but if your desire is for His righteousness and love, He will provide your needs by making grace abound towards you, in all things and at all times so that you have all you need to abound in the good work you do on His behalf. Just as God was trying to get Israel to trust on Him for all their needs in the desert, He's trying to get us to trust on Him for our needs now. It's as if God is saying to us, *"I don't want you to have to worry about necessities like food, clothes, transportation and housing, I'll take care of those things; I want you focused on the important things, the things that have an eternal consequence, therefore focus on righteousness and love and I'll take care of everything else."*

It's really not all that difficult to perceive if you look at it logically. It would be like a young girl going to medical school, but she's compromising her studies by having to work to pay for her education as well as her living expenses. The extremely high cost may even cause her to do things to make money that are against her better judgment, but her need to succeed leaves her with no other options. Yet, her father is telling her that if she stops all that nonsense, and focuses only on school, he will pay her tuition and all her expenses.

> *For I warn you, unless your righteousness exceeds that of the scribes and Pharisees,* **you will never** *enter the kingdom of heaven.* Matthew 5:20

This is a powerful statement on so many levels. First, if Jesus says, *"you will never enter the kingdom of heaven;"* clearly, He is saying that person is not saved. If the OSAS theory was true, then why didn't Jesus say, "For I warn you, unless you confess Me as Lord, you will not enter the Kingdom of heaven?" Next, the Scribes and the Pharisees were the religious leaders of their time; the equivalence of modern day priests, pastors, preachers, evangelists, bishops, deacons and rabbis and just one of their many problems was hypocrisy.

They demanded righteousness through the strict conformance of the 613 laws of Moses, but they themselves could not do it. Like a witch uses witchcraft to manipulate and coerce her victims, the Scribes and Pharisees used the law to manipulate the Jews for their own selfish needs and desires. Jesus is obviously making a generalization here, because there were some Scribes and Pharisees with integrity. Nicodemus was likely one such Jewish leader. As you recall, he secretly visited Jesus to inquire of the "born again" experience in which Jesus ever so sweetly calls him out as being a teacher of the law yet knowing nothing.

> *"How can someone be born when they are old?" Nicodemus asked.*
> *"Surely they cannot enter a second time into their mother's womb*

> *to be born!" ⁵Jesus answered, "Very truly I tell you, no one can enter the kingdom of God unless they are born of water and the Spirit...⁹"How can this be?" Nicodemus asked. ¹⁰***You are Israel's teacher***," said Jesus, **"and do you not understand these things**?*
> John 3:4-9

Just prior to Jesus' crucifixion, He blasts the Scribes and Pharisees for their hypocrisy. It always felt like Jesus was picking a fight with them when I read it. Kind of like He was saying, "Hey guy's, you're going to crucify Me, so get on with it already."

> *"Woe to you, teachers of the law and Pharisees, you hypocrites! You are like whitewashed tombs, which look beautiful on the outside **but on the inside** are **full** of the **bones of the dead** and **everything unclean**.*
> Matthew 23:27

The same would be true of modern day church leaders; they are being deceived by the same spirits, so they are really no different from the Jewish leaders in Jesus' time. They most likely began with good intentions, but lust, greed, selfishness and the like have crept in and stolen the Word that was once in their hearts. Just because someone is behind a pulpit, can fill stadiums full of adoring people, is on TV or even on YouTube does not make them better than you or any other Christian for that matter.

They certainly should not be idolized, adored or exalted in any way, because they are not above reproach. It likely makes them a greater target of the devil and more vulnerable as well. Riddled with sex scandals, fits of rage, jealousy, envy and strife; an overly excessive need for vainglorious sanctuaries, homes, cars and even airplanes has blinded their eyes and hardened their hearts to the reasons they got into the ministry in the first place. The same spirits that deceived the Scribes and Pharisees in the days of Jesus are still at work in the church leaders today, therefore, *"unless your righteousness exceeds that of the Scribes and Pharisees, you will never enter the kingdom of heaven."*

> *Not many of you should become teachers, my brothers, because you know that we who teach will be judged more strictly.*
> James 3:1

If preachers are espousing the OSAS doctrine, it's because they are being ruled by their own sin and in need of an excuse. If they are promoting the prosperity message and not encouraging righteousness, they are simply deceived by the lust of worldly possessions. If righteousness is not what they seek and not an intrical part of almost every sermon, it's likely because the preacher is not walking in it. When righteousness becomes your focus, righteousness is your passion and your calling.

Many believers are seeking after gifts and callings... they're looking to start a ministry or ministries and I get it, when you're a new believer and on fire, you want to use your talents and abilities for the Kingdom, but that's not what's most important... at least not at first.

> *...the gifts and calling of God are without repentance.* Romans 11:29.

This means that you can be *"in sin"* and still have an outwardly effective ministry. You could have a worship leader whose praise and worship is awesome and anointed, all the while he's in an adulterous affair. You could have a boyfriend and girlfriend praying for people and performing miracles in a street ministry while they are living together in fornication. But Jesus warns us to be righteous or else! Or else what? Or else we become just like the Scribes and Pharisees, and we, like them, will not enter the Kingdom of heaven. The Pharisees were masters at appearing righteous on the outside but inwardly He was disgusted with them.

> *He made Him who knew no sin to be sin on our behalf, so that we* **might become** *the righteousness of God in Him.* 2 Corinthians 5:21

Jesus became sin for us so that we **might become** the righteousness of God in Christ Jesus. In the Greek, **"might become,"** means to transition into, manifestation implying growth. "Might become" is not "maybe we become," it specifically implies a present tense transformation into something we are currently in the process of becoming, something completely new. It is not used as a future tense, it is not indicating something that will happen later, after you die and come to be with the Lord; that would do you no good whatsoever. The righteousness of God in Christ Jesus is something we "**are becoming**," something we are expected to transform into upon salvation, but only if we seek it first.

> *You will know them by their fruits.* Matthew 7:16

Children of God are known by the fruit they produce and that fruit is righteousness and love.

> *As obedient children, **do not be conformed to the passions of your former ignorance**, but as He who called you is holy, you also be holy in all your conduct...*
> 1 Peter 1:15

As God was speaking to me about righteousness, telling me to study it and teach it, He woke me up saying this, *"I would not set you up for failure, I would not demand righteousness from you if it were not possible to be so, therefore be holy as I am holy."*

> *For the time will come when men will not tolerate sound doctrine, but with itching ears they will gather around themselves teachers to suit their own desires.*
> 2 Timothy 4:3

The American idealism, the success of this once humble, but free nation has caused it to become a nation of spoiled brats that want to sit in comfy chairs and hear warm fuzzy messages of an idol god they have dreamed up in their own minds, a false god that lavishes bountiful blessings of prosperity on selfish, stubborn, immature children. This false god they have created for themselves will punish all sinner's in the lake of fire, but not them, no-no, they get off scott-free on a technicality. They can sin all they want now, because they have said the coveted "sinner's' prayer. Peter puts this foolish thinking to rest with this Scripture:

> *For it is time for judgment to begin with the family of God; and if it begins with us, what will the outcome be for those who disobey the gospel of God?* [18] *And "If the righteous are scarcely saved, what will become of the ungodly and the sinner?* 1 Peter 4:17-18

Peter is talking to believers about believers while asking a rhetorical question about the fateful end of those that disobey the gospel. He is not talking to or about unbelievers, he did not say, *what will be the outcome of unbelievers?"* He is talking to *the family of God and the judgment that begin with us.* He's talking about anyone in the family of God that does not obey the gospel when he says, *"those who disobey,"* he's talking to believers who are walking in willful disobedience, he's talking specifically to the OSAS. Peter differentiates the saved from the unsaved, but his line of delineation, his dividing line is not a "sinner's prayer"… it is obedience and righteousness! And, the truly scary part is when he says, *"If the righteous are barely saved."* That is why Jesus said to **seek first** the Kingdom of God and His righteousness.

Next, Peter describes the people who will not be saved, *the ungodly and the sinner.* Keeping in mind that Peter was talking to Christians, he places them in two different categories.

- **The Ungodly**. The word for ungodly here is Strong's #765. Asebés. A lack of reverence towards God ("without due respect"), i.e. failing to honor God as one honors a loving parent. To honor a parent is not just to obey them, but to obey with a good attitude.

- **The Sinner**. The word for sinner is Strong's #268. Hamartólos. Sinning, sinful, depraved, detestable. *Falling short* of what God approves, devoted to sin, pre-eminently sinful, especially wicked. People who consider themselves believers but who live in willful disobedient sin.

In Paul's first letter to the Corinthians, he has to deal with some extremely bad behavior in the church. Most people read it and automatically assume he's not talking to the church, but look at the way he begins,

> *Instead, you yourselves cheat and do wrong, even against your own brothers!* 1 Corinthians 6:8

Clearly, we see Paul addressing brothers in Christ about their behavior, and he goes on to say,

> *Do you not know that the wicked will not inherit the kingdom of God?*
> 1 Corinthians 6:9

Why in the world would Paul need to say that to the Christian Church unless wickedness would cause them not to inherit the kingdom of God? But that pales in comparison to what Paul says to them next.

> *Do not be deceived: Neither the sexually immoral, nor idolaters, nor adulterers, nor men who submit to or perform homosexual acts, ¹⁰nor thieves, nor the greedy, nor drunkards, nor verbal abusers, nor swindlers, will inherit the kingdom of God.* 1 Corinthians 6:9-10

Therefore, "If the righteous are scarcely saved, what will become of the ungodly and the sinner? Well... sinner's prayer or not, they will not inherit the Kingdom of God, at least that's what Peter and Paul are saying,

> ***All unrighteousness is sin***, *yet there is sin that does not lead to death.* ¹⁸*We know that **anyone born of God does not keep on sinning;*** 1 John 5:17-18

Righteousness is the line of delineation, it is the measuring stick of one's salvation, not a sinner's prayer, which sounds terrifying at first thought, but if you understand what Jesus is saying when He says, *"Seek first the kingdom of God and His righteousness..."* you begin to see that the only difficult part of this equation is you getting to a place in your life where you want a relationship with your Father so much that your desire is not for worldly things any longer, but your desire is to know Him and His heart.

In desiring to know the heart of your Father, you knock on the door of His Kingdom, "the Kingdom of God," and because it's not about you any longer, you want what He wants for you, so you seek after righteousness because that's what Jesus instructed you to do. Jesus said, *"Seek and you will find."* Now God has you right where He wants you, right where He needs you to be, in a place where He can do **for you** what He has wanted to do **to you** since the Garden of Eden, and that is to once again live **in you**.

He wants to transform you into His likeness, He wants to make you a chip of the ol' block by putting His spirit inside you and living through you. However, as I said earlier, our Father is a gentleman and He never imposes Himself on anyone. He will gently nudge you, but if that doesn't get your attention, He will sear your conscience; He will even allow your bad decisions to bring trouble and heartache upon you; all in an effort to wake you up, but He will not force you to behave righteously. He wants us to *"ask, seek* and *knock"* on our own accord, but if we do, *"it will be given, we will find* and *it will be opened to us."* Our Father is a loving Father and He always responds to us with love.

> ***Ask*** *and it will be given to you;* ***seek*** *and you will find;* ***knock*** *and the door will be opened to you...* Matthew 7:7

If we ask...He gives, *if we seek*...we will find, and *if we knock*...He will open, but it's up to us to take the initiative; we must want Him like He wants us, that's all He requires. Imagine for a moment, being wildly, madly in love with someone, but they do not even notice you let alone love you back; that's how our Father and Jesus feel about us. Then imagine that person you're head over heels in love with, the one you've been pining over, one day, out of the blue, turning around and finally noticing you and saying, "I love you." Imagine how warm your heart would feel at that moment, when the object of your desire finally desires you back.

God wants children who want Him as badly as He wants them. Jesus likened this to a man who learned of a buried treasure in a field, so he purchased the field and dug, and dug, and dug until he found his treasure. What would you do if you learned there was a treasure buried in your back yard? What are you willing to do to establish your relationship as a Child of God?

> *...For with the same measure that you use, it will be measured back to you."* Luke 6:38

God responds to you the way you go after Him. Like all relationships, you will get out of this what you put into it. If He is not important to you, that does not mean that you are unimportant to Him, it just means that He will give you exactly what you are seeking after and according to the vigor in which you seek.

Writing this made me think of a dad who was a great athlete or businessman or whatever and he raises his son to one day walk in his footsteps and carry on the family business or the skill he has developed over decades of hard work, sacrifice and discipline. The father delights in watching his son perform the skill he has passed down, and thoroughly enjoys watching his son excel at the thing that he so loves as he lives vicariously through his child.

And just exactly what is it that our Father loves doing more than anything in the world, what is it that He has perfected, what is it that He desires for us to do now that Jesus has returned to Father? Love & righteousness! Our Father wants to live in us, but not vicariously, not just in His imagination, He literally wants to come and **live in us**, so He can become **love through us** to all His other lost children. God's special skill is His character, His nature; that which He wants to pass to His adopted children is a heart to love His wayward children just as He loves them and to walk in righteousness just as Jesus walked in righteousness.

Jesus blessed and loved and healed thousands upon thousands of people, but He could only make contact with just so many at any one time, because He was only one person. As a seed falls to the ground and dies, Jesus died so He, like a seed could produce much fruit, and we are that fruit. His dying legally allowed God to commute our death sentence and come and live in us so He can be Jesus through us, and only one thing prevents the Father from doing this...US. We have to want it, we have to want Him, and we have to be willing to die to ourselves, so He can come in and overtake our carnality, restore our lost identity, and infuse us with power from on High by filling us with His Spirit. At that point, we are no longer trying to achieve righteousness by acting righteous, but we actually "become righteousness" as He begins to live and love through us.

If we emulate Jesus, we too must die like a seed so we can produce more fruit, however unlike Muslims, Jesus is not asking us to die for Him in the literal sense, we die metaphorically. We die to ourselves so we too can produce much fruit, and like Jesus, our fruit will produce other disciples that will produce fruit as well. This is the gospel of Jesus Christ. We are not told to decrease so he can increase; we die to ourselves so He can live in us and produce even more fruit through us.

This is the offer the Father is making us; this is the deal, take it or leave it, deal or no deal! This offer was never about you living your best life now, that was a big fat lie of the devil, so he doesn't have to worry about the rapid multiplication of dying seeds producing tons of fruit; new children being "born again" into the Kingdom. This thing we are doing is **not about us <u>after all</u>**, in fact, **it's not about us <u>at all</u>**, but it's about our Father and Jesus and their desire to have a

Father/son relationship with all His children. If a seed doesn't fall to the ground and die, it cannot produce, and if we don't die to ourselves, neither will we produce. If it were all about us and our best life now, we are certainly not dying to ourselves and neither will we produce anything.

> *...God our Savior, who desires all men to be saved and to come to the knowledge of the truth.* 1 Timothy 2:4.

The only way that can happen, the only way for men to be saved and come to that knowledge is for the Children of God to let go of their selfish pursuits, knock on the Kingdom door, seek righteousness, die like a seed so they can become love and produce a great harvest. This is God's plan to save mankind and have a family at the same time, and He wants to use us to do it.

> *For the kingdom of God is not a matter of eating and drinking but of righteousness and peace and joy in the Holy Spirit.* John 14:26

Let's be honest here, when Jesus says, *"For the kingdom of God is not a matter of eating and drinking...,"* isn't He is really saying, *"The kingdom of God is not a matter of you living your best life now...."* God is always tugging at the hearts of unbelievers to join His Kingdom, but He is not asking His children to be righteous. Once we have made up our mind to seek the Kingdom of God and be born again, righteousness is no longer a suggestion...it is a requirement. But why? Why be such a taskmaster and demand this thing called righteousness?

As Jesus said, *"...because without righteousness, no one will enter the Kingdom of God."* Whenever God commands something, it's always because it is in our best interest. Righteousness keeps us safe and out of trouble, righteousness wards off worry and doubt, righteousness enables us to walk in authority as evidenced by signs, wonders and miracles and most importantly, righteousness saves our souls from destruction.

Because of the seriousness and urgency to attain this thing called righteousness, Jesus is advising us to seek it as the first thing we should do upon salvation. In Matthew 7:7-8, when Jesus says to *"ask, seek and knock,"* He is telling us to seek for righteousness like one who seeks a treasure. This is confirmed in Matthew 5:6.

> *Blessed are those who hunger and thirst for righteousness, for they will be filled.* Matthew 5:6

In the Strong's Concordance, the definition of hunger and thirst is to crave ardently for, to desire a thing with reckless abandon, as though your life depended on it, but why? Because your eternal life literally depends upon you seeking after and finding His righteousness.

In Matthew 5:6, Jesus uses this analogy of food and water specifically because He knew they would understand the depth of the expression *"hunger and thirst for."* In the Middle East, during the time of Jesus, dying of dehydration and/or starvation was not all that uncommon. When they traveled from town to town, they made long treks through the desert. These journeys were mostly by foot and it took them weeks on end. We have no way of relating to this analogy of hunger and thirst that Jesus uses, because we are so spoiled by modern technology. Most of us wouldn't last a few days let alone one week in their society. All we need to do is jump in the car, check into a hotel, turn on a faucet or stop at a restaurant. Jesus uses hunger and thirst as a dramatic example to stress the importance of seeking righteousness as the very first thing we should do upon salvation, or else face dire consequences, possibly death.

Just as the natural body requires food and water or it will die, so our spiritual body requires righteousness or else it may die...spiritually! Jesus is instructing us to seek the righteousness of God like our life depends upon it, and when He says, *"seek ye **first** the Kingdom of God and His righteousness,"* it's because it is the very first thing we are instructed to do once we repent for our sins, confess Jesus as Lord and are adopted into the family.

> *Anyone who does not practice righteousness **is not of God**...*
> 1 John 3:10

When it says, "...*Not of God*...," it means that they are not of the lineage of God; they are not children by birth or adoption. Jesus said it first, and John reconfirms just how important righteousness is in order to be saved. All this time we've been deceived into using the Word of God to ask for things, when all along we're supposed to be seeking for, longing for, craving for... **His righteousness**! Satan has done a masterful job of turning the message of the cross, this amazing message of love & righteousness, into a message of desire & selfishness. We've bastardized and prostituted the gospel of Jesus Christ, where every sermon is based upon giving, in order to get blessed, and a false definition of grace to excuse youthful lusts.

Instead of becoming a blessing to a lost and dying world and walking in His righteousness, Christians give, but with the sole intention of receiving; then they wallow in willful sin and hide behind the hyper-grace of a false god they have created for themselves, in the futility of their own mind. They are like a man walking around naked but unashamed, because they have been deceived through hypnosis into thinking they are fully clothed. And so, nobody gets offended and leaves the congregation, most Pastors simply give the people more of what they want, sermons about prosperity and grace to excuse the sin they refuse to let go of. Modern Christianity is no longer about saving souls from eternal damnation, but about the size of the church and the amount of tithe that came in that week.

The opposite of love is not hate, it's selfishness; it's a selfish, self-centered attitude where you are the center of your universe. However, you were not made for you; you were made for Him who made you, and when He purchased you with His blood it's no longer supposed to be about you. Walking in love & righteousness is you getting over you and living for Him who gave His life for you, and the grace of God is not a license or an excuse which permits sin...it's the power of the Holy Spirit in us that changes our heart in such a way that we do not want to sin any longer.

Like the rich young ruler, selfishness stems from the hardness of one's heart. Life's experiences, its ups and downs, all the sadness and heartache cause a hardness of our heart that produces an attitude of self-preservation, but when you seek righteousness, God begins working on your heart first, because if your heart does not change, nothing will.

> *Draw near to God, and He will draw near to you. Cleanse your hands, you sinner's, and **purify your hearts**, you double-minded.* James 4:8

> ***Wash the evil from your heart**, O Jerusalem, so that you may be saved. How long will you harbor wicked thoughts within you?*
> Jeremiah 4:14

The first thing that changes in a person who has sincerely given their life to Jesus and seeks righteousness is their heart. The God of all creation comes in and removes all the garbage that has held them in the bondage of sin due to selfishness. It is the hardest thing to describe and the one thing that people of the world will never understand. A heart that truly loves Jesus and seeks righteousness no longer has a desire to hurt anyone, regardless of what they have done or are doing. Their only motive is to love others the same way Jesus loved them. Their hearts are in the process of purification; the evil of selfishness is being washed away and the remnant is a beautiful heart of love; a heart after the Father's own heart.

A Heart to Love

Most people say, "I love you," but they only say it because they are waiting and wanting it said back to them in return. If one truly loves, they don't need it said back to them. Jesus loved everyone, but only a handful of people loved Him; most people just came to see the greatest show on earth with all its miracles. Some came for the free food and the rest just wanted him dead, but Jesus loved them all regardless. Jesus said, *"Love everybody, as I have loved you, love everybody."*

"*If you love Me, you will keep My commandments."* John 14:15

That could also be said this way, *"If you don't love Me, you won't keep My commandments."* But it really hit home when I saw it this way, *"If you don't keep My commandments...it proves you don't love Me."*

You will never hear this message taught in a Mega church; and why not, because they wouldn't be Mega any longer! Mega churches are Mega, for the simple fact that they never confront the subjects of sin and righteousness. Instead, they encourage sin with a false grace god they made up for the sheeple (people who blindly follow like sheep) while they use witchcraft to deceive the church into tithing an uncommon tithe if they want to receive an uncommon gift.

> *...And this is my prayer: **that your love may abound more and more** in knowledge and depth of insight, ¹⁰so that you can discern what is best, that you may be **pure and blameless** for the day of Christ, ¹¹**filled with the fruit of righteousness** that comes through Jesus Christ... Philippians 9-11*

If Paul prayed that our love would abound to such a level of knowledge of the Fathers love towards us that we would be able to discern what Gods will for us was in every situation, then shouldn't we be doing just that? This kind of love walk and understanding would make us pure and blameless, filling us with the fruit of righteousness for the day when we are presented like a virgin bride to Jesus.

> *In Him we have redemption through his blood, the forgiveness of sins, in accordance with the riches of God's grace.* **Ephesians 1:7**

By the blood of Jesus all our sins are washed away and forgiven the moment we die to ourselves and sincerely confess Jesus as our Lord and Savior. If we do as

Jesus says, and seek righteousness, the grace of God works like an etching tool teaching us, convicting us, correcting us and training us to walk in righteousness from that day forward. Not that we are perfect, we're not, but we are expected to strive for, seek for, hunger for and thirst for righteousness.

> *...He restores my soul. He leads me in paths of righteousness for his name's sake.* Psalm 23:3

I took the time to break down every word in this verse with the Strong's Concordance.

He restores my soul - Implies that we had drifted away from Him, but He receives us back into His fold. It is to turn back from evil. It requires repentance on our side and restoration of relationship on Gods side.

He leads me – He leads, we follow. He is not leading us to sin. If we will follow Him, He will lead us into righteousness, but only if we choose to follow Him and not the world. Jesus confirms this when He said, *"My sheep hear My voice and follow Me."*

in paths – A course of action, or life, specifically what is good and righteous.

of righteousness - what is right or just in the eyes of God.

for his name's sake – With the intended purpose of bringing glory and honor to the name of God

Sin

Sin, in the modern church, is not merely overlooked by the hyper-grace movement, in many cases it is tolerated and excused. Even to the point of being glorified by some, as if the more tolerant to sin, the more gracious God is. But what if the modern church has been deceived into a false definition of God's grace? What if the modern church has heaped up for itself a false hyper-grace god to justify a life of sinful pleasure? A life they never gave up after saying a "sinner's prayer," because they were never taught to die to self and seek righteousness. Maybe they got saved in a prosperity driven mega-church and only came to God to get stuff, maybe they were pressured into it because everyone else was doing it, maybe their sin had gotten them in so much trouble, and they were just looking for a way out. Whatever the reason, they never died to themselves, never got hold of righteousness, and therefore, never transformed into the image of God, but remained in the same sinful state they were before they confessed Jesus.

It happens much more often than you think, because the OSAS and prosperity hucksters taught them a doctrine of demons based upon an incorrect definition of grace, but what if the correct definition of grace is not God overlooking or excusing our sin? What if Gods definition of grace is something entirely different from the one we've been taught? What does the word say?

> *How much more severely do you think one deserves to be punished who has trampled on the Son of God, profaned the blood of the covenant that sanctified him, and* **insulted the Spirit of Grace?** Hebrews 10:29

Since the Word of God calls Grace a Spirit, I'll save the in-depth definition and description of the Spirit of Grace for the next chapter, Leg 3 of the altar - Holy Spirit. Regardless, Paul is clearly explaining how willful sin is an insult to the Spirit of Grace. That's a long way from trying to hide behind grace while in willful sin.

> *In Him we have redemption through His blood, the forgiveness of sins, in accordance with the riches of God's grace.* Ephesians 1:7

The word says that Jesus was the embodiment of the Father. In other words, if you saw Jesus, you saw the Father. They were one in the same. Just consider how sweet Jesus was, how caring and kind and considerate He treated everyone. He was so loving and gentle; He never turned anyone away...ever. He was frequently being followed by as many as ten thousand people at a time and He never got frustrated by them or complained about them. Matthew 4 says that Jesus went about proclaiming the good news of the kingdom, and healing every disease and sickness among the people.

> *God anointed Jesus of Nazareth with the Holy Spirit and power, and He went around doing good and **healing all** who were under the power of the devil, because God was with Him.* Acts 10:38

Because God was with Jesus, they were of one mind and one accord. We are so blessed and fortunate that we have a Father who loves us so much that He would go to such lengths to save us. He did it so that He could live in us and do the same mighty works through us that Jesus did. Think about it, the God of all creation comes out of a temple made of stone so He can come into His children and live a life of faith, hope and love towards all of His creation.

God had previously tried to live among His children, but they rejected Him in the desert. They told Moses they did not want to talk to Him directly or they would die, but Moses hadn't died and he spoke to God daily. Moses said, *"It is good to fear God."* Meaning, God wanted to put the fear, the respect, the awe of Him inside them so they wouldn't want to sin against Him anymore. But they rejected that offer, so God moved into a temple and gave them 613 laws and 10 commandments to follow, all because they rejected His initial offer to fellowship directly with them.

> *Do you not know that **your body is a temple of the Holy Spirit who is in you**, whom you have received from God? You are not your own; [20]**you were bought at a price. Therefore glorify God with your body.*** 1 Corinthians 6:19-20

Jesus models Christianity for us and pays the ultimate price on a cross; a price that must be paid so our Father can have a personal relationship with us. If the value of an item is that which someone is willing to pay for it; what price was paid for you? Your Father loved you so much that He asked His Son to give up His divinity, humble Himself to the point of being born of a human, followed all 613 laws as well as the 10 commandments without breaking even one of them, and allowed Himself to be gruesomely tortured and murdered by the most sadistic form of capital punishment ever devised. As it says above, *"you were bought at a price..."* the amount that was paid for you was the greatest amount that has ever been paid for anything in the history of the world; the blood of Jesus. To your Father, you are the most valuable thing in the world.

Now compare what Jesus did for you to what allah requires of his followers. Allah says, "Die for me and I will give you paradise;" the absolute epitome of selfishness, but Jesus said, *"I have come to die for you."* Which one has the character of a loving God?

Jesus paid your fine, a fine you were completely incapable of paying for with your own self-righteousness. What kind of God would do that for His children? A God who loved His children with the greatest love the world has ever known. It never ceases to amaze me; the vitriol that comes from some people when they find out you are a Christian, and I ask them, "what is it about this message of unconditional love that makes you hate so much?" I mean really, what is there to hate about someone willing to die in your place so you could go free; and without so much as a guarantee that you would even accept it?

When you begin to spend time with your Father in His Word, you learn that the God of all creation desires to live in you. As you spend this time in His Word as well as prayer, His Spirit communes with your spirit and He begins teaching you, convicting you, correcting you, encouraging you and training you in righteousness. The absolute most powerful, the most important thing you can do is have communion with the Father, His Son and His Holy Spirit.

"Why do you call Me **'Lord, Lord,'** *but not do what I say?"* Luke 6:46

Lord - Strong's #2962: (koo'-ree-os) – A person exercising ***absolute ownership rights***; this title is given to God, the ruler of the universe. One who has control over a person; the owner or master.

The title Lord was given to or used by very powerful rulers and Kings of the time, but it was recognized by the Jews as being God or as Jesus referred to Himself, the Son of God. If a servant, or a soldier pledged his loyalty to "his Lord," it meant he was giving up his autonomy and going into total servitude to him. From then on, he is no longer his own man; he belongs to his Lord now. With the exception of sleep, he was expected to be on duty 24/7. They were granted times of reprieve to spend with family, but truly dedicated servants would refuse such time, choosing to serve their Lord instead.

This kind of dedication was displayed by Uriah, the husband of Bathsheba, after King David had committed adultery with her and gotten her pregnant. Upon finding out that Bathsheba was with child, David devised a plan to bring Uriah home from the war so Uriah would have sex with his wife, and then Bathsheba could say the child was Uriah's. However, Uriah was so dedicated to his lord, King David that he refused to leave David's side for even one night and simply stayed outside David's living quarters. Even though Uriah was young and they were newlyweds, no amount of persuasion by David could convince Uriah to spend time with his wife.

That is exactly what it means when you call someone Lord. It is your complete and utter devotion of service to them and it is what Jesus expects from us upon salvation. But that is so much to ask, you say. Is it? That's exactly the way you behaved when you were in the world, serving it, lusting after it and wallowing in its filthy pleasures. Before we got saved, sin was our lord, and if we were willing to serve the god of this world so faithfully, a god whose only goal was to kill us, steel everything that is dear to us and destroy everything we love; if we were willing to serve a lord like that, how much more Jesus?

After the price He paid for you, the beating He took on your behalf, the stripes He took to cure the disease of a sinful nature, the crown of thorns He endured so you could obtain the mind of Christ, the bruises He took to forgive your iniquity and death by crucifixion; the most hideous form of death the world has ever known. After all that, making Jesus our Lord is the least we can do and the least He deserves. Jesus did all that for you, and He did it only because He loves you.

Even when you didn't love Him, He loved you. Even when you spoke evil of Him and denied His very existence, He loved you. Even when you deceived, hurt, lied to, stole from, and murdered those whom He loved, He still loved you. And when you consider exactly what He endured on your behalf, not to mention what He saved you from; an eternity in hell to be tortured and burned by a fire that never goes out. Yes, after all that, He expects, no, He deserves your love and utter devotion. Therefore, making Him your Lord, pledging Him your utter devotion is the least you can do for Him.

No Longer a Slave to Sin

> *...he who was free when he was called is now a bondservant of Christ.* 1 Corinthians 7:22

We are called to be Bondservants of Christ. A bondservant is a slave whose freedom was purchased by another, but chooses to serve the one who purchased him, for free. The gift of salvation is free, but you must make Jesus your Lord, you must turn away from the world and towards Jesus with complete and utter devotion, just saying a sinner's prayer is not devotion. If you claim to have said a prayer, but walk like the world, talk like the world, think like the world and act like the world...the world is your Lord.

> *Do not love the world or the things in the world. If anyone loves the world, the love of the Father is not in him.* 1 John 2:15

That is not saying that your Father does not love you. He does. He loves you just as much as He loved His Hebrew children when He took them out of Egypt and destroyed 23,000 of them in the desert because of their sin. He loves you every bit as much as he loved the inhabitants of Sodom and Gomorrah when He rained down fire and brimstone, because of their debauchery. He does love you, that is not what this verse is implying. When it says, "*...the love of the Father is not in him.*" It is **not** saying the Father does not love you, it's saying that if you love the world so much that you won't stop serving it...then you don't love the Father like you say you do. Your allegiance is established by your love and devotion.

> *"No one can serve two masters, for either he will hate the one and love the other, or he will be devoted to the one and despise the other...."* Matthew 6:24

Jesus is drawing a very clear, easy to understand line in the sand here. If you say you love and are devoted to God, then you are supposed to hate and despise the world, but if you are dabbling in the world, you clearly do not despise it. How much time do you spend in your Word reading and praying each day? How much time do you spend in the world doing worldly things? I am not talking about life, your job, your children your spouse; God understands that you have responsibilities. I am talking about your free time. If you spend 3 hours a day watching mindless junk on TV; trash that our Lord died a horrible death to save us from, yet you don't even spend 1 minute in prayer and maybe you read 1 chapter of your Bible...your life is out of balance.

Where you choose to spend your time will determine your loyalty. You are instructed to Love God with everything you have. With all your heart, all your soul and all your mind. The 7th chapter of the book of Romans has long been used to justify sinful behavior. Paul walked more like Jesus that any person recorded in the New Testament. He even rebuked Peter for falling prey to the Jews and expecting new converts to follow some of the law. Therefore, if Paul is admitting to being sinful here, it makes him a hypocrite and disputes his preaching of the ministry of righteousness.

For I do not understand my own actions. For I do not do what I want, but I do the very thing I hate. ¹⁶ Now if I do what I do not want, I agree with the law, that it is good. ¹⁷ So now it is no longer I who do it, but sin that dwells within me. ¹⁸ For I know that nothing good dwells in me, that is, in my flesh. For I have the desire to do what is right, but not the ability to carry it out. ¹⁹ For I do not do the good I want, but the evil I do not want is what I keep on doing. ²⁰ Now if I do what I do not want, it is no longer I who do it, but sin that dwells within me. ²¹ So I find it to be a law that when I want to do right, evil lies close at hand. ²² For I delight in the law of God, in my inner being, ²³ but I see in my members another law waging war against the law of my mind and making me captive to the law of sin that dwells in my members. Romans 7:14-23

What if this entire section was being taken out of context, again, like so many other things we misinterpret in the Bible? The understanding of this text begins when we consider exactly **who** Paul was talking to?

...for I am speaking to those who know the law. Romans 7:1

Paul was talking to the Jews of his time. And the word "know" here is the same word used when a man and woman consummate their marriage with sex. It implies that the Jews he is talking to are married to the law. All this time Romans 7 has been taken out of context and misrepresented as a way to excuse sin, much in the same way the Grace of God has been used by the OSAS to excuse their lust for sin. In this chapter, Paul is describing to the Jews what it is like to try to walk without sin when done without Jesus and under the law. He is telling them from experience, because he used to be one of them, and He too experienced what they are experiencing; a desire not to sin while being unable to stop. No matter how hard one tries in their own strength, the power and authority that sin has over them will eventually win. There is nothing that any man can do to overcome sin without the Lord Jesus, and the Holy Spirit empowering them to do so. In the end, Paul says, but thank God for Jesus, why? Because it's not like that for

Christians any longer, or it's not supposed to be... if they're being taught to seek righteousness as the first thing they do.

> *What shall we say then? Are we to continue in sin so that grace may abound? 2 **Heavens no!** How can we who died to sin still live in it?*
> Romans 6:1

This is actually funny to me, how can the OSAS get around this. Paul asks 2 rhetorical questions but he's asking them sarcastically, because the answer is so obvious, it is ridiculous.

False Conversions

> *We know that our old self was crucified with Him in order that the body of sin might be brought to nothing, so that we would no longer be enslaved to sin. 7 **For one who has died has been set free from sin**.*
> Romans 6:6

Truth hits our heart when we knock and God opens the door exposing His kingdom. In seeking the truth about what our Lord did on our behalf, the punishment He endured in our place, our "old self" is metaphorically crucified with Christ so that sin within us is "done away with," and if it is done away with, it no longer has the same hold over us. Let's focus for a second on the highlighted part, *"For one who has died has been set free from sin."* If and when you make the decision to die to yourself and live for Jesus, the "old self" dies and sets you free from the bondage of sin. Sin no longer controls you because you are not living for you anymore; you are living for Him now. Everyone, please hear me when I say, "You must die in order to live."

> *So **you** also **must consider yourselves dead to sin** and alive to God in Christ Jesus.* Romans 6:11

Righteousness begins when the "old self" dies to sin.

> *Let not sin therefore reign in your mortal body, to make you obey its passions.* ¹³ *Do not present your members to sin as **instruments for unrighteousness**, but present yourselves to God as those who have been brought from death to life, and your members to God as **instruments for righteousness**.* Romans 6:12-13

Paul is not asking them, he is commanding them not to sin and try to get away with it any longer, because if they do, they become an instrument, a tool or resource used by the devil for unrighteousness. But now, Christians are *expected* to *"die to themselves"* and offer their lives to God so He can use them as an instrument, a tool, a resource that displays righteousness to a lost and dying world.

> *What then?* ***Shall we continue to sin*** *if we are not under law, but under grace?* ***Certainly not!*** *Don't you realize that you become the slave of whatever you choose to obey?* ***You can be a slave to sin****, which leads* ***to death****, or* ***you can choose to obey God****, which* ***leads to righteousness****.* **Romans 6:15**

I don't know about you, but that's pretty clear to me; Paul is speaking to believers that have already chosen Jesus as their Lord and he gives them two choices: a) They can be a slave to sin, which leads to death, or b) They can choose to obey God, which leads to righteousness. And just so that we are clear, Paul is talking about spiritual death here. There is no third option, it's either sin & death or obey God & righteousness. It is obedience to God that leads us to righteousness, and it is that righteous obedience which leads to eternal life. The decision to obey and follow righteousness becomes even easier to make when we recall Jesus saying, *"Seek ye first the Kingdom of God and His righteousness."* Is it becoming clearer yet? We really only have two choices once we come to the knowledge of the truth and the Lord God reveals the divinity of Jesus to our hearts.

1. Remain in sin and return to becoming a slave to sin which leads to death, or
2. Obedience to God directing us down the narrow path of righteousness.

It also sounds a lot like Deuteronomy where God tells us to choose between life and death, but let's look at the word for death in Romans 6:15 above, and mind you, this definition came directly from the Strong's concordance. I think you will find it as revealing, as I did.

Death – Strong's #2288 *thánatos* – Literally, it means death of the human host body. Figuratively, it is separation from the life (salvation) of God forever by dying a natural death without first experiencing **death to self** to receive His gift of salvation. Without Jesus, *thánatos* is both physical and spiritual death, but with Jesus *thánatos* is only physical.

Well then, if that isn't a real eye opener. *Thánatos,* the word for "death" that Paul uses to describe what happens to a believer that has never learned to "Die to Self," is eternal separation from God. The OSAS doctrine teaches just the opposite. They believe that once you say a sinner's prayer, you are saved forevermore. They believe there is never any need or expectation to "die to self," and you are under no obligation to righteousness. "Go ahead," they say, "Sin all you want now, you have an OSAS grace license to sin." The whole world will be judged for sin…except the OSAS (sarcasm); they get to sin all they want because they said a prayer…hogwash.

They ignorantly claim that the literal meaning of the word "death" here would be described as your sin possibly causing a physical death, but that has no bearing on your eternal salvation. They teach that your eternal salvation was sealed with a sinner's prayer even if there is no outward manifestation or change in behavior. I suppose they never considered looking up the meaning of the word death before.

The OSAS doctrine teaches that you may do whatever you want, because you're saved by grace. The OSAS believe that there are therefore no more consequences for sin once a sinner's prayer has been said. Remember, that is almost word for word as the motto of the satanic Bible; "Do what thou wilt!" It implies that people are free to do whatever makes them happy, because there is no longer any consequence for their actions or behavior. Isn't that just a little too similar? Yea it is, and it's pretty easy to see who is behind the OSAS doctrine. The OSAS figurative meaning of the word "Death" is death or extreme difficulties to your situation, but again, with no eternal consequence.

Therefore, the OSAS figurative example of death could be described as a pastor who has had an affair that causes a break in his marriage as well as his excommunication from the church, resulting in death to his once wonderful life, but no eternal consequence whatsoever. The OSAS literal example of the word death would be the same pastor's affair, but this time it results in a tragic murder, suicide, but again, with no eternal consequence.

Both the literal and figurative definitions of the word death as taught by the OSAS doctrine are opposed to the Strong's definition, however God has given us the gift of repentance until the day we die. The main problem with the OSAS, besides the fact that they basically condone sin, the main problem is that they feel like they don't have to repent because they are covered by a false hyper-grace idol god that they have created in their own minds, a god who excuses their selfish, lustful lifestyle while punishing everyone else. They are living a lifestyle of sin, making them the same slaves to it that Paul described, and that sin will evolve and grow even more perverse over time, until it destroys everything that is dear to them. And all because they never learned to "die to self" and live for righteousness.

Romans 6:15 says they have become slaves to sin which will ultimately lead them to death; death of their situation, death of their lives, and if they do not repent, eternal separation from the Lord God. In chapters 2 and 3 of Revelation, Jesus is addressing the behavior Paul just described and He pleads with the churches to repent from their sins, turn from their disgusting conduct and return home to Him.

> *Remember therefore from where you have fallen; repent and do the first works, or else I will come to you quickly and remove your lampstand from its place, unless you repent.* Revelation 2:5

Of all 7 churches mentioned in Revelation, only the church of Philadelphia is said to be spared from the trial that is coming upon the whole world, but why? Righteousness, love, faith **and they loved not their own life unto death**. They were willing to die for their faith and not just metaphorically.

> *And if your right hand causes you to sin, cut it off and throw it away...* Matthew 5:30

You know, your hand cannot sin, let alone do anything unless your mind allows it. The early Christian church knew and understood that sin was unacceptable to God and they were expected to seek His power and ability to resist it; repentance was commonplace. Then Satan had the bright idea of becoming the church so he could control it and determine what the masses would learn.

Is it any wonder why the early church forbid the reading of the Bible? People were actually put to death if they were caught with one. That was the dark ages, a time when Christianity almost died out; but God, Martin Luther gets an epiphany, sees the deception and translates the Bible from Latin to German, and it just so happened to be at the exact year the printing press is invented...coincidence? I think not! The reformation begins and Christianity explodes, because as good as the devil is at deception, there is nothing he can do to stop the great harvest of a seed once it has fallen to the ground and died; once a Christian decides to die to self and live for Jesus.

Since that time there have been many wonderful teachers, too many to list, but the hyper grace movement never really got its legs until just recently. It has only been the last two or three decades that the OSAS hyper-grace doctrine of the mega churches, in conjunction with the prosperity gospel has become a doctrine of demons used by Satan to deceive the church into a life of continual sin with no outward fruit of righteousness.

We are called Saints in the Bible, but what is a saint? The actual definition of a saint is a holy one who is sanctified. To be sanctified is to be set apart. Our Father wants us set apart from the world where He can train us up, and mold us into the image... the likeness, the identity of Jesus. I've probably already said it several dozen times, but it's worth repeating here and I'll likely say it a few more times, Jesus never tried to sin and get away with it.

> *...for **He who knew no sin**, became sin for us so we could become the righteousness of God in Him.* 2 Corinthians 5:21

We are instructed by Jesus to seek righteousness daily. To do so we must feed on His word daily. We should desire the pure milk of the Word as we grow in our identity, and as we develop and grow spiritually. By letting go of the things of the world, the youthful lusts that so easily ensnared us, we begin to die to ourselves; growing more and more into the image of our King Jesus. Therefore, whether we see a miracle or not, as Children of God we trust and obey our Father out of loyalty and love. Like a little child, we believe!

Then, as we grow and mature in this place of unconditional love and trust, we begin to feast on the meat of His Word, and learn to discern between good and evil. If Jesus truly is our Lord, and not the world or the things in the world, then out of Love for Him who gave His life for us, we eagerly, gladly, lovingly shun evil and choose good. This is our training in righteousness, His righteousness, not the righteousness of the world whose standards fluctuate and change according to the culture of the time. No, His righteousness is an unwavering standard that has stood the test of time.

We are not called to decrease so He may increase. That is a great example of scripture being taken out of context. When John the Baptist made that statement, he was referring to his ministry working within the confines of the Old Covenant which was decreasing and Jesus' ministry beginning, thereby leading us to the New Covenant, a new law of Love. Nowhere in the New Covenant are we told to decrease so He can increase in us. It clearly says, over and over again that we are to "Die to Self," so He may live in us. If we merely decrease, we will never be able to put to death our sinful nature and the result is disastrous. A mere decrease of me means there is still some of me and my selfish worldliness left and that is a nightmare just waiting to happen. Paul confirms this when he said,

> *"I know that nothing good lives in me, that is, in my flesh..."* Romans 7:18

The reason Jesus wants us to die to ourselves is because "nothing good dwells in us;" He knows that if we simply decrease, the "nothing good" that dwells in us will eventually rear its ugly head and sooner or later we will be conformed again to the likeness of the world from which we came. But when we die to ourselves and seek His righteousness, it is no longer about preserving our life, saving face, being accepted by our peers, winning an argument, being thought of as cool, being needed, wanted or even loved by people at all. Being a man pleaser is the absolute last thing on your mind now, because pleasing Jesus your Lord consumes you.

Through ups and downs we do not lose faith, we do not lose heart, we do not grow weary of doing good, but we trust that our Father has our best interest at heart in every situation. Do not be deceived by the prosperity preachers peddling your best life now lie. That is the exact opposite of what Jesus said repeatedly.

> *If you were of the world, it would love you as its own. Instead, the world hates you, because you are not of the world...* John 15:18

James said, *"Count it all joy **when** you fall into various trials...."* He didn't say "if," he said *"when"* you do, because the Christian life was never intended to be your best life now, a life of prosperity where everything is all peaches and cream. Therefore, whether you are in the middle of a trial, just coming out of a trial or just about to get in one, your only responsibility is to fix your eyes on Jesus and seek His righteousness. If you took a log from one fire and placed it in a fire...nothing changes! If you are on fire for Jesus and you encounter a fire, a trial, a difficult life situation...nothing in you should change either. You should continue to walk, talk, look, think and act like Jesus in the midst of your trial and if you do, just watch how your Father performs miracle after miracle and navigates you through it, leaving you an amazing testimony.

> *You, however, have observed my teaching, my conduct, my purpose, my faith, my patience, my love, my endurance, my persecutions, and the sufferings that came upon me in Antioch, Iconium, and Lystra. What persecutions I endured! Yet* **the Lord rescued me from all of them**.
> 2 Timothy 3:11-12

I am so sorry that you were sold a bill of goods, deceived into thinking that Christianity was a life full of riches and prosperity, blessings, rainbows and lil' lambs...it is not. But what it is, is your road to heaven, your narrow path to your Father.

> *Even though I walk through the valley of the shadow of death, I will fear no evil, for You are with me; Your rod and Your staff, they comfort me.*
> Psalm 23:4

David is not expecting God to navigate him away from the valley of darkness, nor is he asking God to deliver him from it, he is simply confirming that which he knows to be true; that God will comfort him as he goes through his trial, not remove the trial from him. And FYI, the valley of the shadow of death is just a metaphor for whatever trial you may encounter.

> *Indeed, all who desire to live godly (righteous) lives in Christ Jesus* **will be persecuted**, 2 Timothy 3:11

Not some, he said, **"all who desire to live righteously will be persecuted."** Righteousness and persecution will go hand-in-hand, it's one way you know a true believer. Christians back in the days of Paul and the apostles all knew persecution would come for them, it was just a matter of time. Suffering for their faith was a prerequisite, not a choice.

> *But even if you should suffer for righteousness, you are blessed.*
> 1 Peter 3:14

Yes, you will be blessed should you suffer for righteousness, but don't expect to see it in this lifetime. In fact, we are not supposed to do anything expecting to see a return like an investment during our time in exile here. All our blessings, all our returns are being stored up as treasures in heaven where moth and rust do not destroy, and thieves do not steal. *"For where your treasure is, there your heart will be also."*

> **Woe to you when all men speak well of you,** *for their fathers treated the false prophets in the same way.* Luke 6:27

If people of the world love you, it's probably not a good thing. Whenever Jesus uses the word "woe," it's never good, it means great dread. Not that we are trying to be disliked, but if we are walking in the light, children of darkness will feel threatened, because your light will expose their sin, and that goes for deceived Christians as well. Your fifteen coworkers now know you are a Christian, but you're not just a Christian, you seek righteousness, therefore, you are uncompromising and while each one of your coworkers will respond differently to the new you, their reaction will range from hatred to shame and everything in between. However, there will inevitably be someone, maybe only one, but there will be somebody that God has been working on, and your steadfast perseverance and unwavering stand of righteousness will inspire and move them to repentance, and you may never even know it.

Freedom from Legalism

If you are coming out of a church that espouses legalism, a denominational church that refuses to believe in or move in the gifts of the Holy Spirit and you realize that the Holy Spirit wants to live in you and use you, do not neglect the Word of God for the seeking of the gifts of God. I understand that you may feel like you are breaking off shackles, but they were shackles of vapor, a fake prison designed to keep you ignorant and ineffective.

Legalism binds you, it tries to hold you and control you, but relationship with your Father, His Son and the Holy Spirit sets you free. Yes, you are now free, but never forget that your newfound freedom comes with the need to stay in right relationship with your Father. It demands a desire to seek righteousness. Inside this relationship you are compelled to do the will of the Father because He loves you and you love Him. And because Jesus died for you, you now die to yourself, and give your life to Him who gave Himself for you.

However, in order to model Jesus accurately, you cannot live for Him while moving only in the miraculous. You cannot go about prophesying and performing miracles like healing while neglecting the fruit of righteousness. Neither can you live for Him in the truth of righteousness and ignore the miraculous. If I do not live and walk in the fruit of the Spirit, the fruit of righteousness, which comes from a close personal relationship with the Father, and without being grounded in the Word which is an outward reflection of what my Father want me to look like, if I do not walk in the righteousness of God in Christ Jesus, I will grieve the Holy Spirit. On the other hand, if I come to a complete understanding of my righteousness in God the Father but do not walk in the power of God, the miraculous works that Jesus paid such a high price for me to be able to do, I will quench the Holy Spirit.

God wants to raise up a generation, a church without the bars and constraints of legalism that neither grieves nor quenches the Holy Spirit, and the only way He can do that is by us seeking righteousness and establishing a deep understanding and relationship with Him, Jesus and the Holy Spirit by reading His Word and on our knees in prayer.

You can actually live with no fruit of righteousness and still see blind eyes opened, because you are living as an orphan with power like the disciples before the cross. Or, you can be filled with the Holy Spirit and walk in righteousness and love, yet be completely ineffectual in regards to miracles. However, once you learn the significance of righteousness, and seek it with all your heart, it will come in and wreck you.

If you let righteousness get a hold of you, it'll come in and change everything; every job, every relationship, every interaction, every situation and every person you come in contact with throughout the day, all day, every day. If righteousness is your focus, your aim, your goal, if righteousness is what you seek after, it'll come pouring into you like a flood and permeate you to your very soul. Righteousness will shove out every root of bitterness, and begin forgiving and healing; it'll cast off anger, resentment, lust, envy and greed. Righteousness will do all that by putting an abrupt end to selfishness, because selfishness exists whenever and wherever there is an absence of righteousness; selfishness is the root cause of every evil thing.

> *For where jealousy and **selfish ambition** exist, there will be disorder and every evil practice. James 3:16*

Righteousness will literally slam the door on lust as you begin to see people not as objects of youthful pleasure but as orphans in need of a Father, just as you once were. Pornography will have no power over a man who realizes that the women on the screen are merely orphans who are spiritually blind and destined for an eternity of separation from the Father.

Righteousness will enable you to see through the anger, the resentment, the frustration that is being aimed at you by other orphans who are not necessarily angry with you, but orphans who are groaning, crying out for someone to reach out to them and tell them what their spirit longs to hear... that they are children of the King and they no longer have to live like an orphan.

When righteousness comes in, you will no longer try to coerce, manipulate or use people, because you now realize that it's no longer about you getting your way, but about helping those around you get to where you are; in right standing and relationship with the Father and the Son. When righteousness comes in and makes its home in you, your life, and the lives of everyone around you will never be the same.

Righteousness & Grace

God delivering the Hebrews out of Egypt in a miraculous fashion is a mere symbol for our lives in the bondage of sin before salvation. After all the plagues and all the miracles, after parting the Red Sea, when Moses went up the mountain to hear from God, the Hebrews went back to their former lusts and desires. They even made a golden calf to worship and began committing fornication, and all manner of perversion, so that God destroyed thousands upon thousands in one day. This is a perfect picture of the OSAS church.

God does not care about the advancement of "our culture," or that the Supreme Court has ruled it's legal to murder babies. He isn't moved or persuaded by tolerance, becoming progressive or being woke. He's not impressed with money, or fame and I guarantee He's not pleased with the church's newfound acceptance of homosexual pastors and preachers.

> *And don't forget Sodom and Gomorrah and their neighboring towns, which were filled with immorality and every kind of sexual perversion. Those cities were destroyed by fire and serve as a warning of the eternal fire of God's judgment.* Jude 1:17

Allow me to digress for just a moment; a person in a homosexual relationship is no worse than the pastor who is having an affair with his music director or a man that satisfies himself at topless bars instead of going directly home to his wife. Tell me, just what are we thinking? That God has changed His view on sexual immorality just because the world has? The Bible says that God is the same yesterday, today and forever. The book of Jude was written to Christians as a strict warning not to engage in sexual immorality of any kind or suffer the possibility of eternal fire of God's judgment.

The modern Church has become so pampas, so self-righteous; they look down their noses at drug addicts, alcoholics or felons. They arrogantly pray for the homeless or prostitutes while they think in their hearts how weak and depraved, they must have been to be where they are. They puff themselves up, thinking how much better they are because they've never been in trouble with the law or committed such acts.

Yet they gossip about each other behind their backs, they lust after and envy one another. They are greedy for gain and worship the god of merchandise and materialism with grand houses, expensive cars and all manner of excess. They have no need for faith because their money can buy them out of nearly any situation.

Their hearts have grown cold and apathetic to the things of God as they compete with one another for the cares of the world, the deceitfulness of riches and the desire for other things which have entered in and choked the Word that was once in their heart. They have an uncanny ability to apply the Word of God to everyone else's sin…just not their own. If they do it, it's justified by grace, but if it's someone else, by gosh it's sin.

People say, "Life is tough," but that's only because they do not understand why they were created in the first place. They're letting life rule them and decide who they are. They let life speak louder than truth, but your circumstances should not define who you are. Truth is what makes you free and the truth about you and who you are is found in what Jesus accomplished on the cross for you.

The love of God is such a mystery to people even when they understand the purpose of the cross. Believers as well as unbelievers struggle with God's love for them. They wonder how God can love them, because they know themselves and their conscience bears witness to all the things they have thought and done.

They weigh their value based upon their past and love becomes a mystery because they cannot comprehend God loving them for what they know about themselves.

God does not just love you because... He loves you regardless. God loves you unconditionally, no matter what you have done, because He knows who and what you were made to be and that you are capable of becoming the same love with which He loves you to everyone you meet. God does not love you so that you "**feel loved**," He loves you so that you "**become love**" to the unloved. He wants you to know His love for you with such confidence that you become the essence of love everywhere you go to everyone you meet. This is the gospel; to love people unconditionally, and not just the ones that love you back. God does not show us mercy because He's having a good day and feels like being merciful. He shows us mercy, because He is mercy, and He wants you to take the same mercy He extended to you and extent mercy to everyone He brings across your path. His mercy triumphs over judgment, His mercy endures forever.

God will never change His mind about you, your created value, your potential and your destiny. He knows what you would look like if/when He were to live inside you, and He believed you were worth dying for to bring you back from the dead. Yes, I said it, without Jesus, people are literally "the walking dead" and they haven't got a clue. Knowing what we now know about righteousness, how are we going to allow ourselves to be bound up in foolish issues and concerns about "he said this" or "she did what?" When righteousness comes in it'll expose all that for the foolishness that it is and teach you, convict you, correct you and train you to walk in love. God wants you to become like Him, and if God is love, He wants you to become love too.

Mercy woke you up today, but it woke you for a very important reason. Not so you could go to work or take care of the kids, not so you could go fishing, hiking or paddle boarding, mercy woke you up today to give you another day to look like Jesus, to look like love to a lost and dying world. Man was made in the image of God, but Adam fell and we were born into sin. Therefore, what was created to be love in the beginning became selfish and self-serving.

Jesus was a man, in right relationship with God and filled with the Holy Spirit, yet whenever He encountered a demon, they recognized Him for who He was in the Kingdom, "Son of the Living God." He was the ultimate authority and apparently, He had the authority to give the disciples power and authority, yet they had no ability to keep from denying Jesus and fleeing in the garden.

The power and authority Jesus gave them is not the same thing as the Holy Spirit that He breathed on them immediately after His resurrection, or the Holy Spirit that was poured out on them in the upper room. The Holy Spirit they received in the upper room was the full measure of the Holy Spirit, the one responsible for filling them with boldness to not only preach God's Word, but to become the very word they preached. After that, they literally walked as Jesus walked, in righteousness, without offense, and with love for all humanity, while performing signs and wonders in His name.

> *...knock and the door will be opened to you.* Matthew 7:7

God desires to open the door of His Kingdom to all men; He wants to hit their heart with the revelation of Jesus, His death, burial and resurrection; for He is the Way, the Truth and the Life. Salvation is **not** the moment we say a sinner's prayer, but the moment we "die to ourselves;" the moment we give up our selfishness, and all earthly desires for the desires of our King. Seeking righteousness is the moment we enter the cocoon and prepare for the unveiling of our transformation into a butterfly.

Salvation is **not** going after God just to get out of trouble, or improve a bad situation; it is going after God because you love Him more than life itself. It is giving up the pursuit of the things of the world, and surrendering all for the pursuit of righteousness. It is this moment that sends us on our quest for righteousness and positions us to receive the spirit of Grace and Truth, empowering us to walk in righteousness like Jesus.

Obedience Vs Works

> *"The LORD your God is God, the faithful God who keeps covenant and steadfast love with those who <u>love Him</u> **and keep** <u>His commandments</u>, to a thousand generations."* <u>Deuteronomy 7:9</u>

The scripture says we are to love God **AND** keep His commandments, not either or. But you say, "That was before the cross, we have a new covenant." Maybe you missed the last part of the verse, *"... to a thousand generations."* To a thousand generations is a metaphor that implies forever. We're still in the "forever" time zone so this applies to us now!

> *Jesus Christ is the same yesterday and today and forever.* Hebrews 13:8

God has not changed, nor will He. He remains the same regardless of how we feel about it, or if the times have changed, because the Truth is Jesus and Jesus is the Truth and the Truth does not change. What's right is right and what's wrong is wrong, and there just is no right way to do a wrong thing.

> *...For it is **by grace you have been saved** through faith, not of yourselves; it is the gift of God, ⁹**not by works, so that no man can boast.*** Ephesians 2:8

Works - Strong's #2041 (er'-gon) Short Definition: work, labor, action, deed. It implies earning ones salvation by doing good deeds.

"...not by works, so that no man can boast." Nobody will be able to stand in heaven and brag about what they have done to get there. However, is it works when we keep Gods commandments? Certainly not, keeping Gods commandments is not the same as trying to earn one's salvation by works; it simply implies obedience. Works based salvation is thinking that you become eligible for salvation by feeding the poor or giving money to a good cause.

> But Samuel replied, *"What is more pleasing to the LORD: your burnt offerings and sacrifices or your **obedience** to his voice? Listen! **Obedience is better than sacrifice**, and **submission** is better than offering the fat of rams.* 1 Samuel 15:22

Submission - Strong's # 7181 Qashab-To listen **and obey**

God does not care about us doing things for Him, because He knows that we are not really doing it for Him, we are doing it for us out of a selfish heart that is trying desperately to sleep with itself at night. Our sin has brought with it condemnation, and the "good works," only serve as a vehicle to try to clear our conscience. God is not impressed with anything we do to try to feign righteousness, all He wants is for us to submit to His authority, obey His commandment of love and seek His righteousness.

We can't earn His approval by adhering to rituals or man-made traditions. Most religions have very specific "man-made" rules and regulations that must be adhered to, but God is not impressed with anything man dreams up in his futile mind to try to appease Him. God cannot be paid-off with our good works, He's not impressed with our rituals and He can't be bribed by our sacrifices. He wants our love, our loyalty, our devotion, our dedication, but most of all He wants our obedience; everything else is just window dressing and lip service. In the very first chapter of Isaiah, God reveals His heart regarding works and obedience.

> *"Bring your worthless offerings no longer, Your incense is an abomination to Me...I cannot endure your iniquity. "I hate your new moon festivals and your appointed feasts, They have become a burden to Me; "Wash yourselves, make yourselves clean (metaphorically speaking); Remove the evil of your deeds from My sight. **Cease to do evil,** 17 **Learn to do good**; Seek justice, Reprove the ruthless, Defend the orphan, Plead for the widow. "Come now, and let us reason together," Says the LORD, "Though your sins are as scarlet, They will be as white as*

> *snow; Though they are red like crimson, They will be like wool. ⁹ **"If you consent and obey**, You will eat the best of the land; Isaiah 1:13-19*

Just take another look at his list, He is disgusted by our efforts to placate him; the only thing God wants from us is our obedience and righteousness. Here again, God says, *"Consent and Obey,"* not one or the other. The Modern Church has been deceived into thinking that works and obedience were synonymous... they're not. If God is the same yesterday, today and forever, and He demanded obedience and righteousness then, what makes us think He does not demand it now?

If the Altar of Love taught me anything, it's that we are expected to repent, submit and obey. Obeying God is not works; it becomes our desire out of a grateful heart. If we love God, we will want to obey Him. Jesus Himself said, *"If you love me, **you will** keep my Commandments,"* so what are we telling Him when we do not obey?

When asked which commandment was the most important, Jesus rolled all 10 into 2. He said, *"Love the Lord God with all your heart and love your neighbor as you love yourself."* Therefore, when Christians do not love people it is usually a sign that they do not love themselves, because how can you love your neighbor if you are disgusted by your own behavior due to sin? Satan skillfully uses sin to keep us in a constant state of sin, heaping loads of condemnation and self-loathing upon us so we cannot love people as we are commanded.

Like I said earlier, the opposite of love is not hate, it is selfishness. If you love people, you are not going to steal from them. If you love them you will not lie to them. If you love your spouse, you will not leave them or cheat on them. So, love appears to be an easy way to walk out this Christian life. Or is it? Jesus said, *"If you hate, it's as if you murder,"* and *"if you lust, it's as if you commit adultery."* So, we see here that walking in the commandment of love is actually more difficult than following the 10 commandments, because it involves our thought life as well.

As we discussed earlier, by the Law of Moses, you were only considered guilty of breaking the commandment when you actually committed the offense, but under the law of love we are guilty if we contemplate it in the thoughts of our heart. Understand that the devil will plant thoughts in your mind, but that is not where sin occurs. When that happens we are instructed to take every thought into captivity to determine its origin. Is it from God or not? If it is not, we are to cast it down to the obedience of Christ. Sin occurs when we meditate on that thought and begin to plot the action in our heart. Our Father describes how the process works in the book of James.

> *But every man is tempted, when he is drawn away by **his own desire**, and enticed. Then **after desire is conceived, it gives birth to sin;** and when sin is fully grown, it brings forth death.*
> James 1:14-15

Satan knows our weaknesses; he knows exactly what to tempt you with because he's had a demon assigned to you since birth. He knows exactly what is tempting to you and what is not. What he is offering you is only temporary, however, because in the end, it brings death. Think of this thing called sin like crack or heroin. It is said that the first high of either drug is so awesome, because it makes a complete dump of dopamine into the brain causing an unparallel euphoric experience that the user desperately tries to recreate but is physically unable to because the brain cannot recreate that amount of dopamine again. Furthermore, the amount of dopamine decreases with each use causing the user to increase the dosage until they finally overdose. Your Father, on the other hand is offering you peace, joy, hope and eternal salvation.

> *I call heaven and earth as witnesses today that **I have offered you life or death,** blessings or curses. **Choose life** so that you and your descendants will live.* Deut. 30:19

This is a choice, we either choose Jesus and seek the path of righteousness leading to eternal life or we get the devil by default followed by eternal separation from the Father. Who and what we choose is determined by who and what we serve; sin unto death or righteousness unto life and peace. Salvation cannot be obtained by trying to buy your way into heaven with works, or with the mere words of a sinner's prayer. Your Father knows your heart, and nothing is hidden from Him. Expecting God to overlook our disgusting behavior by giving to a charity or claiming to have said a sinner's prayer is like expecting a wife to forgive her husband's adultery without a promise of repentance.

If a man tells his wife he truly loves her but is having casual sex whenever he goes away on business, he does not really love her, does he? He can tell her how much he loves her, he can apologize and try to appease her with gifts, but his adultery says what's really in his heart. Imagine him standing there apologizing to his wife, telling her how sorry he is and how much he loves her. To which she says, "I hear you, but are you going to do it again?" Yet, he never answers her question, he just continues to tell her he is sorry and he loves her, and no matter how many times she asks him, he doesn't answer her question. The fact is, he is sorry... he's sorry he got caught, and he likely does love her keeping his home in order, raising their kids, cooking his meals, and doing his laundry; he loves her, just not enough to honor her and stop the adultery.

> *These people honor Me with their lips, but their hearts are far from Me, in vain do they worship me, teaching as doctrines the commandments of men.* Matthew 15:8

Nowhere in the Bible is the phrase, "once saved - always saved." It is a doctrine of men who wish to excuse their habitual sin; it's as simple as that. Let me say it again, they have created their own god, a false god, an idol, and their own gospel to suit their own lustful desires. It is a doctrine of mega churches designed to tickle the ears of this, "do whatever makes you feel good" culture that is simply looking for excuses to sin. This doctrine is not consistent with the God of Abraham, the God of Moses or the God of David and we know He is the same yesterday, today and forever. A Father, whose mantra from the beginning has been, is, and will always be, **repent, submit and obey.**

> "In **repentance and rest** you will be **saved**, In quietness and trust is your strength. But you were not willing,"
> Isaiah 30:15

Did you notice the result of repentance and rest? Salvation! Furthermore, he says, repentance **and** rest, not either or. We rest in Jesus and stay in continual repentance until righteousness is made perfect and complete, lacking nothing.

> ...¹⁷And with whom was God angry for forty years? Was it not with those who sinned, whose bodies fell in the wilderness? ¹⁸<u>And to whom did He swear that they would never enter His rest? Was it not **to those who disobeyed?**</u> ... "Therefore, **let us fear** if, while a promise remains of entering His rest, **lest any one of you seem to have come short of it.**" Heb 3:17-19

First, whenever Paul says, *"let us fear,"* we know he is talking to Christians, because he is including himself in the discussion when he says us. What I found most interesting was his comment to have, *"fear,"* lest they *"come short"* of it. If we know Paul is talking to Christians, why would they be in danger of falling short of Gods rest, which the Strong's concordance confirms is salvation? Why would he tell them to be careful, lest they come short? Paul is saying that **our rest is in Jesus and obedience to His commandment of love and righteousness, not one or the other.**

Rest-Strong's # 2663 (kat-ap'-ow-sis) Rest, Literally-rest attained by the settlement in Canaan. Metaphorically, the heavenly blessedness in which God dwells, and of which He has promised to make persevering believers in Christ partakers of, after the toils and trials of life on earth are ended:

> "For to us was the gospel preached, as well as to **them**: but the word preached did not profit them, not being mixed with

> *faith in them that heard it." ³ For we who have believed enter that rest, as he has said, "As I swore in my wrath...* Heb 4:2

"Them," who is them? Those who do not mix the Word preached to them with faith/belief. You only **do** the word you **believe**. If you will not do that Word you received through reading your Bible, through a Word of knowledge, through prayer or even a sermon; **if you will not do** the Word of God you heard, you obviously don't believe it, and if you don't believe it, it's because you don't have faith in it. No faith, no rest. *"... They shall not enter my rest,'"... ⁶ "Therefore, since it remains for some to enter into Gods rest, but those who first heard this good news **failed to enter because of their disobedience**."*

They failed to enter into eternity, because of their disobedience. He didn't say they disbelieved this good news, they believed just fine, but what they would not do was obey the new commandment of love and righteousness. They failed to enter into eternity because of their rebellious heart, their refusal to obey Him.

> *"Not everyone who says to me, 'Lord, Lord,' will enter the kingdom of heaven, but **only the one who <u>does</u> the will of my Father** who is in heaven.* Matthew 7:22-24

The only people who will be calling Jesus Lord are people that consider themselves Christians. Muslims, Buddhists and atheists will not be calling Jesus Lord. There is just no way to misinterpret this, these Christians are calling Jesus Lord, and they think they are saved; likely because they said "the sinner's prayer," but according to Jesus they are obviously not saved. Apparently, confessing Jesus as Lord is not enough; these so-called Christians are calling Him Lord, but they are in for a big surprise. Christians are expected to confess Jesus as Lord **AND do His Will** as well. It is not a one-or-the-other deal, it is all or nothing. And just exactly what is His will? His Commandments.

> *Many will say to Me on that day, **'Lord, Lord**, did we not prophesy in Your name, and in Your name drive out demons*

> *and perform many miracles?' ²³Then I will tell them plainly, '**I never knew you;** depart from Me, **you workers of lawlessness.' ²⁴Therefore everyone who hears these words** of Mine **and does them** is like a wise man who built his house on the rock…..* Matthew 7:22-24

It's in verse 23 that Jesus tells them exactly why these Christian believers are not welcome into heaven. Understand that this is not your typical "Christian" sitting in the back row falling asleep every Sunday. No, this is likely someone in leadership, someone that has prophesied, cast out demons and healed people. By the sound of it, it's someone that has moved with power in the gifts of the Holy Spirit. It's the last person that anyone would expect not to make it. He's talking about the Pastor, the deacon, the elder, the prayer partner or the worship leader.

Then Jesus says, "*I never knew you,*" which is to say, "*We didn't have a relationship.*" That is when He tells them exactly why they did not have a relationship, because they were workers of lawlessness. The definition of lawlessness is one who is living contrary to Jesus' commandments, the law of love. Lawlessness is defined as selfish wickedness, the exact opposite of righteousness. A worker of lawlessness is someone who habitually breaks the law of love and practices wickedness by willfully engaging in deliberate, unrepentant sin. Because they think they're saved, it's likely the OSAS.

These people are going to be shocked, devastated even, because in their mind, they are saved by a false hyper-grace god, but they're actually condemned by their unrepentant, habitual sin. This is the once saved- always saved clan of blind guides traveling around the world to make a convert and turning them into twice the son of hell they are. "You're saved," they say, "Go ahead and do whatever you want now because you're covered by grace." They may not actually be telling them to go sin, but that is the inference, and since when is that ever the character of God? It's not!

> And, "If **the righteous are barely saved**, what will happen to godless sinner's?" 1 Peter 4:18

> "...Again I tell you, it is easier for a camel to pass through the eye of a needle than for a rich man to enter the kingdom of God." ²⁵When the disciples heard this they were greatly astonished and asked, **"Who then can be saved?"**
> Matthew 19:24-25

There were times Jesus actually made salvation sound nearly impossible to achieve, so much so that the apostles were under the impression that nobody would meet the standard. What they did not know was that God would send His Holy Spirit to enable us to do what He expected of us.

> Now the works of the flesh are manifest, which are these: Adultery, fornication, perversion, promiscuity, Idolatry, witchcraft, hatred, strife, jealousy, wrath, selfishness, divisions, heresies, envy, drunkenness, orgies, and things like these. I warn you, as I warned you before, that **those who do such things will not inherit the kingdom of God.** Gal 5:19-21

Let us first consider the context of this section; Paul is talking to the church in Galatia, not unbelievers. How many Christians do you know are doing many of these things? All the while thinking they are saved by their false grace god?

> ... The Lord Jesus will come with his mighty angels, In flaming fire taking vengeance on <u>those who do not know God</u>, **and** <u>on those who do not obey</u> the gospel of our Lord Jesus Christ.
> ⁹ **These** <u>shall be punished with everlasting destruction from the presence of the Lord</u> and from the glory of His power.
> 2 Thess. 1:8-9

Unbelievers as well as **believers who do not obey** will end up in the lake of fire. *Jesus is coming to take vengeance on two different groups of people.*

1. ... on those who never took the time to get to know God, and
2. ... on those who do believe, but do not obey the law of love & righteousness.

In the first group, Paul is obviously talking about unbelievers when he says, *"on those who do not know God."* The second group is believers, they do know God, they just choose not to obey Him, falling for the false grace god of sinful pleasure.

> ***"Every tree** that does not bear good fruit **is cut down and thrown into the fire**. Thus you will recognize them by their fruits."* Matt. 7:19-20

Every tree! Jesus said that Children of God would be known by their <u>fruit</u>, not by their confession and certainly not by any works. If every tree is known by its fruit, just exactly what is the fruit we Children of God should be known by?

> *But **the fruit of the Spirit is love**, joy, peace, patience, kindness, goodness, faithfulness, gentleness, and self-control. Against such things there is no Law. **<u>Those who belong to Christ Jesus have crucified the flesh with its passions and desires</u>**.* **Gal 5:22-24**

To crucify the flesh is to put its lusts, needs, wants and desires to death; it's dying to self so you can live forever. Christians are never justified by mere words of a prayer, that's just lip service; we are known by our fruit of righteousness. When you walk in the Spirit you exemplify the fruit of the Spirit for which there is no law. If those who belong to Jesus have crucified the flesh with its passions and desires, then those who don't belong to Jesus continue to satisfy the lust of the flesh. One time the disciples asked Jesus:

> *"Lord, **will only a few be saved?"** He replied, "Make every effort to enter through the narrow door, because I tell you, **many will try to enter and won't be able**. After the master of the house gets up and shuts the door, you will stand outside knocking and saying, 'Lord, open the door for us.' But he will reply, 'I do not know where you are from.' Then you will say, 'We ate*

> *and drank with you, and you taught in our streets.' But He will say, I tell you, I don't know you or where you're from. Get away from Me, all you workers of unrighteousness!'* Luke 13:23-28

These people that Jesus is speaking of must be Christians; they think they have a relationship with Him, but they are in for a rude awakening. They're calling Jesus Lord, but He doesn't know them and once again, He refers to them as *"workers of unrighteousness."* A worker of unrighteousness implies habitual participation in sin, willingly and deliberately, but with no regret, remorse or repentance because they think they're excused from their disgusting behavior by grace. They have no interest in the fruit of righteousness, they are too busy satisfying their flesh with adultery, fornication, perversion, promiscuity, idolatry, witchcraft, hatred, strife, jealousy, wrath, selfishness, divisions, heresies, envy, drunkenness, orgies, and the like.

Is it possible that Jesus was telling a parable about a church ideology 2000 years into the future? When you consider how fast the OSAS doctrine has grown, how far reaching it is now and how big these mega churches have become, I'd have to say yes. The OSAS mega churches may not be formally connected except by ideology, but they may very well be one of the largest religious organizations next to the Catholic Church and they continue to grow exponentially.

> *There will be weeping and gnashing of teeth when you see Abraham, Isaac, Jacob, and all the prophets in the kingdom of God, but you yourselves are thrown out.* Luke 13:28

I just don't know how many times Jesus has to say it before the church actually "sees it." Who do you think Jesus is talking to here when he says, *"...but you yourselves are thrown out?"* He's talking to people who assume they are saved, He's talking to believers. First John is one of the most amazing books of the New Testament, but most people never consider what John is actually saying.

> ***Do not love the world*** <u>***or anything in the world***</u>***. If anyone loves the world****, the **love** of the Father is not in him. ¹⁶For all that is in the world, the lust of the flesh, the lust of the eyes, and the pride of life, is not from the Father but from the world. ¹⁷The world is passing away along with its desires, but **whoever does the will of God remains forever**....*
>
> 1 John 2:15

The first two times the word love is used here it is Strong's #25 agapaó (ag-ap-ah'-o), and it means to prefer, to take pleasure in. The third time love is used, it uses Strong's #26 Agape and it means love, deep affection for. Therefore, reread it again with the properly inserted word for love and notice the difference.

> *Do not **prefer** the world or anything in the world. If anyone **prefers** the world more than they **prefer** the Father, **a deep affection** for the Father is not in him. ¹⁶For all that is in the world, the lust of the flesh, the lust of the eyes, and the pride of life, is not from the Father but from the world. ¹⁷The world is passing away along with its desires, but whoever does the will of God remains forever...*
>
> **1 John 2:15**

Your loyalty, your love of a thing is established by your preference. If you prefer the world, the world is your love and your Lord. Now let's look at it from our Fathers point of view. Whenever the term *"the world"* is used, it is referring to Satan's kingdom, his world system. With that in mind, I saw it like this:

> *Do not prefer Satan's kingdom or anything it has to offer. If anyone **prefers Satan's kingdom** and what he is offering, a **loving affection for** the Father is not in him. <u>For all that is in **Satan's kingdom**, the lust of the flesh, the lust of the eyes, and the pride of</u> life, <u>is not from the Father but from</u> Satan. And Satan, along with his kingdom is passing away as well as his desires, but <u>**whoever does the will of God remains forever**</u>....*

"Whoever does the will of the Father has eternal life," implies obedience. Whoever confesses Jesus as Lord and obeys the law of love and righteousness has eternal life, because your loyalty and obedience establish your preference. It's Jesus and obedience, not one or the other, because your allegiance, your loyalty, your love for the Father is not based upon mere words of a sinner's prayer or any amount of works you do, but upon whom you obey. Will you seek righteousness and obey your Fathers commandment of love, or will you live according to your own passions and desires?

You may hear me say this several times, but for some things, redundancy is the best way to drive home a point. If someone is telling you how much they love you, but secretly they are lying about you, stealing from you, and doing all manner of evil behind your back, they don't really love you now do they? They can say whatever they want, but their actions prove what they really feel. To say a sinner's prayer one time is not a get out of hell free pass, our true intentions are proven by our obedience and loyalty to the Father, and to assume anything otherwise is not just foolish...it's a carefully crafted lie from the pit of hell to deceive hundreds of millions to people into thinking they can have their fun and still be saved on a technicality.

> *"No one can serve two masters, for either he will hate the one*
> *and love the other, or he will be devoted to the one and*
> *despise the other. You cannot serve God and money.*
> Matthew 6:24

Money is just a metaphor for the world; it implies Satan and his kingdom.

For where your treasure is, there your heart will be also. Matthew 6:21

We are not fooling God; He knows what's in the treasure of our heart. He, also, sits in the theater of your soul, recording every thought and deed.

> *For it is impossible for those who were once enlightened* (saved), *and have tasted the heavenly gift, and have become partakers of the Holy Spirit, ⁵and have tasted the good word of God and the powers of the age to come, ⁶ if they fall away, to renew them again to repentance, since they crucify again for themselves the Son of God, and put Him to an open shame.* Hebrews 6:4

In order to keep things in context and within the correct perspective, you have to understand what Paul was dealing with and who he was talking to. This verse has been misused by some to heap condemnation upon backsliders, but that is not Paul's intention. Paul was dealing with Jews that had converted from Judaism to Christianity, but the peer pressure was too much for them and their need to be accepted by the Jews was more important than their need for the Lord. Having once walked in enlightenment, as well as all the gifts of the Holy Spirit, they went back to Judaism and renounced Jesus as the Christ. It is not because they fell into sin, they literally became apostate by returning to the Law.

> "Why do you call Me, 'Lord, Lord,' **and do not do what I say?** Luke 6:46

Why would you call me Lord if you're not going to obey my commandments? If you are not obeying the commandments of God, it's because you desire the things of the world more than God, therefore the world is your lord. Is that simple enough to understand?

> "If anyone's name was not found written in the book of life he was thrown into the lake of fire." Revelation 20:15

> *May they be blotted out of the book of life and may they not be recorded with* **the righteous**.
> Psalm 69:28

Exactly whose names are recorded in the Book of Life? The righteous, that's who, not those who only confess or profess, but those who confess Jesus and walk in love and righteousness.

> *"But **the children** of the kingdom shall be cast out into outer darkness: there shall be weeping and gnashing of teeth."*
> Matthew 8:12

The children of the Kingdom go to hell also? What about the OSAS, how does that reconcile with their doctrine?

> *"But the fearful, the unbelieving, the vile, the murderers, **the sexually immoral**, those who practice magic arts, **the idolaters and all liars**, they will be consigned to the fiery lake of burning sulfur. This is the second death."* Rev 21:8

By imagining a god who overlooks a lifestyle of sin because someone said a prayer long ago, OSAS Christians have broken the first commandment and made a god that suits them; they are the same as an idolater.

> *"If your hand causes you to stumble, cut it off. It is better for you to enter life maimed than with two hands to go into hell, where the fire never goes out."*
> Mark 9:43

If a sinner's prayer could keep someone out of hell, then this statement would not be necessary. If the OSAS hyper-grace doctrine were true, Jesus would not have told them to cut their hand off, He would have just said, "The time is coming when you will no longer have to cut off your hand to keep from sinning, but now I say, 'all you need to do is confess Me as Lord.'"

It almost sounds ridiculously stupid when you put it that way, yet millions have been duped by this doctrine of demons. There are over one hundred more scripture supporting Jesus saying, *"repent, or I will come like a thief in the night"* and *"Why do you call me Lord and not do what I say,"* but those two statements alone should be enough to convince anyone that the once saved mantra is just a man-made doctrine of demons designed to excuse lustful, worldly behavior and to lure us into a life of habitual sin.

Obedience is not works. Works is doing to be approved, but if I am obedient to the commandments, I am **not** doing. I'm not in willful sin, I'm not lying, I'm not coveting, and I'm not lusting after the things of the world. Obedience and works are virtually opposite of one another.

Repentance

The church has watered down the real purpose of the gospel. We leave church thinking things like we're just here to make it to heaven, or we're looking for God to bless us, to protect us and to provide for us, but that's not it at all.

> *...we must help the weak, remembering the words of the Lord Jesus Himself: 'It is more blessed to give than to receive.'"* Acts 20:35

Through Jesus, and what He did on the cross, we receive a new identity from God our Father; a new perspective as it will, and we begin to live in that truth while we seek the righteousness of God. We then take that truth, the goodness, the mercy, the grace, the peace and the joy that we have received from our Father and we give it out to everyone we come in contact with. Giving and receiving has been hijacked by the prosperity gospel and reduced to money and worldly possessions, but what would be better, to give a homeless man a new car or the good news of the gospel so that he comes to the knowledge of the Lord and gets saved? The latter of course.

It's tragic when Christians who sincerely see their need for a savior and believe on the blood for redemption; Christians that understand the sacrifice Jesus made on the cross, but miss the greater point of becoming love to the people in their life and never learn to walk in righteousness. It's an awesome thing to receive the love and mercy of God, but how much better would it be if that child of the living

God got a hold of His mercy to such a degree that he actually became love and mercy to everyone they met?

> ***It's one thing to obtain mercy leading to forgiveness, but becoming mercy is love and righteousness on a whole new level.***

Yet that is supposed to be our goal, the cause we Children of God should be seeking after. To take the blessings we receive from our Father and distribute them to the world around us. To take the gifts our Father has given to us and share them with a lost and dying world while remaining gratefully humble.

What would cause us to want something from our Father that we are not willing to share? Let's take that even farther, why would we want something from our Father that we are not willing to become for others? The answer to that is simple, selfishness. Jesus never said sing to me or pray to me when you are overwhelmed, He said, *"deny yourself and follow me."* Then He went the extra mile to ensure we were able to do what He expected of us and died for us in order to give us His Holy Spirit to empower us, to walk in love and righteousness. Thus, is the point and purpose of this book.

In Matthew 18, Jesus told a parable of a man who could not repay the debt he owed his master, so the master was going to sell him and his family in slavery to repay the debt, but the man cried out for mercy so the master had compassion and forgave him his entire debt. Jesus told that parable as a type and shadow of what was about to happen by way of the cross; that the Lamb of God paid the price for all mankind to not only take away our sins, but to remove the nature of sin for all, once and for all. Not only can guilty men legally go free now because of the blood, but the very nature of sin, the desire for sin can and will be removed by the Spirit of Grace, if we ask.

Do you understand that when you desire change and you wish didn't do the things you did; it means that your heart has turned; you've changed your thinking. You're not the same person who did those things; if you have died to yourself, repented for your past and live for Christ, God no longer sees you as a sinner. When He looks at you now, He sees Jesus who paid your fine for you. It's because of the blood of Jesus that you are now free; your death sentence has been commuted. The nature of repentance is not just being sorry you got caught; it's detesting the behavior to such a degree that the mere thought of doing it again is repulsive to you. Remember, God is always looking at your heart, judging you by what's in it, and not because of an insecure apology or because you said a sinner's prayer under duress.

> *When the righteous turns from his righteousness and commits iniquity, then he shall die in it.* [19]*But when the wicked turns from his wickedness and practices justice and righteousness, he will live by them.* [20]*Yet you say, 'The way of the Lord is not right.' O house of Israel, I will judge each of you according to his ways."*
> Ezekiel 33:17-20

This thing called repentance is actually an amazing gift from God. It allows Him to legally forgive us by way of the blood and the cross, but it's not due to any kind of sinner's prayer, it is solely due to a change in our heart; a desire for righteousness.

> *And a servant of the Lord must not be quarrelsome, but must be kind to everyone, able to teach, and forbearing.* [25]*He must gently reprove those who oppose him, in the hope that God may grant them repentance leading to a knowledge of the truth.* 2 Timothy 2:25

This is so huge and powerful, because we cannot change where we have been or what we've done. We cannot go back and rewrite the script, but who you are can change, so that who you become is no longer the person you were when you did what you did. Next to salvation, repentance has to be the most amazing blessing afforded us by our Father. Most people give all kinds of homage to the mercy of

God, or the blessings of God, but they never stop to consider where they'd be without repentance.

We are not here to get things from God, or to see what He can do for us. We are here to be empowered by His Holy Spirit so we can reveal the Father to everyone we meet, and we do that by looking like Jesus everywhere we go. If we miss that, then we miss the very reason for grace in our life and we are neglecting one of the most important reasons why He came. **He came** that you and I **might become** the righteousness of God in Christ Jesus so that we would walk in love, mercy, forgiveness, and righteousness to everyone we meet.

God does not see you for where you have been, but where repentance and righteousness is bringing you, so that it's not about what you've done, but where you are going. So, how can we walk in righteousness as He is righteous? The answer to that is in the next chapter, Holy Spirit, the third leg of the Altar of Love II.

Die To Self

> *"Truly, truly, I say to you, unless a grain of wheat falls into the earth and dies, it remains alone; **but if it dies**, it bears much fruit."*
> John 12:24

The concept of "dying to self" is not new. It's actually been the theme of Christianity from the beginning and is found throughout the entire New Testament. You'd never know this to be true, however if you were a recent convert into the faith and joined one of those mega churches pushing the prosperity gospel. The concept of "dying to self" would be an oddity, a true anomaly to anyone following the prosperity lie. I mean really, think about it, why in the world would I need to die to myself if I can have "my best life now?" In their world and in their mind, Christianity promises blessings, wealth, jobs, cars, and mansions, so why would the average Joe want to die to all that? It's just one big party now that they're a Christian.

> *For whoever wants to save his life will lose it, but **whoever loses his life for My sake** will find it.* Matthew 16:25

The same is true for the OSAS; they can basically behave any way they want without a worry in the world. They can have their cake and eat it too, so why in the world would they want to die to self when they can indulge all they want and still be saved?

Truly, "dying to self" is the virtual essence of Christianity, in which we take up our cross and follow Jesus. The principle of "dying to self," is, and should be a focal point of becoming a born again believer; the old self dies and a new man is reborn.

> *Jesus answered him, "Truly, truly, I say to you, unless one is **born again** he cannot see the kingdom of God."* John 3:3-7

Clearly, we are not saved unless we are born again, but we cannot even be born again unless we die to ourselves first. First we die, then we are reborn; it seems like a fairly simple concept, so wouldn't it be correct to say that dying to self is essential for one's salvation? Not only are Christians expected to die to self in order to be born again, but we continue dying to self the remainder of our life on earth. It's a part of the process of sanctification. As such, dying to self is both a one-time event and a lifelong process.

Jesus spoke repeatedly to His disciples about taking up their cross and following Him. He made it clear that if they wanted to follow Him, they must deny themselves, which means giving up their lives—spiritually, symbolically, and even physically if necessary. Jesus taught this principle as a requirement, not an option. He did not give them a choice to keep their old way of life and follow Him or they could choose to follow Him and deny themselves. There was no option B, they had to choose, leave everything and follow Him or preserve their life and lose their soul. If Jesus is the same yesterday, today and forever, just exactly when did the church drop this teaching and why?

> *Then Jesus told his disciples, "If anyone would come after me, let him **deny himself**, take up his cross and follow me.* Matthew 16:24

Now just in case you missed His point, He did not say, resist the devil, take up your cross and follow me, he said, *"Deny himself."* The phrase *"deny himself"* was another way Jesus explained the principle of dying to self. The word "deny" is translated from Strong's #533 aparneomai (ap-ar-neh'-om-ahee), it means utterly refusing to recognize the person you once were. That person is not just dead; he's **dead to you** now.

You become dead to you, because the "old you" is so abhorrent to the "new you," that the "new you" wouldn't even associate with the "old you." When you die to yourself you can't even relate to the person you used to be any longer. Except for using the old you as a testimony, you should talk about, and describe the "old you" as if it wasn't you at all. Speak of "the old you" in the third person now, as if that person is dead, because they're supposed to be. The "old you" ought to disgust the "new you."

> *Whoever does not bear his own cross and come after me **cannot be my disciple**.* Luke 14:27

In trying to get them to understand the magnitude of the concept of dying to themselves, Jesus explains it another way when He says that those who are unwilling to *"bear his own cross"* and live for Him cannot even be His disciple. At that time, "a cross" was a symbol of death, and not just any death, it was the most inhumane form of punishment and death ever imagined by man. It was also a form of shame and ridicule, so the phrase, "bear his own cross" had very real, very powerful implications when Jesus said it; it implied way more than just death to a thing, it was shameful, it was torture and it was final.

This is a relationship Jesus is explaining, and it is not separated into disciples and converts where disciples behave like the apostles and minister the gospel and converts live their best life now. You are either a disciple or you are not, and that is exactly what Jesus meant when He said, *"take up their cross and follow Me."* He's asking, "are you in or out, are you a believer, a disciple, or not?" It is no different for us, either we die to ourselves, take up our cross and become a disciple or stay in the world and serve sin, but we cannot have the world and Jesus too; we cannot serve two masters.

Obviously, baptism is not a requirement for salvation, and if it is not, what is the main reason for it? The rite of baptism expresses the commitment of a believer to die to the old sinful way of life and be reborn to a new life in Christ. Jesus knew that we would have a difficult time grasping this concept of dying to self, and of complete surrender. The ritual of baptism, the action of being immersed in the water symbolizes us dying, being buried, and raising again with Christ.

> *We therefore were buried with Him through baptism **into death**, in order that, just as Christ was raised from the dead through the glory of the Father, we too may walk in newness of life. For if we have been united with Him like this in His death, we will certainly also be raised to life as He was. ⁶We know that **our old self was crucified with Him <u>so that the body of sin might be rendered powerless</u>**, that we should no longer be slaves to sin.... Romans 6:4–6*

If the body of sin is rendered powerless then why are so many Christians still bound by it? Because something has been missing, something we were supposed to have been taught was removed by hucksters and selfish, sinful men who took the bait. Baptism symbolizes the death of our "old self" by crucifixion with Jesus, **so that** sin would be rendered powerless...**not so** we would continue in it. Dying to self is the death of your old sinful nature so you are no longer a slave to sin. Most Christians continue in sin because they were never taught to die to themselves. Jesus didn't die so we could continue to sin, He died like He did so sin would not have dominion over us anymore.

In Galatians 2:20, Paul explains this process of dying to one's self, but he uses the phrase "crucified with Christ," Saying, *"...now I no longer live, but Christ lives in me."* By Paul's own words, *"...now I no longer live..."* He's saying that he is dead, right? I mean, if he no longer lives, the logical conclusion is that he is dead, but he's clearly not dead, so what is he? Dead to himself! Paul's old life, with its propensity to sin and to follow the ways of the world, is now dead, and the new Paul is the dwelling place of Christ who lives in and through him.

So, how does one learn to die to oneself? Is it really even possible? Can people really die to themselves, especially in this modern, false grace, self-centered society? Yes, it is possible and it's easier than you think. The ability to truly die to oneself, or not, hangs on the one profound, yet simple commandment...Love. Jesus said,

> *"Love the Lord your God with all your heart and with all your soul and with all your mind.' This is the first and greatest commandment. And the second is like it: 'Love your neighbor as yourself.' On these two commandments hang all the Law and the Prophets."* Matthew 22:37-39

So how is love the key to dying to oneself? Simple, it's a selfish, self-centered attitude that makes dying to oneself an impossibility. The true essence of love teaches us to shift our focus off us and puts it on people other than ourselves. Even the title of the infamous book, "Your best life now," reeks of selfishness. If it's all about **your** best life now, then it's all about **you** living for **you,** and if it's all about you, you're obviously not dead to self; you're living in selfishness.

As I always say, the opposite of love is not hate. The opposite of love is selfishness, and the inability to die to oneself is the epitome of selfishness. Selfishness is also a spirit, it's a spirit of selfishness, and it's one of the very first spirits assigned to a human after they are born. Nobody teaches a 2 year old to throw a tantrum when they do not get their way, so why would they? Selfishness! When you shift the focus off of yourself and put it on the people that God has put in your life, you begin to crucify your own desires by putting the needs of others ahead of you, and the dying to self-process begins. We have to come to the realization that the world does not revolve around us. Esteeming others more highly than ourselves is one of the first ways we learn to die to self.

That is why love (self**less**ness) and dying to self go hand-in-hand; in order to live in love, we must learn to become selfless and to do that we must die to self. This is the main problem with the prosperity gospel, until we understand our focus is not on getting blessed but on becoming a blessing for someone else, then and only then can we truly die to ourselves. If we ever get over ourselves, we will be amazing.

Now, this principle of dying to oneself is in direct opposition to the new modern grace, OSAS doctrine of the Masonic Christian preachers. The prosperity message and the OSAS message, which go hand-in-hand, is nothing more than a deception of Masons who have infiltrated the church to "fleece the sheep." It is designed to rob them blind while it leads them into sin and ultimately to hell through selfishness, greed and disobedience. You won't find a die to self-teaching in these mega grace churches any more than you will find a teaching on tongues or the gifts of the Holy Spirit in a Southern Baptist church. It simply does not fit the hidden narrative of, "do whatever pleases you... your saved, so just live your best life now." It is a spirit of selfishness and rebellion leading most Christians down the broad path to destruction.

Dying to self does not mean we lose our personalities or become insensible; it is possible to become so heavenly minded that we are no earthly good. Rather, dying to self simply means that the old you, your old way of thinking and your old life are put to death. Mainly, the sinful ways and lifestyles we once engaged in; that person is expected to die so that Christ may live in you.

> *"Those who belong to Christ Jesus have crucified the sinful nature with its passions and desires."* Galatians 5:24

Our once sinful nature with its passions and desires pursued selfish pleasures, but now we pursue, with equal passion, that which pleases God. In Scripture, "dying to self" is never portrayed as something we Christians are given a choice to do or not do. It's never an option; it is a commandment for everyone who considers themselves a believer. Jesus didn't say, "Hey guys, if you're thinking of becoming a Christian you might want to consider taking up your cross and following me." When I phrase it like that, it actually sounds absurd, it's laughable, but it is a very real and popular theme of the OSAS and prosperity preachers. Dying to self is the evidence of the new birth, the "fruit" if you will.

> *"Beware of false prophets, who come to you in sheep's clothing, but inwardly they are ravenous wolves. 16 You will know them by their fruits.* Matthew 7:15-16

Clearly, Jesus is saying that fruit is the outward manifestation of the spirit within us. Good fruit = Spirit of God, bad fruit = spirit of the world. *"You will know them"* is referring to our allegiance, either you are dead to yourself and loyal to the Lord God or you live for yourself and are loyal to the god of this world. The evidence of your loyalty is in your fruit which is revealed by your willingness to die to yourself or not. It is the way in which we conduct ourselves, our ability to deny ourselves and walk in love and righteousness, or please ourselves and live our best life now in the world.

> *"Every tree that does not bear good fruit is cut down and thrown into the fire."* Matthew 7:15

If we do not learn to crucify our flesh, die to ourselves, and walk in love and righteousness, we risk the very real possibility of being separated from our Father. No one can come to Jesus unless he lives in obedience to Him, and no man can walk in obedience unless he is willing to see his old life crucified and walk in love. Jesus describes lukewarm followers who try to live partly in the old life and partly in the new life as those whom He will vomit out.

> *So, because you are lukewarm, and neither hot nor cold, I am going to vomit you out of My mouth.* Revelation 3:15–16

That lukewarm condition characterized the church of Laodicea as well as most churches today. Being "lukewarm" is really nothing more than selfishness and rebellion brought about by an unwillingness to "deny oneself." The phrase "vomit you out," is also translated "spit out," and it comes from the Greek word emeo (em-eh'-o), which means to reject with extreme disgust.

When Jesus makes reference to cold and hot, he is not talking about our attitude towards Him. He's not telling us that He would prefer we be on fire for Him or be an atheist; that's absurd. Jesus is comparing us to two different water sources of his time. There was a source of hot springs full of minerals with amazing healing properties, and a mountain river with refreshingly ice cold drinking water, but when the two water sources met, it produced water with no healing benefits that tasted terrible. Therefore, He wished we were either like the hot water for healing or the cold water for drinking, but the lukewarm water like the OSAS and prosperity seekers are good for nothing.

Most Christians understand that Satan is real and they are smart enough to determine they do not want hell, but a lack of urgency to die to oneself and live for Christ is nothing more than a well laid snare of the enemy to keep them in the bondage of *"sin leading to death."* Selfishness is them in rebellion to Jesus, but His heart is crying out to them saying, *"Deny yourself, take up your cross and follow me."* The Christians who say in their heart, "I can do what I want," because I'm saved by grace," are woefully deceived and have simply never learned to deny themselves. They're not prepared to take up anything that doesn't benefit them, let alone a cross of crucifixion.

Let's look at this from another angle, and begin with what Jesus didn't mean. Many Christians interpret, "take up your cross" as some burden they must carry in their lives; a strained relationship, a thankless job, a physical illness or an invalid parent or child to care for. With self-pitying pride, and a misguided attitude they say, "That's my cross, God gave it to me, so I guess I have to carry it." So they carry their burdens on their sleeve like a martyr for all to see, in the hope that people will acknowledge their burden, sympathize, comfort or applaud them. But any need to be comforted, pitied, noticed or applauded is just another form of selfishness and clearly not what Jesus meant when He said, *"Take up your cross and follow Me."*

When Jesus carried His cross to Golgotha to be crucified, no one was thinking it was symbolic of anything. To a person in the first-century, the cross meant one thing and one thing only; death by the most painful and humiliating means possible.

Today, modern Christians view the cross as a cherished symbol of atonement, forgiveness, grace, and love. But in Jesus' day, the cross represented a horrible, torturous death, second to none. The Romans forced convicted criminals to carry their own cross to the place of crucifixion; bearing their cross meant carrying their own device of execution while facing humiliation and ridicule along the way.

Therefore, ***"Take up your cross and follow Me,"*** means being willing to endure whatever shame, whatever humiliation, and whatever persecution comes your way when you decide to die to yourself, seek righteousness and follow Jesus. It is you answering the call of absolute surrender, regardless of the opposition or outcome. As well, when Jesus commanded them to bear their cross in Luke 9:23, He immediately follows it up with:

> *For whoever tries to save his life will lose it, but whoever loses his life for my sake will save it.* Luke 9:24

Without a doubt, this is a hard saying and one the enemy will use against its teaching with words like legalism and faith by works; and while it may be a tough one to come to terms with, the reward is eternal. I've likely said it before and I'll probably say it again, there isn't a soul in hell that wouldn't gladly switch places with you for just one more chance to die to themselves so they could live for Jesus

The Christian life is easy when it runs smoothly, but our true commitment to Him is revealed during trials. Trials separate the mature believer from the posers, the disciple from the hypocrite. Discipleship demands sacrifice, even to the point of death and Jesus never hid that cost. He never tried to deceive His followers by candy coating what would result from following Him with "your best life now" sermons.

> *Jesus said, "Follow me." But the disciple said, "Lord, let me first go and bury my father." ⁶⁰ And Jesus said to him, "Let the dead to bury the dead. But as for you, go and proclaim the kingdom of God." Another said, "I will follow you, Lord, but let me first say farewell to those at my home." ⁶²Jesus said to him, "No one who puts his hand to the plow and looks back is fit for the kingdom of God."* Luke 9:60-62

My favorite example of a failure to die to oneself is found in a parable that Jesus tells in the gospel of Luke.

> *"A certain man prepared a great banquet and invited many guests. ¹⁷When it was time for the banquet, he sent his servant to tell those who had been invited, 'Come, for everything is now ready.' ¹⁸But one after another, they all began to make excuses. The first one said, 'I have bought a field and I need to go see it. Please excuse me. Another said, 'I have bought five yoke of oxen and I am going to try them out. Please excuse me.' Still another said, 'I married a wife, so you know I can't come.'* Luke 14:16-20

The biggest mistake Christians make is by viewing these people as unbelievers, which they clearly are not. These people seemed willing to follow Jesus, so they would definitely be considered Christians, but when it came time to put up or shut up, their commitment was half-hearted at best. They failed to count the cost of not dying to their own selfish needs and follow Him. None was willing to take up his cross and crucify their own self-interests. These are not unbelievers, they are not denying Jesus as Lord, they're just not ready to give up their worldly lifestyle and live for Him.

This is exactly what Jesus meant when He said the road to salvation was narrow and only a few would find it. Dying to self is such a difficult requirement that only a few Christians are willing to do it. On multiple occasions, Jesus appears to almost dissuade His followers by telling them the truth of what was going to happen to them if they took up their cross and followed Him.

> *18 "If the world hates you, know that it has hated Me before it hated you. 19 If you were of the world, the world would love you as its own; but because you are not of the world, but I chose you out of the world, therefore the world hates you. 20 Remember the word that I said to you: 'A servant is not greater than his master.' If they persecuted Me, they will also persecute you. If they kept My word, they will also keep yours. 21 But all these things they will do to you on account of My name, because they do not know Him who sent Me. 22 If I had not come and spoken to them, they would not have been guilty of sin, but now they have no excuse for their sin. 23 **Whoever hates Me, hates my Father also**. 24 If I had not done among them the works that no one else did, they would not be guilty of sin, but now they have seen and hated both Me and my Father. 25 But the word that is written in their Law must be fulfilled: 'They hated Me without a cause... "I have said all these things to you to keep you from falling away. 2 They will put you out of the synagogues. Indeed, the hour is coming when whoever kills you will think he is offering service to God. 3 And they will do these things because they have not known the Father, nor Me. 4 But I have said these things to you, that when their hour comes you may remember that I told them to you.* John 15:18-16:4

Let's take a moment here and consider the highlighted text in verse 23"... ***Whoever hates me hates my Father also.*** " You may be thinking to yourself, "Cool, I'm safe, because I don't hate Jesus," but the word for hate is Strong's #3404 Miseó, and it doesn't really mean hate at all. The correct translation is "love less." Strong's concordance defines it as renouncing one thing in favor of another. It has almost the exact connotation as the phrase "deny yourself." Jesus is saying that we must love everything less than we love Him and the Father by denying ourselves. In order for us to be "right with God," we cannot love anything or anyone more than Him, and that includes ourselves. Unless we die to self, unless we deny ourselves, unless we renounce our own desires and favor the desires of our Father, we will not see the Kingdom of God. God is not messing around with this; we will not live eternally unless we die metaphorically.

If you think that's bad, listen to Paul describe what he had to endure:

> *I have worked harder, I've been put in prison more often, been whipped times without number, and faced death again and again. ²⁴ Five different times the Jewish leaders gave me thirty-nine lashes. ²⁵ Three times I was beaten with rods. Once I was stoned. Three times I was shipwrecked. Once I spent a whole night and a day adrift at sea. ²⁶ I have traveled on many long journeys. I have faced danger from rivers and from robbers. I have faced danger from my own people, the Jews, as well as from the Gentiles. I have faced danger in the cities, in the deserts, and on the seas. And I have faced danger from men who claim to be believers but are not. ²⁷ I have worked hard and long, enduring many sleepless nights. I have been hungry and thirsty and have often gone without food. I have shivered in the cold, without enough clothing to keep me warm.* 2 Corinthians 11:23-27

If I didn't know better, I'd almost think that Jesus and Paul were trying to talk me out of becoming a Christian with these honest portrayals of what can be expected when we die to self and follow Him. If the mega churches taught like Jesus and Paul there would be far less false conversion and they certainly would not be mega-sized any longer. They'd be small church gatherings of a handful of disciples willing to lay down their life for their Lord. Wide is the path that leads to destruction and many find it, but narrow is the path to salvation and only a few find it; what path are you on?

Christian Martyrs

"For me to live is Christ; to die is gain," Phil 1:21

...Said Paul, who was beheaded for his faith in Rome. In fact, all the disciples were violently killed, yet still the message spread and martyrdom never stopped. For anyone reading this that might still be on the fence, why would the disciples be willing to die such horrible deaths for a lie? Seriously, these men lived with Jesus; they almost never left His side for 3 years. They heard all His sermons, and witnessed all His miracles, not to mention His brutal crucifixion. If He was a fraud, surely they would have known it after all that time, so why in the world would every single one of them follow in His footsteps unless Jesus was who He said He was, the Son of God?

Peter was crucified upside down, Stephen stoned to death, and John was boiled in oil but crawled out of the caldron refusing to die. He was finally sent to prison on the island of Patmos where he wrote the Book of Revelation and died of old age. Many were burned at the steak, hung by their necks, sawn in two, fed to lions, placed into ovens and cooked like a roasted pigs.

Cecilia, a noblewoman in Rome was condemned to die by suffocation in the Roman baths. The fires were struck and after a full day she didn't even sweat. An executioner came to behead her, and tried three times but could not get her head off her body. After three days she finally bled to her death but never recanted her faith.

Blandina was arrested along with other Christians as a slave and not a Roman citizen. This is important because if a Roman citizen, death would not include torture but a quick beheading. She withstood so much torture that it is said the perpetrators became tired under her strength. Finally, she was taken to an amphitheater and bound to a stake. Wild animals were let loose. However, they did not touch her. Days past and finally, she was thrown in front of stampeding steer and trampled to death.

At only 18, Catherine, the daughter of the Alexandrian governor was converting hundreds to Christianity. She tried to use her influence to persuade the emperor to end the persecution of Christians. He called for 50 of the best pagan philosophers to debate her regarding her Christian beliefs, but her finely crafted arguments even convert some of the listeners. While in prison, 200 visitors come to see her including the emperor's wife, and all are converted to Christianity. Finally, she is condemned to die by the breaking wheel but when she touches it, it breaks to pieces. In frustration, she is finally beheaded.

Emperor Diocletian had the goal of wiping away Christianity forever. Lucia was one of thousands and thousands of people killed for their faith between 303 A.D. until the toleration verdict by Constantine in 313 A.D. Lucia refused to burn incense in worship of the governor of Syracuse so she was sentenced to die, but when the guards came to take her, they couldn't move her. They even tried using an ox, but she would not budge. They attempted to light her on fire where she sat, assembling straw around her, but she wouldn't burn. Finally, she died by sword.

How different was that from the modern day Gospel presentation sold to us by the OSAS and prosperity peddlers! How many people would respond to an altar call that went something like this, "Come follow Jesus, for if you do, you will likely lose your oldest and dearest friends, get shunned by your closest family members, soil your reputation, lose your career, and possibly even your life? You will be hated; many of you will lose everything, become broke and quite possible even homeless. You'll be beaten, spit on, imprisoned, tortured and even killed." I venture to say that the number of false converts would likely decrease dramatically! But that's exactly what Jesus meant when He said, *"Take up your cross and follow Me."*

The Altar of Love, Part II

Chapter 4

Leg 3 – Holy Spirit

Spirit of Grace, Spirit of Truth, Spirit of Christ

"Truly, I tell you, no one can see the kingdom of God unless he is born again." John 3:3

Jesus, the Homeowner and the Devil

There once was a man that owned a beautiful house. Upon hearing a knock at the door he went to open it and see who was there. As he opened the door a foot quickly slid in and sensing this was a dangerous situation the homeowner immediately tried to close the door, but the foot prevented him from doing so. A struggle ensued, an elbow got in, then a shoulder and boom, the door burst open and a fight broke out. The homeowner fought valiantly, but this was the devil, and the devil is highly skilled and well trained in this kind of warfare.

After awhile the homeowner wakes up and realizes he must have been knocked unconscious; looking around he sees his house is in shambles. Furniture overturned, pictures off the wall and broken glass everywhere. He's sorer than he's ever been in his life with bruises in places he never knew he had. He's got a nasty black eye, a bloody nose with cuts and scrapes everywhere. Tending to his wounds, he hears another knock at the door and fear immediately grips his heart, but he notices that this knock sounds different that the first one, so he opens the door and it's Jesus.

"Come in," says the homeowner, "I've heard about you." Jesus enters and responds, "I saw that you had a bit of trouble so I've come to help." "Oh yes, yes, I could use your help, please come in and make yourself at home. I will give you my master bedroom suite; it's the best room in my house. It has everything you need to be comfortable; it even has its own kitchen." Jesus thanks the man, and retires to His room. Later that day, the homeowner hears another knock at the door and it sounds a lot like the first one, so he cautiously approaches the door and barely opens it, but this time the devil pushes it open with both hands before the homeowner can brace himself and it's on again. The devil is much fiercer this time as the homeowner seems less able to repel the onslaught coming his way. Once again, the homeowner awakens to see his home trashed and once again he is bruised and battered.

Just then Jesus comes down the stairs and the homeowner screams, "where were you when I needed you, didn't you hear all the commotion, how could you just let that happen to me, don't you care about me?" Jesus replied, "I was upstairs in the bedroom you gave me." The homeowner pondered the situation and said, "You're right, I understand, from now on you can have the entire upstairs, I'll take the downstairs because it has my office, it's the only real space I need. It has legal documents, business information and a few other things that are private to me." "Very well," said Jesus, "I'll be upstairs if you need me."

Sometime later there was another knock on the door. The homeowner is now all too familiar with the sound of this knock so he does not even open the door this time; he just looks through the peep hole. Suddenly, the door just explodes off the hinges as Satan bursts in with murder in his eyes, but this time is different than the others; it isn't even a fight as the homeowner is completely dominated, and beaten with the worst beating he's ever taken in his life. Then the devil slid out just before Jesus comes down the stairs. "What... why... how come you don't help me? How can you just allow this to happen every time?"

Jesus replied, "I was upstairs where you assigned me."

The homeowner just sat there dazed and confused when Jesus said, "I have an idea, why don't you give the entire house to me, give me the keys and you can live here for free. Defeated, exhausted and humiliated, the homeowner agrees and hands over his keys to the house. Later that evening there was another knock at the door. The homeowner approached the door and was about to look through the peep hole when he felt a tap on his shoulder. It was Jesus, "Step aside," Jesus said, "This is my house now." Jesus opened the door and the devil looked at Him startled. Leaning back, the devil looked again at the address above the door, then looked back at Jesus and said, "Isn't this 3202 Kingsford Drive?" "Yes, it is," said Jesus. The devil stepped back this time and took a 2nd look at the address in bewilderment. Looking back at Jesus again, he said, "I must have the wrong address," and walked away.

The Helper

> [5]"But now I go away to Him who sent Me, and none of you asks Me, 'Where are You going?' [6]But because I have said these things to you, sorrow has filled your heart. [7]Nevertheless I tell you the truth. It is to your advantage that I go away; **for if I do not go away, the Helper will not come to you**; but if I depart, I will send Him to you. [8]And when He has come, **He will convict the world of sin, and of righteousness, and of judgment:** [9]of sin, because they do not believe in Me; [10]of righteousness, because I go to My Father and you see Me no more; [11]of judgment, because the ruler of this world is judged.
>
> [12]"I still have many things to say to you, but you cannot bear them now. [13]However, when He, the **Spirit of Truth**, has come, He will guide you into all truth; for He will not speak on His own authority, but whatever He hears He will speak; and He will tell you things to come. [14]He will glorify Me, for He will take of what is Mine and declare it to you. [15] All things that the Father has are Mine. Therefore I said that He [c]will take of Mine and declare it to you. John 16:5-15

When the Spirit of Truth comes, where does he go? Is he just floating around like a ghost? No, His desire is as it was from the beginning, to come and live inside us, but there are conditions, there are things we must do to house Him.

> *"no one pours new wine into old wineskins. If he does, the wine will burst the skins, and both the wine and the wineskins will be ruined. Instead, new wine is poured into new wineskins."* Mark 2:2

In order for the Holy Spirit to come into you, you must be "born again," but no one can be born again unless they first die to themselves, and this is where the OSAS misses it most. The old man, the man a person was before they get born again cannot house the Spirit of Truth, as long as they try to hang onto their old worldly ways also known as the spirit of the world. The Spirit of Truth will reside in His own room far away from your everyday life until you decide to give up you, invite Him in and let Him have all of you, not just a part of you. He requires the whole you.

For mature Christians who fell prey to the OSAS or prosperity lie and go back to their former way of sin in the world, the Spirit of Truth will prod you and tug at your heart in an attempt to convict you of righteousness, but you have a free will to choose between the Kingdom of God and His righteousness or the pleasures of the world. Each time you make a decision to follow the world you will get a prompting by the Spirit of Truth to repent, but God is a gentleman and He will not force you to walk in righteousness. Eventually, the Holy Spirit will recede as the voice of the world becomes louder and more influential than the voice of Truth.

> *My sheep listen to My voice; I know them, and they follow Me.* John 10:27

Look carefully at what Jesus is saying here when He says, *"My sheep listen to my voice...."* The whole world will be separated into two groups, sheep and goats; it's as simple as that. Sheep are characteristically passive and obedient, while goats are difficult and rebellious. True and faithful Children of God are likened to sheep because they not only hear the call of God but they are obedient to it. This is a two-part requirement; His sheep listen to His voice and follow Him, not one or the other. To follow means to follow after as a disciple follows his teacher; to become a disciple of one is to abandon everything and submit to the authority and rule of them. In order to "follow Jesus," we must die to ourselves; we abandon our needs, our desires and live for Him who died for us.

People who call themselves Christians, but live like the world are clearly not following Jesus as a disciple. Jesus did not say, "Go into all the world and make converts," He said, *"Go make disciples."* Disciples are loyal to one master and one master only. Owning a Bible, reading it occasionally, going to church, using Christian terminology, wearing a cross, sporting a fish on your car and wearing a Christian T-shirt are all well and good, but none of those things, individually or all together meet the requirements of, nor is it the character of sheep without the obedience of *"follow me."* Quoting scripture doesn't make you a sheep unless you become the scripture you quote.

Demon Spirits

> *When an unclean spirit comes out of a man, it passes through dry places seeking rest and does not find it.* ⁴⁴*Then it says, 'I will return to the* **house** *I left.' On its return, it finds the* **house** *vacant, swept clean and put in order....*
> Matthew 12:43-44

For those that have not read the original Altar of Love, demonic spirits consider us their home. In the scripture above, they are calling this person their house, so I ask you; do you want to be home to a demon? If not, if your answer is no, then your attitude should be, not just "no," but literally "Hell no, and, you've got to go now, in the name of Jesus." Unless you are filled with the Holy Spirit, which most Christians are certainly not, you are home to demonic spirits. In the process of doing the Altar of Love, I have witnessed hundreds of spirits being cast out of people that not only considered themselves Christian, but spoke in tongues and could quote the Bible verbatim. Most people are dealing with spiritual issues because they either don't or won't assume their authority. Authority is there for the taking, if you will not assume it...they will. If you do not make them leave, they are perfectly happy to stay. If you have given your authority to them through willful sin of the present and/or the past, they have the legal right to stay, and that is where authority becomes very interesting and very necessary to comprehend.

There are only two sides to this war, The Kingdom of God or the Kingdom of the devil, AKA "the world," and while there may be billions of spirits in the world, they are loyal to either one side or the other. The entire world and every human being in it are being influenced by either a demon spirit or God's Holy Spirit. There is nothing else under the sun; it's one or the other. Everyone in the world, even most people who consider themselves devout Christians, are being influenced by one or more demon spirits unless or until they are filled with the Holy Spirit.

Don't misunderstand me, demon spirits cannot make you do things against your free will. Many people in my family history were alcoholics, but that spirit never got hold of me, because I hated the feeling of being drunk. I like the taste of a beer occasionally, but rarely ever have more than one, because as soon as I sense even the slightest effects of alcohol, alarm bells go off in me. My free will not to drink is more powerful that the spirit of alcoholism's power to dominate me. Before I got saved, when I was in the world, I had other issues, but when the Spirit of Grace and Truth made their home in me, those spirits were driven out.

> *"...how much more will your Father in heaven give the Holy Spirit to those who ask Him!"* Luke 11:13

ATTENTION, Christians are not automatically filled with the Holy Spirit just because they say a sinner's prayer, or else Jesus would not tell us to ask for Him.

> *...how much more will your Father in heaven give the Holy Spirit to those who ask Him!"* Luke 11:13

Jesus spoke in parables, figures of speech, metaphors, idioms and all manner of different ways in order to hide the truth from the devil, as it is written, *"For had they known, they never would have crucified Jesus."* Even His disciples couldn't understand what He was saying most of the time, but somehow, they knew He had the Words of eternal life.

> *...So Jesus asked the Twelve, "Do you want to leave too?"* *[68]Simon Peter replied, "Lord, to whom would we go? You have the words of eternal life.* John 6:67-68

> *Then the disciples came to Jesus and asked, "Why do You speak to the people in parables?" [11]He replied, "To you it has been given to know the mystery of the kingdom of God; but to those who are outside, all things come in parables,...* Mark 4:10-11

There are so many mysteries in the Kingdom of God that Jesus taught the people; most of which they were incapable of understanding unless He explained himself later. Primarily because the wisdom of God is only revealed by the Holy Spirit and He had not yet been poured out on them. Any revelation they did receive would be on a case-by-case basis as in the Old Testament.

The fundamental meaning of the Kingdom of God was brilliantly hid by the Father behind the principle teaching of Ask, Seek and Knock. For everyone who asks, seeks or knocks will receive exactly what they are searching for. In other words, God is saying, *"I only want a relationship with people who want Me as much as I want them, if you'd prefer a relationship with the world; you are free to do so. If you choose the world over me, I will hide My wisdom from you in such a way that you cannot figure it out. If however, you ask, seek and knock because you are tired of the world and you want what you were created for, a relationship with Me, I will open the door of My Kingdom and my Holy Spirit will teach you what you are seeking to know."*

If you knock on the door of the Kingdom of God, the truth about Jesus will be revealed to your heart, but you still have choices to make. If you are only seeking after God to be your Santa Clause god so you can acquire lots of blessings and worldly possessions, then your knowledge and understanding about Him and His Kingdom will be as shallow as your motives. On the other hand, if your intentions are pure and you **seek** righteousness instead of cars and houses when the door is opened, and if you **ask** to be filled with the Holy Spirit, then your Father will give you what you are seeking after as well as all the things you need in this life, but He also wants to give you many other amazing gifts as well.

These gifts, the gifts that your Father wants to lavish upon you are not gifts as the world sees gifts, these are spiritual gifts. These gifts are so numerous they range from the seemingly inconsequential to the miraculous, but whether small or great, they are awesome, life changing gifts. The gifts of God include, but are in no way limited to: peace for the anxious, faith for the faithless, courage for the fearful, confidence for the insecure, a Husband (Jesus) for the widow, a Father (God) for the orphan, strength for the weak, humility for the proud, forgiveness for the condemned, mercy for the wicked, hope for the hopeless, grace for the lawless, love for the unloved, repentance for the rebellious, and righteousness for the wickedly selfish.

The thing is, there are way too many to list, but your Father knows what you need, so if you knock on the door of His Kingdom and sincerely inquire of the authenticity and divinity of Jesus, He will reveal Himself to you. But it's up to you to make the first move by knocking. If you seek His righteousness, He will pour His love and righteousness into you thereby removing your desire and propensity to sin. If you ask to be filled with His Spirit, He will come and make His home in you so the two of you become one as in marriage. Lastly, He knows you have needs in this world, so He will provide exactly what you need. It may not be a new car, but to the person suffering from anorexia, germ-a-phobia, or a broken heart, it is priceless.

> ***Ask*** *and it will be given to you;* ***seek*** *and you will find;* ***knock*** *and the door will be opened to you. ⁸For everyone who asks receives; he who seeks finds; and to him who knocks, the door will be opened.*
> Matthew 7:7-8

a) First, we Knock on the Kingdom Door and the Father opens it to reveal the truth about Jesus. If we choose to make Him our Lord, we are adopted into the family;

b) Next, we die to ourselves and seek righteousness like we are seeking a treasure and if we seek righteousness, we will find it, but you cannot find something you are not seeking after, especially Kingdom of God things which are not tangible and hidden from everyone but those who hunger and thirst for them;

c) Then, we ask for the Holy Spirit, and the Spirit of Grace & Truth will expel the spirits of the world. Gods Holy Spirit will come flooding in and the transformation process begins.

> *Ask and it will be given... Mathew 7:7*

The word **Ask,** aiteó (ahee-teh'-o) implies begging, a strong petition for a thing because of its great value. It implies asking on behalf of oneself, not for another. Aiteó is used specifically when asking for something to be given **to you**, not done **for you**, thus <u>giving prominence to the thing asked for</u> rather than the person doing the asking. Ask is rarely used and implies asking to the point of begging, because the "thing requested" is so rare, so valuable and so necessary that the requestor relentlessly pursues it without shame.

"it will be given" – **Strong's #1325** didómi (did'-o-mee) Definition: to give. Usage: I offer, give; to give as a gift to the one asking. It means to give to one's care, entrust something of great value. Joined with nouns, didómi denotes strength, power and virtue; it is equivalent to: to endue one with a thing of great value or power.

216

The principle behind the phrase, *"Ask and it will be given,"* is similar to *"seek and ye shall find,"* yet it does not imply a simple request for a thing, i.e.: "please hand me the pen," "may I have a drink?," "can you help me for a minute?" or "Father, can I have the Holy Spirit?" it is more akin to begging earnestly for something of such great value as though your life depended upon receiving it.

> *And when they were gathered together, Jesus commanded them: "Do not leave Jerusalem,* **but wait for the gift the Father promised,**
> Acts 1:4

When Jesus said to the disciples, *"... stay in Jerusalem and* **wait for the gift** *of the Holy Spirit,"* the Bible says, *"With one accord they all* **continued** *in prayer."*

Continued – Strong's #4342 proskartereó (pros-kar-ter-eh'-o) Definition: to attend constantly. Usage: I persist, persevere in, and continue steadfast in; I wait upon.

"They all **continued in prayer***"* (*proskartereō*) means "to continue to do something with intense effort despite difficulty. It is utter devotion while displaying steadfast strength, which prevails in its quest "in spite of" and regardless of the opposition. It is continuing to do something with such intense effort, that nothing could cause you to quit your endeavor.

The disciples knew something remarkable was coming as they waited on the Holy Spirit to baptize them; they were bound and determined to receive this gift no matter what or how long it took, therefore *"they all continued in prayer"* until He came.

> *"Suppose one of you goes to his friend at midnight and says, 'Friend, lend me three loaves of bread, ⁶because a friend of mine has come to me on a journey, and I have nothing to set before him. ⁷And the one inside answers, 'Do not bother me. My door is already shut and my children are with me in bed. I cannot get up to give you anything.' ⁸I tell you, even though he will not get up to provide for him because of his friendship, yet because of the*

> *man's persistence, he will get up and give him as much as he needs. ⁹So I tell you: Ask and it will be given to you; seek and you will find; knock and the door will be opened to you.* Luke 11:5-9

Jesus tells this quirky, almost comical story about persistence that segues into Luke's version of Ask, Seek & Knock, and it's no coincidence, because this is not only our example to seek this thing called righteousness, but a parable of the persistence required for obtaining the gift of the Holy Spirit, connected to the teaching of Ask, Seek and Knock. It is a quest, our quest; a relentless pursuit of such importance that you are willing to do whatever it takes to receive what He is offering. It is you, going in your bedroom, shutting the door and praying without ceasing until the Holy Spirit comes, regardless of how hard it seems or how long it takes. Whether it be minutes, hours, days, weeks, months or even years; it is a gift so valuable, so important and so necessary, if you only knew the half of it you'd never waiver at thought of what it might take to find it.

The Spirit of Truth

> *However, when He, the **Spirit of Truth**, has come, He will guide you into all truth;* John 16:13

When you ask to be filled with the Holy Spirit, your new Father will send the Spirit of Truth. He is a multi-faceted Spirit, and He has many responsibilities and functions.

1. When you knock on the Kingdom door, God sends the Spirit of Truth, and He removes your spiritual blinders so that you can perceive the truth about Jesus. All scripture is spiritually discerned, in that it cannot be understood by mere intellect, it must be revealed by the Spirit of Truth otherwise the message of Jesus and the cross is nothing more than foolishness to those who refuse to knock. The Spirit of Truth ministers the Lord Jesus directly to your heart; something that was not possible until after the cross. This is the moment of reckoning, because now you know the truth, now you must

decide between dying to self and choosing to become a disciple of Jesus or continue being a slave to sin in the world.

2. The Spirit of Truth is not merely truth as spoken, it is truth of idea, reality, sincerity, truth in the moral sense, therefore He is our teacher of what is, and is not righteous. You cannot do what is right if you are confused about what is right, therefore, the Spirit of Truth reveals the Fathers heart to our heart, so that we know and understand what is expected of us in regards to love and righteousness. A really, really bad decision and/or choice is proof of the absence of the Spirit of Truth.

3. The Spirit of Truth guides our walk of righteousness by working in tandem with the Spirit of Grace to convict our hearts of sin while lovingly, gently prodding us to repent in the event we miss it.

4. The Spirit of Truth is the Spirit behind Prophesy, Wisdom and giving us Words of Knowledge.

5. The Spirit of Truth is responsible for giving us discernment and revelation in all things pertaining to God, like His Word for instance. When we read His Word, it is the Spirit of Truth that gives us the revelation to understand it; for without the Spirit of Truth discerning the Word for us, it is nothing more than foolish gibberish to us.

One of the greatest misconceptions of new believers, and one of the dangerous deceptions of the OSAS is the false belief that the Holy Spirit comes to live inside of you the minute you say a sinner's prayer; He does not. Yes, your Father does want His Spirit to come and reside within you; you were created to house Him from the beginning, but it's not automatic. We are required to ask shamelessly and persistently for the Holy Spirit, for without Gods Holy Spirit, something will be missing from your life, and you will never feel complete.

Imagine you had a good friend or a dog even; the best friend in the world or the absolute sweetest dog you've ever owned. Dogs can be amazing companions so it's a worthy example. Then imagine the sadness, the loneliness, the despair one would feel if your friend died. That's how it is for us without Gods Spirit in union with our spirit; the problem is that if you are not filled with His Spirit, you don't know why you feel incomplete, you just do.

Man is first a spirit, with a soul, living in a temporary body, and your spirit was created to have a relationship with your Father. Prior to you establishing that relationship with your Father, your spirit is like a man in a comma; it's there, but it's not awake so it's not really alive.

But when you knock on the Kingdom door and God reveals Truth to you and you take that leap of faith; putting all your hope in the One who saved you from you, your Spirit man comes alive. This is exactly what Jesus meant when He said,

> *"Truly, truly, I tell you, no one can see the kingdom of God unless he is **born again.**"* John 3:3

When you are "born again," the spirit within you, which is likened to being dead because of sin, now comes alive; it is the most amazing experience in the world, because not only are you suddenly energized as if you instantly got 30 years younger, but God's Holy Spirit, the Spirit of Truth begins to reveal wisdom to your heart and mind. It's difficult to put into words for unbelievers, and most of the wannabe Christians like the OSAS and prosperity seekers who have likely never experienced this feeling.

It is exactly why people without Jesus, and Christians who do not believe in the gifts of the Holy Spirit have such a difficult time relating to the passion and the excitement of Holy Spirit filled believers, choosing rather to put them down and speak against them. When the Holy Spirit comes to live in you, He makes you truly alive for the very first time; He literally completes the purpose of your creation from the beginning.

Just prior to my marriage, my wife and I broke up and I was devastated. At that exact time God sent a Christian man to join my school. He shared the gospel with me, but I resisted at first, not being able to see Truth because I wasn't seeking It. I had my opinion, but my opinion was only based upon all the worldly knowledge

I had gained over 30 years. One evening he drove me home from class because my car was in the shop and he asked me a simple question before I exited his car, he said, "You know, what if you're wrong, have you ever been so sure of something only to find out you were wrong? You are basing your eternity on an opinion; you have not one fact to support that opinion, but you are willing to risk an eternity in hell to defend your opinion." He continued, "If I'm wrong, I'm worm food, no big loss, but if you're wrong... Look, I don't even really know you, but I already love you enough to tell you the truth because it's obvious that no one has until now. Let me give you some advice, and you can take it or leave it. Ask God to show you the Truth about Jesus, because I promise you, if you sincerely ask, He will reveal Himself to you as long as you don't ignore all the signs or blow them off as coincidences.

Needless to say, I didn't sleep that night and if I wrote all the signs and miracles that occurred over the next several days after I knocked on the Kingdom door and asked God to show me, it would take up several chapters. Suffice it to say that God did reveal Himself to me and because I'm not an idiot or delusional, I got it. There is an old saying, "God bless the broken road that lead me straight to You." The devastating loss of my future wife was exactly what I needed to knock on the Kingdom door and ask. Within a few weeks of "getting it," I was reconciled with my girlfriend and we immediately got married. But that's not even the point of this amazingly true story.

I was immediately changed, I was not the same person, vulgarity had instantly become repulsive to me and for the first time I could now see all my old friends for who they truly were as well as the sin they engage in, and it made me sick to my stomach to even be around them any longer. At this point, I wasn't knowledgeable enough to minister to them, so my first impulse was to get away from them.

I began going to church, reading my Bible, and making new friends, but my wife was not on the same page as me, so things were not hunky dory at home. She was

100% sold out to the world with all of its lustful pleasures of drinking, partying, cussing and the sort; and me, I'm walking on a tight rope between trying to appease her without giving in to the sin while getting to know my Father. From 1991-1999 it was a rollercoaster ride as we'd get along for the most part, but there would be frequent, violent explosions of rage and anger because to say the spirit of the world inside her was not comfortable with the Holy Spirit inside me is a major understatement. Many times I looked in her eyes only to see a demonic spirit looking back at me like it wanted to kill me, because it probably did.

I'm not going to sugarcoat it, it was not good for quite a while, but I really loved this woman to such an extent that even with all the anger, the hatred, the verbal and physical abuse, I would have given my life for her, because the love of Jesus had taken out my heart of stone and replaced it with a heart of flesh, a heart that loves like He loves...unconditionally. I figured that Jesus didn't give up on me even after 30 years, neither will I give up on her, so I made up my mind to just love her whether she ever got it or not. I was determined never to give up, but 8 years of living in turmoil seems like an eternity when you're going through it. The key here is love and patience.

After arriving home from a vacation, one in which she absolutely ruined with frequent fits of rage and constant drunkenness, I was at my wits end, so I asked God to please change her, and immediately He answered me. In a clear audible voice He said, *"She's my responsibility, I will deal with her, you concern yourself with you."* Just then, my life began flashing before my eyes and all the sin I was still compromising on was revealed to me in an instant. No, I wasn't the same person I used to be, and yes, I had come a long way, but He showed me all the places in my life where I was still trying to hold onto things of the world and He was ever so sweetly telling me to surrender completely. In that moment, I understood that in order for my marriage to come alive, I had to die to myself.

> *"Truly, truly, I say to you, unless a grain of wheat falls into the earth and dies, **it remains alone**; but if it dies, it bears much fruit.*
> John 12:24

As long as I tried to live with one foot in the Kingdom and the other foot in the world I would remain alone, but if I was willing to die to myself it would bear much fruit in my marriage. Up to then I had only incorporated Jesus into my life, but remember, we are not instructed to decrease so He can increase; we are required to die so He can live in us and through us. If my wife was ever going to "get it," I was going to have to deny myself, take up my cross and live completely for Jesus. Trying to get her to eat the fruit of righteousness off my tree would never happen unless I actually had fruit to offer her. In order for me to produce the fruit of righteousness, I had to become righteousness, and in doing so, she would eventually come and pick fruit from my tree, willingly.

The following Sunday, my pastor's sermon was on seeking righteousness, therefore, from then on, I made it my goal to seek the Kingdom of God and His righteousness as a man seeks a treasure. The next few years were amazing as the Lord began speaking to me in audible voices and doing miracle after miracle after miracle to the point where I was in a constant state of amazement. Don't get me wrong, nothing had changed at home between my wife and I, but me. My wife was still angry, abusive and she was still drinking excessively, but God had given me a supernatural ability to love her unconditionally and within time I began to notice cracks in the walls she had erected for self-preservation.

There were so many outrageous miracles happening in our life daily that she'd have to have been an idiot not to notice and be affected by them, and she was no idiot. I could literally write an entire book just on the miracles in our life at that time. I'm not talking about mere coincidences that are likely not coincidences at all, I'm talking about the impossible, the amazing, the supernatural, and they were happening daily.

About 9 years into our marriage she expressed interest in attending a Bible study that our pastor, Jim Scalise was teaching every Wednesday. After 6 months or so, I noticed that going to Bible study had become so important to her that instead of skipping it when something else arose, she carefully adjusted her schedule around it. She had finally gotten to a place where she was knocking on the Kingdom door, and because God is faithful to His Word, He opened the door and the Spirit of Truth was about to reveal His truth to her heart.

One Wednesday evening I arrived home from teaching but, she had not yet arrived home from Bible study. The phone rang, I picked it up, and it was my Pastor Jim Scalise. He asked, "Have you seen your wife yet?" Totally confused by his question, I said, "No, why, did something happen to her?" He laughed the sweetest laugh and said, "Well, I felt the Holy Spirit tell me to just start praying, so we all closed our Bibles and I began walking up and down the rows of chairs praying over people when I came to Angela and the Holy Spirit told me to touch her.

To the best of my recollection, he said that as soon as he touched her, she fell out of her chair and just lay on the ground for minutes as Jesus breathed the Holy Spirit upon her. At the exact moment he's telling me that story, Angela walked in the front door. As I turned to look at her, I am amazed to see she is virtually glowing; lit up like a Christmas tree. I do not know if I can accurately articulate what I saw, but the woman who walked in my front door that day was not my wife; she was a new creation, her spirit which was dead to sin, had come alive and it was the most beautiful thing I have ever seen, even to this day. She looked at me and instead of the usual look of indifference, she smiled a smile so big, so warm, and so loving, it was the first time in a decade that I felt she actually loved me.

She had been transformed from a caterpillar to a butterfly in an instant; and unless you were there, unless you were involved in our lives, you'd have no way of understanding just how great a miracle it was. People don't just change; have you ever heard the old saying, "a leopard cannot hide his spots too long?" Apart from an actual spiritual transformation, apart from Jesus imparting the Holy Spirit upon us, any attempt to change one's personality is futile and temporary at best. This woman had changed for real, and from that day forward we had the most awesome, the most amazing, and the most loving marriage I have ever known. Over the next 12 years, I never met anyone with a better, more caring, selfless marriage than ours, as she grew into the most amazing woman I have ever known.

Being filled with the Holy Spirit is a power so incredible that it can move mountains, stop time, hold back water, slay a giant, heal cancer, restore sight to the blind and life to the dead (physically and spiritually), and as in my case, it can heal a broken heart, renew a dead Spirit and make beauty out of ashes. If just one member of the marriage is filled with the Spirit of God it is hugely powerful, but the power, the authority, the abilities of two Spirit filled believers in marriage is a force so great that all hell shudders in fear of its potential.

Therein lies a very big problem, because the devil is freaking out about now and he cannot have a dynamic duo going about destroying his kingdom wherever they go. A marriage of this sort will have Satan's best, most cunning agents assigned to it; no resources will be withheld. Destroying this marriage becomes his number one priority, because if these two ever come to the understanding of their true identity and just how powerful they are together, nothing would be impossible for them.

So, Satan plots and plans and schemes; he sows lies and deception looking for a chink in their armor. And if he finds one, if there is even a sliver of selfishness, if he can get their focus off Jesus and on their situation or themselves individually; that's all he needs to divide them. If he can uncover something to exploit... IT IS ON, THIS IS WAR, IT'S BLITZCRIEGE! He will throw everything he has at them and he will do it all at once. Within no time at all their life will look like Job's, different circumstances maybe, but very similar in outcome.

This is where identity comes in, because regardless of what is going on in your life, a proper understanding of your identity, who you are as a Child of God and what you were created for, will enable you to keep your eyes on Jesus, not on your situation or each other. Any "Job-like" trial is nothing more than an opportunity to squeeze Jesus out of you and get Him all over everyone and everything confronting you. Just exactly what do you think happens when, in the midst of a trial, you are squeezed and Jesus comes out? That right, miracles, upon miracles, upon miracles.

My brethren, count it all joy when you fall into various trials... James 1:2

If you are filled with your Father's Holy Spirit and you are fortunate enough to have a spouse who is filled as well, may I suggest that you not turn to the left or the right, but only forge ahead in a relentless pursuit of righteousness, being careful to never forget your identity. This thing that you have is so rare, so valuable and so wonderful that nothing, apart from the love of Jesus, nothing is comparable to it. If you don't have it, pray for it, and trust that your Father has your best interest at heart. He knows better than you and He also knows the future, so feel free to tell Him what you want, but just like Jesus in the garden, acquiesce to His will.

For those that once had it and lost it, I don't know what to tell you other than, never give up hope, because with God all things are possible. Jesus said,

Therefore what God has joined together, let man not separate. Mark 10:9

For those of you with a difficult marriage, those in the middle of a divorce or those that have already divorced, the verse above is not taken out of context; it comes directly on the heels of Jesus teaching about marriage. The Jews were trying to frame Jesus with the law regarding divorce, because they wanted to justify divorcing their wife for a younger one. Jesus had a 0-tollerance policy in regards to divorce with the only exception being adultery, and they knew it, but they contended that Moses had given them the legal right to divorce. Jesus brilliantly counters with Gods original plan for marriage.

> *Everyone who divorces his wife and marries another woman commits adultery,* Luke 16:18

I found this verse to be completely out of place, because it was not in context with what Jesus was talking about whatsoever. Jesus was trying to reason with the Pharisees who were scoffing at Him. From there He says, *"God knows your hearts. For what is prized among men is detestable before God."* Then He mentions the law and the prophets, and from there He just drops this divorce bomb out of nowhere and immediately segues into the story of Lazarus in paradise and the rich man in hell.

> *But Jesus told them, "Moses wrote this commandment of divorce for you* **because your hearts were hard**. *⁶However, from the beginning of creation, 'God made them male and female.' ⁷'For this reason a man will leave his father and mother and be united to his wife...*Mark 10:5-7

Moses permitted them to divorce because of the hardness in their heart, but Jesus was trying to get them to understand that the law of the land does not supersede Gods law regarding marriage from the beginning of creation. I find it interesting that most devout Christians would never consider an abortion because they know it is not God's will, yet they will divorce at the drop of a hat. In doing so, they once again break the first commandment by worshiping a false idol god that favors one of His laws over other.

> *"...and the two will become one flesh. 'So they are no longer two, but one flesh."* Mark 10:8

Selfishness, due to an absence of the Holy Spirit will make any heart grow cold and hard, it's as simple as that. If my wife wasn't filled with the Holy Spirit that awesome day in 1999, the next 12 years are likely more difficult than the first.

Just one touch washed away every worry, every doubt, every resentment, every root of bitterness, every lie, and every lustful, greedy, selfish desire and filled her with His love and righteousness. Some of you know what I'm talking about; some of you have had it, but time, life, children, work, trials, sin and selfishness have stolen it from you. But God is faithful, if he did it once, what makes you think he cannot do it again? He can, He does and He will if you seek Him and His righteousness like your life depends upon it.

> *"Behold, I am the LORD, the God of all flesh. Is anything too difficult for Me?* Jeremiah 32:27

Zoe Life

> *The thief comes only to steal and kill and destroy. I have come that they may have **life**, and have it more abundantly.*
> John 10:10

We live in the devil's kingdom, even Paul admitted that Satan was the god of this world, but your Father brilliantly figured a way to get his Son into Satan's system and by the cross, Jesus legally purchased that which Satan had lured away in the insurrection. There was an insurrection, but Jesus died and was resurrected, so we could be reconciled by His blood back to our Father. In the passage above, the highlighted word "**life**" is translated from the Greek phrase, Zoe life. Jesus begins the passage by telling us the goal and motive of the devil for us, then He contrasts Satan's offer with what Jesus is offering. *"Satan comes to kill, steal and destroy, but I come to offer you **Zoe life**."*

Jesus is referring to the "born again" experience; the moment His Spirit infuses your spirit with eternal life thus giving you His Zoe life. Everyone without this Zoe life is literally "the walking dead." Those who were once enlightened but have abandoned Jesus for the fading delicacies of Satan's world will begin dying a slow spiritual death until their spirit, which was once alive, is now dead unto sin as before. If we, who were once made alive unto Christ, return to sin like a dog returns to his vomit, we will die to it again, it happens all the time, which is why Satan does not just give up tormenting believers after they get saved. Don't fall for his lie, the only thing Satan and his world system has to offer you are temporary pleasures followed by ultimate destruction.

A big home, vacations in the Caribbean, new cars, money in excess and all manner of worldly treasures and pleasures are very enticing, but people who go after such things, Christian or not, have no idea what lies ahead. They are being slow cooked, basted and marinated for the final banquet for which they are the main course. My heart breaks for all the gullible Christian souls that have fallen prey to the OSAS and prosperity lies. Those who were once saved and filled with His Spirit, but have chosen to go back to the world and have died again unto sin, but they don't even know it. Unbeknownst to them, their fate will be much worse than before they had known, having known and rejected the ministry of righteousness.

> ***Jesus took what you deserved so you could get what He deserved. He became what you were so you might become what He is...righteousness!***

I know a few people like this; once devout, Spirit filled believers that life has beaten down. They call themselves Christians, they might even go to church occasionally, they love the thought of the way they were when they loved Jesus back in the day, and they still considered themselves believers, but they serve the world and all its pleasures now. They are dead again unto sin, but like the rest of the world, they can't see it, because the Holy Spirit which reveals discernment has been removed.

This is a seriously dangerous place to be, because before they were enlightened, God was calling them, beckoning their heart and something within them told them that they needed Him. This is the great deception behind the OSAS doctrine. Before OSAS, backsliding Christians would have sensed the loss of His Spirit and conviction would prick their heart, but now they are under the false pretense that they can have Jesus and mammon (sin) at the same time, so as He calls to them to come home, they falsely think they are already home when in fact, they are a million miles away. The Bible says, *"Let God be true and every man a liar,"* and *"It is impossible for God to lie."*

> *God will not be mocked, whatever a man sows, that shall he reap.* Galatians 6:7

If we sow to the flesh through willful, wanton sin without a sincere, heartfelt repentance, we will reap corruption in our flesh by reestablish ourselves as slaves unto sin as well as eventual separation from our Father. If, however, we sow into righteousness which produces a selfless love for all, we will reap peace, hope and joy followed by eternal life.

Jesus never promised us a rose garden, on the contrary, if you read many of Jesus' quotes and Paul's letters, you see a very familiar warning that not only will our life not be perfect; it will very likely become much more difficult. That's when Jesus reminds us to keep this life with all its ups and downs in perspective.

> *What will it profit a man if he gains the whole world, yet forfeits his soul? Or what can a man give in exchange for his soul?* Matthew 16:26

For Christians who have backslidden, no job, no man or woman, no car, no amount of prosperity is a sufficient trade for your soul. When Jesus said, *"I have come that they may have **Zoe** life...* in John 10:10, He's describing what happens when His Spirit comes into your spirit, and your spirit comes alive. You were lost but now you are found, you were blind but now you see, you were spiritually dead, but now you are alive with Zoe Life. And just in case I have not sufficiently proven the OSAS lie, King David, a man after Gods own heart wrote this in

Psalms:

> *Cast me not away from Your presence;* **take not Your Holy Spirit from me.** Psalm 51:11

When you are "Born Again," Gods Holy Spirit enters you and your spirit comes alive with Zoe Life, however we were created with a free will, so you are perfectly within your right to reject the Father's offer and live for Satan and his world system if that is what you prefer. Furthermore, if you were previously saved and filled with His Spirit, you are well within your rights and privileges of free will to go back to the selfish, sinful, wickedness of the world like an addict returns to his drugs. If it were not so, why would David say, "...*take not Your Holy Spirit from me?*" Why even make the statement if it were not a possibility? The fact of the matter is...it is possible to return to the world, but if you do, you will become a slave to sin as before and God will take His Spirit from you; people do it all the time, you'd be surprised.

It is also possible for believers to become apostate, because just like repentance, free will doesn't end when you get Zoe Life.

> *At that time* **many will fall away** *and will betray* **and hate one another,** Matthew 24:10

Fall Away – Strong's #4624. Skandalizó (skan-dal-id'-zo) Definition: to put a snare in the way, to cause to stumble, to give offense. Usage: I cause to sin, cause to become indignant, offended. To cause a person to begin to distrust and desert the One (Jesus) whom he ought to trust and obey; **to become apostate is to abandon the faith for another or the world.**

> *Now the Spirit expressly states that in later times* **some will abandon the faith** *to follow deceitful spirits and the teachings of demons,* 1 Timothy 4:1

To abandon the faith means they were once Christians, but they abandoned that belief to either believe a lie or they simply returned to the world; they have become apostate. One of the signs of this condition is "hate." The new commandment for all Christians is "love," therefore, "hate" has no business even being part of our vocabulary. Jesus said, *"If you hate it's just as if you committed murder."* Hate is a byproduct of the worlds system, and a fairly good indication that a former Christian has returned to the world and become apostate. As we learned earlier, when Christians reestablish their friendship with the world, they make themselves an enemy of God, and exactly what do you think it was that caused them to abandon the faith? They were...

> *...influenced by the hypocrisy of liars, whose consciences are seared with a hot iron.* 1 Timothy 4:2

But Jesus said,

> *But the one who perseveres to the end will be saved.* Matthew 24:13

In the verse below, Paul acknowledges the dire consequences as a result of a believer filled with Zoe Life who either never dies to themselves and continues in sin or they end up going back to becoming a slave to it. Paul is including himself in the equation when he says, "**If we**..." so we know he's talking to believers about believers.

> ***<u>If we</u> deliberately go on sinning <u>after</u> we have received the knowledge of the truth, no further sacrifice for sins remains,*** *²⁷but only a fearful expectation of judgment and raging fire that will consume all adversaries.*
> Hebrews 10:26-27

I highlighted and underlined the text I wanted you to pay careful attention to. I'm not really sure I can express the urgency of what you will face without a heartfelt willingness to die to yourself and seek righteousness before it is too late to do so. So, just exactly what does Paul mean when he says, *"If we deliberately go on sinning...?"*

Deliberately – Strong's # 1596 (hek-oo-see'-ose) to sin willfully, tacitly, as opposed to sins committed inconsiderately, and from ignorance or weakness.

The meaning is clear, if we engage in behavior that we know is wrong, behavior we know is sinful at the time we are doing it...it's a serious problem, it has the very real consequence of hell if there is no heartfelt repentance. Paul puts it in perspective when he says, "*...after **we** have received the knowledge of the truth...*"

Knowledge – Strong's # 1922 (ep-ig'-no-sis) Knowledge gained through first-hand **relationship**. The knowledge of His Holy will and of the blessings which the Father bestows on men through Christ.

Of the truth – Strong's # 225 *(al-ay'-thi-a)* The word denotes what is true in things appertaining to God and the duties of man.

And this is where it can easily be misunderstood, because it is true that most Christians never come to the knowledge of the truth. They've been so deceived by denominationalism, the OSAS lie and the prosperity gospel that they are mere babies regarding the truth of the gospel and have almost no knowledge whatsoever. So, does that make them exempt from judgment?

Jesus said, *"I am the way, the truth, and the life...,"* therefore, "the knowledge of the truth" is referring to one who has an understanding of the relationship that Jesus died on the cross for us to obtain. It is acknowledging the Father-son relationship between us and our God, and the adoption that took place upon conversion from serving the world to serving your Father. Now, if that be true, there might be a case to be made for someone to say, "I didn't know, my church, my pastors misled me," but that argument would be settled by Paul in Romans 1:18-20...

> *The wrath of God is being revealed from heaven against all the godlessness and wickedness of men who suppress the truth by their*

> *wickedness. ****¹⁹For what may be known about God is plain to them, because God has made it plain to them.*** *²⁰For since the creation of the world God's invisible qualities, His eternal power and divine nature, have been clearly seen, being understood from His workmanship, **so that men are without excuse.**...* Romans 1:18-20

The ungodliness and unrighteousness of men is due to the fact that they are suppressing the truth, because of the wickedness in their heart. The word "truth" is Strong's #225, and the same word Paul used in Hebrews 10 when he says, "...*after we have received the knowledge of the truth*..." Paul goes on to conclude that men are without an excuse, because God's eternal power and nature is plain for all men to see.

Most Christians are literally playing Russian roulette with the world system and an enemy that wants nothing more than to kill them and take them to hell as food for a race of locusts. If you have not gotten it by now, if you have read this far and His Words (not mine) have not woken you up and convinced you to come out of the world and run into the loving arms of Jesus without looking back...then may I suggest you at least reason within your heart to **Knock** on the door of His Kingdom and request His Spirit of Truth reveal all Truth to you, **Ask** your Father to remove the spirit of error that may be blinding your eyes, and **Seek** His wisdom and counsel like your life depends upon it.

Because...what if you're wrong? What if you have been deceived, lured back into deliberate sin and OSAS really is a big fat lie? If the Spirit of Truth is the one who discerns spiritual things to us so we can understand them; what if you cannot see the danger you are in because God has removed His Holy Spirit from you, and *"practicing lawlessness"* (habitual sin) has blinded your heart by making you dead to sin again.

And what if, in the midst of life's trials and tribulations, you bought into the OSAS lie, thinking that your Father loves you just as you are, but He's just not happy with you? That He's OK with you ***deliberately sinning even after you received***

the knowledge of the truth, even though He's telling you otherwise all throughout his Word. It's all a lie; you have been lied to on every level, because even when you are at your most depraved, your Father sees you by the potential that is within you if you get filled with His Spirit. His heart goes out to you, loving you, prodding you, beckoning you back to Him, but the longer you are away, the quieter His voice sounds to you, until it's less than a whisper in a raging wind.

When Jesus said He would give us Zoe Life, he's talking about a rebirth of everything; all of our thoughts, our emotions, our feelings, our heart, our mind and our conscience. It's what makes us different than the zombies in the world who move about without the Spirit of God, without remorse, without empathy, without love for anyone that does not love them back. We're not called to be that way, because the same Spirit that raised Jesus from the dead is now in us, breathing Zoe life into us. We have been made alive with Zoe Life, so now we are free to love the unlovable, free to forgive the unforgiveable, free to hope and believe the best in all people.

This new Zoe Life is both amazing and sad at the same time, because your new spirit will bring to life feelings and emotions that have been dead for a long time. Your joys will be more joyful, but so will your trials be more heartbreaking, because you are alive with Zoe Life. That is what Jesus meant when He Said,

> *I have come that they may have life,* **and**
> **have it in all its fullness.** *John 10:10*

Becoming alive with Zoe Life means you are no longer the walking dead, every feeling and every emotion will be in all its fullness, because you are no longer dead...you are alive with Zoe Life. When people do something selfless for you, you will feel an overwhelming sense of joy for the love they displayed, but if a loved one disappoints you, it too will be magnified, it will cause you to hurt and morn like you've never known. You will experience life to its fullness, good and bad, happy and sad, but it's better than being dead inside and feeling numb. Besides, if you get the part about dying to yourself and loving people, they no longer offend you when they hurt you, because it's not about you any longer. Don't ever let what someone else does not perceive about who they are and what they were created for, be an excuse or reason to cause you to sin. Never let their lack of identity change, alter or affect the righteousness within you. Remember, they're just orphans who are groaning.

The only reason sin abounds to the degree with which it does is due to the absence of Gods Holy Spirit from people, Christians and non-Christians alike.

Atheism

There is an old saying, but it is absolutely correct; and it goes like this:

***It is easier to deceive a person, than to convince
them they've been deceived!***

What if God is God and you have simply fallen for a cunningly crafted lie of atheism? A lie which has not one shred of evidence to support it. There are literally thousands upon thousands of archeological findings to factually prove and support every Word in the Bible. There have been over 1000 very specific, detailed prophesies in the Bible come true; kingdoms, rulers, wars, times, dates and places; and all of them with amazing accuracy. Academia calls believing in God an act of faith, but the truth of the matter is, it requires waaaaaaay more faith to believe in evolution without one shred of factual evidence than it does to believe in the God of Abraham, Isaac and Jacob.

They are correct when the say "the theory of evolution," because evolution is only a theory, but evolution ought to be recategorized as a religion, because without blind, ignorant faith based upon no physical evidence, only a child is gullible enough to believe a lie that big. But Jesus said, *"Satan is a liar, and the father of all lies,"* "Just like it says in the communist manifesto: "Tell a lie, make it so big that nobody would dare to question it, tell it often enough and the sheeple will soon believe it."

The Bible boasts mountains of physical and archeological evidence proving every word is true, not to mention the 2500 manuscripts of the New Testament alone. People believe Plato and Socrates were actual living beings because of the 7 and 9 manuscripts they wrote, but even with 2500 exact copies of the New Testament, Jesus is sold to us as a myth by academia and the media. But don't be surprised, remember, Satan is the god of this world; he runs everything, media, news, academia, politics, sports, music and Hollywood. If it's on TV, if it's in pop culture, if it's trending on Google, YouTube, Instragram, or Twitter...it's a lie, and it's from you know who.

Here's a fabulous litmus test, whoever the mainstream media and pop culture is promoting, is likely your enemy, and whoever they are railing against may be trying to actually help you, but you'd never know it. They are masters at exulting the most depraved and vile people while vilifying anyone that opposes them. Whatever they are telling you is a lie and the opposite is likely true. Unfortunately, you will likely never see the actual truth until Truth hits your heart and the Holy Spirit reveals actual Truth to you. It's nothing more that the blind leading the blind, and the very reason we are instructed to die to our selfish desires obtained from Satan's sick and perverted world; a world designed to fill you with a heaping helping of his lusts, his thoughts, his mental disorders and his wickedness.

Receive the Holy Spirit

> *While Apollos was at Corinth, Paul passed through the interior and came to Ephesus. There he found some disciples* [2]*and asked them, "Did you receive the Holy Spirit when you became believers?" "No," they answered, "we have not even heard that there is a Holy Spirit."* [3]*"Into what, then, were you baptized?" Paul asked. "The baptism of John," they replied.* Acts 19:1-3

The Corinthians were believers; they were baptized into Jesus as the Christ but had not received the Holy Spirit, proving that the Holy Spirit is not automatically given to you upon believing. This is not the only such instance either; Peter and John also encountered believers in Christ without the Holy Spirit. Some may say, "I have the Holy Spirit because I speak in tongues," but that is not necessarily true. The Bible says,

> *All of them were filled with the Holy Spirit and began to speak in **other tongues** as the Spirit enabled them.* Acts 2:4

When the Bible talks about the disciples speaking in *"other tongues"* in Acts 2:4, it means they were speaking in a language other than their native tongue. The Holy Spirit gave them the supernatural ability to speak a language previously unknown to them. Babbling sounds is not necessarily speaking in tongues, any unbeliever off the street could do the same, and therefore babbling is not evidence of the Holy Spirit. Miracles, like speaking a different language instantaneously, make it easy to determine if someone has the Holy Spirit, but how can one be sure if they are being run by the Holy Spirit or a demon spirit apart from the miraculous? Our flesh, the human host body, is a virtual mask, hiding the identity of the spirit running the individual, so just how can you discern what kind of Spirit is behind the mask of everyone you meet, Christian or non-Christian?

> *By this all men will know that you are My disciples, **if you love one another.**"* John 13:15

Holy Spirit filled Christians should be easily recognizable from the world. The way they walk, the way they talk, the way they think and the way they act should be a consistent walk of love and righteousness. Holy Spirit filled Christians look, act and think... just like Jesus. Love, joy, peace, patience, kindness, goodness, faithfulness, gentleness, self-control, mercy and forgiveness are all virtues of a Spirit filled believer.

> *...Jesus went around doing good and healing all who were oppressed by the devil,* Acts 10:38

But you say, "How could anybody do what Jesus did, He's Jesus, of course He walked without sin...He's Jesus!" I know that sounds right and you'd likely get no argument from just about every preacher in the world regarding that statement, but God would not say, *"be holy as I am holy,"* if it were not possible for us to be Holy. Nor would He tell us to pluck out our eye if it was causing us to sin, if sin would not send us to hell.

> *If your right eye causes you to sin, gouge it out and throw it away. It is better for you to lose one part of your body than for your whole body to be thrown into hell.* Matthew 5:29

Now let's be logical for just one second; if sin would not cause us "*...to be thrown into hell,"* then why would Jesus even say this? Why wouldn't He just tell us to say a "sinner's' prayer?" I'm serious, stop for a second and think about it. If OSAS was true, Jesus would never have said this at all. He would have said, "If you eye causes you to sin, do not worry, just confess me as your Lord and all is well." But He didn't do that at all, did He? No, because sin is unacceptable to Him and the Father.

The reason Jesus could do the miracles He did is not because He was God walking in a man suit. Yes, Jesus is God, but He gave up His divinity when He came to earth and became a man. He could not have accomplished the goal of setting us free from the curse of sin, He could not have restored our Identity as Children of God, He could not have made it possible for us to die to ourselves, He could not have made righteousness available for us, He could not have gotten back our authority and He could not have gotten the Holy Spirit into us if He had done so as a God.

This is a very difficult concept to grasp, but it is vital if you want to walk in love and righteousness like you are commanded. There is no sacrifice if Jesus did what He did as a God. When one considers all the amazing miracles God did throughout the Old Testament, then Jesus walking without sin and enduring the cross is not all that remarkable if He did it as a God. People teach that, *"Jesus went around doing good and healing all who were oppressed by the devil,* but they leave off the first part which explains how He did it.

> ***God anointed Jesus of Nazareth with the Holy Spirit and with power,*** *and Jesus went around doing good and healing all who were oppressed by the devil,* ***because God was with Him.***
>
> Acts 10:38

What makes what Jesus did so amazing is that He did what He did as a man not as a God. Jesus became a man and walked out all 613 laws of Moses and all 10 Commandments without sin, but He didn't do it as God; He did it as a man walking in love and righteousness, filled with the Holy Spirit and Power from on High, and that, in a nutshell should be our goal and the purpose of this book. The fact that Jesus did not do any miracles until after He was filled with the Holy Spirit at 30 years old is further proof of that. The Pharisees hated Jesus because they said he was a man that made Himself God, but they had it backwards. Jesus was God (the Son), who made Himself man. Jesus' life was our example, an example of a man living a life of love and righteousness while being filled with the Spirit of God. Our goal should be to look like Jesus, talk like Jesus, think like Jesus, and be just like Jesus. A goal that is attainable if we truly love Him and follow His carefully detailed instructions of how things operate in the Kingdom of God by Asking, Seeking & Knocking.

> *...on earth as it is in heaven.* Matthew 6:10

There is not one recorded miracle before Jesus is baptized by John the Baptist in the Jordan River and the Spirit of God descended upon Him like a dove. If you are filled with the Holy Spirit and you meet another believer who is filled with the Holy Spirit, you will know it immediately. There is something special, something remarkable about them in every way. Call it kindred spirits, I don't know how else to explain it; you just know, that you know, that you know, and if you can't tell or if you're not sure, chances are...they're not. Not so for the OSAS and Prosperity Christians; that does not mean they don't believe in Jesus, I'm sure they do, they're just like the Corinthians and others in the New Testament who were baptized into the name of Jesus but never baptized with His Holy Spirit.

> *"...no one can enter the kingdom of God unless they are born of water and the Spirit."* John 3:5

Satan's greatest deception of the modern church is the OSAS and prosperity gospels; it's all about an altar call, a simple sinner's prayer, but they are never taught to die to self and seek righteousness. If people never die to themselves, or seek righteousness, there is no renewing of their mind, and the end result is no outward transformation. Without transformation, there can be no Holy Spirit, because you cannot put new wine in old wine skins.

There are "Full Gospel" churches that encourage people to pray for the Holy Spirit after they get them to say the coveted "sinner's prayer," but they largely drop the ball in regards to teaching any form of identity, and neither do they teach the importance of righteousness. For these unfortunate souls, it is a lesson in futility. Crafty too, because in not doing so, the slave is never set free and simply moves from being a slave to sin, (a slave to the world) to being a slave of a religious doctrine while continuing to wallow in willful sin excused by grace. This is the same spirit that kept the Jewish Rabbis in darkness when Jesus appeared. They were more concerned about their religious doctrine than the Truth, so when the Truth was made manifest, they couldn't see it.

> *Paul explained: "John's baptism was a baptism of repentance. He told the people to believe in the One coming after him, that is, in Jesus."* ⁵*On hearing this, they were baptized in the name of the Lord Jesus.* ⁶**And**

> **when Paul laid his hands on them, the Holy Spirit came upon them, and they spoke in tongues and prophesied.** Acts 19-4-6

The Holy Spirit is a piece of your Father, something He longs for you to have; it's something you desperately need to have if you plan on living an effective Christian life. The Holy Spirit is something Jesus died for you to have, but God, being a gentleman, never imposes Himself on us. You have to want the Holy Spirit bad enough to go after Him with all the gusto and fervor you can muster. Jesus told us to Ask, Seek, Knock; He paid the price and *"It is finished."* His job is complete, the ball is in your court now; it's your responsibility to pick it up and run with it, and you can either run towards Him or back to Him whichever the case may be.

> *"for everyone who asks, receives."* Matthew 7:8

What Are You asking for?

> *If you ask Me anything in My name, I will do it. ¹⁵If you love Me, you will keep My commandments. ¹⁶And* **I will ask the Father,** *and* **He will give you another Advocate** *to be with you forever.* John 14:14-16

This is just another one of those verses taken out of context and used by prosperity pimps for acquiring things of the world. Jesus is not telling them to ask for worldly things to satisfy their lustful desires, He is instructing them to ask for Godly things. Remember, there are only two kingdoms, the kingdom of the world, and the Kingdom of God. Your Father does not want you asking for the things of the world, things that satisfy the lust of the flesh, the lust of the eyes and the pride of life. He is opening the door and making available to you the wonderful things of His kingdom. Your Father, by way of the cross is allowing you to ask for anything in His Kingdom. Paul says it this way in Romans,

> *For the kingdom of God is not a matter of eating and drinking, but of righteousness, peace, and joy in the Holy Spirit.* Romans 14:17

Paul uses eating and drinking as a metaphor for the things of the world. God is not concerned if you have a beautiful new Mercedes Benz or a 20 year old junker, He's concerned about your attitude while you drive the car. Are you appreciative for the clunker? Are you haughty and high-minded while driving your Mercedes, looking down at others less fortunate? These are the things God is concerned about; He's looking at your heart and He also sees into the future, so He knows what you do and do not need, to help you along the path of righteousness.

Your Father sees the bigger picture, He sees past this life to our eternal life and His goal is to make you look as much like Jesus as He can in whatever time you have left. He's trying to get you ready for the rapture and an eternity in Heaven, because He knows what hell it will be like on earth when the Holy Spirit is removed, and the locusts are released; not to mention what hell it will be like in hell itself. When Jesus says, *"If you ask Me anything in My name, I will do it,"* He's talking about Kingdom minded things, things like righteousness, peace, joy, patience, virtue, honor, integrity, forgiveness and the ability to love everybody, not just those who love us back. He's talking about spiritual gifts like prophesy, healing, words of wisdom and knowledge.

If you read the scripture very carefully, and in context, it is quite revealing after all.

> *If you ask Me anything in My name, I will do it.* ¹⁵*If you love Me, you will keep My commandments.* ¹⁶*And* **I will ask the Father**, *and* **He will give you another Advocate** *to be with you forever.* John 14:14-16

Do you see it? It jumped of the page at me when He says, *"If you ask Me anything in My name, I will do it,"* then He says, ¹⁶*And* **I will ask the Father**, *and* **He will give you another Advocate** *to be with you forever.* Here's what I found interesting, both statements regarding asking and receiving are conditional. What do I mean by that? They're sandwiched between, ¹⁵*If you love Me, you will keep My commandments.* Coincidence? Not bloody likely! This amazing gift, this promise of the Holy Spirit is based upon you loving Him to such an extent that you willingly give up the world and all it offers, die to yourself, seek righteousness, follow Him and in doing so, keep His commandments. And this is where most Christians miss it, because they are unwilling to give up Satan's delicacies, and *"keep His Commandments,"* therefore they never receive what the Father is desperately trying to give them, His Holy Spirit and all the wonderful gifts that accompany Him.

The deception of the prosperity peddlers becomes obvious when you look at it through glasses of righteousness. They lust after the things of the world and it shows in their doctrine. They say, "Give us your money, and God will give you many worldly things," fulfilling the lustful desires of a heart that has no desire to keep the commandments of God and therefore no need for righteousness. But that is not the heart of the Father. Your Father does want to bless you abundantly, He does want to lavish gifts on His children, and He has given you permission to ask for things; just not the things of the world, the things that will steal your attention away from Him and draw you back into sin. He's trying to get us out of the world and the sin that so easily ensnares us, not give us a weekend pass to sin and a fist full of dollars to party in Vegas like its 1999.

Why in the world would Jesus encourage us to ask for worldly things, things that He died to deliver us from? It doesn't even make any sense when you consider it logically. The entire Prosperity doctrine falls flat on its face when you take into account everything He suffered to deliver us from, and look at it through His eyes, the eyes of righteousness.

Like almost everything the devil does, the OSAS and prosperity preachers take all their supporting scripture out of context in their attempt to separate you from your hard-earned money like a witch casting spells on the ignorant masses. Confirmation comes when Jesus says, *"If you love Me, you will keep My Commandments."*

Our Father does not want us asking for the things of the world; we are being instructed to ask for the things of God, things that are heavenly minded not earthly minded. Jesus is coaching us on the things that are important to the Father, the things He wants for us, and the things He wants us to want and seek.

> *The world is passing away along with its desires, but* **whoever does the will of God remains forever.** James 2:17

Who remains forever? Whoever **does** the will of God, and just exactly what is His will...His commandments! We need to come to terms with the fact that the world as we know it is nothing more than a temporary matrix that is coming to an end very quickly, but Gods Kingdom is eternal. People are seeking after and desiring things of the world, but all those things will perish, and much sooner than you think. They are selfish, lustful desires of worldly, demonically inspired things that have no eternal value whatsoever. Furthermore, the devil uses those things to draw you into sin and away from a relationship with your Father as well as the people He placed in your life, the people He gave you and entrusted to you to love unconditionally.

Our Father wants us to wake up, come out of this fake world matrix and into the light of His glorious everlasting Kingdom. He wants us Kingdom minded, not worldly minded. He wants us focused on Kingdom principles, Kingdom goals and Kingdom gifts like the gifts of the Spirit. He wants to give us the gift of the "Holy Spirit" so He can get us "the gifts of the Spirit," with the ultimate goal of molding us into the image of Jesus. All He really wants from us, is for us to want His gifts as much as He wants to give them to us, so He's telling us to Ask, Seek and Knock for them.

Consider for a moment, what the Holy Spirit did for the disciples in the upper room when He fell on them all. They were instantly changed; like a caterpillar being transformed into a butterfly. Before the Holy Spirit, they had all kinds of issues; they were lazy, weak, lacked faith, high minded, quarrelsome, selfish and disloyal, but after the Holy Spirit they were the embodiment of Jesus. Your Father wants to give you the same gift that so completely transformed the apostles into the likeness of Jesus, and all you have to do is knock on the door of the Kingdom of God, seek His righteousness and ask to be filled with His Spirit.

Seeking His Kingdom and His righteousness shows Him you are serious, that you mean business; it is proof to the Father that you can be entrusted to house something as awesome, as powerful, as immense as the Holy Spirit. Let's not forget what His Holy Spirit is capable of; it was the Holy Spirit that empowered David to kill a lion and a bear with his bare hands, not to mention a giant with a slingshot. It was the Holy Spirit that empowered Sampson to defeat 1000 Philistines with the jawbone of an ass, and it was the Holy Spirit that gave Joshua the strength of a young man at the age of 80 to finally take the Promised Land in battle. It was the Holy Spirit given to random individuals all through the Old Testament so they could do mighty works on Gods behalf and because of what Jesus did on the cross, He is offering that same Holy Spirit to everyone who Asks, Seeks and Knocks.

The things of the world, however, will take our focus, our attention and eventually our loyalty away from our Father and His Kingdom. Satan will use the cares of the world, the deceitfulness or riches and the desire for other things to obscure and distract us from our Fathers wants and desires for us. God's not about to give you excessive amounts of money and worldly things when He considers everything it took, everything He had to do to get your attention and out of the world in the first place. Many of the things we consider a blessing from God are just the opposite.

> For ***the love of money*** *is the root of all kinds of evil.* ***By craving it, some have wandered away from the faith*** *and pierced themselves with many sorrows.* 1 Timothy 6:10

Once again, we have a verse here that everyone is familiar with, but I'll bet you did not know it was written by Paul as a warning to believers about believers that had wandered away from the faith because they craved money. That's right; Paul was dealing with the prosperity lie 2000 years ago. As I told you before, all the same spirits are still roaming the earth doing what they do best; lying, cheating, stealing, killing and destroying. Money itself is not evil, but the love of it is, and for anyone who has not learned to die to themselves and seek righteousness, money will pierce them with many sorrows. Money causes roots to grow in your heart like a tree, and as the tree grows it produces fruit, but the fruit a money tree produces is greed for even more money, lust for even more pleasures it can buy and a desire for bigger and better toys. It sure gives new meaning to the phrase, "money tree."

How many marriages are ended because of money, how many partnerships, friendships and even family members are estranged due to money? Satan will use whatever it takes to keep you away from righteousness, especially money. He knows how powerful you would be if you ever began seeking after and walking in righteousness, but that is nothing compared to the awesome power available to and through a righteous believer filled with Gods Holy Spirit.

Therefore, Satan's most aggressive attack is against people who make the decision to knock on the Kingdom door and seek righteousness, because he knows if he can derail you there with religion, prosperity or hyper-grace, you will never get to the place where you are filled with the Holy Spirit. Satan uses lust through illicit sex, he will challenge your identity through worldly relationships, and he will even use money if he thinks you have a propensity for desiring it. He will go after you from a thousand different angles until he finds your weakness and once he sees where you are vulnerable, he throws everything he has at you.

That is why dying to yourself is so important. Dying to yourself takes all Satan's hooks away. If you have a stronghold Satan can use against you, it's because it is an area that you have not died to, however if you have settled within your heart to die to yourself as well as everything the world has to offer, then there is nothing that Satan can use to lure you away with. If you want to call yourself a Christian, if you want to be able to say honestly, "I am a believer of Jesus Christ, I am a Christian," you must die to yourself first. Jesus does not even consider you a disciple unless you make the decision to die to yourself in order to follow Him. As I said earlier, Jesus did not say, "Go into all the world and make converts," He said, *"Go into all the world and make disciples."* Therefore, if you want to be on team Jesus, you have to reason within your heart that you must become a disciple, and in order to do that, you must die to yourself. Nothing less will do; you cannot hold onto anything in this world and make it to the next, it is that simple. I truly believe this book is for the sole purpose of getting Christians saved.

> *"If anyone would come after Me, he must deny himself and take up his cross and follow Me. Matthew 16:24*

A new job, with a huge pay raise seems like a blessing from God, but if it works you for such long hours that you no longer spend time in fellowship with the Lord, if it fractures your relationship with your spouse and your children, if it places you in compromising positions with shady individuals, it's not from God. God is not giving you anything that takes you away from Him, because He knows what's at stake. Everything you love and cherish, everything that is important in your life, hangs in the balance, even your very soul.

This is why it is so important to get born again after we knock on the Kingdom door and seek righteousness. Walking in unconditional love and obtaining righteousness is paramount but it is also an **impossible** task to accomplish in your own human strength, and God proved just that when He gave us the 10 commandments. 10 simple rules: don't lie, don't cheat, don't steal, don't murder…, and it seems simple enough, but not one person in the history of the world was able to pull it off, but Jesus. That alone, proved to us that we not only needed a savior, but we also must have the Holy Spirit living inside us to empower us to walk in love and righteousness or else we will fail, just as the apostles failed before the cross.

This is exactly what Paul was alluding to in Romans 7 when he was talking about wanting to do good, but sin ultimately reigned supreme. Without Jesus we are unable to be filled with Gods Holy Spirit, and without Holy Spirit, we are incapable of walking in righteousness as proven by the 10 commandments. If we seek righteousness and ask for the Holy Spirit, it is a sign that we have come to a place of maturity where we want, we need, we desire more important things than the things of the world, and we want the things of God.

> *So you also must consider yourselves **dead to sin** and alive to God in Christ Jesus.* Romans 6:11

The following verse really needs no explaining, but it's one of those that most people read over just as fast as they can. They never give it a second thought, or they are avoiding it on purpose, nevertheless, it is-what it is. I recommend that you not just read it, but read it and reread it and reread it one hundred times if that's what it takes for you to understand what Paul is saying.

> ***Let not*** *sin therefore reign in your mortal body, to make you obey its passions.* ¹³ ***Do not*** *present your members to sin as instruments for unrighteousness, but present yourselves to God as those who have been brought from death to life, and your members to God as instruments for righteousness.* ¹⁴ *for **sin shall no longer be your master**, since you are not under law but under grace.* Romans 6:12-14

Surely by now you are beginning to see it come together. Paul is telling us how sin will no longer have dominion over us; sin can't control you now, or force you to do anything against your will if you move from trying to obey the 10 commandments in your own strength and are filled with the Holy Spirit, the Spirit of Grace & Truth which will supernaturally empower you to die to yourself and live in righteousness. Your righteousness obedience moves you out from under the law and under grace.

If, however, you are constantly being lured back into sin, it will be your master, and then you are in bondage to the flesh. Such a one is not walking in the spirit and therefore, they are still under the law. Condemnation comes flooding in by way of sin leading to death, but Gods Holy Spirit sets us free from the law of sin and death.

> *Therefore, there is now no condemnation for those who are in Christ Jesus. ²For in Christ Jesus **the law of the Spirit of life has set you free from the law of sin and death.** Romans 8:1-2*

When people first knock on the door of the Kingdom of God and He reveals the truth in and to their heart, God uses the law to reveal your sinful state, but this is not where your Father wants you to stay. He does not want you sin conscious, He wants you Son conscious, but most Christians never get to this place, because of their lack of identity. It is a place where righteousness abounds and the law was nothing more than a tool that sets us on the narrow path of righteousness by way of the Holy Spirit.

> *For what the Law was powerless to do in that it was weakened by the flesh, God did by sending His own Son in the likeness of sinful man, as an offering for sin. Thus He condemned sin in the flesh. Romans 8:3*

If you stay focused on the law after you receive the knowledge of the truth, you will remain sin conscious which leads to condemnation and a constant cycle of sin and repentance. Christians who seek blessings and prosperity in place of righteousness and the Holy Spirit remain sin conscious because they set their minds on the "things of the flesh." They continue to "walk in the flesh" daily, satisfying the "lusts of the flesh," just as they did when they were unsaved.

Many who fall victim to the OSAS lie, even go all the way back to their pre-enlightenment state of sin, and some go even farther. The biggest problem for people such as these is finding their way home again, most never make it and suffer with the fate of the world. A spirit of stupor establishes a great delusion to cloud their eyes and harden their heart, as in the case of King Saul when he wanted to kill David. An evil Spirit will be allowed to enter them and hinder their ability to see their own demise. To reverse course now would be to admit they were wrong; that they made a mistake and those prideful demonic spirits that now rule them will resist any attempt of that person to repent. It's a heart wrenching but all too common scenario as these once enlightened brothers and sisters in Christ, who still consider themselves Christians, will be used as instruments of unrighteousness.

Seeking righteousness and the Holy Spirit takes your focus off you and the law and puts it squarely on Jesus thus becoming Son conscious, whereby, He condemns sin in your flesh, so you literally become righteous as He is righteous.

> *Those who live according to the flesh set their minds on the things of the flesh; but those who live according to the Spirit set their minds on the things of the Spirit.* Romans 8:5

It is critical that we become Son conscious, because whatever you set your mind upon is that which you will serve. If you set your mind on prosperity and worldly things, the things of the flesh, you will serve them and live accordingly. However, becoming Son conscious is to set your mind upon Jesus (the things of the Spirit) and you will live according to the Spirit. That is, you will be infused with power from on High to live righteously; a life full of miracle power and authority over all the power of the enemy.

> *The mind of the flesh is death, but the mind of the Spirit is life and peace,* Romans 8:6

Son consciousness brings life and peace, but sin consciousness brings forth death. Whether you are a new believer or a long-time Christian, when you seek the things of the world as opposed to righteousness and the Holy Spirit you are setting your mind on fleshly, worldly desires and your mind will actually become hostile towards God. It will allow bitterness towards God when things don't go the way you prayed, it will allow you to become offended with God or people when you fall into trials and tribulations and it will allow you to grow angry at

God and imperfect people when life's disappointments occur and reoccur with an ever increasing frequency due to a selfish desire for the things of the world.

> *...because the mind of the flesh is hostile to God: It does not submit to God's law...* Romans 8:7

We are required to submit to God's law, but that is impossible unless we first die to our worldly desires, because motive is everything in the Kingdom of God. Selfishness breeds sin which give birth to death, but righteousness brings peace which produces life. Selfishness is the broad path that leads to death, but righteousness is the narrow path unto life.

> *But if Christ is in you, the body is indeed dead on account of sin, but the Spirit is life on account of righteousness.* Romans 8:10

If Christ is in you, you are dead to sin, therefore if you are not yet dead to sin, if you are in willful, deliberate sin, Christ is **not** in you, and you are only deceiving yourself if you think otherwise. As long as Satan is allowed to remain the god of this world, sin will rein and a slow decay until death for all things is inevitable. If, however, Christ Jesus has made His home in you, if you have made Him Lord over your life by desiring to keep His commandments, if you get to know Him through time in prayer and reading His Word, He will come to know you; then righteousness gives life to your Spirit and it quickens your mortal body.

> *Therefore, brothers, we have an obligation, but it is not to the flesh, to live according to it.* Romans 8:12

Just as a good soldier is obligated to his king, we are obligated to our King. We are either loyal to our flesh or we are loyal to our Father, and Paul equates our loyalty with our willingness to resist the sinful pleasures of the flesh. But why, what has one thing to do with the other?

> *For if you live according to the flesh, you will die; but if by the*
> *Spirit you put to death the deeds of the body, you will live.*
> Romans 8:13

Paul already addressed how our bodies must die to sin, so the use of the word "die" here is spiritual death. We cannot go around willy-nilly, living according to our flesh and expecting a false grace god to give us a free pass to sin. If you are ruled by the sinful pleasures of your flesh it will have eternal consequences. Romans 8 absolutely destroys the OSAS lie; a summary of it is as follows, but let's first remember that Paul was talking to Jews who had been converted to Christianity and eventually went back to Judaism. So, we see here that 2 Laws exist:

> **...*the law of the Spirit of life has set you free***
> ***from the law of sin and death.*** Romans 8:1-2

Law of the Spirit vs. Law of Sin

1. The law of the Spirit that leads to eternal life (AKA spiritual life) and the law of sin which leads to eternal death (AKA spiritual death).

2. If you seek righteousness, Jesus will set you free from the law of sin and death, but if you seek your own made-up god that excuses sin because of a one-time prayer or the god of blessings and prosperity, the law of sin becomes your ruler.

3. By seeking righteousness, you set your mind on the things of the Spirit of God, but if selfishness rules you and becomes your god or if you seek the god of blessings and prosperity, you will set your mind on the things of the flesh.

4. If you set your mind on the things of the Spirit you will live according to the Spirit (righteously), however if you set your mind on the things of the flesh, you will live according to the flesh (selfishly).

5. If you set your mind on the things of the Spirit to live a life of righteousness according to the Spirit, your reward will be eternal life and peace, however if you set your mind on the things of the flesh, to live a life of selfishness according to the flesh your reward will be spiritual death.

This is confirmed in Galatians which also exposes the lie of the OSAS and prosperity gospel preachers.

> *So I say, walk by the Spirit, and you will not gratify the desires of the flesh. For the flesh craves what is contrary to the Spirit, and the Spirit what is contrary to the flesh. They are opposed to each other, so that you do not do what you want. But **if you are led by the Spirit, you are not under the law.*** Galatians 5:18

At the risk of being redundant, I'm going to go through this verse several times from different angles, because this is vitally important, but it's also extremely complex. Please listen carefully to what Paul is saying: If you are filled with the Holy Spirit, the Spirit of Grace and Truth, you won't gratify the flesh through sinful behavior. He is not saying it's ok to sin, he's saying you won't want to sin if you are filled with Grace and Truth. He goes on to say, "however, if you are in willful, deliberate sin, you are fulfilling the lusts of the flesh, therefore a man engaging in premeditated sin is obviously not being led by the Holy Spirit, and if you are not being led by the Holy Spirit, there is only one other spirit which can lead you ... the spirit of the world, AKA a demonic spirit. It's an either / or, you are either led by the Spirit of God or the spirit of Satan, and the proof of your leader is willful, premeditated, deliberate, habitual sin. He is not talking about getting frustrated and loosing you cool with someone in a stressful situation; that is not willful, habitual nor premeditated, so don't freak out.

Paul then says, "If you are filled with and walk in the Holy Spirit, you are being led by the Spirit of Grace," and the evidence, the proof that a person is being led by Grace is the fact they will not engage in premeditated sin. But doesn't that also imply that if you are engaging in deliberate sin, you are not being led by the Holy Spirit? Instead, you are walking in the flesh, being filled with and ruled by the spirit of the world.

That is exactly what Jesus was addressing when He said, *"If you love me, you will keep my commandments."* People can say anything they want, but the proof is in the pudding. As my earthly father used to say, "don't talk about it, do it."

Christians have all these deep philosophical discussions about how difficult it will be to determine who is saved and not, and only God in His infinite wisdom can do it. And while that part is true, the actual determination will be much easier that we think; "did you, or did you not even try to keep my commandments?" Keep in mind, God knows our weakness; you are not able, nor does he expected you to walk in righteousness and keep His commandments without being empowered by the Holy Spirit, and Jesus told us exactly how to go about getting Him when He said to Ask, Seek, Knock.

So fearful of the power of the Holy Spirit within us was Satan that he inspired whole denominations to teach doctrine that believes the Holy Spirit is not available to us today, that Jesus was somehow lying when He said He would go, but that He would send us "the Helper" (Holy Spirit) in His absence. I don't understand that doctrine, did the Holy Spirit just vanish when the last apostle died? Is that written anywhere in the New Testament and confirmed in the Old Testament? No, it is not, it is a doctrine of demons meant to keep Christians powerless, ineffectual and in a constant cycle of sin, condemnation and repentance. The validity of their doctrine is further dismantled when you consider that the apostles prayed for the Holy Spirit to fill **everyone** they ministered to. As well, Jesus said, *"...how much more will your Father in heaven* **give the Holy Spirit** *to* **those who ask Him**?"

One day I read Galatians 5:18 and I heard the Lord tell me to reverse engineer it. At first, I was not sure what He was saying, I understand what it means to reverse engineer something, but how do you reverse engineer scripture? Apparently, you take the meaning and consider not just what it **is** saying, but what it **is not** saying as well. For instance, if you told your child you would take him for ice cream, but only if he cleaned his room. That would also imply that if he did not clean his room, he would not get ice cream, but there is no need to actually say that, because it is implied and clearly understood.

Ok, stay with me here, because this gets really good. Paul says, *"If you walk in the Spirit, you will not gratify the desires of the flesh,"* simple enough, so if I reverse engineer it, it also implies that if I am gratifying the desires of my flesh through willful sin, I am obviously not walking in the Spirit, right? Paul goes on to say, "But **if you are led by the Spirit, you are not under the law,**" but that also means, if I am gratifying the desires of my flesh, I am most certainly not being led by the Spirit of God and therefore I am walking in the flesh, so if I am walking in the flesh...**I am under the law.** This totally destroys the OSAS, because...

> *...no one will be justified in His sight by works of the Law.* Romans 3:20

So, let us review, because this is huge! Paul is saying, "If you are knowingly, willfully fulfilling the lusts of the flesh, you are not being led by the Holy Spirit and if you are not led by the Holy Spirit, you most certainly are under the law and not grace any longer." And, if no man is justified by the Law, where does that leave you? This also makes so much more sense when you consider the actual purpose of Grace as defined in Titus.

> *...**grace instructs us** to renounce ungodliness and worldly passions, and to live sensible, upright, and godly... Titus 2:12*

If you recall, Jesus already told us that He was sending the Holy Spirit to teach us all things, therefore the Spirit of Grace is not a covering or an umbrella to sin, He is our instructor, and His number one purpose is to teach us to **renounce** ungodliness. Ungodliness, by the way is the opposite of righteousness, so if you reverse engineered that, it would read, "Grace instructs us in righteousness."

> *But the Helper, the Holy Spirit, whom the Father will send in My name,* ***He will teach you all things****...*John 14:26

It is the Spirit of Grace that supernaturally teaches us how to walk in righteousness and renounce wickedness. This is why the devil rails against the Holy Spirit so hard; he knows that if you ever get filled with the Spirit of Grace, he's done for. A seed of righteousness will die in you and it will produce even more Spirit filled believers who also seek righteousness instead of the selfish desires of the world. In Titus 2:12, Paul expounds upon what Jesus meant when He said, *"The Holy Spirit will teach you all things."*

Therefore, the Holy Spirit, sent by the Father was commissioned to teach us,
1. To renounce ungodliness = Righteousness
2. To renounce worldly passions = Righteousness
3. To live sensible, upright, and Godly = Righteousness, Righteousness, and more Righteousness.

Like I've been saying all along, the purpose of Grace, was never to cover or excuse our sin, it is and always has been for the sole purpose of teaching us to renounce sin and walk in righteousness. There is not one verse, not one single example in the Bible that defines Grace as a free pass or excuse to sin, but our Father never expected us to walk in righteousness in our own power or ability. God is good and He understands we are here with a monster, so He is giving us the ability to do what no man besides Jesus has been able to do since the beginning of the world. He has empowered us to walk in righteousness by His Holy Spirit, but the Holy Spirit can only be found if we Ask, Seek and Knock.

Another Advocate

*...**He will give you another Advocate** to be with you forever.* John 14:14-16

So, who is this other advocate the Father will give us when we Knock on the door of His Kingdom, get born again, die to ourselves, seek righteousness and ask for the Holy Spirit?

*...**the Spirit of Truth.** The world cannot receive Him (Truth), because it neither sees Him nor knows Him. But you do know Him, for He abides with you **and will be in you.*** John 14:17-18

The reason people fall for the OSAS or the prosperity lie, the reason people believe in evolution, or Buddhism, the reason they fall for the lie of New Age, or reincarnation or whatever futile god they have concocted in their mind is because they do not have the Spirit of Truth. For that matter, the only reason that once faithful believers have fallen back to their worldly ways is an absence of the Spirit of Grace. It is the Spirit of Truth that reveals the truth about Jesus, so without Truth, there's no way for unbelievers to know unless they Knock on the Kingdom door. The only thing that God requires from us is to simply Knock, Seek and Ask, because he who asks, receives.

When you knock on the Kingdom door, become a disciple of Jesus, when you seek righteousness and ask to be filled with Gods Holy Spirit, the Spirit of Grace & Truth will come and abide with you and in you, teaching you, convicting you, correcting you and training you in this new man you have become, a man of righteousness.

So many things changed right after the cross, but one thing is for certain, it was finished, the hard part was over, now Jesus simply needs to gather the disciples together and complete the process of their transformation into His image, but to do that He needs to address one last obstacle.

> *"And now I will send the Holy Spirit, just as my Father promised. But stay here in the city **until the Holy Spirit comes and fills you with power** from heaven."*
> Luke 24:49

It has always been assumed that Jesus was talking about the power to cast out demons and to heal the sick, but what if He had already given that power to the disciples before the cross?

> *Then Jesus called the Twelve together and gave them power and authority over all demons, and power to cure diseases.* Luke 9:1

While Jesus had given the disciples power to cast out demons and heal the sick before the cross, He did not give them the Spirit of Grace & Truth at that time. Jesus would give them more of the Holy Spirit after His resurrection on two separate occasions. Outward proof of this fact is the way the disciples all fled Jesus out of fear in the garden and denied of Him at His trial.

> *God anointed Jesus of Nazareth with the Holy Spirit and **Power**...* Acts 10:38

The Holy Spirit and Power was given to Jesus at the time of His baptism, but it was not that way for the disciples. Notice that Power is listed as a separate anointing from the Holy Spirit. The disciples were given Power in Luke 9:1, but no Holy Spirit, but why, why didn't Jesus just pour out the full measure of the Holy Spirit upon them when they made the decision to follow Him?

The entire time the disciples were with Jesus they acted just like all the other people of the world with no understanding. They were still carnally minded, they rarely, if ever understood what Jesus was teaching unless He took them aside and explained it to them personally, and even then, they still didn't get the true revelation until the Spirit of Truth revealed it to them after the cross.

> *...the Holy Spirit, ...**will teach you all things** and remind you of everything I have told you.* John 14:26

Up until the Holy Spirit was poured out on the disciples in the Book of Acts, they behaved like prepubescent children and looked then, like most Christians look today. They argued amongst one another about foolish things, Jesus was constantly chastising them for their lack of faith, and at the first sign of trouble, they all fled like cockroaches when the light is turned on.

> *And no one pours new wine into old wineskins. If he does, the wine will burst the skins, and both the wine and the wineskins will be ruined. Instead, new wine is poured into new wineskins."* Mark 2:22

Because Jesus was not yet crucified, the Holy Spirit could not fit in the disciples without destroying them. There must have been something about them, (when I say them I mean all humans) that prevented the Holy Spirit from dwelling within us prior to the cross, something that would have harmed them, otherwise Jesus would not have said, *"the wineskins would be ruined."* We are the wineskins, and something Jesus did on the cross and thereafter enabled us, empowered us, changed us so we could receive the full measure of the Holy Spirit. Jesus used another example to describe this as well.

> *No one sews a patch of unshrunk cloth on an old garment. If he does, the new piece will pull away from the old, and a worse tear will result.* Mark 2:21

Both the new wine and the new patch represent the Holy Spirit, but there must be some reason that both of these metaphors have the original (old) garment or wineskin ruined by the new wine or new patch. This Holy Spirit patch not only covers us, but it fills a void within all of us; a desperate loneliness that can only

He can fill. Without the Holy Spirit, people will try to fill their void with all kinds of worldly things like, money, possessions, toys, sex, drugs, careers, movies, music, hobbies, education and pretty much anything that can and will give their soul only temporary satisfaction, but nothing can complete in us what only the Holy Spirit patch was designed to do.

I personally think the analogy to wine and wineskins is very interesting as well. If we are the wineskins, then the Holy Spirit is the wine. It is obvious that Jesus drank wine, but there is no account of Him being drunk. They accused Him of being a wine bibber, so they obviously saw Him drinking it and He does not deny it. It's important to note that clean water is vital to live, but it was not as plentiful to them as it is for us. Alcohol is distilled making it 100% pure, and clean drinking water was probably difficult to come by for them. That is why Paul tells Timothy to drink the wine instead of the water when Timothy was likely suffering with digestive issues due to the impurity of the water.

Drinking wine as in all alcohol does not automatically make someone drunk, there are different stages and a level of the influence that alcohol has over people. I can say from experience that being filled with the Holy Spirit is a similar feeling to the very first stages of the influence of alcohol. It's like the feeling one might sense after only one glass of wine. When you are filled with the Holy Spirit, your whole body tingles, there is unspeakable joy, a heightened sense of your surroundings, a feeling of amazing ability that is difficult to explain, pure humility and a general sense of euphoria. If only people could experience it one time, they'd likely abandon all their futile, worldly quests and seek that which they were created to have; a relationship with their Father, and His Holy Spirit by way of Jesus.

So, just what was it that Jesus needed to accomplish or what was it about us that had to change in order for the full measure of the Holy Spirit to dwell within us?

Perfect Love

There is no fear in love, but perfect love drives out fear, because fear involves punishment. The one who fears has not been perfected in love.
1 John 4:18

After the cross, the disciples were in hiding, for fear of the Jews that had killed Jesus. Jesus appears to them and breathes on them a portion of the Holy Spirit. But it still was not the full measure of the Spirit that would come in the upper room after His ascension to heaven. It must have been necessary and important, because Jesus never did anything without a reason or benefit towards us.

Have you ever wondered why the disciples were not waiting at the tomb on the 3rd day? He told them over and over that He would be crucified and raised again. Why weren't they there waiting for him to come out? Mary was there, so she must have remembered, but not His disciples, so what prevented them from wanting to see if He would rise from the dead just like He said?

Wouldn't you be curious? I know I would, and it's not like He didn't have the credibility. Think about it, how many miracles had he performed, how many prophesies had He fulfilled, how many times had He made known even their own thoughts? He was credible, very credible, so why didn't any of them go to the tomb to see if He would do what He said He would do...raise from the dead? All the accounts are slightly different, because they're each telling it from a different point of view, but if stitched together, they seem to tell the whole story.

In the Gospel of Mark, it says, *"Mary Magdalene, Mary the mother of James, and Salome bought spices so they could go and anoint the body of Jesus."* They encounter an angel who tells them Jesus has risen, and more specifically to go tell the disciples **and Peter** who must have been in major condemnation because of his betrayal.

Referring to Mary, John's gospel says, *"She came running to Peter and the other disciple, the one whom Jesus loved."* You've got to love that about John, he always knew how much Jesus loved him. Peter and John ran to the tomb, John is faster than Peter, so he gets there first, but he's afraid and doesn't go in, choosing rather to look inside only. Peter, with all his boldness goes right in and sees that Jesus is missing. John finally gets up the courage to go in and he sees as well. Then the Bible says, *"Both of them believed," "but they still did not understand Jesus had been raised from the dead."*

After they leave, Mary is still standing there weeping when she bends down to look inside and sees two angels sitting there. Then she turns around and Jesus calls her name. Mary goes to hug Him, but He tells her not to touch Him because He has not gone to the Father yet. Mary is the very first person to see Jesus resurrected.

> *"Do not cling to Me," Jesus said, "for I have not yet ascended to the Father. But go and tell My brothers...* John 20:17

Matthew 28:8 seems to contradict John's account, but not if you look at it closely. While at the tomb, Mary sees Jesus and He tells her not to cling to Him, but go tell the others. Remember, Jesus traveled with more than just the 12 disciples, the Bible says He had about 70 people with Him most of the time. Mary leaves and does what she is told, but she has only her feet for transportation so it could have been hours before she got to her destination. In the spiritual realm, it would have been more than enough time for Jesus to present His blood to the Father and return.

> *...So they hurried away from the tomb in fear and great joy, and ran to tell His disciples. ⁹Suddenly Jesus met them and said, "Greetings!" They came to Him, grasped His feet, and worshiped Him.* Matthew 28:8-9

Here, they grabbed the feet of Jesus proving it happens after the first encounter where she was forbidden to even touch Him. Just as the Jewish high priest brought the blood of spotless animals into the Holy of Holies, and sprinkled it on the altar for the remission of sins, so Christ had to offer His blood in heaven, at the mercy seat before the Father as the final sacrifice and offering for all sins. Therefore, in Mary's first encounter, there must have been some kind of defilement that would have occurred if Mary had touched Jesus, but now they are free to worship Him.

Jesus presented Himself to Mary first because she went there looking for Him; as it written, *"Seek and you will find."* She likely remembered Him saying He would rise on the 3rd day; maybe she didn't really expect it to actually happen, but there must have been a smidgen of hope, so she went. When she tells Peter and John, they see the tomb is empty, but they did not actually see Jesus. The women then go and tell the rest of the disciples, but they do not believe it is true, so Jesus presents Himself to them all at the house they are staying in.

> *Jesus came and stood among them... As the Father has sent Me, so also I am sending you."* ^{22}*When He had said this,* **He breathed on them and said, "Receive the Holy Spirit.** ^{23}*If you forgive anyone his sins, they are forgiven; if you withhold forgiveness from anyone, it is withheld."...* John 20:21-23

So why didn't any of them go to the tomb to see if Jesus would do what He said He would do...rise from the dead? Weren't they the least bit curious? You'd think that they would have been camping out there from day one.

> *When the disciples were together* **with the doors locked** *for* **fear of the Jews,** *Jesus came and stood among them...* John 20:21

The reason they were not there like Mary, is fear! The disciples were terrified that the Jews were going to kill them in the same manor they killed Jesus, but for some reason Mary wasn't afraid. The disciples were hiding out in a room with the doors locked trembling with fear while Mary was at the tomb. History shows that the Romans didn't crucify women or children unless they were traitors or rebellious slaves, but I have a feeling that Mary just didn't care anyway. For whatever reason, Mary didn't allow fear to prevent her from going to the tomb, unlike the disciples.

Jesus had to know that the disciples were afraid of the Jews who crucified Him. They just witnessed Him endure the most horrific torture and murder the world has ever known, so they were probably thinking they were next. The Romans made execution public for the sole purpose of putting fear into the masses of people so they would not want to rebel, making them easier to rule. Understand, this was not the typical crucifixion, what they did to Jesus was beyond anything known to man, so Jesus had to remove all fear and any doubts they might have about preaching the good news, and He does it by breathing on them "Perfect Love," the Spirit of Love.

> *There is no fear in love, but* **perfect love drives out fear,** *because fear involves torment. <u>The one who fears has not been perfected in love.</u>* 1 John 4:18

This portion of the Holy Spirit that Jesus breathes on the disciples solves a multitude of issues within them as well as providing many benefits for them. The first thing the disciples receive is the Spirit of Adoption which reveals their identity as Children of God. This is their "born again" experience, something impossible before the cross. For the first time they fully understand who they are, and what they were created for.

Next, His Holy Spirit drives out the spirit of fear and selfishness by filling them with Agape love and righteousness. By pouring out His love on the disciples they literally became the righteousness of God the Father in Christ Jesus. Fear is present in an absence of love and selfishness is present where there is an absence of righteousness which is why Jesus stressed the importance of loving everybody and seeking righteousness as soon as the Kingdom door is opened to you. Fear and selfishness work in conjunction with one another resulting in the bondage of self-preservation, holding us in a prison of hopelessness. However, Jesus breathes on them the Holy Spirit, adopting them as children, so perfect love and righteousness can supplant fear and selfishness, setting them free from the yoke of sin and death. This is what the modern church has been missing; this is why Christians keep falling into a never-ending cycle of sin, condemnation, and repentance.

> *For God has not given us a spirit of fear, but of power and of love and of a sound mind.* 2 Timothy 1:7

If I've said it once, I've said it a thousand times, "the opposite of love is not hate it is selfishness." The love I am referring to here is the "perfect love" of the Holy Spirit. Perfect love is the God kind of love; it is a selfless love that prefers the needs of others above its own needs. Perfect love is a mature love and can only happen when we make the decision to die to self. It is a love that sees through a person's fault so you can properly minister to their need. Perfect love doesn't run out on someone when they mess-up or make a mistake; it loves them through it, because it sees people the way God sees them, the way they would be if perfect love was in them and the only desire of perfect love is for that person to see themselves the same way Jesus sees them also. However, fear and selfishness combine to produce an attitude of self-preservation making everything all about them, but when Jesus breathed the Holy Spirit upon the disciples, He perfected their love so they could walk without fear.

> *And they have overcome him by the blood of the Lamb, and the word of their testimony; and* **they <u>loved not</u> their own life unto death.** Rev. 12:11

When the "perfect love" of the Holy Spirit gets in you, all manner of self-preservation goes out the door, and you no longer care what someone says, thinks or does to you if you are about your Father's business. Any fear in evangelizing, praying for, or healing people in public is a lack of "Perfect Love." If you are self-conscious about praying for a random stranger in a wheelchair when the Holy Spirit prompts you, you are in self-preservation mode and loving your own life, and your own reputation; you have selfishly made it about you. I say this not to heap condemnation upon you, but to encourage you to ask your Father to send you "Perfect Love," driving out all fear. These are the things Jesus is telling us to ask for when he says, Ask, Seek, and Knock. Not things of the world, things like jobs, houses, cars, women (men) or money; Jesus has authorized us to ask for the things of God, things like "Perfect Love." He said, *"Ask and it shall be given."*

The disciples were in hiding because fear and selfishness kept them focused on preserving their own lives, but Jesus didn't call us to preserve our lives, He is asking us to give our life to Him just as He gave His life for us.

> *When He had said this, **He breathed on them** and said, "Receive the Holy Spirit."* John 20:22

Breathed – Strong's # 1720 - Emphusaó (em-foo-sah'-o). Definition: to breathe into or upon.

This incident where Jesus breathes on the disciples the Holy Spirit is strikingly similar to the event surrounding God's creation of Adam in the book of Genesis.

> *And the LORD God formed man of the dust of the ground, and **breathed into his nostrils the breath of life**; and man became a living soul.* Genesis 2:7

God breathed His Spirit into Adam thereby giving him eternal life. At that moment, Adam was created a son, filled with love, righteousness and Gods Holy Spirit. Later, God anoints Adam as king and ruler of the earth when He confers dominion to him. There is likely no mention of Adam having power to perform miracles because it wasn't necessary before sin entered the world. If everything is perfect, where's the need for a miracle. Miracles are only necessary in a fallen world. When Jesus breathed the Holy Spirit on the disciples, He is partially restoring them back to the place Adam was before the fall. I say partially, because there would be more Holy Spirit to come in the upper room. When Jesus breathes the Holy Spirit on the disciples, it is their born again experience, their moment of Adoption. Adam was born a son, but believers are adopted as children.

"God has not given us a spirit of Fear..."

Fear is a demonic spirit and the spirit of fear is so powerful that it can literally incapacitate a person who is without "Perfect Love." Have you ever heard the phrase, "frozen with fear?" It is not just a saying, it is reality, and after what the apostles had witnessed with the scourging and crucifixion of Jesus, they were literally frozen with fear and bound to their living quarters. Jesus knew exactly what they were feeling and what they needed at that moment for them to get in a position for Him to give them the gift He's wanted to give them; the gift He died to get in them, His Holy Spirit. Before He can get His Spirit into them, He has to get the spirit of fear out of them. Fear is unbelief, it is the opposite of faith and He needs them full of faith for the mission ahead. What Jesus breathed on them was "Perfect Love" and the "Spirit of Adoption," adopting them and driving out the spirit of fear, so they could function again.

> *For you did not receive a spirit of slavery **that***
> ***returns you to fear,** but you received the Spirit of*
> *Adoption (Sonship), by whom we cry, "Abba! Father!"*
> Romans 8:15

"Returns you to fear...!" This was bombshell revelation to me when I saw it for the first time. You cannot be returned to fear unless you had been previously delivered from it. All people, everyone in the world are enslaved by the spirit of fear until they **knock** on the door of the Kingdom of God and the Spirit of Truth reveals Jesus to their heart. If they choose to receive Jesus as their Lord and savior by speaking it with their mouth and believing it in their heart, the spirit of the world, and the spirit of fear is expelled, but for most Christians now it's only temporarily. This is where the devil pulled off his greatest deception, because the modern church stopped moving past this step to the next two vitally important ones. Step two should have been the church teaching new believers about their identity as a Child of God and the paramount need to die to themselves, to give up their former selfish, worldly desires and **seek** righteousness with the same urgency as a man seeking a treasure. But the process is still not complete until they **ask** to be filled with Gods Holy Spirit.

The great revivals of the 50's, 60's and the 70's saw many new Holy Spirit filled churches spring up everywhere, but Satan cunningly slithered in and stopped that revolution by the late 80's and early 90's with the false hyper-grace and prosperity lies. I don't propose to know the mind of the devil or what all his plans to undermine the church are, but he successfully managed to deceive the new Spirit Filled Christian pastors and teachers into ending their pursuit of Jesus with a simple sinner's prayer, and a lust for money thereby slamming the door on the once great revival.

The aftermath... "Holy Ghost" (Sarcasm here) mega churches with millions of <u>professing</u> Christians but no knowledge of their identity, no righteousness and a misguided, mistaken belief that performing miracles and casting out demons are proof of an indwelling of the Holy Spirit. The modern church looks and acts just like the Apostles did before the cross; like spoiled little brats who can cast out demons and heal the sick, but otherwise have no outward appearance of Jesus whatsoever.

So, let's look at Romans 8:15 again and we can see the result of a church that does not teach identity, righteousness or the Holy Spirit.

> *For you did not receive a spirit of slavery that **returns** you to fear, but you received **the Spirit of Adoption** (Sonship), by whom we cry, "Abba! Father!"* Romans 8:15

By leaving out identity and righteousness, new professing Christians are never filled with the Spirit of Adoption. Without the Spirit of Adoption, Satan waits for the perfect opportunity, a temptation, a test or a trial, and his spirit of slavery reenters them returning and delivering them back to the bondage of the spirit of fear again. The end result is a professing Christian living a lifetime of fear, sin, repentance, temporary joy, trial, fear, sin, repentance, temporary joy, trial and on and on it goes. All because they were taught to seek hyper-grace and ask for prosperity as opposed to seeking righteousness and asking for the Holy Spirit.

Clothed with Power

> *And behold, I am sending the promise of My Father upon you. But remain in the city until you have been <u>**clothed**</u> with power from on high."* **Luke 24:49**

When studying this out, my initial thought was to look at the word power, but the Holy Spirit urged me to take a closer look at the word ***"clothed"*** first, and what I found was quite interesting.

Clothed - Strong's #1746 Enduo (en-doo'-o). Two words forming a compound word, En and Duno. First, Duno, means ***"to put on,"*** but the deeper meaning is ***"to step into."*** Secondly, the word En, means ***"from within."*** So, Jesus sent the ***"promise of the Father,"*** the ***"Holy Spirit"*** to ***"clothe us with power from on high,"*** and we ***"step into"*** this power like a soldier steps into a suit of armor. The awesome part is what happens when we "step into" or "put on" this Holy Spirit suit of armor; it **infuses us with supernatural power "from within;"** the same power and ability that Jesus had, so we are able to walk in righteousness just as He walked. All this time Satan has deceive us into thinking we can be righteous in our own strength, which only sets us up for failure; when all the while we have had the permission, and authority to request God's Holy Spirit power (Enduo) to empower us to be holy as He is Holy.

> *And behold, I am sending the promise of My Father upon you. But remain in the city until you have been clothed with <u>**power**</u> from on high."* Luke 24:49

Power – Strong's #1411 - (doo'-nam-is) is the root word for dynamite. It is the **ability** to perform; for the believer, it is the Lord's *inherent abilities* **working in and through us, giving us power** to achieve righteousness. Not in our own ability, but in His ability. *Dýnamis* is needed in every area of our life in order to grow in sanctification (holy, set apart) and prepare for heaven (glorification).

With Dynamis power we are supernaturally empowered to walk in righteousness, and love. With Dynamis, we literally become the fruit of the spirit and are enabled to perform all manner of miracles as we exercise all the gifts of the Spirit. Without Dynamis, however, we are mere mortals who are easily offended, impatient, greedy, lustful, full of envy, bitter, jealous, petty, angry, unforgiving and down-right rude.

If you have ever wondered why you never reached the same level of anointing as the apostles, this is it. This is what the devil has hidden from the church since the days of Acts of the Apostles. A power that is only attainable when we choose to die to self, seek righteousness and desire the Holy Spirit.

Therefore, this *"dynamite power"* that we step into like a suit of armor, is God's inherent power, the same power that enabled Jesus to walk without sin, the same power that raised Jesus from the dead, this dynamite power that was given to the disciples in the upper room at Pentecost is available to us when we ask for and receive His Holy Spirit. This *"power"* that is *"put on"* like a suit of armor was prophesied in the Old Testament and confirmed by Peter in the New Testament when, immediately after receiving it, he led 3000 to salvation in his first sermon where he quotes from the book of Joel:

> *"In the last days, God says, '***I will pour out My Spirit*** on all people. Your sons and daughters will prophesy, your young men will see visions, your old men will dream dreams.'"* Joel 2:28

Jesus himself said this about the Holy Spirit and the "Dynamis Power" that was soon to be available to the disciples, a power that Jesus demonstrated daily.

> *For truly I tell you, many prophets and righteous men*
> *longed to see what you see but did not see it, and to hear*
> *what you hear but did not hear it.* Matthew 13:17

The prophets of the Old Testament knew something awesome was coming and they had such joy for us knowing that the power and ability of the Living God was going to be available for us. Now consider the modern church as we look at the letter Paul writes to the church at Corinth.

> *For when I come, I am afraid I may not find you as I wish; I fear*
> *that there may be quarreling, jealousy, rage, rivalry, slander,*
> *gossip, arrogance, and disorder.* 2 Corinthians 12:20

Sound familiar? As in most churches, greed and lustful pleasures have squelched any semblance of righteousness in the body of Christ. The elders of the Old Testament didn't have the Holy Spirit living inside them, but they were glad for us because they knew it was coming. We have the Holy Spirit available to us, yet we behave like we do not. They didn't have Holy Spirit and were glad, we have access to the Holy Spirit and we are sad; there's something wrong with this picture.

> *And behold, I am sending the promise of My Father upon you. But*
> *remain in the city until you have been clothed with* **<u>power from on high.</u>**" Luke 24:49

"Power from on High" is the power of the Holy Spirit, miracle Power from Heaven and Holy Spirit ability made available to and in us so that we can do what is impossible to do in our own strength; to be holy as He is Holy and walk in love and righteousness.

Nobody is outside the goodness, mercy and grace of God the Father. To say that God loves you just as you are is totally true, but true grace commands change, it demands transformation, and any grace preached that does not encourage transformation is worldly and demonic. Grace that **does not** involve a change from worldly lusts and desires to love and righteousness, is not grace from God, because grace empowers truth to happen and truth happens when the power of the Holy Spirit comes in and makes His home in you. Then your mind gets renewed, and when your mind gets renewed with the Word, it begins transforming into the mind of Christ.

> *...But we have the mind of Christ.* 1 Corinthians 2:16

The gospel of Jesus Christ is here to set you free from you, because you are your own worst enemy. Jesus paid the price so you could finally be free, and when you are free from you, you are free from others, and nobody is your problem. If you have a problem with someone, anyone, it's not them, it's you. Jesus had more right to be offended than anyone in the history of the world. His own creation is mocking Him as they are crucifying Him and yet He asked the Father to forgive them.

> **Be imitators of God,** therefore, as beloved children, ²and **walk in love**, just as Christ loved us and gave Himself up for us as a fragrant sacrificial offering to God....
> Ephesians 5:1-2

Let's face it people, we are the problem, and if we can figure out how to get out of our own way, we will be amazing. The word does not say deny the devil, pick up your cross and follow him, it says, **"deny yourself,"** because your-self, self-seeking, selfishness, self-righteousness, and all the selfish wisdom of the world is both sensual and demonic. Selfishness prevents us from becoming the righteousness of God in Jesus.

I do, what I call, "cases," in the Altar of Love, where demonic powers are cast out and strongholds that have been given authority through sinful behavior are removed. The body of Christ is in shambles, a virtual mess, because the leadership has led them astray. It's almost as if they want their congregation ignorant and in need, assuring that they will return and tithe the following week. With all the cunning of a serpent, these prosperity pimps seduce the ignorant sheep into lusting after the things of this world, convincing them that if they want a bigger blessing, they have to sow a bigger seed. As Jesus Himself said, *"It's the blind leading the blind."*

It may be 2000 years later, but the same religious spirits still roam the earth looking for liars and thieves to fool the sheep. Jesus called the leaders of His time, blind guides. They said, *"Are you calling us blind?"* but Jesus said, *"If you were blind, you'd have no sin, but because you say you can see, your sin remains."* Another time, Jesus rebuked them saying, *"you travel all over the world looking for converts, just to make them twice the son of hell that you are."* And please do not misunderstand me, the Word says, *"Do not forsake the gathering of one another."* We are supposed to meet and fellowship, and attending church is biblical, but Satan has done a masterful job of confounding the purpose and direction of the modern Church.

Sometime after the Lord told me that time as we know it was up, He urged me to leave the church I was currently attending. Now, my brother and I are very close, and he was attending this same church, but he decided to stay and see if he could change the culture there. It was a lovely little church, the pastor was a typical Baptist preacher, intelligent, trained at seminary, well-spoken and always prepared, but there was no life in that church. No gifts, no miracles, no move of the Holy Spirit.

As time went by and my brother became more involved, he was put in a position to pray for the pastor that was under considerable stress. My brother, being filled with the Holy Spirit, prayed a prayer that must have rocked the pastor, because he invited my brother to preach one Sunday night and guess what he preached on...The Holy Spirit. It is possible for one person to change the entire culture of a church. Our job is to be the salt and the light everywhere we go. We are not, however, instructed to be overbearing and force ourselves on people in the process, but out of a loving, selfless, humble heart we are to display the fruit of righteousness and the Holy Spirit will move on people to come and pick our fruit.

How many Christians go from church to church looking for a place where they are loved? When you ask them, they say things like, "I just wasn't feeling the love there." But my response is the same, "Well you should have, because you were there." We are looking at this thing all wrong; we are not supposed to go anywhere looking for love, because we are called to become love. My brother became love to a dead church and changed the culture in the process. I'm sure I've said it several times already, but if someone offends you at church or on the job or wherever you may be, it's only because they don't understand their identity. If they knew who they were as Children of God, they'd never behave in such a way, but if you understood your identity, you'd never let them offend you again. However, doing this by sheer willpower alone is impossible, because it will get the better of you, but if you get filled with the Holy Spirit, He will empower you to walk without offense.

> *But you have received the Holy Spirit, and He lives in you, so you don't need anyone to teach you what is true. For **the Spirit teaches you everything** you need to know, and what He teaches is true, it is not a lie. So just as He has taught you, remain in fellowship with Christ.* 1 John 2:27

That does not imply that we're not supposed to gather for church. The Bible says, "*... do not forsake the gathering together.*" It just means that you now are a temple where the God of all creation can dwell in you and He is pleased to dwell there. You are the church if His Holy Spirit dwells in you, and everywhere you go is church. God has given us men and women to teach the Word, but we should not place or esteem them in higher authority than the Father, the Son or the Holy Spirit. In other words, if you spend all your time listening to the teaching of men because you are too lazy to get in the Word and read and pray for yourself, you will fall prey to demonic doctrine like the OSAS and the prosperity message.

Neither of those false doctrines would have become as prevalent as they are today if the sheep had not relied on men to tell them what to think and how to feel instead of seeking their Father for guidance and asking the Holy Spirit for instruction.

Read the Word, but before you read the Word, ask the Holy Spirit to teach you the meaning of what you will be reading. If you read something and you do not understand it at first, do not just forget it and move on, stay with it, seek it out, ask the Holy Spirit for revelation. Some of the most awesome revelation I have ever gotten is from the things that I did not understand when I first read them, but through dedication, discipline and a desire to know the Truth, wisdom was poured out and the knowledge was amazing. This book is one such example. Don't ever forget, *"Seek and you will find."*

Make Disciples

Jesus did not say, "Go into all the world and make converts." He said, *"Go make disciples...."* It's a huge difference, because a convert is someone that has said a sinner's prayer, joins a church, praises God and claims to love Jesus, yet there is no outward transformation, because they never sought righteousness or received the Holy Spirit and they continue living in willful sin, much like the world. Converts like this are on the wide path to destruction.

To make disciples - Strong's #3100 *mathēteúō* - To train someone to progressively learn the Word of God to become a mature Christian. Literally, a true Christ-follower (as opposed to a false or deceived follower). To train people to be Disciples of Christ **not only in belief but in practice also**.

This immediately brought to mind,

> *Be doers of the word, and not hearers only.*
> *Otherwise, you are deceiving yourselves.*
> James 1:22

John 3:16 says, *"...whosoever believes in Him, shall have eternal life."* The Bible says that Jesus is the Word and the Word is Jesus, however, the only Word you believe is the Word you actually do. Satan doesn't care if you read your Word; he just doesn't want you being a doer of the Word you read. Satan doesn't care if you go to church; he just doesn't want you becoming church wherever you go. Attending church doesn't make someone a Christian any more than sitting in their garage makes them a car. Satan doesn't even care if you quote scripture, he just doesn't want you becoming the Word you quote. Jesus didn't just die to get you into heaven, He died to get heaven into you so you could look, think and behave just like Him. As it is written, *"On earth as it is in heaven."*

We were created to have a relationship with the Father to *"train us up in the way we should go,"* as well as the Holy Spirit to *"teach us all things."* The Bible tells us two important things that most Christians ignore:

> *...do not call anyone on earth your Father, for **you have one Father, who is in heaven**. Matthew 23:9*

> *But you have received the Holy Spirit, and he lives in you, so you don't need anyone to teach you what is true. For **the Spirit teaches you everything** you need to know, ... 1 John 2:27*

You are now a temple the God of all creation can dwell in and He is pleased to do so. He patiently waited 4000 years to restore things to the place where He can live in us again. Church is not a building made of brick and mortar, we are the church now, and we are the temple of the Holy Spirit, not some vainglorious building.

The 5 Fold Ministry

> *Now these are the gifts Christ gave to the church: the apostles, the prophets, the evangelists, and the pastors and teachers.* **¹²*to equip the saints for works of ministry, and to build up the body of Christ...***
> Ephesians 4:11

The 5 fold ministry, the apostles, the prophets, the evangelists, and the pastors and teachers, all have a very important purpose in the church.

When new converts come into the church, the 5 fold ministry has the responsibility to equip them and build them up in their Identity, a complete and full understanding of who they are as Children of God. It has the awesome job of teaching them what power and authority is now available to them as Children of God; the power to cast out demons, power to heal the sick, power to raise the dead and power to move mountains.

The 5 fold ministry should be teaching these new converts the power that their own words have. The power that the devil has is the power we give him by the words we speak. The very same power our Father used to create the earth, He placed within His children, and therefore, the five-fold ministry must train the church to be men of few words. Our words have power to give life or death, to change any situation either for or against us and our words can either give up or retain our authority.

The 5 fold ministry must convey the importance of dying to self so they can walk in love just as Jesus walked in love. The 5 fold ministry must be able to model love for new converts, so they see what Godly, unconditional love looks like.

The 5 fold ministry is faced with teaching the depth of Sonship, to be filled with the Spirit of Adoption so new believers become well-grounded in their new and very personal relationship as a beloved child of the Father, the Son and His Holy Spirit. They need to educate new converts in the wisdom of God so the Holy Spirit can teach them, convict them, correct them, and train them in righteousness.

The 5 fold ministry has the ever important task of conveying to new believers that the first quest is to seek righteousness before the things of the world, that they may walk blameless in a wicked and perverse generation. The 5 fold ministry, by example, has the responsibility of properly teaching about and inviting new believers to receive the Holy Spirit, the Spirit of Grace and Truth.

Lastly, they have the responsibility of teaching about the awesome power of God, the laying on of hands for healing and the working of miracles. Lastly, they should tell new believers about praying in the spirit as well as prayer in their native tongue, the importance of reading the Word and fasting.

In totality, the ultimate responsibility of the 5 fold ministry is to take new converts and train them up to be disciples, so they are well able to go and do the same for everyone they meet. THAT, is the purpose of the church and the 5 fold ministry, and it is imperative that believers get plugged into a Truth teaching, Holy Spirit filled, Bible based church that neither grieves nor quenches the Holy Spirit so they can grow into faithful children that walk and talk and act and think and look just like Jesus, to a lost and dying world. I could go on and on about the purpose of the 5 fold ministry, but Paul explains it perfectly in Ephesians.

> ***And He Himself gave some** to be **apostles, some prophets, some evangelists, and some pastors** and teachers, ¹²**for the equipping of the saints** for the work of ministry, for the edifying of the body of Christ, until we all come to the unity of the faith and of the knowledge of the Son of God, to a perfect man, to the measure of the stature of the fullness of Christ; ¹⁴that we should no longer be children, tossed to and fro and carried about with every wind of doctrine, by the trickery of men, in the cunning craftiness of deceitful plotting, ¹⁵but, speaking the truth in love, that we may grow up in all things into Him who is the head–Christ– ¹⁶from whom the whole body is joined and knit together by what every joint supplies, according to the effective working by which every part does its share, causes growth of the body for the edifying of itself in love.* Ephesians 4:11-16

The mystery that has been revealed is that Jesus paid the price so that He could come and dwell within us. God didn't live in us, He lived in a temple made of stone, but He wanted to have children He could live in, so He sent His Son to die on a cross and when the veil was torn, God came rushing out looking for temples of flesh, children that His Spirit could come and live in and do miracles through, just as He did with Jesus; on earth as it is in heaven.

> *For the eyes of the LORD roam to and fro over all the earth, to show Himself strong on behalf of those whose heart is fully devoted to Him.* 2 Chronicles 16:9

The Father is looking for children He can use to show Himself strong in, Children who are fully devoted to Him and not the things of the world. The Word says that Jesus was the embodiment of the Father. In other words, if you saw Jesus, you saw the Father. They were one in the same. Just notice how sweet Jesus was, how caring, kind and considerate; Jesus was patient, loving and gentle. Matthew 4 says, *"Jesus went about proclaiming the good news, and healing every disease and sickness among the people."*

> *God anointed Jesus of Nazareth with the Holy Spirit and power, and he went around doing good and healing all who were under the power of the devil, because God was with Him.* Acts 10:38

Because God was with Jesus, they were of one mind and one accord. We are so blessed and fortunate that we have a Father who loves us so much He would go to such lengths to save us, but He did not do it just to get us into heaven, otherwise He would have taken us out of here the minute we got saved. He did it so He could live in us and do the same mighty works through us that Jesus did. Think about it, the God of all creation comes out of a temple made of stone so He can come into His children and live a life of faith, hope and love towards all of His creation, and He's using us to do it.

God wanted to live among His children Israel, but they rejected Him in the desert. They told Moses they did not want to talk to God directly or they would die, but Moses didn't die, and he spoke to God daily. Moses said, *"It is good to fear God."* Meaning, God wanted to put the respect and the awe of Him inside of them so they wouldn't want to sin against Him. But they rejected that offer, so God moved into a temple and gave them 613 laws and 10 commandments to follow and all because they were afraid.

Therefore, Jesus models Christianity for us and pays the ultimate price on a cross; a price that must be paid so our Father can have a personal relationship with us. When you begin to spend time in your Word and the God of all creation who wrote the Word lives in you, His Spirit will commune with your spirit and He will begin teaching you, convicting you, correcting you, encouraging you and training you in the way that is right to Him, the way of love and righteousness, but it is your responsibility to seek Him. God did not make us robots and He never forces Himself on us. He has given us free will to choose. We can either choose to have a relationship with Him or not, and we can choose to seek His righteousness or not.

> *I call heaven and earth as witnesses against you today that I have set before you life and death, blessing and curse.* ***Choose life so that you and your descendants may live.***
> Deuteronomy 30:19

How awesome is our Father? He could have been a taskmaster and He would have been well within His right to do so; after all, He is the creator of the universe, and we are His creation. Does the pottery have the right to tell the potter what his spout should look like? The Lord God also gave us free will to choose Him and His righteousness or the world and all it offers. Not only does this display an enormous amount of confidence and security in Himself, but it also displays His deep love towards us. He loves us so much He has given us the right, the freedom to make these eternal choices, and just in case we are not sure what to choose, He offers His Godly advice when He says, *"Choose life so that you and your descendants may live."*

In regards to whom you will serve, you only have two choices, you either choose *Life* by choosing Jesus or you choose Satan and get eternal death. If it's Jesus you have chosen, you have a third choice now; you must choose to die to yourself, become His disciple, seek righteousness and be filled with his Holy Spirit or you can be a Christian wannabe, a poser per-say and live a life of delusion thinking you are saved while lusting after the gain and access of worldly possessions and pleasures. And for those of you agnostics that do not believe, but you don't disbelieve, those who might say, "I don't choose either, I am not ready to commit to Jesus, but I certainly do not choose the devil." Do not be deceived, by not choosing, you will get the devil by default. Failure to make Jesus Lord of your life is the same as rejecting Him, therefore I urge you to choose now and choose wisely. You need to choose Jesus as your Lord, the Lord of your life, and then you need to choose to seek righteousness instead of blessings, because…

> *Pursue peace with all, and holiness, **without which no one will see the Lord.*** Hebrews 12:14

When Paul says, pursue peace and holiness, he's describing the attributes of righteousness. You must pursue righteousness and you must pursue it now, you cannot afford to go another day without His love and righteousness coursing through your veins. The absolute most powerful, the most important thing you must do when you receive Jesus as Lord is seek righteousness and ask for the Holy Spirit, because, "…*without which no one will see the Lord.*"

> *When the enemy shall come in like a flood, the Spirit of the LORD shall lift up a standard against him.* Isaiah 59:19

This verse always used to bother me, because it seemed to give too much weight, too much credence to the devil, saying he comes in like a flood. Floods are powerful and there is virtually nothing anyone can do to stop a flood except try to survive it. However, *"greater is he who is in us the he who is in the world,"* and we've been given power and authority over the devil now. Jesus said,

> *Behold, I have given you authority to tread on serpents and scorpions, and over all the power of the enemy, and nothing shall hurt you.* Luke 10:19

If we know this to be true, and if Satan has no power over us except the power we choose to give him when we hand over our authority, then just maybe we are reading Isaiah 59:19 all wrong. We know that the punctuation is not there in the Hebrew, so it very well could read like this:

> *When the enemy shall come in, like a flood the Spirit of the LORD shall lift up a standard against him.* Isaiah 59:19

Instead of the enemy coming in like a flood, *"...Like a Flood, the Lord lifts up a standard when the enemy tries to come in."* That sounds a whole lot more like our Lord.

The Spirit of Grace & Truth

> *For the Law was given through Moses;* **Grace and Truth** *came through Jesus Christ.* John 1:17

Grace – Strong's # 5485 *xáris* (khar'-ece) Grace is a gift or blessing brought to believers by Jesus Christ. Grace is to be favorable towards, or to share benefit"). It is God *freely extending His favor* to His children, His *predisposition* to bless them because of what Jesus did to pay a fine they could never pay. It is His capacity and ability given to His children, the extremely diverse powers and gifts granted to Christians, the divine influence upon the heart of a believer, and its outward reflection in their life.

The Grace of God

Grace is one of the most misunderstood and improperly defined words used by Christians. As we have now learned, it is never used as the excuse of, or overlooking of sin, rather it is the supernatural capacity and God given ability by the Spirit of Grace to the Children of God who seek righteousness and ask for the

Holy Spirit to renounce sin so they are not a slave to it any longer. This next verse out of the book of Jude uncovers the nakedness of, and should put to rest the OSAS lie.

> *For certain men have crept in among you unnoticed, <u>**ungodly men**</u>, <u>**turning** the **grace** of our God **into a license for sin**</u>.* Jude 1:4

If Satan did it back then, the same spirits still roam the earth to do it now. The slick hyper-grace preachers are simply being used and manipulated by demonic spirits to confuse the purpose and meaning of grace so they can infiltrate the church turning the grace of God into a license for sin.

Grace is the diverse and awesome power of an almighty God working in and through His children. It is Gods influence upon our hearts to be seen through our lives. Grace is a Spirit and He desires to come live in us, because Lord knows, we cannot walk righteously without Him. Grace is Gods etching tool, teaching us, correcting us, convicting us and training us how to walk in righteousness.

The Truth

At this point, most people are thinking, 1 John 1:8:

> *If we say we have no sin, we deceive ourselves, and **the truth** is not in us.* 1 John 1:8

1 John 1:8 is the verse that most people, especially the OSAS will point to, to justify their sin, and scream legalism, but what if they never actually looked at the verses before or after it to get the full context? Remember, it's always about context, so let's first take a look a few verses back.

> *God is light; in Him there is no darkness at all. If we say we have fellowship with Him yet walk in the darkness, we lie and do not practice **the truth**.* 1 John 1:5-6

Truth – Strong's # 225 alétheia (al-ay'-thi-a) In ancient Greek culture, (alḗtheia) was synonymous for "*reality*," the opposite of illusion, i.e. fact. Objectively, Truth is what is true in any matter under consideration (opposed to what is false or a lie. Subjectively, Truth is personal excellence (righteousness); sincerity of mind and integrity of character.

In 1 John 1:5-6, John is laying the groundwork for a life of Truth expressed through our walk of righteousness while using darkness as a contrast to prove his point, and he's not talking to unbelievers when he makes this comparison. This is a person under the false impression that they are saved; a perfect illustration of the OSAS, because walking in darkness is just another way of saying they are in willful sin. Walking in darkness is a Christian who knows what they are doing is sinful, yet they do it anyway, thinking that they are covered by the false hyper-grace of an idol god they have created in the futility of their mind. John is describing the guy who considers himself a believer, yet he is having an affair on his wife, or living in fornication excusing himself with God's grace. That man is walking in darkness and does not practice "**the Truth.**" Jesus is the way, "**the Truth**" and the life, therefore if a man walks in darkness (willful, deliberate sin) and **"the Truth"** is not in him, Jesus is not in Him and he is not saved.

> *But if we walk in the light as He is in the light, we have fellowship with one another, and the **blood of Jesus** His Son **cleanses us from all sin**.*
> 1 John 1:7

If the blood of Jesus cleanses me from sin, why would I still be in it? If we walk in the light, we have no fellowship with the darkness, we are not in willful sin, and the blood of Jesus cleanses us from all sin. Remember, Gods definition of "good" is much different than ours; we may sin multiple times a day without even knowing it, and this is where the blood of Jesus cleanses us from all sin. We are being judged by everything we do and think, therefore a haughty look, an insensitive remark, an inappropriate gesture, or an impure thought, no matter how seemingly insignificant it is to us, is all sin, but it's not willful and/or premeditated. Indiscriminate, unintentional sin falls under God's grace, not willful deliberate sin, sin that I know is sin, yet I do it anyway. Furthermore, even indiscriminate sin occurs less often as I grow in love and righteousness, because most of those sins result from selfishness.

The blood of Jesus does cleanse us of sin, but only if we have **no** fellowship with darkness (willful, premeditated sin) and if we walk in the light. To walk in the light is to seek righteousness and walk in love, but in order to do that we must eagerly desire to be filled with His Holy Spirit so we can walk in and exercise the gifts of the Spirit out of a heart of love for all people. If I am cleansed from all sin, why would I still be in deliberate sin? I wouldn't, so if I am in willful, deliberate sin, I must not be cleansed and the reason I am not cleansed is because I am still in fellowship with darkness; I'm not walking in the light. Walking in the light is also referred to as walking in the Spirit. Walking in darkness is also commonly referred to as walking in the flesh.

Exactly what is John saying when he says, "*If we say we have no sin, we deceive ourselves, and the truth is not in us?*" This is one of the most misunderstood verses in the Bible and the one responsible for billions upon billions of people sinning and excusing it with false hyper-grace. What if that's not what John is saying here, what if, like so many other verses in the Bible, this one has been cherry-picked out of context to excuse a lustful life of sinful behavior.

Self-Righteousness

John is talking to the self-righteous, the people that feel they are good people and have no need for the blood of Jesus. The Donald Trumps of the world that feel like they don't need to repent. Caveat, I am A-political; I am not saying anything about Donald Trump, good or bad. I am merely referring to an interview where he said he had no need to repent for anything because he basically lives a "good life," and always tries to be fair and honest. In all fairness to him, that was 2016 when he was campaigning to become President, and it is a fact that he has surrounded himself with many Christian pastors and preachers and asks them to pray from him daily, and we all know, *"with God anything is possible."* Regardless, we should reserve no judgment on him one way or the other; it's not our place, because he's not our son.

Self-righteousness is best defined as people who believe their salvation is based upon them living a "good life" and "doing good" for other people. It is salvation by works and idol worship, because they have created a false god who grants salvation to "good people." We tend to forget about the self-righteous people that think like this, focusing rather on damnation for the wicked only but there are an awful lot of self-righteous people in the world, believers and unbelievers alike and John is addressing them here and now, which he confirms several more times in the next few verses.

> *If we say we have not sinned, we make Him out to be a liar, and His word is not in us.* 1 John 1:10

When John says, *"...not sinned,"* he is using the past tense. If we falsely believe that we have never sinned, ever in our life, because we are a "good person" and any sin we engage in, well... those are just minor indiscretions (I am saying this with sarcasm from the point of view of the self-righteous), then we are saying we have no need for the blood to cleanse us because of our good intentions.

> *If we say we have not sinned,* **<u>we make Him out to be a liar,</u>** *and His word is not in us.* 1 John 1:10

Self-righteous people don't consider their sin as sin, just minor indiscretions; therefore, they have no need for the blood of Jesus, which is like calling God a liar, because His word says:

> *Surely there is no righteous man on earth who does good and never sins.* Ecclesiastes 7:20

God says that all have sinned, that no man on earth does good, but the self-righteous disagree, feeling like their good outweighs their bad and therefore they don't need the blood of Jesus to cleanse them from unrighteousness. Now, somebody is right and somebody is wrong. Either God is right and all have sinned and fallen short of the glory of God, or the self-righteous are right and their goodness is sufficient to save them. I guess we might be at what is called an impasse here. Hmm, how do we judge this? How do we figure this one out? I know, what does the Word say?

a) *Let God be true and every man a liar.* Romans 3:4
b) *God is not a man, that He should lie;* Numbers 23:19
c) *...it is impossible for God to lie...* Hebrews 6:18

Well, I don't know about you, but that settles it for me. Now let's look at the next two verses and confirm it.

If we confess our sins, He is faithful and just to forgive us our sins and to cleanse us from all unrighteousness. 1 John 1:9

If I am honest enough to admit that I am a sinner when I knock on the Kingdom door and the Spirit of Truth reveals the truth of the Lord Jesus to my heart, and if I confess those sins, He is faithful to not only forgive me, but if I seek righteousness and ask to be filled with the Spirit of Grace, He will come inside me and cleanse me of unrighteousness which empowers me to walk in love and without sin. This is the missing link; this is how Satan pulled off his greatest deception, by getting the church to seek conversion and money, instead of seeking righteousness and asking for the Holy Spirit. When we are cleansed from all unrighteousness, we no longer desire to be in willful sin! To remain in willful, deliberate sin, is unrighteousness, so either I am cleansed or I'm not; which one is it? Unrighteousness is also defined as wickedness, so there are some real contradictions here if the conventional teaching is used. Have I been cleansed from all wickedness...or not? Is John contradicting himself, or is he just about to confirm his point?

> *My little children, I am writing these things to you **so that you will not sin**. 1 John 2:1*

This proves, beyond a shadow of a doubt that John was not giving us a grace license to sin in verses 8 & 10. He was speaking to believers, but he was speaking about a completely different group of them, the self-righteous who think that their good works can do what only the shedding of the Blood of Jesus was ordained to do for us, which is to cleanse the world of unrighteousness so that we are no longer a slave to sin.

John was using this analogy to show new believers that the righteous blood of Jesus will empower them not to sin. The problem with self-righteous people stems from the fact that they believe they are already righteous and therefore they have no need to be cleansed of unrighteousness. In their unbelief, they won't receive the cleansing they need, to be transformed into His image, which is the righteousness of the Father in Christ Jesus.

> *But **if** anyone does sin, we have an advocate with the Father, Jesus Christ the righteous. 1 John 2:1*

Notice John is **not** saying, *"when we sin,"* he says *"if we sin."* Huge difference, because *"when"* implies that sin is a guarantee, it's just a matter of *"when."* *"When you sin,"* would involve premeditation, and would only serve to prove the point of the OSAS.

Workers of Lawlessness

> *Many will say to Me on that day, 'Lord, Lord, did we not prophesy in Your name, and in Your name drive out demons and perform many miracles?' ²³Then I will tell them plainly, 'I never knew you; depart from Me, **you workers of lawlessness!'** Matthew 7:22-23*

"Workers of lawlessness," is defined as people who practice sin habitually, people under the false impression they are excused by grace. They are obviously Christians as evidenced by the fact they call Jesus Lord. Buddhists, Muslims, atheists, etc., do not call Jesus Lord, only Christians do, also proven by their shock, confusion and bewilderment that He is not letting them into the Kingdom. They refer to all their gifts and miracles as proof of their loyalty to Him, but He counters with, *"I never knew you; depart from Me...."* They are "OSAS and prosperity Christians," among other deceived believers; they are habitual sinner's thinking they were saved on a technicality, a "one time" sinner's prayer, a virtual get out of hell trump card as it were. They are under the false illusion, or should I say "delusion" that certain kinds of sin or a certain amount of willful sin is acceptable to God as long as they said their coveted prayer of salvation.

Sin is a very divisive issue for believer and unbeliever alike. Unbelievers are in habitual sin because they do not believe in God or a final judgment. For most of them, it doesn't really matter what they do, as long as they are not hurting anybody, no harm-no foul. Sin in the church is a much more difficult issue, because most churches refuse to even mention it for fear of offending someone. God forbid their feathers get ruffled and the church loses a tithing member. The sad but true fact is that the modern church no longer sees people as brothers and sisters in the faith, but as dollar signs.

A *"worker of lawlessness,"* is not someone who loses their cool in a stressful situation, and upon conviction of it, they repent; that is grace at work in them. A *"worker of lawlessness"* is someone who sins often and without remorse or repentance, assuming "all is well," they are saved by grace. A very popular, but dangerous OSAS pearl of foolishness goes like this, "My Father loves me, He's just not happy with me right now." Remember, friendship with the world is **you making you** an enemy of God. You did it to yourself, by lusting after the world instead of seeking after righteousness. Remember, *"... you cannot serve two masters;"* you must choose whom you will serve.

Yet, it is never too late with God, 1 John says, "*But **if** you sin, you have an advocate in Jesus.*" In the event you slip-up, don't let condemnation get a foothold, simply repent and make the situation right. Then, thank your Father that you are not that person anymore. Thank Him that you were made in His image, in His likeness and that you were created for Him to be used by Him. You are learning from each and every misstep, and you might not be perfect, but praise God you're not who you used to be and you're becoming more and more like Him every day. You have the mind of Christ now, so confess it continually; that'll drive the devil nuts.

> *How much more severely do you think one deserves to be punished who has trampled on the Son of God, profaned the blood of the covenant that sanctified him, and insulted the **Spirit of Grace**?* Hebrews 10:29

Notice again that Grace is referred to as a Spirit, and by engaging in deliberate sin without remorse is insulting to Him; "*How much more severely do you think one deserves to be punished?*" The Father desires children whose heart is so filled with love for Him who did not spare His own Son, but delivered Him up on a cross, so they could be free from sin, not so they could wallow in it like a pig in mud. Christianity is coming to the understanding that we need a savior, repenting for past sins, and choosing to leave behind the lust of the flesh, for a life of love with a Father who first loved them. It's seeking righteousness and asking for the Holy Spirit, so the Spirit of Grace can come in and clothe us with power from on high. The result is a heart that responds to such unconditional love with love itself and a desire not to sin is birthed within us.

That is why John said, "*If you sin,*" not "*when you sin,*" because sinning against Jesus, who was tortured beyond recognition as a man, tortured more than any man in the history of the world; sinning against Him after He did that to acquit you of your guilt is almost inconceivable to you now that love for Him consumes you. The mere thought of willful, premeditated sin offends your very heart now; so that you would almost rather die than do that to Him.

Before the tragic ending of my 25 year marriage, I recall being so "in love" with my wife that the thought of cheating on her or having an affair was repulsive to me. I would literally shield my eyes if a beautiful woman came into view. I never even wanted her to see me gazing upon or take a second look at another, because I never wanted my wife to ever wonder if she could trust me. My love and dedication towards her was so pure that loyalty and devotion was my only goal. However, Jesus said,

> *"Whoever loves father or mother more than me is not worthy of me..."* Matthew 10:37

If we can love a spouse, or a child or a friend to such a degree that we would not sin against them, why don't we have the same loyalty towards our Father? It doesn't even make any sense if you think about it. Our true devotion is proven in our love.

> *"If you love me, obey my commandments.* John 14:15

Doesn't this also imply that if I don't obey His commandments, I probably don't love Him the way I say I do? Seriously, think about it, if I said I loved my wife, but I was having casual sex on the side, isn't that proof that I don't really love her like I say? If I walk in darkness, unrighteousness, disobeying the 10 commandments, which Jesus said was now rolled into the two commandments, love God and love people; if willful disobedience to Gods law is standard practice for my life, isn't it just proof that I don't love Jesus like I think I do? When people smile at you and call you their friend, but deceive you behind your back, do you judge them by their friendly words or devious treatment of you?

Now, before you get all riled-up thinking I am espousing works based salvation; this is not about works, it's about obedience. Works is about what you do to be justified, but as we learned earlier, obedience is "not doing;" it is **not** walking in willful sin. Works is trying to earn your salvation by doing things to impress God with your "sacrifices."

Sacrificing your time volunteering at church or shelters and sacrificing your money to feed the poor or to give to the church in the form of a tithe is all good and well, but it does not impress God. Walking in willful sin and pointing to your sacrifices for redemption is like a disobedient child trying to excuse his bad behavior saying, "but my room is clean." Trying to gain redemption or favor from God because you're giving money to the church is doubly tainted because most people gloat about it. To make matters worse, they are only giving, because they're expecting a return like an investment. If any of this sounds even remotely familiar to you, repent right now, because salvation is nothing to mess with. It is the biggest decision anyone will ever make in their life. Let's be honest with ourselves, we should want to know how the Father feels about obedience vs. grace or works.

Jesus did not die on a cross so we could be sinner's saved by grace, that's just twisted; it's demonically inspired thinking. We are children of the King, being transformed into His likeness so we can live righteously in and amongst a wicked and perverse generation, with the power of an almighty God flowing in and through us so we can be a light, a replica of Jesus to a lost and dying world. If our attitude is "hurry up and get me out of the forsaken world," then we are in selfishness mode. A proper attitude towards the end of time would be, "Father, empower me with your Holy Spirit that I may walk in love and righteousness everywhere I go, so I can display Jesus to everyone I meet, and give me more time to do it." Jesus wasn't in a hurry to get back to heaven, so neither should we be.

Tribulation

> *...In the world you will have tribulation. But take courage;*
> *I have overcome the world..."* John 16:33

Jesus was honest with them, He never told anybody that their life would be awesome; He warned them that they would have trouble for as long as they were in the world. He is saying, *"You will go through trials in your life, a lot of them, but display your faith, your belief, your hope in Me by maintaining a good attitude in the midst of the trial."* If you have a log that is on fire and you put it in a fire...nothing changes, right? Well, neither should we. We are not supposed to be emotional rollercoaster's; we are instructed to be steadfast and consistent in our attitude and behavior regardless of our situation. But how, how can we be confident and steadfast in tragic situations?

> *If the Spirit of Him who raised Jesus from the dead is living in you,*
> *He who raised Christ Jesus from the dead will also give life to your*
> *mortal bodies through His Spirit, who lives in you.* Romans 8:11

The same Holy spirit, the Spirit of Grace and Truth that empowers you not to sin is the same Spirit that quickens you, strengthens you, and empowers you to endure any and all tribulations that may come your way. Whether we see a miracle or not, as Children of God we trust and obey our Father out of loyalty and love, clothed with "power from on high," power of the Holy Spirit. We simply believe! If you squeeze an orange, orange juice will come out. If you squeezed an orange and apple juice came out, that would be strange. If you squeeze a Christian, Jesus should come out. If you squeeze a Christian and anything other than righteousness and love comes out, there is a different spirit ruling him. The only thing that comes out of a man's mouth is what is in his heart. If Jesus is truly in your heart, Jesus will come out when you are squeezed by a trial. Your words, your actions, your decisions will reflect what is inside you.

> *If then the light within you is darkness, how*
> *great is that darkness!* Matthew 6:23

Christians are supposed to be the light of the world. The children's song may say, "This little light of mine," but we are not called to be "little lights," we are called to be raging infernos as bright as the sun. We are called to be a beacon of light unto a dark and depraved world, a lighthouse for poor souls in peril, facing the potential disaster of being shipwrecked and certain death. But God sent His Son to be the light of the world and if He lives in us, then we manifest that light unto our world, our circle of influence, our job, our home, and everywhere we go. Darkness within us is nothing more than willful sin we tolerate and excuse. If therefore, the light within us is darkness, how great is that darkness?

If a room is dark and you turn on a light, what happens to the darkness? Nobody ever says, "Who turned on the darkness." Darkness is simply a metaphor for a lack of Jesus; an absence of righteousness in any situation. If you are a Child of God and you walk in a room, your light should permeate that room and all darkness will flee, because you are a reflection of the light of the world, Jesus. On the contrary, if you are in willful sin and condemnation covers you like a blanket, nobody can see your light. If, in an absence of your light, darkness prevails, just how great is that darkness?

This is not an indictment on any man's physical appearance; this is the inner man being projected outwardly. If an attractive looking person walks in a room, people will notice them and even be attracted to them, because of their outward appearance. Yet, if they are without righteousness and the Holy Spirit, they have nothing to offer anybody but worldly wisdom, and lustful desire, because darkness rules them.

Our Weaponry

The Lord God is God, the God of all creation, the great God, and He knows everything, He is omnipresent, in that, He is everywhere, all the time. Satan cannot do that, but Satan has demonic entities and earthly scorpions everywhere, reporting to him constantly. God knows every thought of your heart and mind. Does Satan know your thoughts? Well, the truth is, Satan's minions have the ability to place thoughts in your mind, but you have free will, so you have the ability not to dwell on their demonic, twisted thoughts, and the Word of God instructs us how.

> *The weapons of our warfare are not like the weapons of this world. Instead, they have divine power to demolish strongholds. We tear down arguments, and every presumption set up against the knowledge of God; and we take captive every thought to make it obedient to Christ.* 2 Corinthians 10:4-6

We are instructed to take every thought into captivity and make it obedient to Christ, but what does that even mean? It means, take every thought and ask yourself, "is this from Jesus?" The answer is always a simple yes or no. If your boss sticks you with the absolute worst task in the office, the one job everybody hates doing, one he has given to you the last 8 times because you are "a Christian" and you're not supposed to complain about ANYTHING, EVER. But this time your day has not gone well to begin with and your thought is to make a case for yourself about how he is abusing your good nature, and you feel like giving him a piece of your mind. That thought is not from God, get over it, and cast it down.

You are never supposed to give anyone a piece of "your mind;" you're instructed to give them a piece of "His mind." The only time you are allowed to give anyone a piece of your mind is if you are "walking in the Spirit" to such an extent that you have "the mind of Christ," and that is the mind you give them. Remember, you are the light of the world, so let your light shine, because in doing so, somebody will be touched by your patient endurance. People are watching you, people you least expect, and the way you handle yourself in every situation, even the smallest, seemingly most insignificant scenario, speaks volumes to them. Your actions and reactions to life are a better witness than actually witnessing itself.

You can go about preaching the gospel all day long, but if you are not walking it out, if you are not behaving like what you are preaching, you are doing more harm than good for the Kingdom. If you are saying one thing, but doing another, you would be better off just not telling people you are a Christian at all; at least not until you come to terms with the fact that you no longer live to satisfy you, but now you live for Him who died for you and purchased you with His blood.

Does the devil know our thoughts? That depends!

> *For who among men knows the thoughts of a man except his own spirit within him? So too, no one knows the thoughts of God except the Spirit of God.* 1 Corinthians 2:11

Therefore, no one knows the thoughts of anyone except the spirit that resides within them. As we discussed earlier, there are only 2 spirits in this world:

a) The spirit of the world, AKA the spirit of the devil or

b) The Spirit of God, AKA the Holy Spirit.

All people are either filled with or controlled by one or the other. I say it all the time, this is **not** the Star Trek Enterprise, and there is no Neutral Zone. You either choose to love your Father and accept His free gift of salvation by making Jesus your Lord, or you get Satan and what he is offering behind door number 2, and it's not pretty.

Please excuse me while I deviate, yet again, for a minute. LISTEN TO ME CAREFULLY HERE, and for the sake of being redundant, people do not have to choose Satan to get Satan, they get Satan by default if they fail to make Jesus their Lord, AND SEEK RIGHTEOUSNESS. Everyone needs to make this decision, so do not procrastinate. Death is an enigma, and for anyone without the Lord Jesus, eternity is a long, long time. For death knows no boundaries, sees no color, cares not for your title, honors no fame and is no respecter of age. It comes when it wants, shows up where it wants and takes whomever it wants, so you might as well decide right now, before it's too late.

> *But if you refuse to serve the LORD, then choose today whom you will serve. Would you prefer the gods your ancestors served beyond the*

> *Euphrates? Or will it be the gods of the Amorites in whose land you now live?* ***But as for me and my family, we will serve the LORD.****"*
> Joshua 24:15

Getting back to my first point; if no one knows the thoughts of a man except the spirit of the man that is within him, it only stands to reason that the way to determine if Satan can read your mind is whether or not you have the spirit of the world or God's Holy Spirit, and we know now that a tree in known by its fruit, so the fruit of righteousness or unrighteousness will determine if Satan can read your mind. For the righteous with Gods Holy Spirit, we know that Satan has the ability to place a thought in your mind, but he cannot make you dwell upon it.

> *Now we have not received the spirit of the world, but the Spirit from God, that we might understand the things freely given us by God.* 1 Corinthians 2:12

If you knock on the door of the Kingdom, seek righteousness like one who seeks a treasure and ask to be filled with His Holy Spirit, He will come in to you, and dwell in you so that you can understand the things of God, the Word of God, and the Wisdom of God. These things are foolishness to the people of the world, because they do not have His Holy Spirit.

> *When we tell you these things, we do not use words that come from human wisdom. Instead, we speak words given to us by God's Holy Spirit, using the Spirit's words to explain spiritual truths.* 1 Corinthians 2:13

A 7 year old girl filled with the Holy Spirit would be able to explain the most complicated things in the Bible, while an unbelieving college professor, with several PHD's would babble incoherently if asked to explain even the simplest things, but why?

> *The natural man does not accept the things that come from the Spirit of God. For they are foolishness to him, and he cannot understand them, **because they are spiritually discerned**.*
> 1 Corinthians 2:14

Unless the Professor has the Spirit of God residing within him to discern or explain what the spiritual meaning of the Scripture is, it's just gibberish to him. Paul describes this very clearly in the first book of Corinthians, so you can see for yourself how it works.

> *And my message and my preaching were very plain. Rather than using clever and persuasive speeches, I relied only on the power of the Holy Spirit, so that your faith might not rest in the wisdom of men but in the power of God. Yet when I am among mature believers, I do speak with words of wisdom, but not the kind of wisdom that belongs to this world or to the people of this world, who are dying and soon forgotten. No, the wisdom we speak is the mystery of God—His plan that was previously hidden, **but He made it known to us** <u>for our glory</u>. God's wisdom, which none of the rulers of this age understood. For if they had known it, they would never have crucified the Lord of glory.* 1 Corinthians 2:4-8

Paul didn't enter a town and begin debating with the Jews or engaging in long philosophical sermons or discussions, rather, he began healing and doing miracles which got their attention and established his credibility so that they would listen when he did begin teaching. If an atheist has a torn ACL and it gets healed, he's going to have difficulty holding onto his atheism when the facts prove otherwise. His knee was injured, now it is not. Now, if it were to happen to his friend, at least then he can reason it away, but if it happens to him, it's a difficult thing for him to ignore, and this is one of the main reasons for God giving us the power and ability to perform these kinds of miracles.

Paul then explains that the reason why Jesus spoke in parables, idioms and figures of speech was to hide the wisdom of the cross from Satan, for if Satan had known what Gods plan for restoring our identity, regaining our authority, providing our righteousness, making it possible for the Holy Spirit to reside within us and ultimately lead us to salvation; if Satan had known all that, he never would have crucified Jesus. The disciples and those listening to Jesus did not understand anything He was saying before the cross, because those things are spiritually discerned and the Holy Spirit had not yet been sent to teach them. Once they received the Spirit of Truth, He would bring all the words of Jesus flooding back to their remembrance and everything would suddenly make sense to them.

So, when it comes to thoughts, begin with this approach:

> *Finally, brothers, whatever is true, whatever is honorable, whatever is right, whatever is pure, whatever is lovely, whatever is admirable—if anything is excellent or praiseworthy, think on these things.*
> Philippians 4:8

This is the point where the true understanding of your identity takes over. This is the time when you completely ignore the lies which make up the thoughts and you begin talking to your Father; thanking Him that you are not that person any longer, that you are a Child of God, filled with His Holy Spirit, walking in love and righteousness. The following scripture is a very important strategy that Jesus taught besides just thinking on good things, a biblical principle that must be employed every day of your life.

> *"Truly I tell you that if anyone says to this mountain, 'Be lifted up and thrown into the sea,' and has no doubt in his heart but believes that it will happen, it will be done for him. Mark 11:23*

When one of Satan's minions tries to place a thought in your head, a thought of fear, worry, doubt, unbelief, sadness, despair, frustration, or maybe he's trying to talk you into a behavior you are in the process of transforming out of or even an old behavior that once held you in bondage. It is not enough for you to just think about good things, **you must speak them as well**. The Bible says that Jesus was tempted in every way just as we are.

> *For we do not have a high priest who is unable to sympathize with our weaknesses, but we have one who was tempted in every way that we are, yet was without sin.* Hebrews 4:15

If Jesus was tempted the same way we are, He likely didn't actually see Satan in bodily form, but was tempted with thoughts in His mind. Why, because if people actually saw Satan in the flesh, it would be a lot easier to resist him. For most people, not all, but for most people that have done really stupid things they later regret, it's because they had no idea Satan was behind it.

Take a married woman with an awesome family; if Satan visually presented himself to her with the goal of getting her to have an affair with her boss, she likely would have declined, knowing what a scoundrel and a liar Satan is. But that's not the way he works, Satan plants suggestions in the form of thoughts, and he very cunningly does it in such a way that she thinks it's her thoughts. Thoughts like, "my husband isn't paying me enough attention," or "he doesn't appreciate me like he used too," or "it doesn't have to mean anything, but it will further my career and my husband will never know." Satan is very cunning and subtle, and he knows just how to word the suggestion so you can rationalize it. It's brilliant actually, and it works the exact same way as subliminal advertising except it's much, much more powerful.

If a thought comes in and you know it isn't from your Father, you cannot only think on "good things" to make it go away, that is not what Jesus did. It is a three-fold strategy:

1. First, we take the thought into captivity; that is, we recognize something out of the norm is taking place. We capture it by scrutinizing the origin of it; is it from God or Satan?

2. Next, we think on good things, and do as Jesus did by determining what God says about the matter.

3. Finally, we again do what Jesus did when He said, "It is written," and we speak out loud what God has already spoken regarding our problem.

> *...no one knows the thoughts of God except the Spirit of God.* 1 Corinthians 2:11

If we are filled with Gods Holy Spirit, Satan does not know our thoughts, but he does know what he's whispering in our ear and he knows we hear him.

This is where we must do what Jesus did. He responded to Satan's thoughts verbally. Jesus was likely sitting there, His stomach was growling from the hunger of fasting when this thought popped in His head, *"You're the Son of God, why don't you just turn this rock into bread?"* And even though it was a thought, Jesus took it into captivity, thought about good things (the Word of God), and responded verbally with, *"It is written, man shall not live by bread alone....."* Jesus knew that thought was not His thought, so He responded with the Word of Truth.

When Satan plants a suggestive thought in your head designed to lure you into sin or depression or whatever stronghold he has used against you in the past; your best defense is going on offense. Begin responding with your identity. "Father, I thank you that I am the righteousness of You in Christ Jesus. I thank you that the Spirit of Grace and Truth empowers me with Power from on High, and I'm just not that person any more. I thank you that I am a new creation made in the image and likeness of my Lord Jesus by virtue of the cross. No longer will I allow myself to be manipulated by lies of the enemy, I am a Child of God, an heir to the throne, and I am seated in heavenly places with Christ Jesus and Satan is my footstool. Now go little demon, be bound in chains, torn limb from limb and cast back to your pit in hell, be bound there till you are cast to the lake of fire, never to be released, and never to return, in Jesus name." One more demonic soldier down for good; that ought to get their attention.

Old Testament Spirit vs. New Testament Spirit

> *Elijah the prophet approached the altar and said, …³⁷Answer me, O LORD! So this people will know that You, the LORD, are God,… ³⁸Then the fire of the LORD fell and consumed the sacrifice, the wood, the stones, and the dust, and it licked up the water in the trench. ³⁹When all the people saw this, they fell facedown and said, "The LORD, He is God! The LORD, He is God!"* 1 Kings 18:36-39

Elijah was filled with the Holy Spirit. "The Spirit of Elijah" was a familiar phrase used by the sons of the prophets. When the angel of God spoke to Zacharias, the father of John the Baptist, he could find no better illustration of the presence of the Holy Ghost than to say, *"He shall go before Him in the Spirit and Power of Elijah"* (Luke 1:15-17).

The ministry of Elijah was not due to any inherent qualities in himself but to the extraordinary indwelling of the Holy Spirit given to him as well as other holy men of God in the Old Testament, through faith. If we could have that same Spirit in an **equal measure**, shouldn't we be able to repeat his marvelous deeds? Do we have a smaller measure? What if we had a greater measure? The real question for the modern church is whether the Holy Spirit is working in and through us like He was with Elijah? If He is, then why is our nature so paltry and weak? Why are Christians in the modern church so much less effective than Old Testament prophets?

> *Jesus has received a much more excellent ministry, just as **the covenant He mediates is better** and is founded on better promises.* Hebrews 8:6

As awesome as Elijah was, he was discouraged that the miracles on Mount Carmel did not change the hearts of Jezebel and others. The Lord then taught

Elijah that spiritual, heart-changing experiences are not always in "strong winds," or "earthquakes," or in miracles, but in "the still small voice" (1 Kings 19:11–12). The Spirit does not usually get our attention by shouting or shaking us with a heavy hand. Rather it whispers; it caresses so gently that if we are preoccupied, we may not hear it at all.

> *"Behold, I will send you Elijah the prophet **before the coming of the great and dreadful day of the Lord**: And he shall turn the heart of the fathers to the children, and the heart of the children to their fathers, lest I come and smite the earth with a curse."* Malachi 4:5-6

John the Baptist was sent before the first coming of Jesus Christ in the Spirit and Power of Elijah (Luke 1:17). This time period was described as the day of repentance, mercy and forgiveness, not the great and dreadful day of the Lord. Therefore, the scripture in Malachi is referring to the time period just after the rapture. It seems fitting that God would send His Spirit in such a way to turn more hearts back towards Him right before the end of this present age when Jesus returns to judge the world. Jesus, referring to John the Baptist, stated that the spirit of Elijah had already come, and He added that it will come again in the future as well.

> *"And His disciples asked Him, saying, "Why then do the scribes say that Elijah must come first?" Jesus answered and said to them, "Indeed, Elijah is coming first and will restore all things. But I say to you that Elijah has come already, and they did not know him but did to him whatever they wished. Likewise the Son of Man is also about to suffer at their hands." Then the disciples understood that He spoke to them of John the Baptist."* Matthew 17:10-13

The Spirit of Elijah had already come in John the Baptist, but Jesus is referring to Himself when He says, *"the Spirit of Elijah is coming first and will restore **all things**."* "*All things*" is referring to all the things that were taken from the

Children of God in the Garden of Eden; all the things that Jesus is going to restore by His death, burial and resurrection.

1. Our Salvation
2. Our Identity as Children
3. Our Righteousness
4. Our Authority with Power
5. His Holy Spirit living in and through us

In the Old Testament, God poured out his Spirit on individual men like Elijah as He saw fit. After the cross, the Holy Spirit was made available to all believers who seek righteousness and ask for His Spirit. What most people do not know is that when the rapture occurs, the Holy Spirit will be removed with the righteous bride that has made herself ready, because the antichrist spirit cannot do his thing as long as the Holy Spirit is present.

> *For the mystery of lawlessness is already at work; only **He** who now restrains will do so until **He** is taken out of the way.*
> 2 Thessalonians 2:7

Notice that "He" is capitalized in each place the Holy Spirit is addressed. It is Holy Spirit filled believers presently restraining the antichrist from being manifest. Once the true bride of Christ is removed (Holy Spirit filled seekers of righteousness) and the Holy Spirit within them, then the antichrist is free to delude the rest of mankind.

> *And you know what is now restraining **him**, so that **he** may be revealed at the proper time.* 2 Thessalonians 2:7

The "him" and "he" are not capitalized here indicating Paul is referring to the antichrist spirit. Holy Spirit filled believers who know their identity and walk in righteousness is *"the bride of Christ"* and they must be removed at the rapture so that the antichrist can appear. The left behind books are complete fiction, not all

"Christians" go in the rapture, but only those who have died to themselves, sought after righteousness and are filled with the Holy Spirit will be taken; all others will be left behind. Then, **just *before*** Jesus returns to put down the rebellion at the ***"great and dreadful day of the Lord,"*** the Spirit of Elijah will be poured out one final time to turn more hearts back to Him.

> *God desires all men to be saved and to come to the knowledge of the truth.* 1 Timothy 2:4

Elisha Receives a Double Portion of the Holy Spirit

> *After they had crossed over, Elijah said to Elisha, "Tell me, what can I do for you before I am taken away from you?" "Please, let me inherit a double portion of your spirit," Elisha replied.* 2 Kings 2:9

> *Elijah took his cloak, rolled it up, and struck the waters, which parted to the right and to the left, so that the two of them crossed over on dry ground.* 2 Kings 2:8

Both Elijah and Elisha had been blessed with the ministry of the Holy Spirit; but it is in this age alone, from the day of Pentecost till now that the Holy Spirit is available to all men who seek righteousness and ask for Him. Now every believer, even the humblest and the weakest, may be bathed in His power, ability, righteousness and authority; but in Elijah's time, only the elite of the household of faith knew what it meant to be filled with the Holy Spirit.

> *"Holy men of God spoke as they were moved by the Holy Ghost"* 2 Peter 1:21

> *The Holy Ghost was not yet given; because Jesus was not yet glorified"* John 7:39

Once Believers knock on the Kingdom door and are born again, they must choose to die to self, seek righteousness and ask for the Holy Spirit.

> *...how much more will your Father in **heaven give the Holy Spirit to those who ask Him!**"* Luke 11:13

But just how much Spirit is available to believers of the modern church? Elijah had fire rain down, Elisha parted a river and Jesus walked on water but is anyone in the modern church doing anything even remotely close to those things? Are we even capable of such feats? Do we have some kind of Jr. Holy Spirit, one who is less able than theirs? What does the Word say?

> *For the One whom God has sent (Jesus) speaks the words of God, for **God gives <u>the Spirit without limit</u>**.* John 3:34

Elijah had a portion of the Holy Spirit, Elisha had a double portion of the Holy Spirit, but Jesus had the Spirit without limit. Other versions of the Bible use the phrase, *"without measure."* Unlike the Old Testament prophets who received the Holy Spirit in portions and for certain events to further the purpose of the Father, Jesus had no limitations whatsoever. He had the gift of prophesy, healing, gave Words of wisdom and knowledge, performed random miracles like turning water into wine and fed 5000 men with the leftovers of a 2 piece fish dinner from Long John Silver. Jesus not only had discernment of demonic spirits but authority over them as well. He had the ability to teach, preach and evangelize, and He could speak death or life into people or things with just His words. Jesus had the Holy Spirit without measure, on earth as it is in heaven.

So, what about us? Do we have a more inferior Holy Spirit than Elijah or a double portion like Elisha? Just exactly how much Holy Spirit does a Christian receive when they ask for and receive the Holy Spirit?

> *The Spirit of God, who raised Jesus from the dead, lives in you. And just as God raised Christ Jesus from the dead, He will give life to your mortal bodies by this **same Spirit living within you**.*
> Romans 8:11

Therefore, if Jesus had the Spirit without measure, and we have **the same** Holy Spirit as He, then we have the Spirit without measure too. If we have the Spirit without measure, shouldn't we be doing the same works as Jesus?

> *"Truly, truly, I say to you, whoever believes in me will also do the works that I do; and greater works than these will he do, because I am going to the Father. John 14:12*

Wait a minute...if that is true, why is the church not doing the miracles that Jesus did? Why are we so ineffectual?

> **But seek first the kingdom of God and His righteousness**, *and all these things will be added unto you.* Matthew 6:33

So just exactly why are we so weak spiritually; because of righteousness, or a lack thereof. If we desire to seek righteousness and ask God to be filled with His Spirit, He will enable us to walk in righteousness. By sincerely following Jesus' plan to Ask, Seek & Knock, we show our Father that we can be trusted to be used by Him for **His glory** and not our own selfish ways. This life was never intended to be "our best life now," but "**His best life in us for His glory**," whatever that may be, and righteousness is the key, it is the determining factor for the level to which the Holy Spirit is able to perform within us. Any void or lack of righteousness is filled by selfishness and selfishness will quench the awesome Power of Holy Spirit.

Faith notwithstanding, I am convinced that the level we demonstrate the gifts of the Holy Spirit is directly related to the degree with which we seek righteousness and walk in love. The more selfish we are, the more we seek our best life now, the more we make everything about us, the less we are capable of doing. A great example would be Smith Wigglesworth. Smith was reputed to have raised 23 people from the dead in front of many witnesses. Smith prided himself on seeking Gods Kingdom and walking in righteousness. Once he was converted, he vowed never to read anything except his Bible, nor did he listen to any music that was not old school gospel. He paid no attention to world events, politics or pop culture and as a result, he walked more like Jesus than any man in modern times.

We Were Made to House the Spirit of God

> *Then the LORD God formed man from the dust of the ground and breathed the **breath** of life into his nostrils, and the man became a living being.*
> Genesis 2:7

Breath - Strong's# 5397. neshamah (nesh-aw-maw') Intellect, soul, spirit.

God made man from dirt like a skilled potter makes a vessel, but man was not yet alive. God then breathes into him the breath of life, His Holy Spirit and man comes to life, physically and spiritually when he is filled with the Spirit of God. Man, now has a mind with a personality, intellect, a will and emotions. Man is a complete being with a soul and a body that houses a partnership between His own spirit and the Spirit of God, much like a marriage. When sin enters the scene through Adam and Eve, God removes His Spirit from man and death is activated. Anytime the Spirit of God is removed, death enters in to fill the void. God's Spirit is the breath of life and when His Spirit was removed so was eternal life... but Jesus.

Kingdom Fruit

> *"You will know them by their fruits.* Matthew 7:16

Jesus uses this statement to describe false profits, the OSAS and prosperity hucksters, calling them wolves in sheep's clothing; a statement He makes right on the heels of telling them to enter into the narrow gate because wide is the gate and broad is the way to destruction. It's probably not a coincidence either, because He then turns right around and contrasts that with this:

> *Likewise, every good tree bears good fruit, but a bad tree bears bad fruit. Matthew 7:17*

> *So then, by their fruit you will recognize them.* Matthew 7:20

Because Jesus had not yet gone to the cross, and therefore the Holy Spirit had not yet been given to them, He was speaking prophetically here. Mind you, Jesus is not talking about the Spirit of Adoption, the born again experience. He is referring to the time in the near future when they would be *"clothed with power from on high."* Jesus is talking about their transformation from a caterpillar into a butterfly. In Galatians, Paul describes what the fruit of the spirit looks like.

> *But the fruit of the Spirit is love, joy, peace, patience, kindness, goodness, faithfulness, 23gentleness, and self-control.* **Against such things there is no law....** Galatians 5:22-23

It wasn't until the Spirit of Grace and Truth fell on them in the upper room that they were filled with the fruit of the Spirit and transformed into the image of Jesus. Until that day, they had no ability to walk in love and righteousness. They tried, they really wanted to, they watched Jesus do it, and they knew they should, but they could not. Just like the modern church, as soon as tribulation arose, they resorted to the flesh.

The upper room was their butterfly moment; it's here that the metamorphous was complete. It was time for the cocoon to open and the new creation in the likeness of Christ Jesus to emerge. It was the moment that changed not just the disciples but the whole world forever; the moment all men were afforded the right and ability to become the express image of the Father. Sadly, the modern church in no way resembles this image, the image of Jesus, because the Holy Spirit has either been quenched by unbelief or misrepresented and grieved by liars and hucksters.

Unbelief comes when whole denominations teach that the gifts and miracles ended when the last apostle died, but Jesus said,

> *Truly, truly, I tell you, **<u>whoever</u> believes in Me will also do the works that I am doing.** He will do even greater things than these,*
> John 14:12

You'd think that when they read their Bible they'd notice Jesus said, *"**Whoever** believes in me,"* not just the apostles. Funny how people will take scripture out of context and/or just ignore other parts altogether to justify their own weaknesses. Jesus also said,

> *And these signs will accompany those who believe: In My name they will drive out demons; they will speak in new tongues; ¹⁸they will take up snakes with their hands, and if they drink any deadly poison, it will not harm them; they will lay their hands on the sick, and they will be made well."* Mark 16:17-18

There's actually an awful lot going on in this verse we can discuss, and much of it has been completely misunderstood, even to the point of men creating churches that handle deadly venomous snakes as some kind of proof of faith. The first and most obvious thing to notice is the reference to signs, wonders and miracles following *"those who believe."* Once again, we see that miracles will follow anyone who believes, not just the disciples.

The main reason many pastors and whole denominations do not believe in miracles is because they themselves do not have enough faith to believe they can. They have no real faith in themselves, so they project their unbelief upon their church and the result is a church without the Holy Spirit. A church without the Holy Spirit is a church devoid of the authority and power that Jesus died to give us. But why, why don't some pastors believe in miracles? Selfishness! They have made it all about them. If they pray for healing and the person does not get healed, they assume the church will think their faith is lacking. It is a reflection of weakness in their flesh, so it's easier to just not believe; that way they never get embarrassed if they pray and nothing happens.

The problem with this line of thinking is that we don't heal anyone anyway, God does. We are just the conduit for the Holy Spirit, the extension cord between the person in need and the source of the healing, God's Holy Spirit. Ultimately, it comes down to a failure to seek righteousness. Any void of righteousness is filled with selfishness and selfishness either destroys or corrupts everything and anything if given enough time.

Take Up Snakes

For the early church, casting out demons and healing the sick were the very first signs new believers did to display their faith. All that said, I feel compelled to address the much misunderstood and sometimes misrepresented part in Mark 16:17 where Jesus said, *"They will take up **snakes** with their hands."* The word snakes is translated from the Greek word ophis, but we have improperly defined it; and in doing so, changed the entire meaning of this phrase.

Snakes - Strong's #3789 - Ophis (of'-is) Literal use: a serpent, snake. Figurative use: The devil or Satan.

If Jesus is not talking about actual snakes here, but referring to Satan and the demonic forces, then the real meaning of this statement begins to open with understanding. Let's look again at the verse and then take a look at the Strong's meaning and you will be shocked when you see the definition of *"take up."*

*"They will **take up** snakes with their hands."*

Take up - Strong's #142 airó (ah'-ee-ro) Definition: to raise, take up, lift. Usage: I raise, take up, lift up, **take away, I remove**. <u>**Euphemistically, to *"pick up"* is to cause our sins to cease, i.e., our desire to sin is removed**</u>, while we enter into fellowship with Christ, who is free from sin, and abide in that fellowship.

If the most common and frequent usage of the phrase *"take up"* is to take away or remove, then to pick up snakes is to remove Satan's power of sin over us by removing our desire for sin. *"They will take up snakes **with their hands**,"* might actually throw a wrench into this vein of thought until you take it apart as well.

*"They will take up snakes **with their hands**."*

With their hands - Strong's #5495 Cheir (khire) Definition: the hand. Usage: a hand, from the root meaning "to lay hold of."

After coming out of Egypt and into the wilderness, the children of Israel were being killed by a curse of snakes in their camp, but the curse was canceled when they looked upon Moses as he "lifted up" a snake on a pole. By looking upon Moses *"take up"* or "lifting up," the snake on a pole they lay hold of Gods promise to remove the curse.

> **Let us fix our eyes on Jesus,** *the author and perfecter of our faith,...* Hebrews 12:2

As Israel looked at the snake on the pole to "lay hold of" their deliverance, likewise, when we *"take up snakes with our hands"* we are delivered from the curse of sin in us, because we fix our eyes on Jesus. Therefore, one of the signs that would follow true believers is that the curse of sin no longer holds them in bondage to it and they are free to live in righteousness. A literal interpretation of taking up poisonous snakes is nothing short of ridiculous. There is not one story or scripture of any kind to support the taking-up or handling of snakes, therefore this cannot be a literal meaning.

There is one story of Paul getting bit by a snake in the book of Acts, but he wasn't trying to pick it up; it bit him by surprise, so that does not count. Now let's reread Mark 16:17-18 again and see if we notice just how out of place His reference to snakes is; does it even fit with the rest of the list?

> *In My name they will drive out demons; they will speak in new tongues; ¹⁸**they will pick up snakes with their hands**, and if they drink any deadly poison, it will not harm them; they will lay their hands on the sick, and they will be made well."*
> *Mark 16:17-18*

Do you see how out of place it is? If *"Taking up"* is to remove, and *"Snakes"* is referring to Satan, then *"taking up snakes"* is Gods promise to remove the curse; Satan's power that sin has had over us our entire life. *"With our hands"* means we *"lay hold"* of something, we acquire something we are seeking after. Within the phrase, *"They will pick up snakes with their hands,"* is Jesus' promise to remove the power that sin has over us.

When we *"seek first the Kingdom of God and His righteousness,"* and fix our eyes on Jesus, He cancels the curse against us by removing Satan's power of sin from us. That is the meaning of "Take up snakes…." If you seek righteousness and are filled with the Spirit of Grace & Truth, righteousness becomes part of your personality, not just something you try to do. In our seeking of righteousness, we *"take up"* or *"lay hold of"* righteousness and the power of almighty God infuses us with His ability to *"go and sin no more."*

Good Gifts

Along with the same Spirit that raised Jesus from the dead, we are promised to receive wonderful gifts from our Father. Jesus described them as *"good things"* in Matthew and *"Good gifts"* in Luke.

> *So, if you who are evil know how to give good gifts to your children, how much more will your Father in heaven give **good things** to those who ask Him!*
> *Matthew 7:11*

But just what exactly are the *good things*, we will be given?

> *So, if you who are evil know how to give **good gifts** to your children, how much more will your Father in heaven **give** the **Holy Spirit** to those who **ask** Him?"* Luke 11:13

The Holy Spirit is the gift from the Father, the gift that gives good things. If you think about it, He is giving us a gift that gives; a gift that gives you a new identity as a Child of God, a gift that provides you power and authority to cast out demons and heal the sick, a gift that empowers you to teach, preach, evangelize, exhort and prophesize, a gift that gives words of wisdom, knowledge and the ability to recognize demonic or heavenly beings also known as the discernment of spirits. The Holy Spirit clothes us with power from on high giving us the ability to walk in righteousness.

The level to which we operate any of these gifts is based upon our commitment to walk in love and righteousness; that is to walk in the light as He is in the light. These gifts are given not so they may be horded; these are for us to share with all men. The more generous you are in blessing others with these gifts; the more prosperous you will be in them. Jesus said, *"Freely you received, now freely give."* These gifts were given as a free gift for you to give away, not sell. The Gospel is never supposed to be a for-profit organization; woe to the prosperity pimps.

> *Give, and it will be given to you. A good measure, pressed down, shaken together, and running over will be poured into your lap. For with the measure you use, it will be measured back to you."* Luke 6:38

This verse is often used by prosperity preachers to cast spells upon the ignorant church to seduce their hard earned money away from them. On the surface, it does appear like a verse about giving money in order to receive money, but what if Jesus is not talking about money at all? What if this verse, like so many others, is not being seen in the correct context? How would we know, seeing there is no direct reference as to what we are giving and receiving? The best way to determine the true meaning of a verse is to look at the verses leading up to it, but that was no help, because this seems to come out of left field.

Jesus starts by telling them to *"love their enemies"* in verse 27, *"bless those who curse you, and pray for those who mistreat you"* in 28, *"turn the cheek"* in 29, *"give to everyone who asks and don't ask for it back"* in verse 30, and *"do unto others and we would have them do unto you"* in 31. He frames verse 32 as a rhetorical question followed by the answer when He says, *"If you love those who love you, what credit is that to you? Even sinner's love those who love them."* He expounds on these a bit more in verse 33 and 34, by again comparing our character to that of sinner's in the world. In verse 35, Jesus tells us why it is important to conduct ourselves in this manor when he says, *"But love your enemies, do good to them, and lend to them, expecting nothing in return. Then your reward will be great, and you will be sons of the Most High; for He is kind to the ungrateful and wicked."* In verse 36 and 37 Jesus tells us to *"be merciful as our father is merciful* and *do not Judge if we don't want to be condemned,"* followed by *"forgive and you will be forgiven."*

That is when Jesus says, *"give and it shall be given...,"* so I found nothing before it that framed a concept for it. Then I looked at the verse following it, and that is when the Holy Spirit showed me what it was.

> *Jesus **also** told them a parable: "Can a blind man lead a blind man? Will they not both fall into a pit?* Luke 6:39

Also – Strong's #2532 – A conjunction connecting it to the previous saying or thought; *moreover, even as.* It **never** means "however" ("but"), which opposes or cancels the previous thought.

Therefore, when it says, *"Jesus **also** told them a parable,"* the parable He tells them was to explain the previous thing He said.

> *Jesus also told them a parable: "Can a blind man lead a blind man? Will they not both fall into a pit?* Luke 6:39

Jesus often described the Scribes and Pharisees as blind guides, and that is who He was referring to in Luke 6:39. He is saying that the people are blind but their religious leaders are also blind so both of them will fall into a pit which represents hell. Our Father wants to give us *good gifts,* so we can emulate Jesus and use them to love on other people He brings along our path. We are given good gifts, so we can bless people with those good gifts, and the more we give, the more we receive. In fact, if we freely give what we have received, we will receive so much more it will be overflowing within us. That is how we get to the place where our measure of the Holy Spirit becomes greater than the Old Testament saints and equal to the apostles.

The same demonic spirits that blinded the Scribes and Pharisees are blinding the OSAS and prosperity preachers. The church is blindly being led by the blind into a pit, because they never learned to die to self, seek righteousness and ask for the Holy Spirit so they can position themselves to receive good gifts.

> *Now about spiritual gifts, brothers, I do not want you to be ignorant. ...⁴There are different gifts, but the same Spirit. ⁵There are different ministries, but the same Lord.* 1 Corinthians 12:1-5

> *For to one is given the word of wisdom through the Spirit, and to another the word of knowledge according to the same Spirit; ⁹to another faith by the same Spirit, to another gifts of healing by that one Spirit,...¹⁰to another the working of miracles, to another prophecy, to another distinguishing between spirits, to another speaking in various tongues, and to still another the interpretation of tongues. ¹¹All these are the work of one and the same Spirit, who apportions them to each one as He determines.* 1 Corinthians 12:8-11

Baptism of Fire

As I write this section regarding the Baptism of Fire, the date is 01/06/20, and I have already finished this book, but I am performing several rereads, looking for errors, redundancies and general irregularities and mistakes. I got up to write and edit yesterday, Sunday at about 3am, the same time I do every day, but by 7am I began to feel drowsy, so I closed my laptop and decided to take a quick nap before going to the gym. As I drifted off, I very clearly heard the words nine-eleven while seeing a 911 visually at the same time. My first thought went to Revelation 911.

> *They were ruled by a king, the angel of the Abyss. His name in Hebrew is Abaddon, and in Greek it is Apollyon.* Revelation 9:11

There was just no way I would be able to sleep after that, so I got up and began to get ready for my day. I assumed I was done with this book, but I'm never quite sure God is, so I've been asking Him if there is anything else He wanted to add. As I was tinkering around the house, I heard the Holy Spirit tell me to write about the Baptism of Fire. There is only one verse in the Bible that makes reference to Baptism in Fire, and only a handful of people I know say they have actually experienced it; so I did what Jesus instructed us to do, I asked, "If you want me to write about it, please baptize me in it."

> *I baptize you with water for repentance, but after me will come One more powerful than I, whose sandals I am not worthy to carry.* **He will baptize you with the Holy Spirit and <u>with fire</u>.**
> Matthew 3:11

As I sat there contemplating all this, it suddenly occurred to me to look up 911 in the Strong's Concordance, and you will not believe what it is.

Strong's # 911. Baptó. Baptism – Baptism of Fire maybe?

Isn't that just a little too coincidental? The 911 I saw was confirmation of what He wanted for me and what he wanted me to add to this project. I went about my day as usual, but whenever I thought about it, I continued to ask for it until I went to sleep that night. Suddenly I am awakened by the most intense feeling I have ever experienced in my life. Every muscle, every ligament, every tendon and even my bones were under great duress, the likes of which I can hardly explain. It was very strong, and my body was in severe distress, but it's not like it was painful. Imagine restless leg, over your entire body X 10 and that does not even come close to describing it. There is a saying gym rats use when performing a really heavy squat or bench press; it's called getting your muscles to fire. It's the instantaneous blast of energy and motion needed to drive the weights to the desired end. While I was in agony, I also felt incredibly powerful, like I would have been able to access superhuman strength. My muscles wanted to fire, all of them and all at once.

At this point, I'm not associating what I am experiencing to what happened earlier in the day, so I'm rolling back and forth in bed, frantically trying to figure out what in the world is happening and I'm making every effort to get comfortable with all my muscles firing to the max. Finally, I decide that I've got to get up, I've got to do something, because the feeling is now intensifying. I could barely endure the initial wave, but now it is growing stronger and my mind is wondering if I was going to even survive at this point. Finally, I jumped out of bed and began to walk around when it suddenly dawned on me, "this is the baptism of fire I've been asking for." Now, I'm wavering between asking for more, and asking Him to make it stop, because it is almost intolerable, but something tells me to go back to bed and let what's happening, happen.

For the next hour or so, I lay in bed and worshiped Jesus while I was being baptized with fire. I had an inward knowing that there was more, but I would not have been able to endure it, so I believe I was given only what I could handle. The next day I asked God to give me whatever was held back, I wanted it all. Sure enough, that evening, I woke to the same thing all over again, only this time it was not quite as intense, but it was extremely uncomfortable.

So just exactly what is the purpose of baptism of Fire? The Strong's concordance gives an excellent explanation of the word fire used here and it perfectly lines up with everything I have been trying to convey in this book.

Fire – Strong's #4442 Pur (poor). Like with the "fire of God" which **transforms all it touches into the *light* and *likeness with itself*.** *God's Spirit*, like a holy fire, enlightens and purifies so that believers can share more and more *in His likeness*. Indeed, the *fire of God* brings the *uninterrupted* privilege of being *transformed* which happens by experiencing *faith from Him*.

That definition is straight out of the Strong's, but if I were to put it in my own words, I'd have to say that the baptism of fire is God's refining fire; burning up everything and anything associated with the world in order to complete the transformation of us into His image, and making us ready for our homeland, because it's time to go home. It is the purification of our identity as Children of God, by burning with fire every and any connection or desire for this world. I'll be honest, I am not the same man I was yesterday, something is seriously different.

The Altar of Love, Part II
Chapter 5
Leg 4 – Power & Authority
Miracles, Healing, Cast out Demons, Gifts of the Holy Spirit

Sin entered the earth the day Adam and Eve handed over their authority in the Garden of Eden, and Satan became the god of this world.

> *The god of this age (Satan) has blinded the minds of unbelievers so they cannot see the light of the gospel of the glory of Christ...*
> 2 Corinthians 4:4

After Adam's fall, Gods Holy Spirit was removed from the earth, because He can have no part of sin. Over the next 4000 years, the Spirit of God moves in and out of chosen individuals to perform His will. After Israel's exodus from Egypt, God desires to be near His children, so He has them build Him a temple that His Spirit can reside in, but His desire was to live inside them, not in a temple made of wood and stone. That is exactly what He did with Jesus after His baptism in the Jordan River, what He did with the disciples in the upper room in the Book of Acts and what He wants to do with us.

> *I am sending the promise of My Father upon you. But remain in the city until you have been clothed with power from on high."*
> Luke 24:49

In the Book of Acts, Jesus told the disciples to go to Jerusalem and wait there for the Holy Spirit, but God had been telling the Jews this day was coming all throughout the Old Testament; a day when authority is transferred back to its rightful owner, the Children of God, and they are infused with power from on High, the power of Almighty God enabling them to renounce youthful lusts and walk in righteousness.

> *...until the Spirit is poured out upon us from on high.* Isaiah 32:15

From the time of Adams fall until Gods Holy Spirit is poured out on all mankind, the earth is in shambles. Gods beautiful creation is in complete disarray; a downward spiral of decay and destruction.

> *Her towers will be overgrown with thorns, her fortresses with thistles and briers. She will become a haunt for jackals, an abode for ostriches.* Isaiah 34:14

Anytime Satan has a hand in anything, it will degrade. Everything he touches begins to die, until...

> *...**until** the Spirit of God is poured out upon us from on high. **Then** the desert will be an orchard, and the orchard will seem like a forest. ¹⁶Then justice will inhabit the wilderness, and righteousness will dwell in the fertile field.* Isaiah 32:15-16

Salvation by the blood of Jesus transforms us from a dry lifeless desert into a glorious orchard abounding in marvelous produce. As time passes, this orchard we have become grows into a lush, Christ like forest due to the Holy Spirit within us. As we walk in justice, we affect change for the good and the love and righteousness we display changes even the wilderness we inhabit into fertile fields.

Satan introduced wickedness to Gods perfect creation which began its degradation, but the Spirit of God brought justice wherein righteousness restores life. Unless we are filled with His Spirit, life is nothing more than a slow degradation unto death; physical and spiritual. That does not imply Christians will not see physical death in their human body, they will, but a physical tent which houses the Holy Spirit has many advantages over one that does not.

Sickness and disease have no place, no power and no authority over a Child of God filled with His Spirit. Oh, it can try, but it will never get a foothold.

> *... when sin is fully grown, it brings forth death."* James 1:15

Just as a desert becomes an orchard when the Spirit of God is released upon it, so too is a human host body transformed from a sickly, frail vessel of death into a marvelous host body for the Holy Spirit; a tent renewed with life once it becomes infused with power from on High.

> *He who raised Christ Jesus from the dead will also **give life** to your mortal bodies through His Spirit, who lives in you.*
> Romans 8:11

Give life – Strong's #2227. Zóopoieó (dzo-op-oy-eh'-o) Definition: I make that which was dead, come alive. It is particularly used of God *infusing His life in the believer*. The Lord infuses eternal life (*zōē*) into us each time we receive (obey) *faith from Him*. This enables *living with God* – not just *for* Him.

Power to do the Miraculous

Power from on High and authority is what Jesus and Paul used to win over the masses of people they preached to in every city and town they went. Performing miracles, healing the sick and casting out demons with authority in the name of Jesus is the absolute best way to get the attention of non-believers.

> *...God our Savior, who desires all men to be saved **and** come to the **knowledge of the truth**.* 1 Timothy 2:3

However, power & authority without identity, righteousness and the Holy Spirit is a recipe for disaster. Obviously, the most important thing for every man is to seek ye first the Kingdom of God; the moment our spiritual eyes are opened, and we see Jesus for who He truly is and what He did on our behalf. When revelation hits your heart and you willingly, consciously, publicly declare that

Jesus is your Lord; Leg 1 is complete, Son-ship is obtained, you have been adopted into the family as a Child of God. Leg 2 is coming to the knowledge of the truth; it is dying to yourself and seeking righteousness. Leg 3 is being filled with His Holy Spirit, the Spirit of Grace & Truth.

Power and authority is the 4th Leg and it is very important to any Christian serious about their faith, but lacking it will not keep you from the Kingdom of God. On the contrary, any void of righteousness will be filled with selfishness, and a self-centered desire for the things of the world will eventually reemerge renewing a friendship with it. As we've already learned in James 4:4 that any friend of the world **makes themselves** an enemy of God. 1 John 3:10 says, anyone who does not practice righteousness is not even of God, and it does not take a rocket scientist to figure out what you are if you're not of God. Therefore, righteousness is essential for one's salvation, and its discovery will unlock your potential; a potential that can never be obtained without it.

We know that the Holy Spirit is necessary for salvation because Jesus said, *"...unless we are born of the Spirit we cannot see the kingdom of God."* Furthermore, it is the Holy Spirit of leg 3 that empowers us with the ability to walk in the fruit of righteousness so the righteousness of leg 2 is an impossibility without being filled with Holy Spirit power from On High in leg 3. Which brings us to leg 4; the Power and Authority of Leg 4 is the only leg we can be without and still be assured of our salvation. It is quite possible to live a happy and productive Christian life without moving in miracles, healing the sick and assuming one's authority over all the power of the enemy. With that said, the question that begs to be asked is not whether or not we can live without power and authority, but why would we want to?

God showed me in the Altar of Love part I that power and authority was given to the disciples well before they even got saved, understood their identity, had even and inkling of righteousness or were filled with the Holy Spirit. They were performing various kinds of miracles, yet Jesus had not even gone to the cross.

God confirmed this fact for me on two different occasions when the Holy Spirit prompted me to have unbelievers pray for 2 different injuries I had and they both got healed. In one case, I prayed for a woman first and she got healed, then I had her pray for my injury and it got healed. In the other case the script was reversed, first I asked a random woman to simply speak to my leg and it grew out; ending almost 2 years of hip pain. The woman didn't even know who Jesus was, but after He healed me, He healed her torn rotator cuff and she became a believer.

One could argue that the healing was manifest only because I am a believer, and that is true, however, on several occasions I have witnessed a brother in Christ have one unbeliever pray for another unbeliever and they were healed. The more I contemplate miracle power and authority, the deeper and more complex I find it. From my earliest memories of becoming a believer, power and authority was commonplace, but as years passed, the miracles seemed to fade.

A few years before God moved on me to write the Altar of Love part I, He prompted me to begin moving in miracle power and authority like never before. It seemed like everywhere I went He was giving me words of knowledge and performing many miracles. People were reaching out to me from all around the world to pray for them, but I constantly had to remind myself that it was not me, I was nothing special, and I can do nothing without the Holy Spirit inside me. The experience was good though, because I saw just how dangerous power and authority has the potential to become unless we are grounded in our identity as Children of God and righteousness.

How easy it would be to begin thinking more highly of ourselves than we ought when miracles flow through us effortlessly, and the opening it provides for Satan to infiltrate and manipulate us with conceit. I am convinced that power and authority without a full and complete understanding of one's identity, as well as being rooted and grounded in love and righteousness is a recipe for disaster. Just as the disciples fled and denied Jesus even after everything they witnessed, likewise will any believer fail their day of winnowing without a solid foundation of their identity, love and righteousness.

I recall the first time God manifest this renewed healing gift through me for a young lady in a grocery store. It was inspired entirely by the Holy Spirit; every moment scripted, right down to the words spoken. Afterwards, she asked me how I did it, and His response has been etched in my memory ever since. I said, "I did not do it, the Holy Spirit did, I am no better than you, I have no more power than you, the only difference between us is that I believe I can and if you believe you can, you will as well." She gratefully thanked me about a half dozen times, so I took the opportunity to ask her to do something for me. Astonished, she nodded her head yes, in agreement. "Always remember what happened here," I said, "and how it happened, because you can do it as well." "I want you to pray for someone else in need today, will you do that for me?" She enthusiastically agreed and walked away without a limp.

I say this not to glorify myself in any way, but to highlight what the Holy Spirit did and said through me, because none of it was any of my doing. Before we prayed, she was limping and grimacing in pain with every step. Apparently, she dropped some piece of heavy equipment on her foot, crushing several bones, and was in one of those surgical boots up to her knee. First, He drew her to me, I did not go looking for her; our paths crossed and I saw she was in pain so I asked if I could take it away. I didn't even invoke the name of Jesus the first time I prayed and her pain went from a 12 to a 2 on a scale of 1-10 (her words, not mine). The second time I prayed, I prayed in the name of Jesus and all her pain left.

I began using that event like a pattern and it was very helpful and inspiring for me. I stayed with that very same approach for the next several months, but over time I realized that particular event was mainly to build my confidence. If we make ourselves available the Holy Spirit will use us in different ways and for all different kinds of situations, so we shouldn't box Him into any one approach.

It's likely things unfold the way they do because that is the best way to get the attention of the person in need, so I learned to just go with the flow of the Spirit and let Him do His thing, as He wills.

After a few years, however, I noticed fewer and fewer opportunities to do the miracles. It almost felt like the gift was being removed from me, but I soon realized that I was being removed from it... temporarily. Initially, I thought it was so I could focus more on seeking righteousness in order to stay grounded, but its purpose was to lead me to begin writing this book.

I'm such a guy, whatever task I do, I do with excellence, but I can only do one thing at a time. I am not very good at multitasking; if I try to do too many things at once, they all suffer, so I tend to focus on just one thing. My Father knows that about me, He made me this way, so I believe He led me through a season of miracles so I could experience it, then took me from it (He didn't take it from me, He took me from it) so I could focus on writing about it from the experience of having done it. Theory is good, but nothing beats practical, on-the-job experience.

Righteousness is Superior to Power & Authority

My oldest and dearest friend is a man of the utmost integrity; he has a good understanding of his identity as a Child of God, he is a man that seeks righteousness and walks in it daily, he believes in and is filled with the Holy Spirit, but he does not generally walk in miracle power. I do not know why, maybe it's just not part of his personality, but he is probably the most honorable man I have ever known and I'd trust him with my life because of his Godly integrity and his endless pursuit of righteousness.

Nevertheless, he never fell for the prosperity lie, but put his heart into seeking after righteousness and ironically, he became the most successful persons I know. I believe that his desire for the righteousness of God, not the things of the world, proved to his Father that he could be trusted with great wealth and it not corrupt him. Years after becoming a multi-millionaire, he is still the sweetest, kindest, best man I know. He is a man of great honor, integrity and humility, and a man who seeks after righteousness like one who seeks after a treasure. Doing miracles and assuming one's authority is awesome, but to the Father, those things pale in comparison to a man or woman who walks in love and righteousness.

He is not overly vocal of his faith, but neither is he ashamed of it. He may not go around preaching the good news, but he will defend his belief with wisdom and confidence. His witness of the gospel is almost never in a loud proclamation, but in his quiet walk of humility and selflessness. He doesn't need to go around boasting about his faith, because his walk of righteousness is so obvious and pure, it is his witness.

In contrast, I know other people in the Kingdom that exhibit power and authority daily, miracles abound everywhere they go but righteousness is an after-thought and it shows in their life. They are a mess, immature, complainers, fighting and quarreling, dishonest at times and generally worldly. I'm not talking about tribulations due to their lack of righteousness, because Jesus said we would all go through trials. Even my good friend has gone through some difficult times, but he does so with a steadfast, faithful perseverance and a righteous attitude towards God. Righteousness is not dependent upon what he's going through, it is his way of life.

All that notwithstanding, the question I hear the Holy Spirit asking is not, "can you lead a happy and productive Christian life without walking in power and authority," but rather, "why would you want to?" If Jesus died to get us to the place where we are "like Him," shouldn't we want all He suffered to give us? From my experience, moving in miracles and authority is the heart and nature of the Father to "love on" His hurting children.

In 1 Corinthians 14:1, Paul writes, *"Let love be your highest goal!,"* because as we grow in righteousness we should grow into His likeness. If we know that God is love, and He loves to love His children, then love for His children should be our highest goal as well. In that chapter, Paul goes on to write all the blessings and benefits of tongues, but he begins by telling them that prophesy is better, because tongues is for your benefit, but prophesy is for the benefit of others. Tongues builds up your inner man; you spirit man is becoming more and more like Jesus, which is exactly what we want, but prophesy benefits the hearer. Therefore, according to the law of love, prophesy is more selfless, making it more preferable to the Father.

Likewise, is power and authority to do miracles. If we truly want to look like Jesus then we would most certainly be praying for people like Jesus did, everywhere, and all of the time. To do so would be to mimic the heart of our Father towards His suffering creation. Miracles are selfless acts of love towards Gods own children and therefore our Father wants us doing them. It's His nature to love on, to heal, to help His creation in times of trouble; just not at the expense of righteousness, therefore, seek ye first the Kingdom of God and His righteousness, but desire the gifts of God, desire to do miracles.

> *While Jesus was in one of the towns, a man came along who was covered with leprosy. When he saw Jesus, he fell facedown and begged Him,* **"Lord, if You are willing,** *You can make me clean."* ¹³*Jesus reached out His hand and touched the man.* **"I am willing,"** *He said. "Be clean!" And immediately the leprosy left him.*
> Luke 5:12-13

The testimony of the leper above displays the very heart of the Father; *"He is willing"* to cleanse us, to heal us, to help us if and when the devil comes to kill, steal and destroy us. When it comes to healing and miracles for His beloved creation, it is His will, but Jesus is no longer here; His seed died so we "might become" the likeness of Him and do all the works He did, in His stead, to the benefit of His children. That is the heart of the Father, and by **not** wanting to do the same miracles for His children, are we **not** rejecting the heart of the Father to love on His creation? A case could be made that **not** doing the miracles Jesus died for us to do could be considered an act of self-preservation, but only God knows our heart.

Power & Authority has its place in the Kingdom

As we discussed in the previous chapter, the apostles had various kinds of power & authority when they walked with Jesus. Before He breathes on them the Holy Spirit and they are born again, before they get even an inkling of righteousness and before they have received the Spirit of Grace and Truth in the upper room, Jesus gave them power & authority...but why?

> *Then Jesus called the Twelve together and **gave them power and authority over all demons, and power to cure diseases**. ²And He sent them out to proclaim the kingdom of God and to heal the sick.*
> Luke 9:1-2

Why were these two gifts the first ones given, even though the apostles were clearly not mature enough to handle them? And for those that assume it was some kind of special anointing only the 12 apostles possessed, the following verse should clarify things nicely.

> ***The Lord appointed seventy-two others** and sent them two by two ahead of Him to every town and place He was about to visit. ²And He told them, "The harvest is plentiful, but the workers are few...³Go! I am sending you out like lambs among wolves...*
> Luke 10:1-3

From the time I noticed that Jesus gave power and authority to the apostles before they had received the Holy Spirit, I was quite curious as to the whole process. Before they were saved, before they understood their identity, before they knew to seek for righteousness and well before they were filled with His Spirit in the upper room, they were performing miracles. The only logical explanation I could determine was to show and prove to them what was available in the Kingdom of God, thereby motivating them not to quit, not to give up and go back to their former lives after the horror of the cross. By performing some of the same miracles that Jesus did, it would have inspired confidence in them to achieve all that He was and did. Then I remembered something Paul said, and I believe it sums it up best.

> *My message and my preaching were not with persuasive words of wisdom, but with a demonstration of the Spirit's power,* ⁵***so that your faith would not rest on men's wisdom, but on God's power.***
> 1 Corinthians 2:4-5

If the Bible says, *"Without faith it's impossible to please God,"* then acquiring faith is obviously paramount; God uses His power to do miracles through us to establish faith in us as well as everyone around us who witnesses them.

Paul was well educated, he claimed to be a Pharisee of Pharisee's, in other words, he was a teacher of the teachers; likely equivalent to a professor with several PHD's. Yet even with all his education and human knowledge, Paul let the power of God do his talking for him, so the faith of the people would be in the power of God and not him. This is probably the absolute best reason for us to pursue miracles, because it takes us out of the equation and puts the focus on God. If we stay grounded in our identity and seek righteousness, any and all miracles will be attributed to God thereby giving Him all the glory.

Expounding on Paul's reason for doing miracles, one could argue that not seeking such power may also be construed as an attempt to exalt oneself if their ministry is based upon preaching only. If miracles display the power of God giving Him the glory, then not allowing yourself to be used to do miracles places all the weight on our ability to minister the gospel, which could potentially be used by the devil to glorify one's self. I am not saying it is the case, but I've learned not to ever underestimate the enemy.

So we see here a dichotomy exists; on one hand, power and authority can go to our head, puffing us up with self-glorification by doing miracles without a proper understanding of identity and righteousness, but not doing them is like us doing ministry in our own wisdom and knowledge thus denying God the opportunity to reveal His power and love towards His children, thereby denying Him all the Glory.

The fact is, God is a good, good Father and He not only wants all of us saved, He wants us healed as well. If we remember that, and the fact that we are not the ones actually doing the healing or the miracle, it takes all the pressure off of us and puts it squarely on Him. Our job is to allow ourselves to be used like an extension cord that connects the Holy Spirit power source with the person in need.

> *Earnestly pursue love and **eagerly desire spiritual gifts**, especially the gift of prophecy. 1 Corinthians 14:1*

> *And now, Lord, consider their threats, and enable Your servants to speak Your word with complete boldness, ^{30}by stretching out Your hand to heal and performing signs and wonders in the name of Jesus." Acts 4:29-30*

The disciples wanted more boldness to preach His Word so they prayed the Father would stretch out His hand to heal in the name of Jesus. Considering that Jesus gave the disciples power and authority to perform miracles well before the cross, I can see no conclusion other than to assume that our Father wants us to desire to do miracles as well. Always keep in mind that moving in miracles with a lack of one's identity as an adopted Child of God as well as a pursuit of love and righteousness will set you up to fall just like the disciples in the garden. We are only the facilitators of miracle power, a conduit our Father uses to reach the lost, the poor, the broken and the needy. We requisition the power of God on behalf of the one in need. Therefore, we should diligently seek for and ask for power to do miracles but not at the expense of knowing your identity, walking in love and seeking righteousness.

Fire from heaven

Casting out demons and healing the sick are unselfish acts within themselves, but the disciples had other power as well; they had the power to rain down fire if need be, and that, in the hands of the immature, is scary indeed. It would be dangerous enough to give firecrackers to a 6 year old, but this power the disciples had was like giving him dynamite; close supervision is paramount.

> *He sent messengers on ahead, who went into a village of the Samaritans to make arrangements for Him. ⁵³But the people there refused to welcome Him, because He was heading for Jerusalem. ⁵⁴When the disciples James and John saw this, they asked,* **"Lord, do You want us to call down fire from heaven to consume them?"** *⁵⁵But* **<u>Jesus turned and rebuked them,</u>** Luke 9:52-55

Can you imagine a bunch of undisciplined children with the power to rain down fire on someone that offended them? Remember, the apostles were a mess, behaving as adolescents; in many ways the disciples before the cross looked just like the "Spirit Filled - Full Gospel" churches after the OSAS and prosperity hucksters sank their greedy little talons in them and defiled them. These once awesome, faith filled houses of God have become nothing more than a den of thieves. It's the blind leading the blind.

There was a time when the "Full gospel" movement was full of power and authority, preaching righteousness, being filled with the Holy Spirit and exercising all His gifts. I was saved at the very end of that era and it was awesome. Miracles abounded in these once faith filled bastions of hope and love, but Satan crept in with his den of thieves and their OSAS and prosperity lies, putting an end to a very "Acts like" church movement.

Now most, not all, but most of the full gospel churches are a mere shadow of their former selves. Selfishness abounds because no one teaches the need to die to self and seek righteousness. They greet people with a smile, but lust for the things of the world has produced within them a selfish, loveless heart. False grace messages give birth to sin so seeds of righteousness can never take root. The result is an orphan with no understanding of their identity, no Godly wisdom and no knowledge. They do espouse the Holy Spirit, but it's almost as if they are ashamed to do so; in fear of seeming weird and running off a potential "customer." I use the word "customer" here because that is exactly the way people are being treated by the church leadership now. They are selling feel-good-ism and the hope of an uncommon blessing that can be **purchased** with an uncommonly huge monetary gift to a parasitic preacher.

Any Holy Ghost experience is largely limited to speaking in tongues now, which is nothing more than ineffective incoherent rambling, because they don't teach the intended purpose or the benefits thereof. Most likely because the preachers either don't know themselves or have forgotten just how powerful, and beneficial tongues are in the Spiritual realm, as well as how important tongues is in establishing a personal prayer language with the Father for the edification and maturity of their own spirit man. All that is gone now, lost to selfishness and a quest for wealth, and it all began when they lost their identity because they stopped seeking righteousness.

Authority is no longer taught for obvious reasons. The OSAS and prosperity doctrines are a doctrine of demons and they have no desire for you to learn who you are and what authority you have over devils, so every message is nothing more than a motivational seminar followed by an offering. You have to hand it to Satan, his plan worked...almost. Almost, because I believe there is a new movement back to the Kingdom of God and His righteousness. Albeit small, there is a remnant church seeking after, hungering and thirsting for righteousness, and they are the bride to be raptured; the few on the narrow path of righteousness.

Ever since my YouTube videos began emphasizing righteousness, my viewership dropped by 90%, and to be honest, I really couldn't care less; I never produced videos to become popular anyway. Obedience and righteousness is not a sexy message, but it is necessary to get the bride ready to go home for the wedding feast.

> ***Blessed are you*** *when people insult you, persecute you, and falsely say all kinds of evil against you because of Me.*
> Matthew 5:11

Regarding righteousness, never allow what people do not perceive, affect what you do. The fact is, most Christians will not understand this message, and when I say most Christians, I am speaking literally. Christians have been taught from their conversion that they are just sinner's saved by grace and therefore they have a sin conscious outlook on life; they just expect to sin. Any message of righteousness and living a life without habitual sin is like blasphemy to them. Their response is much like the Pharisees response to Jesus and the apostles when they preached the truth about the kingdom of God. On several occasions they tried to stone Jesus but the Holy Spirit intervened and got Him out of harm's way. The apostle Steven was not so lucky; He called them out for their unrighteousness and for murdering Jesus and their response was ridiculous and juvenile.

> *At this **they covered their ears, cried out in a loud voice,** and rushed together at him.* ⁵⁸*They dragged Steven out of the city and began to stone him.* Acts 7:57-58

They covered their ears and cried aloud? Picture that… it sounds like a bunch of snowflakes needing a safe space to hide when an opposing view is expressed. Jesus didn't die such a horrific death so we could continue to sin, he did it to deliver us from sin, to take the nature of sin away from us so we would no longer want to sin. I find it interesting that most believers have awesome testimonies about how they miraculously stopped drinking, doing drugs or whatever, but they continue to live in fornication or other things that are obvious sin. The miracle power of God was able to deliver them from one sin but not all the others, and the ones they continue to engage in are somehow OK with God now because of their false definition of grace?

No, the sin we willfully engage in is nothing more than the sin we refuse to die to. It is selfishness at its finest hour, doing what selfishness does best... fulfilling the lust of the flesh. Seeking righteousness exposes our sin as sin and the Holy Spirit empowers us to rule over it, not the other way around.

> *Enter through the **narrow** gate. For **wide** is the gate and **broad** is the way that leads to destruction, and **many** enter through it. ¹⁴But **small** is the gate and **narrow** the way that leads to life, and only a **few** find it.*
> Matthew 7:13-14

Most people automatically assume that Jesus is speaking about believers and unbelievers here, the saved and the unsaved, but what if that is not the case? There were times when Jesus was preaching to the masses of people, but there were also times He preached privately to only His followers. Likewise, I truly believe that Jesus is speaking to the church and not the whole world when He uses the narrow and wide analogy. In it He paints a very vivid picture of two roads; one road with thousands upon thousands on it, and another road with only a few, 3 to 5 people on it, but that does not accurately portray the balance of confessing believers to unbelievers. 85% of all Americans believe in the God of the Bible, and 45% of those are confessing Christians, who claim to be members of a church, so that does not jive with the broad and many, narrow and few picture that Jesus paints.

What if, like all the others, we are taking these verses out of context too? What if Jesus is not talking about believers and unbelievers? What if He is talking specifically to the church? What if the church was divided into these two roads, one heading towards destruction and another heading to eternal life? What if

Satan had successfully infiltrated the church with a doctrine of demons leading most people who consider themselves Christians down a path of separation from the Father? What if this illustration is **not** regarding Christians and non-Christians? What if Jesus is comparing the righteously obedient Christian with Christian workers of lawlessness who practice unrepentant, willful sin? If context is the best way to determine who Jesus is talking to, then Jesus would seem to confirm He is speaking to the church and not the whole world a few verses later when he says,

> *Many will say to Me on that day, 'Lord, Lord, did we not prophesy in Your name, and in Your name drive out demons and perform many miracles?' ²³Then I will tell them plainly, 'I never knew you;* ***depart from Me****, you workers of lawlessness!' Matthew 7:22-23*

Only Christians call Jesus *"Lord, Lord,"* and these Christians are told to, *"depart from Me, you workers of lawlessness!"* "Not possible," you say, "the church can't possibly be deceived to that extent." May I remind you of a time just prior to Martin Luther when the Catholic Church actually killed people if they were even suspected of reading a Bible.

In Revelation 2 & 3 Jesus pleads with the seven churches to come back to their first love (Him) or suffer dire consequences, yet only one out of seven churches heeds his warning and is spared from the tribulation to come, thus confirming the wide and narrow illustration is more likely an indictment on the church than the whole world. If one considers the state of the modern church and how Satan has deceived the masses with his OSAS & prosperity lies, it becomes far more likely that many confessing Christians may be in for a rude awakening on that fateful day, and Jesus' prophesy here only confirms what is set to transpire.

Remember, context is everything, so if we go back a few verses, beginning in Matthew 7:6, we get a better picture regarding the audience of Jesus' message.

> *Do not give dogs what is holy; do not throw your pearls before swine. If you do, they may trample them under their feet, and then turn and tear you to pieces. ⁷Ask and it will be given to you; seek and you will find; knock and the door will be opened to you.*
> Matthew 7:6

Now the whole thing about casting your pearls before swine is a bit tricky to explain, because while God does desire all men to be saved, there are some people that actually commit sin unto spiritual death, but the first point to make here is that Jesus is obviously talking to his followers, not just anybody. He's talking to his future church.

> *If anyone sees his brother committing a sin not leading to death, he should ask God, who will give life to those who commit this kind of sin. There is a sin that leads to death; I am not saying he should ask regarding that sin.* 1 John 5:16

So, we see here that there is a sin, just one, that leads to death and we are not supposed to cast our pearls, the wisdom of God, the Word of God before the people who commit such sin. This sin that John is speaking of has been somewhat of a mystery to the church, and I feel like God has just given me revelation regarding it, but let me get back to my first point and I'll tackle this later. I believe Jesus is talking to believers because He's not going to tell unbelievers not to share the wisdom of God with certain unbelievers; that doesn't even make any sense. Then, He immediately goes into the process of how to become like Him; He tells them to ask, seek and knock which was the very inspiration behind this book, and further proof that He is speaking to His church, not the world.

> *For everyone who asks receives; he who seeks finds; and to him who knocks, the door will be opened. ⁹Which of you, if his son asks for bread, will give him a stone? ¹⁰Or if he asks for a fish, will give him a snake?*

> ¹¹*So if you who are evil know how to give good gifts to your children, how much more will your Father in heaven give good things to those who ask Him!* ¹²*In everything, then, do to others as you would have them do to you. For this is the essence of the Law and the prophets.* ¹³*Enter through the narrow gate.* Matthew 7:8-13

For me, this has a way different feel than when Jesus is speaking to the Pharisees and the unbelieving Jews. The tone in this passage is as one speaking to a loved one or a beloved child. I believe the confirmation comes when He makes the comparison of giving good gifts to children. He is referring to them as His children, and as I confirmed earlier, I believe Jesus is talking to His church when He uses the analogy of the wide and narrow road due to the context of the entire section.

If Christians are the subject matter of Jesus' warning of the broad road to destruction, then it would only stand to reason that most confessing Christians are on the wrong path. It's probably no coincidence that His warning comes directly on the heels of His Ask, Seek, & Knock lesson which also leads directly into seeking first the Kingdom of God and His **righteousness**.

Unless we cherry-pick Jesus' warning of the wide path to destruction out of its place in context, it appears like the narrow path that leads to life is the path of righteousness, but can we confirm that in the Word?

> **There is life in the path of righteousness,** *but another path leads to death.* Proverbs 12:28

The "life and death" spoken of in Proverbs here is not physical, it's righteousness leading to spiritual life or unrighteousness leading to eternal death, and here's the problem, almost nobody is preaching righteousness, even though it is obvious that righteousness is the narrow path leading to eternal life that Jesus speaks of. A church that condones pedophilia by simply moving the offenders to a different church isn't about to touch righteousness. The Christian

Science, Unity and most denominational churches with their inclusive, do whatever makes you feel good theology is staying as far away from righteousness as they can get. The OSAS and prosperity preachers have no desire for their sheeple to seek righteousness, for righteousness would open their eyes thus exposing their fraud. If the righteous path to life is narrow and only a few find it, don't be surprised if hardly any of the people you know and love will perceive what you perceive, believe what you believe, and seek righteousness too.

Simon the Sorcerer

In the book of Acts, we read about a man named Simon who practiced sorcery in the city of Samaria and astounded the people there. He claimed to be someone great, and all the people, from the least to the greatest, heeded his words and said, *"This man is the divine power called the Great Power."* However, when they heard the apostle Philip preach the gospel of Jesus Christ, they believed and were baptized. Simon himself believed, was baptized and followed Philip closely; being astounded by the great signs and miracles he observed.

When the apostles in Jerusalem heard that Samaria had received the word of God, they sent Peter and John to pray <u>for them to receive the Holy Spirit</u>, because the Holy Spirit had not yet fallen upon any of them; they had simply been baptized into the name of the Lord Jesus. When Peter and John laid their hands on them, **they all** received the Holy Spirit. The moment Simon saw that the Holy Spirit was given through the laying on of hands, <u>he offered them money</u> and said, *"Give me this power as well, "so that everyone on whom I lay my hands on may receive the Holy Spirit."*

But Peter replied, *"May your silver perish with you, because you thought you could buy* **the gift of God** *with money!* **You have no part or share in our ministry, because your heart is not right before God.** *Repent, therefore, of your wickedness (unrighteousness), and pray to the Lord. Perhaps He will forgive you* *for the intent of your heart. You are poisoned by bitterness and captive to iniquity."*

Peter was given a word of knowledge to discern what was in Simon's heart. Simon would have likely used this power to exalt himself, not the Kingdom of God, so Peter rebukes him, and exclaims that Simon is a *"captive to iniquity,"* which is defined as bound in unrighteousness in the Strong's concordance. Therefore, even though Simon was baptized into Jesus, even though he said "the sinner's prayer" and confessed Jesus as his Lord, Simon was not given the Holy Spirit because he was held captive to unrighteousness, confirming that the Holy Spirit is not automatically given upon ones profession of faith. The main purpose of this book is to reveal the proper order of a believer's journey upon revelation of Jesus as Lord.

1. Seek the Kingdom of God
2. Die to Self
3. Seek Righteousness
4. Ask for the Holy Spirit
5. Desire Power and Authority
6. Repent daily
7. Do not grow weary of doing good

In Acts 5:1-11, Confessing Christians, Ananias and his wife Sapphira were killed by the Holy Spirit for the unrighteousness of simply withholding money and lying about it, yet Simon is not killed for his evil, even though he was found to have wickedness, bitterness and iniquity in his heart. So, why was Ananias and Sapphira killed, but not Simon? All three were confessing believers in Jesus Christ, all believed in His life, death, burial and resurrection, and all are rejected, but two killed and the other only rebuked, but why? Simon is spared because of his contrite heart.

> *Then Simon answered, **"Pray to the Lord for me, so that nothing you have said may happen to me."** Acts 8:24*

Thankfully, God is so very patient and forgiving, and He is always looking at the condition of our heart; whether it be hardened or repentant. Ananias and Sapphira showed no remorse for what was in their heart, proving that God is more concerned with what is going on inside your heart than your confession. People say one thing and do the opposite all the time. Salvation is not guaranteed by merely saying a sinner's prayer; it's not even so much what you have done or what you do, but how you feel about it afterwards as proven by Simon. God loves a repentant heart. If you mess up and temporarily go back to something you thought you were free from, was there sorrow and remorse? How did it make you feel, because there was a time when it didn't even bother you? So, if it bothers you now, that is a good thing, because there must be a seed of righteousness growing inside you.

> *A broken and a contrite heart, O God, You will not despise.* Psalm 51:17

If that is you, do not let condemnation in; don't even give it an inch. Instead, rejoice, praise your Father that righteousness is growing within you. Thank Him that you are not that person any longer; you are a new creation in Christ Jesus, one who seeks righteousness over the things of the world. Virtually nobody responds like that, and it will drive the devil insane.

The following is a fictitious depiction of Satan's conversation with the demon assigned to a Child of God who understands their identity and seeks righteousness:

Satan: *Did you get her to sin?*

Demon: *Yes boss.*

Satan: *Did you then get condemnation, guilt and depression to assist you?*

Demon: *Yes, boss, they did join me afterwards.*

Satan: *Remember, the goal with this one is to get her so depressed that she takes her own life; the spirit of suicide is waiting for you to prepare her for him so he can finish the job.*

Demon: *Yes boss, I know, but...*

Satan: *But what?*

Demon: *Well...her response was not the same as usual, and frankly, I'm confused.*

Satan: *What do you mean, what did she do? How did she respond to condemnation?*

Demon: *She praised Je...sus!* (they have a difficult time saying His name without shuddering in fear)

Satan: *She what? She praised His name? Nobody does that, they're selfish, it's all about them, it's one big pity party. Sin, followed by Self-loathing and condemnation has worked on this one since she first believed.*

Demon: *I know, but not this time boss, I think she finally figured out that she is a child in authority, and she's begun confessing it daily, even when...no, especially*

if I get her to sin which is less and less now that she is seeking after righteousness. And I gotta tell ya boss, she's driving me, selfishness and condemnation crazy; they're talking about leaving her alone and moving on to someone who's more gullible.

Satan: *UUUGH! Damn those Christians who know their identity and seek righteousness. Ok, new strategy, leave her alone for awhile, get to work on your next assignment, but when you're done with them, go back to this one and see if she has forgotten who she really is. I'll stop blocking that promotion she's been praying about and make her so busy with her new job she won't have time to pray. Then we'll send prosperity her way, she's quite ambitious, maybe we can trap her with the deceitfulness of riches and a desire for worldly things. I've seen this before, but eventually they grow weary of doing good. We'll see how long she can keep this up; I give her 1... 2 years at best.*

Power in the Gifts of the Holy Spirit

*Brothers and sisters, I want you to know about the gifts of the Holy Spirit... ⁴ **There are different kinds of gifts**. But they are all given to believers by the same Spirit... ⁸ To some people the Spirit gives a message of **wisdom**. To others the same Spirit gives a message of **knowledge**. ⁹ To others the same Spirit gives **faith**. To others the Spirit gives gifts of **healing**. ¹⁰ To others He gives the power to do **miracles**. To others He gives the ability to **prophesy**. To others He gives the **discernment of spirits**. To others He gives the ability to speak in **tongues** (different kinds of languages) they had not known before. And to still others He gives the **interpretation of tongues** (the ability to explain what was said in those languages). ¹¹ All the gifts are produced by one and the same Spirit. He gives gifts to each person, just as He decides.* 1 Corinthians 12:1-11

1. *The Gift of Wisdom* – This is the gift that Solomon asked God for and he was given wisdom to such an extent that he was considered the wisest man in the history of the world (second only to Jesus). The gift of wisdom is supernaturally knowing the exact right thing to do or say at any given moment. When confronted with two women each claiming that a certain baby was theirs, Solomon ordered the baby be cut in two and each woman be given half. One of the women cried out, "no, give the baby to her." Solomon knew immediately who the real mother was and she was given her baby back.
2. *Gift of Knowledge* – The gift of Knowledge is when the Holy Spirit tells you something about someone so that you may better minister to that person. My friend Ralphena travels all over the world preaching, and occasionally she gets words of knowledge about sin involving church leadership, often the pastor himself. Words of knowledge aren't always about sin; I get a word of knowledge sometimes about a sickness or injury affecting a person. When

you ask them if they have a knee or back injury and they actually do, it gets their attention and provides the opening necessary to pray for them. This is especially helpful for unbelievers making them more receptive to minister to after they get healed. First you heard something about them without knowing it prior, then they get healed of the thing you heard, now their defenses are down and their ears are open. I encourage you to seek words of knowledge, but as with all the gifts, never let it go to your head and only desire to use it for the kingdom, not for your own selfishness.

3. *Gift of Faith* – Jesus said you can move mountains with faith the size of a mustard seed. A mountain is simply a metaphor for a difficult trial, and faith the size of a mustard seed expresses the awesome power of God contained in the smallest amount of faith. A mustard seed is as small as the head of a pin, therefore the principle behind the saying is this: *"If you don't have at least that much faith, you likely don't have any faith at all."* Yet the Bible says that God has given us a measure of faith, so we all have more than enough faith to move whatever mountain we face. Don't be afraid to ask for a greater measure of faith, for Jesus said, *"ask and it shall be given."*

4. *The Gift of Healing* – Personally one of my favorites because it is such a great opportunity to preach the gospel. Who's not going to listen to you tell them about the Jesus that just healed them of an injury or sickness they had for years, seeing all their symptoms gone as well? Besides, it's exactly how Jesus and Paul used to get the people's attention, so it must be an effective witnessing tool. Along with authority over demons, healing was the first power given to the disciples. Furthermore, in Mark 16:17, healing is listed as one of the signs that would follow **all** new believers in Jesus.

5. *Power to do Miracles* – While healing is a miracle, the power to do miracles is not the same as healing. I met a young man in a convenient store one day when God gave me a word of knowledge about an injury to his knee. Lo and behold, he had blown it out playing football in high school so that he could no longer bend it because it had a steel rod in it. After I prayed for him, he

squatted to the ground with ease. Not only did God heal the ACL in his knee, but He also removed the steel rod from it. That is a miracle completely independent of the healing of his ACL. If God simply healed his ACL, but does not perform a miracle by making the steel vanish, he still can't bend his leg so what good is that to him? If I have faith that God will heal an ACL, then I ought to have faith that the metal be removed too. All that notwithstanding, for me, the real miracle came when the two Muslim cashiers who witnessed the event asked me to pray for them as well. For which I agreed, but only if they allowed me to minister Jesus to them, to which they readily accepted.

6. *Gift of Prophesy* – Is the ability to foretell events before they happen. Many people dream prophetically, others get day visions much like a day-dream. Having been in the ministry for 30 years now, true prophets are few and far between. Miss Ralphena has given me some remarkable prophesies over the years that were right on the money, but it is a gift that has become extremely rare in the body of Christ. Paul said we should earnestly desire spiritual gifts, especially the gift of prophesy, and when writing about the many benefits of tongues, he states that he would rather have us prophesy.

7. *Gift of Tongues* – Tongues is the very first gift the apostles displayed after receiving the Holy Spirit in the upper room on the day of Pentecost. It is the most misunderstood and maligned of all the gifts, but it is a gift of God none-the-less, therefore we should desire it.

> *...with stammering lips and another tongue will He speak to His people.* Isaiah 28:11.

Tongues are one of the ways God speaks to you. It is a vehicle He uses to reveal mysteries to you. Praying in tongues is also referred to as *"praying in the spirit."*

> *Praying **always** with all supplication **in the spirit**.* Ephesians 6:18

Everywhere Paul says, *"Praying in the spirit,"* he is referring to "praying in tongues," and Paul instructs us to pray in tongues, always!

One day I received a phone call, out of the blue, from the headmaster of Encourager Christian Academy. He asked me if I would teach about tongues to his high school classes. I had been speaking in tongues a lot, but I wasn't quite sure how or what I would teach on, so I asked God to teach me some of the many benefits of tongues that I could pass on to the students.

The following day, while in prayer, I received a vision from the Lord. I saw Jesus lying on the ground prostrate and He was in great sorrow. I immediately knew He was in the garden of Gethsemane, just before they came to take Him for His trial. He was sobbing and I could almost feel His heart breaking as He literally cried tears of blood, begging the Father to take this cup from Him or make another way. He did not want to go to the cross, and He pleaded with God, but in the end He said, *"Yet not my will, but Your will be done."* Just then I heard, with a clear audible voice, *"Just as my son prayed my will over this, likewise do you pray my will over the issues of your life when you pray in tongues."* When we pray in tongues, we are praying the Fathers will over our situation, and if we know His will is perfect, why would I **not** pray in tongues?

Not long afterwards, I woke one evening with an unusual feeling of emergency, almost to the point of great dread. I tried falling back asleep, but urgency would not allow me, so I got up to pray, and noticed it was 4:00 am. As I began to pray the sense of danger only seemed to heighten, and I immediately felt the need to pray in tongues. I am not sure if I prayed for 5 minutes or 50 minutes, but suddenly I saw the image of one of my closest and dearest friends, who was residing out of State at that time. After a few moments, the image went away along with all the urgency and dread, so I went back to sleep.

When I called them 2 days later, my friend's wife answered the phone and after exchanging pleasantries, I told her what had happened with me and asked if her husband was okay. She said, "He had a heart attack that night." Apparently, at 4:30, he woke up and said he felt thirsty, so he went to get a drink, took a few steps and collapsed. She called 911 and proceeded to do CPR. At the hospital the following day, the doctor asked him how he felt and he said he felt perfectly normal. The doctor responded by telling him they knew he had a heart attack, because the monitors proved it, but they had run test after test and there was absolutely no damage, they had no reason to keep him there any longer, he was free to go home. When you pray in tongues, you have no idea who and what your Father may be using you to do, it's up to you to be obedient and allow yourself to be used. You never know, your Father may be using you to cover a brother in Christ halfway around the world.

When you pray in your native tongue people can understand you, but who else can understand you? Satan can, and the 10th chapter of the book of Daniel is a fascinating depiction of how things actually work in the spiritual realm.

I highly recommend that you go read it, but I'll synopsize it here:

It begins with Daniel fasting and praying without ceasing until his answer comes from God 21 days later. When the angel arrives, Daniel responds with, "Dude (modern vernacular here), 21 days? It took you 21 days to respond? I have been fasting and praying for 21 day, what in the world took you so long? The angel said, "Oh Daniel, greatly beloved of God…, dude, don't even go there, because from the moment you set your heart to pray, God sent me, but because Satan understands your language, he sent the Prince of Persia to stop me (A fallen angel powerful enough to rule over an entire country), and there I did battle for 21 days. Yet, because you continued to speak words of faith, because you did not doubt in your heart, God sent Michael the arc angel on my behalf, and there I did break free, so now I have come with your answer."

This is a most enlightening description of the way it works in the spirit realm when we pray. God sends the answer immediately, but Satan sends up a roadblock with the express purpose of causing a delay. In Mark 11:23 Jesus said, *"Whatever you speak with your mouth and believe in your heart, these things will come to pass...."* In other words, you will have whatever you say, so if you speak doubt after you pray, you will not get anything, it's as simple as that. When our answer is delayed, Satan sends a spirit of doubt to us with the hopes of getting us to speak doubt over our situation. "Gee, it's taking a long time; I guess it's just not His will." That is all Satan needs to bring an accusation of doubt against us, and stop our answer before it gets to us.

> *...he who doubts is like a wave of the sea, blown and tossed by the wind. ⁷That man should **not** expect to receive anything from the Lord.*
> James 1:6-7

When we doubt, we are our own worst enemy, but Satan does not know the language of tongues, therefore he cannot stop it, he cannot send up a roadblock to our prayer request when the request itself is made while praying in tongues. Furthermore, when we pray in tongues, we don't know what we are praying for so we can't doubt it, and if we cannot doubt it, even we can stop it. This makes praying in tongues the most powerful and effective form of prayer in the world because it cannot be stopped by the devil or us for that matter.

God is a genius, and He knew we were here with a monster whose hatred for us and wickedness towards us is so much worse that we will ever know. Our Father did not leave us here with a psycho defenseless; God gave us weapons to defeat him; and one of those weapons is tongues. That is why so many church leaders have been deceived into preaching against tongues, because tongues basically neuters the devil and leaves him powerless against us.

> *For if I pray in tongues, **my spirit is praying** (praying in the spirit), but **I don't understand what I am saying**.*
> 1 Corinthians 14:14

The Bible says, when I speak in tongues, I speak directly to God.

> *For **he who speaks in tongues does not speak to man but to God**, for no one understands him; however, in the spirit he speaks mysteries.*
> 1 Corinthians 14:2

How can any serious believer with a normal functioning frontal lobe say that speaking directly to God through the medium of tongues is bad in any way? Now if a mystery is something previously unknown, then praying is tongues is just another way our Father reveals the mysteries we are seeking after.

> *The one who speaks in a tongue **edifies** himself...* 1 Corinthians 14:14

When we speak in tongues it literally edifies our spirit man, thus molding us, and transforming us into the image and likeness of Jesus.

Edify – Strong's #3618 oikodomeó (oy-kod-om-eh'-o) The building up of character: I encourage. It implies to build or to remodel your moral fiber as one would build or remodel a house.

Speaking and praying in tongues is essential for the development and growth of one's own spirit thus building their character into the likeness of Jesus.

> *But you, beloved, by building yourselves up in your most holy faith and praying in the Holy Spirit...* Jude 1: 20

How many times have you prayed for something and it did not come to pass, and we thought gee, I guess I did not have enough faith? We know how important faith is to every situation, but what is Jude referring to when he says, "...our most holy faith." As we learned earlier, when we pray in tongues, we are praying Gods will for us and our situation. If Gods will and faith is perfect for every situation and we are praying His will and faith as we pray in the spirit or in tongues, then praying in tongues is perfect faith or the "most holy faith" that can be displayed by a human. It cannot be stopped by Satan, it cannot be doubted and therefore stopped by us and it is Gods perfect will and faith in our situation; therefore, it is a "most holy faith."

The benefits of tongues are:

1. We pray Gods wisdom when we pray in tongues.

2. The Father will use us to intercede and do miracles on behalf of others.

3. Tongues edify our spirit man so that we can grow in righteousness, look like Jesus and flow in the Gifts of the Spirit.

4. As our spirit man grows into the likeness of Jesus, it also becomes more sensitive to His voice and keeps us in-tune with God's Holy Spirit, so that we are able to hear and , if and when, danger is approaching.

5. Like Jesus in the garden, when we pray in tongues, we pray Gods perfect will over our situation.

6. Paul refers to tongues as the language of angels, but Satan and his hoard of demons do not understand it, in fact, it's the only language that they don't understand, and they can't stop what they don't know.

    7All people have a propensity to doubt if prayers are not answered immediately, and God's timing and our timing are almost never in agreement. Because we do not know what we are praying for when we pray in tongues, we are not capable of doubting what we do not know, so even we can't stop it.

7. When we pray in tongues, we are praying Gods most holy faith over our situation, so the result is always perfect; even if it is not the result we wanted or were expecting, it is Gods will and therefore perfect will.

*Earnestly pursue love and **eagerly desire spiritual gifts**...*
1 Corinthians 14:1

I want you to seriously consider for a moment, if tongues was the first spiritual gift given to the disciples at Pentecost, and Paul urges us to desire it, why in the world is there so much resistance to it? Whole denominations rail against tongues, making all kinds of ignorant claims regarding it. I have literally heard Christians say that tongues was from the devil! So many people oppose tongues because it does not fit into the doctrine they were raised in, but Paul said, "<u>For he who speaks in a tongue does not speak to men, but to God.</u>" How can it be from the devil if I am speaking to God? Are people even reading their Bibles when they say such things, or do they just skip the 14th chapter of Corinthians altogether? And if they did read it, you'd think that it would immediately cause them to discard their foolish doctrine, but for some odd reason they are dogmatic about it even though Paul names it as a spiritual gift we should desire earnestly.

I personally think speaking against any gift of the Spirit is a dangerous position to take. If scripture says that tongues are a gift given by the Holy Spirit, wouldn't we be grieving the Spirit by rejecting it, and would it not also be a form of blasphemy of the Spirit? Yes, and yes. Furthermore, condemning tongues is the very definition of a delusion; holding onto an idiosyncratic belief, even in the face of overwhelming evidence (Gods Word) to prove otherwise.

For anyone that is still holding onto the belief that tongues is from the devil or not for this present age; it's my advice that you keep it to yourself, just in case you are wrong. If you choose not to do it, that is fine, but don't risk speaking against the Holy Spirit based solely upon an opinion or the opinion of a misinformed, faithless preacher; it's not worth the risk. Besides what if you are wrong, have you ever been so sure about something only to find out later you were wrong?

So why would the body of Christ be so opposed to a gift that provides them the opportunity to speak directly to their Father in such a way that it literally edifies (builds up, strengthens) their own spirit and in a language Satan does not know and cannot stop? I believe it is for that very reason; Satan knows that the God of all creation has made a way for His Holy Spirit to live in you now that the cross is complete. Satan also knows that if he can keep you from righteousness and being filled with the Spirit of Grace and Truth, he can eventually drag you back to his world system and destroy you. However, when you pray in tongues, your Spirit is being edified by Gods Holy Spirit and you will begin to look more and more like Jesus and that scares the hell into him.

The absolute last thing Satan needs is more people looking like Jesus; that's why he hates righteousness and why most churches won't touch the subject. It was bad enough he had to deal with Jesus and the apostles 2000 years ago; he certainly doesn't want to go through it again. While tongues have many functions, the first was the ability to minister the Gospel to people of other languages. Paul dedicates almost the entire 14th chapter of 1st Corinthians to the benefits of tongues and encourages them to eagerly desire it. Some of the most amazing miracles I have ever witnessed came after much time spent praying in tongues. Let me leave you with one last quote from Paul about tongues.

> ***I wish that all of you could speak in tongues,...*** 1 Corinthians 14:5

8. *Interpretation of tongues* – I don't want to say this was common when I first got saved and began going to a Spirit Filled Church, but it wasn't uncommon either. Within a few years, and just after the prosperity gospel took root, interpretation of tongues virtually vanished. Here's one way it worked: A man or woman of God (usually an elder), would stand up and begin speaking in tongues as the Holy Spirit prompted them. The pastor would just stop preaching and wait. Almost immediately thereafter, a different person would then get up and give the interpretation. Sometimes it would be a prophesy about a world event, other times it would be a word of wisdom or knowledge for a brother or sister in the church, but the accuracy was always dead on.

I once met an evangelist from Romania named Daniel Matea. He was saved in the days of communism before the Berlin wall came down and was instructed by God to flee with his family to America where he would learn "all things" and return to preach the gospel to Romania. He successfully and miraculously escaped, but when he arrived in America, he was confounded by the fact that he could not understand the language.

After some time praying in the spirit (praying in tongues), God began translating the English that was being preached to him into Romanian for his understanding. This was not a gradual learning either, one day he could not understand and the next day he could. On top of that, God also took the opportunity to supernaturally teach him to read, write and speak English beautifully. The first time I met Daniel his English was so good, I was under the impression he had been in America for decades, only to find out it was less than a year.

"Ask and it shall be given..."

When Jesus said this, He wasn't talking about a spouse, a job, a house or a car; in fact, He wasn't talking about worldly things at all. Jesus was talking about spiritual things; He was talking about the gifts of the Holy Spirit. Example: When my friend Ralphena decided to go into the ministry full time, she began by preaching in the prisons. She had a burning desire to use song as an opening to get people's attention so she could preach to them more effectively. Her desire to sing was completely unselfish, but the problem was that she couldn't really sing all that well, so she asked God for the ability and one day she just woke up singing.

> *So if you who are evil know how to give good gifts to your children, how much more will your Father in heaven give good gifts to those who ask Him!* Matthew 7:11

Miracles

Miracles, whenever they occur are awesome, and they come in many different ways. Sadly, some Christians go their entire life and never get to witness a single miracle. I have personally witnessed hundreds of them, small, great and everything in between. From the very first day of my walk with Christ, I always just expected to see them, because it was the way I was raised. My mentor, Jim Scalise did them everywhere he went so I just assumed it was normal and expected of Christians.

> *Truly, truly, I tell you, whoever believes in Me will also do the works that I am doing. He will do even greater things than these, because I go to the Father.* John 14:12

I probably heard Jim give his testimony a hundred times and it never got old. Lying on the floor of his prison cell where he expected to remain for the rest of his life with 17 life sentences; Jim was dying of pneumonia. He begged the guards to take him to the infirmary, but they just mocked him. Finally, one guard said to him, "You were man enough to get yourself in here, be man enough to heal yourself." Remembering he had a Bible his mother gave him at his sentencing, He randomly opened it to Mark 16:17 and began to read,

> *And these signs will accompany those who believe: In My name they will drive out demons; they will speak in new tongues;* ^{18}*they will pick up snakes with their hands, and if they drink any deadly poison, it will not harm them;* **they will lay their hands on the sick, and they will be made well."** Mark 16:17-18

He said the Words literally came off the page in 3D, "… <u>these signs will accompany those who believe: In My name</u> … they will lay their hands on the sick, and they will be made well." He said he noticed that there were three things required for this to work. First, one must believe, second a hand was involved, and third, a sick person. He thought, "I have no clue what I believe, but I have a hand and I am sick, so I have two out of three; those are pretty good odds." He said to himself, "God, if you are real, show me." Then he held up his hand and began lowering it to his forehead, as he touched his head he said a warm wave came over his entire body and he was instantly healed from head to toe.

I believe it was Jesus breathing His Holy Spirit on Jim as He did to the disciples when they were in fear of the Jews after the cross, because Jim was not only healed of his infirmity, but Jesus completely took every vestige of anger, and resentment out of his heart in a moment. All his addictions were removed, along with every form of lust, greed, and selfishness; everything...gone in an instant. It was Jim's road to Damascus moment. He said he just laid there and cried for hours, vowing to serve Jesus the rest of his life, and from that day on Jim spent every day at chapel and reading his Bible. Soon afterwards, his attorney notified him of a problem with his case. In court, the judge shocked everyone when he dismissed all the charges; 17 life sentences were vacated in an instant and Jim was released. From that day onward, Jim was a walking miracle just waiting to happen.

Jim was literally transformed from a super-villain into a carbon-copy of Jesus in an instant. I always thought of Jim as a modern day Paul with his road to Damascus miracle.

This salvation was first announced by the Lord, was
confirmed to us by those who heard Him, [4]and was affirmed
by God through signs, wonders, various miracles, and gifts
of the Holy Spirit distributed according to His will.
Hebrews 2:3-4

Miracles are also referred to as Signs and Wonders in the New Testament.

Signs – Strong's #4592 Sémeion (say-mi'-on) Definition: a sign. Usage: a sign, miracle.

Wonders – Strong's # 5059 Teras (ter'-as) Definition: a wonder, marvel. Usage: a wonder.

Miracles – Strong's #1411 Dunamis (doo'-nam-is) Definition: (miraculous) power, might, strength. Usage: physical power, force, might, ability, powerful deeds, deeds showing (physical) power, marvelous works.

> *"Men of Israel, listen to these words: Jesus the Nazarene, a man attested to you by God **with miracles and wonders and signs** which God performed through Him in your midst, just as you yourselves know.* Acts 2:22

One of the most frustrating religious spirits for me is the one that refuse to acknowledge miracles, healing and the gifts of the Holy Spirit. Those who believe and teach the last miracle ended when the last apostle died. What incredible nonsense and the following verse completely refutes that line of reasoning.

> *So if you who are evil know how to give good gifts to your children,* **how much more will your Father in heaven give the Holy Spirit to those who ask Him!"** Luke 11:13

I do find it interesting, however when you pray for them, they still get healed even in their unbelief. Their faith or lack thereof has nothing to do with anything, it's our faith they will rely upon, not their own. People can be in the middle of saying, "I don't believe in all that stuff," while they are getting healed.

But why would a preacher preach against healing and miracles? Like I said before, in doing so, their lack of faith is not exposed. They never have to be embarrassed when it does not work for them. They don't realize that they're not the ones doing the healing, so they're off the hook anyway. All they need to do is show up and be used. It's really nothing more than an identity crisis; they're still orphans pretending to be children. They have no idea who they are in Christ Jesus or how much He loves them. Their position of leadership has developed within them a "god complex," assuming they are something more than they ought.

It is so important to stay grounded in your identity as a Child of God, whether you are being used by Him to do miracles or not. In doing them, it's not you doing the doing, so a proper understanding of your identity is vital to keep you from getting filled with pride. As well, even if you are not walking in miracles, don't allow what you do not see prevent you from praying for people in need; knowing that God is the one on the hook to perform. Any period of time not seeing miracles is just His way of preparing your heart for the time He begins doing them mightily.

A gentleman introduced himself to me at the gym one day, saying that he saw me stop and pray for a random person who was walking into the gym as I was walking out. This gentleman was a devout Christian, but he had never considered doing anything like that, nor had he seen anyone do it and it convicted his heart. He didn't stay to witness any miracle, but just the act caused him to reevaluate his own faith and said it inspired him to become bolder with his witness. You have no idea how your Father plans to use you, so just make yourself available and don't even give a second thought to the outcome.

Authority

When describing what happens to a demon as it comes out of a human, Jesus said, "***it passes through dry places seeking rest.***" Humans are 98% water; so maybe, demons being without a human host is like us being in the desert, but whatever the case, demon spirits consider us their home.

> *When an unclean spirit comes out of a man, it passes through dry places seeking rest and does not find it. Then it says, 'I will return to **<u>the house</u>** I left.' ²⁵<u>On its return,</u> **it finds <u>the house</u> swept clean** <u>and put in order.</u> ²⁶Then it goes and brings seven other spirits more wicked than itself, and **they go in and dwell there**. And the final plight of that man is worse than the first."* Luke 11:24-26

Demons are the offspring of the fallen angels, however, unlike their fathers, they were not immortal. Even though their mothers were the daughters of Adam, their DNA was far different than that of their human ½ brothers. They did possess one important quality of their fathers; they were sadistically wicked by nature. The Bible refers to them in different ways, most notably as the Nephilim, and they are genetically predisposed to do evil; it was part of their DNA, it's who they were and what they now do. It's what caused Cain to kill Abel. Like a Pit Bull is bread to fight, so were the Nephilim bred for wickedness.

In the very first chapter of the Book of Enoch, God tells Enoch to write down all His words, saying that the book he would write was not for his generation, but would be opened at the time of the end. The Book of Enoch was taught by the early Jewish Rabbis, but virtually vanished until a copy was found in the Dead Sea Scrolls in the late 21st Century. Shortly afterwards, an exact copy was found in Ethiopia by a missionary.

To date, there are three known identical copies of the book of Enoch. Jesus and Peter both quote out of the Book of Enoch, thus confirming its authenticity. The Book of Enoch gives us an in-depth description of the events surrounding the first 200 angels that defected and exactly what sin they introduced to man. It details their lust for the daughters of Adam and how they were able to change their appearance into the likeness of their husbands, thereby deceiving the women into having relations with them.

The act was not consensual at first, but the after-effects were devastating. If there was ever a case to be made for abortion due to rape, it would have been then. Enoch goes on to say that the pre-flood Nephilim grew to gigantic proportions, even up to 300 cubits which is approximately 450 feet tall. Enoch describes how exceedingly wicked the Nephilim were and after they had nearly eaten everything on the earth, they noticed man, and so they began to eat him. In doing so, they began to crave the blood of man. Every form of wickedness and lawlessness was being conceived and practiced on earth at this time. Finally,

God has seen enough and He condemns the traitorous angels to be bound in chains in Antarctica for 4900 years, and their offspring to roam the earth as demonic vagabond spirits upon their spiritual death.

The very first thing you need to understand is that these foul vermin consider you "their home." Are you home to a demon spirit? You may be and don't even know it. Demons want, no, they need a human host body to possess; in doing so, they fulfill their two main objectives.

Their first objective is to kill you, steel all you have worked for, and destroy all that you hold dear. They are masters at this game, because they have been at it for 4000 years. Imagine how good you'd be at something if you had 4000 years to practice at it. They excel at this game because they are sadistically evil by nature and seriously enjoy what they do.

They have no remorse, feel no pity, never grow weary of doing evil, don't need rest, never get hungry, take no vacations, have whatever time is necessary to complete the task, are immortal now, cannot be stopped by human strength or with guns and bullets and they are extremely patient; they are the perfect employee. They have known you since you were born, so they know you like the back of their hand. They know what makes you happy, sad, emotional, angry, frustrated and impatient, and they use their powers of persuasion to elicit all your emotions while they work you like a skilled musician works an instrument.

They can move easily, by touch, in and out of anyone not filled with the Holy Spirit. All the while they are whispering suggestive thoughts in your ear that you mistake as your own. Thoughts that enrage you further, thoughts that depress you deeper, thoughts that arouse and entice you, and thoughts that control and manipulate you like a puppet on a string.

They are not as wise as their fathers, the fallen angels who fell with all knowledge of the universe, but they're not stupid either. They are cunning and crafty, working in conjunction with many others like them, all with different skills and abilities, but they do have a tendency to overplay their hand from time-to-time. That is to say that sometimes they push a person so far to the brink of disaster that they finally have no other option but to look up and ask God for help. If the demon spirit had just backed off a bit they could have kept that person in perpetual torment, but in their crazed frenzy to kill and destroy, sometimes they push people right into the waiting arms of Jesus; fortunately for us, they just don't know when to leave well enough alone.

Their second main objective is one they absolutely love doing, attaching to you with the ultimate goal of entering in you. In doing so, they get to live out their sick, twisted, greedy, selfish, lustful, murderous, hateful fantasies through you. Most of them have been residing in their host body for so long that the host has adopted the demon's personality traits as his/her own. If you can think of any one thing that you do, but you wish you did not do, a fear, a phobia, a bad temper, a tendency to drink too much, overeat, severe depression, lying, cheating, stealing, cussing, lust, greed, promiscuity, procrastination, unforgiveness and the like, it's because it's not your natural personality, it's them, projecting on you and through you.

We were made in the likeness and in the image of our Father, but because of the negative influence of these monsters, we have taken on all of their sick, twisted, perverted and wicked traits. As in the case of my friend Jim, when the Holy Spirit comes in to you He forces out all the evil spirits from you and our natural personalities emerge again. For some people, they've been that way so long, they don't even remember who they were before the infiltration and therefore, they have to get to know themselves all over again.

> ...***be transformed*** *by the renewing of your mind. Then you will be able to discern what is the good, pleasing, and perfect will of God.*
> Romans 12:2

By renewing your mind with the Word of God, you will be transformed from the image of Satan back into the image of Jesus. You were made in the image of God, but Satan uses everything in the world to conform you into his image. This is an epic battle over your identity, remember, it's all about your identity, and why identity is the first leg. God made you to look like Him, but Satan wants to give you a makeover so that you look like him. Who do you look like? Just because you say you are a Christian, or because that's who you want to identify as, does not necessarily mean that is who or what you really are.

"For each tree is known by its own fruit." Luke 6:44

If it walks like a duck, quacks like a duck and looks like a duck…it's a duck. If you walk in and among the world, talk like the world, and behave like the world, you are a Christian in name alone, but Jesus is not your Lord. A persons Lord is the one they follow, the one they honor (with more than just their lips), the one they emulate and obey; that is their Lord.

Sometimes, there are people like my friend Jim who get so filled with the Holy Spirit upon conversion that every evil spirit is removed immediately and they look absolutely nothing like the person they were before. They have new DNA; new Godly fruit growing off their tree and it is clearly evident for all to see, but it does not always work like that. Sometimes, there is no noticeable difference in that person's behavior.

But why, why are some people radically changed while others look no different; choosing rather to linger in their same sin for years afterwards? There's probably more than one answer to this question, but the main reason is motive. It is a condition of their heart. What was their motive for coming to God in the first place? Many times a person's motive is initially honest, but Satan's deceptions cause them to be conformed back again to a world that Jesus died to deliver them from in the first place.

A group of passengers going on vacation are given a big bulky backpack weighing one hundred pounds and told to wear it during their flight. In the pre-flight instructions, the flight crew tells them it will make their flight experience amazing, it is the best gift they could get. An hour later, the bulkiness and weight of it has made them very uncomfortable; their back is hurting, they're restless and miserable. The backpack has not made their trip amazing at all; it's more like an albatross around their neck. Finally, the discomfort is unbearable and most of them strip it off to settle in and get cozy. Shortly thereafter, turbulence rips the top of the plane clear off and everyone who took off the backpack is ejected to their death.

The backpack was actually a parachute and everyone who retained it was saved from certain death. This is a portrayal of the deception of the OSAS and the prosperity gospel. Telling everyone that receiving Jesus is the road to blessings and prosperity is setting them up for failure and a rude awakening. Confessing Him in a "one time prayer," but living selfishly in the world is like taking Him off to enjoy the ride.

> *I have told you these things so that in Me you may have peace.* ***In the world you will have tribulation.*** *But take courage; I have overcome the world!"* John 16:33

Jesus never tried to get anyone to say a one-time prayer; permitting them to remain in the same perverted state they were in previously. What Jesus actually said was, *"Go and sin no more...."* There was no such thing as a "sinner's' prayer" in the early church; that was concocted by man about 80 years ago. Jesus said,

> But **the one who perseveres to the end will be saved.** Matthew 24:13

Likewise, Jesus never promised anyone that following Him was going to make anything better except your eternal life. He warned them continually about just how bad it was going to get if they chose to follow Him; claiming that they would likely lose everything they owned and be, not just shunned, but even hated by everyone they loved, saying,

> *If the world hates you, understand that it hated Me first. ¹⁹**If you were of the world, it would love you as its own**. Instead, the world hates you, because you are not of the world, but I have chosen you out of the world.* John 15:18-19

Now let's take the same situation from a different point of view. Each passenger boarding the plane is given the same heavy, bulky backpack but told it is a parachute that will save their life because tragedy is inevitable. In the pre-flight instructions they are told not to take it off under any circumstance, regardless of how uncomfortable they may be. There will always be a few rebels willing to risk taking it off, thinking they can do so temporarily and get it back on before anything bad happens, only to be caught off-guard in the end. Most, however, will keep that bulky, heavy beast of burden on because they had the proper warning, not being tricked by a false sense of safety and/or pleasure.

Who do you resemble?

> *Do not be conformed to this world...,* Romans 12:2

It is a warning for all believers to never grow weary of doing good, choosing rather to go back to the world like a dog returns to its vomit. Satan does not give up when you get saved, he just changes his strategy. When a person gets a true understanding of the cross and accepts what Jesus did on their behalf, Satan's not going to waste his time telling you God is not real, and he's no longer trying to convince you that if your good outweighs your bad, that's good enough. He knows that you know the truth, so his new goal is to subvert or pervert your growth and maturity as a believer by keeping you from righteousness.

First, he tries to keep you from reading your Bible, so you never learn your identity, but if that fails he's got a million other deceptions up his sleeve. Ultimately, he'll use every skill he has developed and every demon at his disposal to ruin everything in and around you so that you give up and go back to the world, thus re-conforming you to it. But why, why don't they just give up on us when we come to the knowledge of the truth and become a disciple of Jesus? Because they know something we are unwilling to see and accept.

But the one who perseveres to the end will be saved. Matthew 24:13

Salvation is not guaranteed upon conversion and there are many instances of former apostles of Jesus from the book of Acts and beyond that left the faith and went back to the world, becoming apostate. Jesus said many things that eluded to this fact, and God is the same yesterday, today and tomorrow, so where else did He say it.

If a righteous man turns from his righteousness and practices iniquity, committing the same abominations as the wicked, **will** *he live?* **None of the righteous acts he did will be remembered.** *Because of the unfaithfulness and sin he has committed,* **he will die (a spiritual death)**.
Ezekiel 18:24

All of the apostate followers of Christ were being controlled and manipulated by demonic spirits to kill them, steal their salvation and destroy everyone and everything they hold dear in their lives. It's what these demons do, it's all they live for; they are virtually living vicariously through their human host, and unless you get a full understanding of your identity as a Child of God, seek righteousness with all your heart, and get filled with the Holy Spirit, you will come out on the losing end of life's wars, battles, trials and tribulation because of them. Christian or not, you will lose most of the time because they have the extreme advantage of stealth. Humans cannot see them and because we are heavily dependent upon our five senses, we tend not to acknowledge anything we cannot see or physically prove. However, just because they cannot be seen does not mean they are not there.

> *For we do not wrestle against flesh and blood, but against principalities, against powers, against the rulers of the darkness of this age, against spiritual hosts of wickedness in the heavenly places.*
> Ephesians 6:12

Therefore:

> *While we **do not look at (consider, acknowledge) the things which are seen, but the things which are <u>not seen</u>**. For the things which are seen are temporary, but the things which are not seen are eternal.*
> 2 Corinthians 4:18

There has been a demon assigned to you since you were born; taking notes and recording your every action and reaction to his schemes. It is his job, and he will suffer at the hands of Satan himself if he is not effective in deceiving you. Yet, your demon really does not need to be motivated, bribed, or threatened to do this job better, he is happy to do it because in you he gets to live again.

I explained how this works in great detail in The Altar of Love part I, so I'm not going to go deep into it here. As Children of God, we have been given authority over them, so we have the legal right to cast them off, but the first best line of defense is to prevent them from taking up residence in the first place. To do so, we must seek to walk in righteousness immediately upon conversion, and ask to be filled with the Holy Spirit.

> *"I have given you authority to tread on snakes and scorpions, and over all the power of the enemy. Nothing will harm you."*
> Luke 10:19

By restoring authority back to its rightful owner, Jesus has given us the legal right to completely dominate the devil and all his demon forces. Authority changes our position from the hunted to the hunter. We are the Sherriff now, with a badge, a gun, and a SWAT team of heavenly angels to back us up.

Furthermore, we are the judge, jury and executioner. It is our responsibility to judge them guilty, set the punishment and commands that punishment to be carried out. The angels of God do not work for us, they hearken unto "His Word," but we are the ones here speaking "His Word" now so it is their job to carry out "the Word" we proclaim.

"I have given you authority to tread on snakes and scorpions..."

While authority confers the legal right back to us, to "tread on" implies complete domination, therefore we have the legal right to completely dominate all demonic forces. Congratulations, you have been deputized! Snakes refer to all spiritual demonic forces that attempt to attach to us in the hope of entering in us, but scorpions connote a different class of enemy altogether. Scorpions are humanoid sentries that report back to the demons who report to the fallen angels. Scorpions are modern day Nephilim as well as human witches, sorcerers, Satanists and Luciferians working on behalf of the devil. Many times they are assigned to masquerade as Christians, infiltrating churches to cause division and strife.

If a Christian walks in willful, habitual sin, they give their authority (their legal right) back to the enemy just as Adam and Eve did. Now that demon has the legal right to enter the believer and stay in them to do as they please, and trust me when I say that they do not have your best interest at heart, and they will not stop terrorizing you until everything in your life is destroyed and/or you are dead. They will go after your kids, your spouse, your marriage, your friends and relatives; everything and anything that you hold dear to you is in their crosshairs, and you can rebuke the devil until your rebuker wears out, but that thing doesn't have to go anywhere if you have handed over your authority due to willful sin.

In the Altar of Love Part I, I described 5 ways Christians give their authority back to the demons. As in the garden, sin provides the enemy the legal right to gain entry back into them **and stay**. I'm not talking about unintentional sin, I am referring to the sin that Jesus spoke of when, speaking about Christians, He told them to "go away," calling them, "workers of iniquity. It implied they were sinning habitually, deliberately, and without remorse. They were behaving just like the world while calling themselves Christians. They are the OSAS.

The counter to giving away your authority is another awesome gift God has given us called repentance. Once we repent for our rebellious behavior and ask forgiveness, authority is immediately transferred back to us, and now you are free to expel the varmint. For a complete, detailed process, see The Altar of Love part I.

God has blessed us with authority, and by law, He too is obligated to follow it. God is not a "do as I say, not as I do," God. If God makes a law, he follows it. Many Christians are angry at God for not healing them or coming to their rescue when they cried for help; they blame Him for all the misfortune in their life when all the while it was within their authority to do for themselves? How embarrassed will they be when they stand before God and He shows them they were angry with Him for something He put under their authority to do? Millions upon millions of Christians have cursed God and fallen away from the faith because He didn't deliver them from their situation. I witness it almost every time I take on a new case. This is what Jesus meant when He said, *"My people perish for lack of knowledge."* It's the authority you don't assume that prevents you from receiving your victory.

Ignorance is not an excuse either; we cannot argue and say, "But that's not fair, I didn't know I had authority." We are expected to study to show ourselves approved; it is our responsibility to assume authority whenever and wherever it has been given to us by our Father. God understands that Satan is a narcissistic, egotistical, maniacal, sociopath, surrounded by hordes of equally sadistic demons whose main goal is to kill, steal and destroy us.

Therefore, God has not left us here without the power and ability to utterly destroy the works of the Devil. When a believer understands his identity, decides to die to self, seeks righteousness and is filled with the Holy Spirit, authority becomes as natural as a walk in the park, and he becomes a victorious force for good in the kingdom of God. Like Jesus, Paul knew his identity, sought righteousness and was infused with the Holy Ghost to such an extent that the awesome miracle power of God was available whenever he assumed his Authority.

Authority that we either do not know we have, do not know how to use, are too lazy to use or are afraid to use, gives the Devil the legal right to take it and use it against us. Let's consider this from another angle; if I offered to give you $10,000 as a one time-gift, or I offered to give you a business that made $10,000 a week, which would you prefer? If you were wise, you'd take the business. Likewise, is the authority given to us by God; He could have made it so that we had to approach Him for every single request, but instead, He gave us the authority and ability to do it ourselves. Instead of having to petition God for every little thing now, we can, in our authority, do it ourselves, as long as we do it in the name of Jesus.

You have to admit, it's much better this way, but it does take a certain level of maturity. The church has no business teaching prosperity until it first teaches maturity. Unless a Christian is fully matured in their Identity, unless they die to self and seek righteousness, unless they get filled with the Holy Spirit, unless they learn to control their tongue and walk in Love they will remain as orphan children and money would only destroy them.

> *When I was a child, I spoke like a child, I thought like a child, I reasoned like a child. When I became a man, I gave up childish ways.*
> 1 Corinthians 13:11

We must first become mature, adult believers before we ever consider being worthy stewards of vast sums of money. This is the brilliant deception behind the prosperity message. It's like giving the keys of a Corvette to a 9 year old boy and not even warning him to be careful. He'll be dead before the day is done, because the power and temptation to test the limits of the speed is beyond his ability to control it. Maturity must come before any amount of prosperity.

Keep in mind that the devil is not stupid, so if we begin to exercise our authority he will regroup and come at us from a different angle. The easiest way for him to knock us off our high horse of authority is to draw us back into sin, and lawfully take back the authority we use like an atomic bomb to destroy his kingdom. He wants your authority, he needs your authority; it is vital to his plans against you and everyone else around you he's been plotting and planning to take out. He can do nothing without it, and he will stop at nothing to get it back from you; this is war so you had better resolve yourself to that fact and expect resistance from all sides at all times…however? However righteousness! Righteousness and our Fathers Holy Spirit are the best foundation, and your greatest weapon for this spiritual battle; I used to think authority was our greatest weapon, but it's not, it is righteousness. If I walk in righteousness, I will rarely have need to exercise my authority.

> ***Submit yourselves, then, to God.*** *Resist the devil, and he will flee from you.* James 4:7

Most people quote the second half of this verse only, "<u>Resist the devil, and he will flee</u>…," and that is true, but as we discussed in the 2nd Leg of righteousness, doing so in your own power and ability is futile without being endowed with power from On High. This is precisely why James says, *"Submit yourselves to God,"* first.

Submit – Strong's #5293. Hupotassó (hoop-ot-as'-so) Definition: to place or rank under, to subject, to obey. Usage: I place under, I submit, put myself into subjection.

Submit, Hupotassó, is a military term, and it describes a soldier placing himself in subjection to, or under the authority of one higher in rank. It implies an absolute yielding to God's admonition, advice, plan, rules and regulations. If that be the case, what did Jesus advise and admonish us to do? To *"Seek ye first the kingdom of God and His righteousness."* Therefore, our ability to make the devil flee is solely dependent upon our ability to resist him, which is only possible when we submit to God by seeking righteousness.

Seeking righteousness is the absolute best way to make the devil flee from you, however, for your educational purposes, I will list the ways he can assume this awesome superpower called authority away from you.

5 Things that will Hand Over Your Authority

1. If you do nothing
2. Practicing Sin
3. Your Words
4. Selfishness
5. Witchcraft of the Heart

1.   Doing Nothing

The first way you give up your Authority is literally by doing nothing. Most Christians fall into this category, because almost nobody teaches on authority, certainly not the OSAS and prosperity hucksters. The most amazing thing I learned from the Altar of Love regarding authority was the fact that authority is there to be assumed, if you do not assume it, Satan will. Picture a demon standing next to you, arms folded and he's tapping his fingers on his bicep, saying, "What are you going to do here? Authority is available in this situation. Are you going to assume it? Because… if you don't, I will."

When God conferred authority to Adam in the Garden of Eden, it became spiritual Law, and when God decrees a law, even He will not break it. Adam sins and gives his authority to Satan, but 4000 years later, Jesus lawfully gets it back for us on the cross. When something is under your lawful authority, God will not "step in," and do it for you. First, because God would be breaking His own law and second, because He would be undermining you if He does. Being the lawful owner of authority means nothing if you don't use it, and Satan is happy to assume authority that is lawfully yours if you:

- Do not know you are the one in authority in any given situation.
- Know about authority, but don't understand how it works.
- Know what authority is and how it works, but are reluctant to use it for fear of retaliation from the devil (thinking that if you don't mess with him, he won't mess with you)
- Attempt to use it without a proper understanding of your identity.

If you are a baby Christian and do not yet understand how authority works, your Father has made provisions for you. For new Christians in spiritual huggies, all you need to do is cry out for help and your authority is transferred to God, thus enabling Him to help you without breaking the law. He will do that for a relatively short period of time, however, because there is an expectation of maturity on your part.

God is a good parent, He's actually much better at it than we are, and just as you would not allow your 32 year old son to live in your basement without a job, playing video games all day, your Father will not do everything for you when He has given you everything you need to dominate within this world system; He expects you to mature spiritually and begin assuming your authority.

Babies cry when they are hungry because they're unable to feed themselves and have not yet developed the verbal skills to articulate their need to eat. If my 9 year old is crying at the counter because he's hungry, I'm likely to scold him saying, "If you're hungry, tell me, but don't just sit there and cry." If my child comes home from college and says, "I'm hungry," I'm likely to say, "You're a big boy now, make yourself lunch." As in life, Christians cannot continue to behave like infants, asking God, begging God to do everything for them, we are expected to mature spiritually; we are expected to assume our authority.

A young Christian couple rushes their 4 year old son to the hospital with a temperature of 105. The cultures have determined that the child has meningitis, his temperature is still rising, they're losing him…he's dying. Spiritually, this child has done nothing to give authority to the enemy to kill him, but authority unassumed is authority acquiesced. They've been members of one of those mega churches for years, faithful tithers and givers, but this is way out of their league, they have no knowledge, no understanding of what, how and why this is even possible. They pray, "Father, we don't understand, how can this be allowed to happen to us, we tithe faithfully!" Time for a wakeup call, tithing has nothing to do with anything here, this is war and the winner of this war is the one with the best weapons and the knowledge to use them.

The fate of their child rests not on the money they tithed, or how many people from church come to pray for and console them, the fate of that child rests in the parent's knowledge and ability to assume the authority that is rightfully theirs, or not. The prosperity gospel they've been force-fed at church for the last 4 years cannot save their baby. If they are newbie Christians and are fortunate enough to even know a mature brother in Christ with the knowledge and the selflessness it takes to get involved in the matter, and if they have enough sense to acquiesce their authority to such a brother, God is likely to grant their request, but otherwise, this battle for their son is theirs to win or lose. Honestly though, the number of Christians who are knowledgeable enough and prepared to take on a battle of this magnitude is miniscule; 1 out of 100,000 at best.

Authority that you do not assume, for whatever reason, gives Satan the legal right to use it, and he will use it against you. God has given us the authority and ability to do **most things** ourselves. Instead of having to petition God for every little thing, we can, in our authority, do **most things** ourselves, but only in the name of Jesus.

I say, "most things," because our authority is limited, we do not have authority over everything, so we must learn what we do, and do not have authority over.

Please take note here, **where authority ends, prayer begins**, and knowing the boundary is vital. There were times Jesus took authority and simply spoke to something and there were times He prayed to the Father.

You have to admit, it's waaaay better to have authority than not, but it takes a high level of understanding, confidence and faith to know how and when to use it properly. Power & authority is like dynamite in the hands of a little child unless they are fully matured in their identity, seek righteousness with all their heart, and get filled with the Spirit of Grace and Truth. Just like the disciples in the garden, Christians experiencing a trial without identity, righteousness and the Holy Spirit will fold like a bad poker hand.

Most Christians do not even know what authority is, let-alone that they have it. Some Christians know about Authority, but they have no real understanding of how it works. A few know what Authority is and how it works, but life in the world has worn them down; they've forgotten its power and leave it on the table for their enemy to use. The most frustrating group are the ones that think, by leaving Satan alone, he will leave them alone. Nothing could be farther from the truth; Satan is an equal opportunity destroyer, and like all bullies, he preys on the weak and helpless. The only thing demons respect, the only thing that keeps them in check or at bay is an adopted child of the Most High God, walking in righteousness, filled with the Spirit of God while exercising power & authority. Everyone else is easy prey; they're roadkill for vultures.

2. Practicing Sin. The second way you give up authority is by practicing sin. Jesus said, "Go away you workers of iniquity." As with all sin, be quick to repent and ask forgiveness. Sinful behavior to stay away from includes but is not limited to: Everything and anything associated with the occult, lying, cheating, stealing, lust, drunkenness, revelries, drugs, vulgarity, whoredom, harlotries, fornication, adultery, gossip, manipulation, intimidation and rebellion.

Just as Adam's sin gave away his authority in the garden; our sin hands our authority away as well. Participating in any form of occult activity no matter how innocuous it seems, is sin. While sin comes in a multitude of improper actions and behavior, the two main ways we give up our authority through sin is occult activity and sexual immorality or sex outside of marriage. These are not the only two, but they are the main two and upon this behavior, authority is given to a demonic spirit that will be allowed to enter you if it is habitual and if you do not repent. They are not stupid; they will not enter you and immediately begin freaking out, because that would be too noticeable; they are cunning, crafty and extremely patient. They can and will lay dormant within you for years before they rear their ugly head in the form of sickness and disease. Behavior modifications will be subtle at first, growing ever more rebellious over time.

Entrance is not granted immediately upon sin, your Father will give you a grace period, an opportunity to repent for the foolish behavior. He will prick your heart with conviction, but after awhile, if repentance is not made, your authority is handed over and the demonic spirit will gain entry. Once entry is granted, it has the legal right to stay until its authority is taken away and it is expelled. Attempting to expel it without removing its authority has no effect, nor does repenting to gain and assume authority without actually commanding it to be removed. In other words, if you realize you have given up your authority and repent for the behavior, thus returning authority back to you, but you do not expel the varmint, you are still not free; it'll stay as long as you let it.

People that say a Spirit cannot enter a Christian have no clue what they are talking about. They can and do, all the time. I know this, because it happened to me many years ago, and I have also witnessed it hundreds of times while doing Altar of Love cases. In my case, I was ministering to a friend that was dealing with a spirit of depression. In hindsight, I think I was his real target to begin with, because after 2 hours of speaking the Word to and over him, he shook my hand and transferred it to me. I immediately sensed something amiss, but in my lack of understanding of authority, I did not pray right away, and its influence over me grew stronger with each passing hour. Finally, much later that evening, my wife took one look at me and instantly noticed something was on me and prayed over me. The moment she touched my hand and said, "In the name of Jesus;" it had to leave because I had not done anything sinful to give it my authority. I was only trying to help a friend, but it transferred to me by touch and was allowed to stay because of my lack of understanding.

> *"You are to consult neither mediums nor familiar spirits. You are never to seek them—you'll just be defiled by them. I am the LORD your God.*
> Leviticus 19:31

I would soon learn that sin, in the form of occult activity, is the main cause of mental and emotional issues, but they can also usher in other spirits that bring affliction and disease as well. Sexual sin caused most, if not all of the physical ailments that afflicted my case subjects, but occult activity opens the door to demonic spirits that afflict the mind in the form of extreme sadness, depression, schizophrenia, suicide, anger, rage and even murder. In order to evict these demonic spirits, authority must be taken back and this is where repentance and forgiveness come in.

> *But the man who was healed did not know who healed him...*
> *14Afterward, Jesus found the man at the temple and said to him, "See, you have been made well. **Stop sinning**, or something worse may happen to you."* John 5:13-14

Sickness and disease also comes by way of occult activity. All the people who had dabbled in the occult, but had not committed sexual sin outside marriage still had many physical ailments as well as many mental problems. Sexual sin on the other hand, is mainly sin against your own body, and affected my case subjects with severe physical ailments but not necessarily their mind. This is confirmed by Paul in 1 Corinthians,

> *"Flee from sexual immorality. Every other sin a man can commit is outside his body, but **he who sins sexually sins against his own body**."*
> 1 Corinthians 6:18

Sinning against your own body is equivalent to deliberately injuring yourself. I know there are spirits that self-mutilate but most people would not willingly inflict serious, long-lasting harm to themselves, yet, that is exactly what sexual sin does in the spiritual realm. A Christian who engages in fornication for example is like a person who cuts off his thumb to spite his index finger. As with occult activity, sexual sin hands over your authority to a demonic spirit to enter you and causes a number of sicknesses and diseases as well as physical ailments.

I found it interesting that many of my case subjects were unlawfully sexually active in their younger years at college, but had been faithful since their marriage for the last 20 or 30 years. It was only after all that time that the physical ailments and disease began to manifest, because the spirit that was given authority through the behavior lay dormant for all those years. The process of the Altar of Love and the wisdom of the Holy Spirit enabled us to connect the sin to the ailment, once we did and repentance was made, authority shifted back to the rightful owner and the spirit fled immediately.

So why is it that nobody is teaching about a believer's authority and the power therein? Why is the church so focused on prosperity? Because prosperity is being used as a distraction to deceive the church into seeking after the things of the world thus never becoming like Jesus. In seeking prosperity and their best life now, they never grow and mature, they never learn to love unconditionally, or count it all joy when they fall into a trial and they never learn to forgive. They never seek righteousness, dying to themselves would be a cruel joke, and they falsely assume they received the Holy Spirit when they said their "sinner's prayer."

3. Your Words. The power (Authority) the Devil has is the power (Authority) we give him by the words we speak. Death and life are in the power (Authority) of your tongue. Everything you say can and will be used against you by the devil.

> *"...out of the abundance of the heart the mouth speaks."* Matthew. 12:34

Everything we see, everything we listen to, and everything that we experience; all of it goes into our heart and out of the abundance of our heart our mouth speaks. When people say foolish things, hurtful things, evil things, deceitful things, it is because that is what they have been putting into their heart. Much like the people of the world, well-intentioned Christians say dumb or insensitive things, because they have been putting worldly junk into their heart for their entire lives and that is the only thing that can come out. If they seek righteousness however, and renew their minds with the Word, it will happen less and less often, until it happens no more. One must continually remind oneself to be patient with new believers and not let their remarks offend them.

> *"For where your treasure is there your heart will be also."* Matthew 6:21

> *"A good man out of the good treasure of his heart*
> *brings forth good things, and an evil man out of the*
> *evil treasure of his heart brings forth evil."*
> Matthew 12:35

God refers to your heart as a treasure, so how are you treating the treasure that is your heart? When I think of a treasure, I think of a chest filled with precious gems like diamonds, rubies, and emeralds. I picture it overflowing with gold coins and gold jewelry so valuable that one could not put a price tag on it. If you had a treasure like this, how would you treat it? Would you just leave it out in the back yard where the sun would fade its brilliance and the rain, dust, dirt would tarnish it? Would you use it as a toilet in your house? Absolutely not! You would place it in a safe, or lock it in a vault, and give it the utmost care. That is the way we should care for our heart, letting nothing enter it that may corrupt it, because out of our heart, out of our treasure, we speak.

When you have a problem, don't talk about it, but rather take authority over it and command it to line up with the will of God. If someone you know comes to you with a problem, don't allow yourself to be dragged into a discussion about it, simply ask them if they would like to pray about it and **<u>let it go</u>**! Many times, I have prayed for people and immediately after prayer they would start talking about their problem again. This can be very tricky since you do not want to seem insensitive; however, you have to be careful that you do not nullify everything you just prayed for by talking about or feeding the mountain you are trying to move. Also remember that, when someone has a problem and you pray for them, it blesses them and you as well.

> *"Do not be deceived, God will not be mocked, for whatever a man sows, that shall he also reap."*
> Galatians 6:7

Unselfishly praying for others will sow seeds for yourself, and there may come a day when someone will pray for you when you need it most. Take no thought repeating what the Devil is whispering in your ear. Have you ever had an old song go through your mind all day because you heard it briefly on the radio? All the words and the melody come flooding back, and no matter how hard you try, you just can't stop replaying that song in your mind. That does not even come close to the suggestive power the enemy has over us. While that song may replay in our minds because we heard it one time, Satan has a demon stationed near you to repeat a lie over and over and over. As well, he will likely usher in several other demon friends who specialize in similar fields of suggestion and persuasion with the intent to break down your will power.

All this effort, all this time is devoted to one cause…to get you to say **"It."** He needs you to say **"It!"** Say what? Say **"It!"** What is **"It?"** **"It"** is the very thing he is trying to get you to say, so that he can take your authority and use **"It"** against you. "I have cancer," "You're a loser," I'm stupid," "I hate you," "I hate myself," "You'll never amount to anything," "I guess God didn't hear my prayer," etc. If it's mean, hurtful, negative, condemning or faithless he's trying to get you to say it, because when you do, he can legally take your authority and use it against you. Remember, the power the Devil has is the power we give him by the words that we speak. The power God is referring to here is our authority, our superpower. He's after our superpower by hijacking our words.

> *... the weapons of our warfare are not carnal but mighty in God for pulling down strongholds, casting down arguments and every high thing that exalts itself against the knowledge of God, bringing every thought into captivity to the obedience of Christ.*
> 2 Corinthians 10:4-6

Paul says it perfectly here. Your fight is not with your boss or your neighbor or your coworker or even your spouse. Just like you, they are under bombardment with suggestions to lie, cheat, steal, cuss, and fornicate; you name it and they're going through it too. God is instructing us in how to handle this assault by telling us to take every thought into captivity and hold it to the standard, which is the Word, to see where it comes from. But how many Christians, even mature ones, do you think have the wisdom to do that? The number is miniscule.

First of all, most believers never even think of doing this. They've been in church for years and the only thing they know about is prosperity. Second, the ones that have read and learned of this verse never considered actually putting it into practice. The third and final group just don't put it into practice, but not because they don't know how; more likely than not, it is because they're tired. They've been fighting the good fight of faith for decades, but the enemy has worn them down. This is a most difficult task to do alone, and one of the main reasons we are encouraged to attend church; we need each other.

We are instructed to take **<u>every</u>** thought into captivity to the obedience of Christ. Every thought! Hello, every thought! How many thoughts do you think we have in a day? 10,000? 30,000? 50,000? I really don't know, but the mere thought of that alone is exhausting. Maybe that's what Paul meant when he said, *"do not grow weary of doing good."*

God has placed within us the power of the spoken Word, the same power He used to create the Earth, but modern man has misused this power. Every negative statement, every rude comment, every cuss word, everything that comes out of a man's mouth and does not edify another is used by Satan against the offender and the offended.

> *"Let no corrupt word proceed out of your mouth, but what is good for necessary edification, that it may impart grace to the hearers."* Ephesians 4:29

Satan has nothing, no power or authority over us what-so-ever, except that which we give him by the words that we speak. Yet, he brilliantly figured out how to get us to speak against ourselves thus transferring our authority back to him in the process, and he does it by the power of suggestion. For most people in the world, believers included, he simply suggests it, and because there is very little to no self-control these days, they either repeat it, or do it.

> *Let no unwholesome talk come out of your mouths, but only what is helpful for building up the one in need and bringing grace to those who listen.* Ephesians 4:29

> *But I tell you that men will give an account on the day of judgment for every careless word they have spoken.* Matthew 12:36

4.   Selfishness. The opposite of love is not hate, it is selfishness. God so loved the world that He gave His son to die in our place that we may be freed from this prison of sin. Jesus did not ask us to love people, He instructed us to love them, and not just the people we know, not just our family & friends or those we like and get along with. He said, *"love everybody,"* and everybody means everybody, but this is impossible for the typical believer apart from righteousness and the Holy Spirit.

When we allow ourselves to act or react selfishly, we give up our authority. I am not referring to a "one-time," stress induced incident. I am referring to habitual selfishness, the immature Christian who got saved in a prosperity, OSAS or denominational church and was never taught to die to self. They may talk about love, but they'll never be able to walk it out, because the opposite of love is not hate, it is a selfish spirit. Seeking after wealth and the things of the world will foster and feed a selfish spirit so true, selfless love can never be attained. Selfish feelings and emotions that can give away your authority include, but are not limited to: anger, rage, resentment, bitterness, contentions, selfishness, haughtiness, arrogance, pride, indigence, envy, strife, jealousy, unforgiveness and greed.

5.   Witchcraft of the Heart. Days before I sent the Altar of Love part I to the publisher, I asked God if there was anything regarding authority that He wanted me to add. Up to that point I only knew of 4 ways to give up authority and figured it was complete, so I closed my eyes, fanned through my Bible to 1 Samuel 15, and verse 23 jumped off the page at me in 3D.

> *For rebellion is like the sin of witchcraft, and*
> *arrogance is like the wickedness of idolatry.*
> 1 Samuel 15:23

Rebellion is not like making a simple mistake; it is knowing the difference between good and evil, and choosing to do the evil in spite of what God says, and what you know to be right. We've all had a child who was deliberately rebellious, so it should be easy for any parent to understand why it's so displeasing to God. It was this very sin that caused God to keep Israel in the wilderness for 40 years. God considers rebellion a form of witchcraft which is also referred to as divination in the Bible and God is disgusted by it. One third of Gods angels rebelled in the insurrection.

Next, arrogance is referred to as the wickedness of idol worship, and wickedness is the opposite of righteousness. Isn't it interesting how almost everything seems to come back to righteousness or a lack thereof? Arrogance is pride on steroids, so if pride comes before the fall, what will the outcome be for arrogance? If rebellion and arrogance got Satan and his followers exiled from Heaven, what will the outcome be for Christians who know they should be walking in love but rebel against Gods Word and/or behave arrogantly. Arrogance must be a really big deal to God if He compares it to idolatry, because idol worship is addressed in the very first commandment.

> *"You shall have no other gods (idols) before Me."* Exodus 20:3

In the Old Testament, witchcraft is also referred to as divination. In the New Testament, Paul's list of the "Works of the Flesh," are also considered witchcraft of the heart. One might expect witchcraft of the heart and the works of the flesh to be sin relegated to unbelievers and baby Christians only, but unfortunately, they are not. From baby Christians to mature believers; witchcraft of the heart is commonplace in the modern church, because wickedness abounds wherever there is a lack of righteousness.

Witchcraft of the heart could also be seen as an extreme form of selfishness; if my goal is to coerce someone into doing my will, it's all about me and that's selfishness. Whenever Christians are behaving selfishly it's because there had to be a breakdown somewhere in their seeking of righteousness as well as their love walk. It could be they rebelled and rejected correction, choosing to abandon the faith and go back to the world. Maybe they were not fortunate to have good Bible-based instruction as they developed, or they just neglected to till the soil of their heart and let the world be their lord and master again. Regardless, the Devil has sown seeds in the form of demonic behaviors like rebellion, seduction, arrogance, lust, bitterness, quarreling, drunkenness, carousing, self-seeking etc.

When these things exist within believers, Satan uses people like pawns to bring division and offense into the body of Christ. I highly advise that you search your heart circumspectly and see if you exhibit any one of these behaviors. Many times, they are generational and passed down from family member to family member. If you notice one or more of these in your personality, repent, ask forgiveness, seek righteousness and ask to be filled with Gods Spirit of Grace and Truth.

Witchcraft and divination were the first sins that the fallen angels taught humans in the insurrection. Practicing witchcraft is attempting to gain power or authority by way of Satan, thus replacing your dependence upon God as your provider, but the authority Jesus obtained for us on the cross supersedes any form of witchcraft, so why would anyone want to go after an inferior power source when a superior one is available? The reason people seek the power of witchcraft is because Satan has done a masterful job of hiding our true authority from us. If people had a proper understanding of the awesome power of their authority, they wouldn't be so quick to seek an inferior power.

Most people automatically think of Gods distain for witchcraft as being limited to rituals like casting spells and hexes, using psychic's, mediums and palm readers, or playing with Ouija boards, tarot cards and the like, but God views witchcraft of heart exactly the same; it's all a form of idolatry to Him. Any time a person intimidates or bullies another into doing their desire; it is a form of witchcraft of the heart.

The very definition of witchcraft is the practice of magic and the casting of spells, but its purpose is to force, compel or intimidate someone to do something that would normally be against their natural will. A man bound in pornography has succumbed to the sin of lust, and while his lust is exceedingly sinful, it's usually private and relegated to affecting just him. However, in his lust, if he seduces a coworker into an adulterous affair, the seduction is an added layer of sin far more dangerous and deadly than the porn itself; it is as the sin of witchcraft. Seduction is witchcraft of the heart, and it is especially dangerous, because it not only brings judgment upon the seducer but the object of the seduction as well.

If you coerce someone into persuading another person into doing something, it is witchcraft. Simple, harmless flirting, and dressing in such a way as to arouse or entice someone is also witchcraft of the heart. I'm not saying everything is your fault, most men can be aroused by a woman in a potato sac, so just don't do it intentionally. Try to be conscious and careful not to knowingly do anything to arouse, entice, intimidate or coerce anyone into anything against their natural will. In the eyes of your Father, it is no different that worshiping false gods.

Authority Misconceptions

Satan has successfully stolen the authority away from some believers by duping them into thinking that they are not supposed to engage the enemy, quoting this verse in Jude out of context,

> *"But Michael the archangel, when he disputed with the Devil and argued about the body of Moses, did not dare pronounce against him a railing judgment, but said, '"The Lord rebuke you!"'"* Jude 1:9

Sounds correct, right? No, Michael and the other two-thirds of Gods angels did not fall; they stayed faithful to God and have a very special place in His heart. Angels are spiritual beings bound by a different set of laws than we are, because they are from outside this world system. We humans, on the other hand, fell, were redeemed by the cross, and adopted as children from within Satan's world system. Angels were not given dominion and authority to rule and rein as Kings and Queens in this system, but we were. We are vessels that God can come into like He did with Jesus, for the purpose of preaching the gospel to other lost souls while wreaking havoc on Satan from within his matrix system. That is precisely why Jesus had to give up His spiritual divinity and become a human, so He could lawfully enter the world system and restore that which was lost; our identity and our authority while providing a road to salvation.

Because angels are spiritual beings, they are not subject to natural laws as we are; they only need to abide by spiritual laws. They do not grow weary, they don't get sick, grow old, feel cold or hunger, they are not subject to gravity or bound to this planet in any way. I'm not saying our task is more difficult than theirs, because I obviously do not know everything required of them, however we operate within natural laws while trying to learn spiritual ones as well. Much of our problem is due to the fact that we cannot see the spiritual realm and we tend not to acknowledge anything we cannot see. Gravity is a natural law and we can't see it, but we can see the effects of it, so we can get our minds around it even though it is invisible.

Another difficulty comes as we wrestle with the fact that spiritual laws always supersede natural laws. Examples: Jesus walking on water, turning water into wine, miracle healings, signs and wonders, etc. God has different expectations for us than He does for the angels. We have different tasks, different motives, different goals, a different cause, and we were given different responsibilities. Angels come in different classes, they are different sizes and they have different functions in the Kingdom. There are guardian angels, ministering angels and warring angels among others. God's holy angels as well as their fallen counterparts can assume any image they desire, and they possess superhuman strength. Biblical accounts describe one angel killing tens of thousands of human soldiers within minutes. We are no match for angels which is why God has given us authority as a weapon.

If this is war, you could equate us to the infantry that was parachuted behind enemy lines with the goal of destroying as many enemy targets while saving as many innocent civilians as possible. The angels are like our support lines, our intel, our ammunition supply depot and our air support. They provide whatever supply or support we need to complete the mission, but they cannot do the mission for us. Just as Jesus had to take on the likeness of a natural man walking in love and righteousness and filled with the Holy Spirit to make a way of salvation, the job of spreading the gospel to the rest of mankind must be done by a natural man from within the system as well, therefore it's our responsibility, not the angels.

We are natural beings fighting a spiritual war and the weapons of this war are not carnal; this fight cannot be won with kicks and punches or guns and bullets. Our weapons are spiritual, but they are mighty indeed; our weapons are love, righteousness, forgiveness, faith, hope, authority, the name of Jesus and the Word of God.

The Bible says that angels hearken unto the spoken Word of God, so it is their job to carry out His Word. Jesus said we were given authority, so if we are the ones here speaking the Word of God, you could say they indirectly work for us. Therefore, one of their jobs is to perform the Word that we sow (speak). In Mark 4, parable of the sower, Jesus illustrates the kingdom of God as a man who scatters seed. We are that farmer and the seed is the Word of God that we sow in the form of prayer or authority. Binding and loosing come into play here as well. When we bind the works, powers and plans of the enemy, we are not the ones holding the Devil accountable, the angels are. They facilitate that which we bind or loose.

> *Bless the LORD, O you His angels, you mighty ones **who do His Word**, obeying the voice of His Word!* Psalm 130:20

Whether we are praying, binding, loosing or assuming authority, it's the job of the angels to make it happen. Each Christian has two angels assigned to them for the sole purpose of ministering to us, guiding us, protecting us, facilitating the answer to our prayers and assuming the authority we take. That is, providing we are within our legal right, our authority, to do so. If we attempt to assume authority over something we have no authority over, whether out of ignorance or arrogance, then our angels are under no obligation to perform that task. Everything we do must be within our lawful right to do, otherwise our angels are powerless.

After the Cross

The cross was an amazing day for mankind as God made a way for Him to commute man's death sentence by sending His Son as payment for sin. Man was hopeless before the cross, but now they have hope and they have Satan to thank, because it was his stupid idea to kill the Son of the living God. Satan's plan to destroy Gods creation was thwarted because of his extreme hatred and jealousy of God. I can just imagine all the fallen angels and their demon offspring converging on Satan to kill him for the blunder of killing Jesus. But Satan has an epiphany, and he reminds them all about how easy we are to deceive, how gullible we are; how selfishness, lust and greediness can be used to keep us in sin, and full of every evil thing. He admits that God outsmarted them, and now man can legally be redeemed, but he appeals to their naturally sadistic nature and challenges them to keep us ignorant of that fact. If they keep us from learning our identity, out of righteousness and in deliberate sin, it will prevent us from seeking to get Gods Spirit in us, and keep us in a continual state of slavery to sin and bondage. The demons agree, a new plan is formed, and the war is back on.

Now, demons are given another, more important mandate by utilizing the authority of unbelievers, hiding authority from unlearned believers and looking for opportunities to assume the authority from even mature believers. They know how valuable and powerful it is, and they certainly do not want you using it against them.

In order for us to operate successfully in the Kingdom of God, we must line up with and according to the laws which govern us as well as the Word and the will of God. Unlike angels, we are Children of God, co-heirs to the throne with authority over all of God's creation as well as all the power of the enemy.

Therefore, you cannot compare our role to that of the angels, we are children and they are servants.

An accurate analogy would be comparing the difference between a child and an employee of a business owner. The owner may love his employees, but they are still just employees. No matter how loyal and faithful they may be, they will never take the place of the child. Even if the child is not acting all the way right, they are still the one that receives the inheritance. If an employee messes up, repentance or not, he's likely to get fired, however, if a child messes up, and asks forgiveness, he's forgiven, no matter how many times it happens, because it's a totally different relationship.

There are some things not under our authority, so it is important for us to understand what things we have authority over and what things we do not. Where does authority end and prayer begin? As we already learned, Jesus said we had authority over Satan and all demon powers and over all diseases. That's easy enough, if it's demonic or illness, it's under our authority. But what about people? Do I have authority over people? No and yes! Because God made us with a free will, I have no authority over another person unless they are under my authority as children or unless they give their authority to me.

A person can acquiesce their authority to another if they ask that person to pray for them. If they allow me, I can take authority over any demonic spirits that are afflicting them as long as the demonic spirit is there without authority or if the person repents, thereby taking back authority that was given away in the first place. If that person refuses to let me pray for them, I have no authority to bind the spirits that may be afflicting the person and cast them off. In areas not under our authority such as this, your only recourse is prayer. This is one area where authority ends and prayer begins.

Now that you know you have authority, you must begin to use it. It is time to take off your "spiritual huggies" and put on some "big boy" pants. God is not going to do everything for you now that you know what authority is and how it works.

While this world (matrix) system is real, it is only temporary, and it has very specific laws which govern all of its functions; laws of physics, biology, gravity, chemistry, mechanics and such. Humans are bound to operate within the governing laws of this world system, except for signs, wonders and miracles. A miracle is simply a defiance of a natural law. When God parted the Red Sea, it was a defiance of the natural laws and properties of water. When Jesus turned water into wine, it defied the natural properties of water molecules by converting them into molecules of wine. In both cases, God and Jesus exercised their authority and the natural law was forced to obey them, because the one assuming authority had the legal right to do so, and faith is the substance that makes it happen.

> *Now faith is the substance of things hoped for, the evidence of things not seen.* Hebrews 11:1

Faith is being fully confident in what we hope for, the thing we just took authority over or prayed for and our full assurance it will come to pass, even if we do not see it yet. The only reason we are able to do miracles at all, is when a believer stands in faith and assumes authority in opposition to a natural law, therefore, faith and authority go hand-in-hand. You cannot assume your authority over something unless you have faith to do so, neither will faith work without knowing you have authority. The main reason the modern church sees very few miracles now is due to the fact that they do not teach authority. If you do not know what you do and do not have authority over, how can you then have faith to change it?

The way we are able to rule over Satan's matrix world system is the same way God rules in heaven; we assume our authority over it by faith.

> *"...on earth as it is in heaven."* Matthew 6:10

This may be Satan's kingdom, but we have been given authority to rule in it by virtue of our son-ship, and by way of the cross. This is where identity comes in. Just as you cannot perform miracles without faith and authority, neither will you see them without knowing who you are as Children of God. One would assume that Christians automatically know what it truly means to be a Child of God, but Satan has hidden all that Jesus actually overcame and accomplished on the cross to restore what Adam gave away.

It's why Satan attacked Jesus' identity in the desert and why he is constantly questioning ours. He knows if we waiver in our identity, even a smidgen, he can break our confidence, shipwreck our faith and undermine our authority. THAT, is why the OSAS and prosperity messages will not teach a believer's identity, righteousness and authority, and further proof they are a doctrine of demons.

Parable of the Growing Seed

In the gospel of Mark, chapter 4, Jesus gives a perfect illustration of how He is able to perform miracles in defiance of natural laws while living within a system governed by them. The bulk of the chapter is thoroughly broken down in the Altar of Love part I, but I wanted to focus on the second part of the parable; the section that most Christians tend to overlook. Well…maybe it's not so much that they overlook it, but they are not associating it as being an extension, a continuation of the parable of the sower. And why is it important to know the two are connected? Because of the importance Jesus places on the parable of the sower when He said,

> *"Do you not understand this parable? How then will you understand all the parables?"* Mark 4:13

This question that Jesus asks here is way more important and revealing when we reverse engineer it. Basically, He is saying, *"If you don't understand this parable, you won't understand anything I tell you."* With that in mind, we must ask ourselves, "Just how important is the parable of the sower, and exactly what is Jesus trying to teach us?" I won't go into it here, because I already did it in the Altar of Love part I, but suffice it to say, it is vitally important in understanding how the Kingdom of God operates regarding faith, identity, authority, the Word of God and the working of miracles. The parable of the sower essentially takes everything needed to see and perform amazing miracles and wraps it all up into an easy to understand story about a farmer.

> *And He said, "The kingdom of God is as if a man should scatter seed on the ground, 27 and should sleep by night and rise by day, and the seed should sprout and grow, he himself does not know how. 28 For the earth yields crops by itself: first the blade, then the head, after that the full grain in the head. 29 But when the grain ripens, immediately he puts in the sickle, because the harvest has come."*
> Mark 4:26-29

Seeking first the Kingdom of God and becoming adopted as a Child of God has many amazing privileges; authority being just one. Knowing one's identity and authority empowers and emboldens the believer to confidently exercise their faith and operate within Satan's fake, temporary matrix system, like Jesus. Understanding our authority by way of our identity as sons and daughters is the fuel for our faith, and gives us the confidence to speak to mountains, with the expectation that they will move. Not because "I said so," but because Gods law has granted me "authority to say so," and Gods law supersedes all natural laws.

Just look at the attitude of the farmer after he planted his seed. He didn't worry or doubt, he planted his seed and slept soundly, because he knows that if he puts a seed in the ground and it has sunlight and water, it will grow. That same confidence the farmer has towards the seed is likened to the same confidence we have as children in authority when we speak to a mountain or pray over something. It's not a matter of "if it grows," but a matter of "when it grows." This is the same attitude we are expected to take whenever we have to operate within Satan's fake matrix world system.

Prayer begins where Authority ends

Another truly remarkable benefit of being an adopted Child of God is prayer. Prayer is an entirely different process than authority and works on a different level altogether. There are some things that we do not have authority over, so where authority ends, is where prayer begins, and this is explained by Jesus in Mark 11:24.

> *Truly, I say to you, whoever says to this mountain, 'Be taken up and thrown into the sea,' and does not doubt in his heart, but believes that what he says will come to pass, it will be done for him.* ²⁴ *Therefore I tell you, whatever you ask in prayer, believe that you have received it, and it will be yours.* Mark 11:23 & 24

Verse 23 indicates Authority, but verse 24 indicates prayer. In 23, He is simply directing us to speak in faith as Children of God to the thing under our authority. He's not instructing us to ask God to do it, he's telling us to assume our authority by faith with our words, because we are children. As long as we know our identity, as long as we know our authority and as long as we believe (faith) what we've taken authority over must obey us, we will have whatever we say.

On the other hand, in verse 24, Jesus is **not** just being redundant, He is not just saying the same thing in a different way because we are thick-headed, He is describing how prayer works, and He put them together to show us how interconnected the two are. Where authority ends in verse 23, is where prayer takes over in verse 24. He says, *"Whatever we pray for, if we believe we will receive, we will have it,"* because we are children of faith in authority. While all this is amazing revelation, and you may very well be jumping with joy at the prospect of going out and doing miracles and moving mountains now that you understand your identity and believe by faith in the authority that has been given to you as a child. Even with all this amazing knowledge and understanding regarding identity, faith and authority, it's all just a waste of time if you are not walking in love and righteousness.

> *If I have the gift of prophecy and can fathom all mysteries and all knowledge, and if I have absolute faith so as to move mountains, but have not love, I am nothing.*
> 1 Corinthians 13:2

Regarding both prayer and authority, it is imperative that we consider what Gods will is for any matter. This may seem like an impossible task, but I assure you, it is easier than you think. God's will is His Word. If you read, and study his Word diligently, if you seek righteousness with all your heart and if you get filled with the Holy Spirit, you will begin to know His will. Occasionally, you will face a situation that is out of your realm of expertise or knowledge. When that happens and you do not know what to do because you don't know what Gods will is, that's a perfect time to pray for wisdom.

> *"If any of you lacks wisdom, let him ask God, who gives generously to all without reproach, and it will be given him."* James 1:5

Adam and Eve gave their dominion (their authority to rule and rein as Kings and Queens over the earth) over to Satan when they sinned. Satan wielded authority with an iron fist for the next 4000 years until Jesus regains it for us on the cross. Jesus did not regain authority for everyone however; this awesome super-power called authority is only for Children of God with the Spirit of Adoption. Seeking the Kingdom of God and being adopted into the family is the only way to position yourself to become authorized to dominate snakes and scorpions again.

Stop for just one moment and consider the magnitude of what Jesus did by going to the cross. His selfless act of love allows us, mere humans, to completely dominate Satan and all his demon forces. Even though they have supernatural powers we probably don't even know the half of, Jesus has granted us the authority to rule over them from within their own system, a system that Satan is god of! If you ever wondered why Satan hates us so much... now you know.

As we discussed earlier, snakes refers to Satan and the demon forces, and they have certain kinds of spiritual abilities; most notably is the ability to lie to you, influence you and entice you to sin, all by stealth. It is a subliminal attack on your subconscious mind, they are very good at it and it is an extremely effective strategy. Satan's scorpions (modern day Nephilim (human hybrids) are witches, masons, Satanists and Luciferians using spells, curses, hexes and various kinds of white and black magic to influence and intimidate the targeted victim. Their success, their effectiveness is dependent upon these variables:

1. Their dedication and expertise within the occult.
2. A proper understanding of our identity as adopted Children of God.
3. Our understanding and usage of our authority.
4. Faith in our identity and authority.
5. Our walk of love and righteousness.
6. Our being filled with His Holy Spirit, the Spirit of Grace & Truth.

If the object of their assault is not a Child of God, that poor soul is at the mercy of the abilities of the black arts practitioner unless they are new at it or just dabbling in it. In that case, it's likely they are not very effective, however if they are serious in their endeavor and have made a covenant with the devil, they can be very dangerous and successful against Christians who do not understand their identity and authority.

All of that notwithstanding, the power & authority of an adopted Child of God trumps anything and everything Satan throws your way. Nothing they have, no weapon, no plot, no plan, no skill, no curse or hex has any power or ability greater than the authority of a believer. Furthermore, when you walk in love and righteousness as a child in authority, full of faith and filled with Gods Spirit, you are surrounded with a shield of favor as well as 2 sixteen foot angels whose only job is to protect you.

> *For surely You, O LORD, bless **the righteous;** You surround them with <u>a shield of your favor.</u>* Psalm 5:12

An interesting side note: The Hebrew word for shield here is Strong's # 6793 tsinnah (tsin-naw') It is described as a full body shield that protects all sides leaving no area exposed. That said, notice now just exactly who is eligible for a shield of favor... those who walk in righteousness.

Now, prayer is powerful, but it is not more powerful than ones free will. Usually, if a person refuses prayer, it's because the spirit ruling them has such a hold over them that they do not want it removed. They have grown quite fond of the spirit, they like the behavior they are engaging in and do not want to stop. You cannot make someone want to be free from the yoke of sin if they are enjoying the sin, they are engaging in. For such a case, the best you can do is explain the dangers that lie ahead, and pray that God open their eyes of understanding.

If you are tired of living a life ruled by a bunch of demons, you can choose to be free of them and filled with God's Holy Spirit. However, you are free to hold onto them as well; choosing rather to fulfill the lust of the flesh because you are not yet ready to give up Satan's sinful pleasures. Your Father has given you free will, but unlike the OSAS liars and prosperity pimps, I have no ulterior motive other than your true conversion and eternal life. I don't need anything from you, so I'll just tell it to you plainly. If you want to see eternal life, abandon the world and all it offers, and seek ye first the Kingdom of God and His righteousness.

The signs, wonders and miracles Jesus performed were just an expression of His love for people, the natural byproduct of a life of love & righteousness while being filled with the Holy Spirit. Power, authority and miracles are part of your new DNA once you get born again, die to self, seek righteousness and get filled with His Spirit. Your Father has deposited new talents and abilities within you now that must be trained and exercised, just like any other talent or skill.

The Altar of Love, Part II

Chapter 6

All 4 Legs of the Altar

Identity & Son-ship, Wisdom & Righteousness, the Spirit of Grace & Truth, Power & Authority

If God is for us, who can be against us? Romans 8:31

Moreover, if God is for me...<u>who cares</u> who is against me!

Looking at Matthew 6 and the seeking of righteousness, I was drawn to the part where Jesus says, *"and all these things will be added to you."* "What things," I wondered, so I took another look at the verse just prior to that and He says this:

'...Therefore do not worry, saying, 'What shall we eat?' or 'What shall we drink?' or 'What shall we wear?' Matt. 6:31

Jesus is listing necessities only. There is no excess in what we will receive because excess will lead us back into unrighteousness. It is a supernatural contentment regardless of our current situation which allows us to focus on seeking righteousness and walking in love. Once righteousness is attained, excess is less likely to cause sin, but as we will see shortly, it still happens, even to the best of us. I love Paul's practical outlook on life here, and it should be our model as well:

I know how to live on almost nothing or with everything. I have learned the secret of living in every situation, whether it is with a full stomach or empty, with plenty or little. Philippians 4:12

The secret that Paul learned, the secret of living contently in every situation, whether on almost nothing or with plenty is found in Matthew 6:32 *"... for your heavenly Father already knows all your needs. ³³But seek first the kingdom of God and His righteousness and all these things will be added unto you."* Paul knew, that God knew what Paul needed before he even asked, and he also knew that God would provide all his needs *"...according to Gods riches and glory in Christ Jesus;"* as long as Paul set his heart to seek for righteousness and walk in love.

The more time we spend worrying about stuff, praying for stuff, and striving to acquire stuff, the less our focus will be on love and righteousness. Our Father wants us free from the bondage of sin brought on by the pursuit of the pleasures of this world, so we are free to pursue His righteousness and walk in love.

> *Beloved, if our hearts do not condemn us, we have confidence before God, ²²and we will receive from Him whatever we ask, because we keep His commandments and do what is pleasing in His sight.*
> 1 John 3:22.

"Beloved," proves that John was speaking to believers. *"If our hearts do not condemn us,"* is our walk of righteousness. One's heart is condemned when they are in willful sin, but if you seek after righteousness you will have confidence before God, because what is pleasing in His sight is for you to walk in love & righteousness. God is Love, and Jesus was the very definition of righteousness. When John wrote, *"... and we will receive from Him whatever we ask,"* is where most Christians who put all their hope as well as their hard earned money in the prosperity lie, miss it. This is not your queue to ask for stuff, on the contrary, we are told by Jesus to seek righteousness and **ask for** the Holy Spirit and all the wonderful gifts of the Spirit. John is telling his brothers in Christ how to position themselves to get filled with the Holy Spirit.

Altar of Love, Part II *Ask, Seek & Knock*

> *...how much more will your Father in heaven give the*
> *Holy Spirit to those who ask him!* Luke 11:13

Then He confirms it with, *"because we keep His commandments and do what is pleasing in His sight."* In other words, because you have obeyed the commandment of love and are seeking after righteousness, you have positioned yourself to receive the Holy Spirit, the Spirit of Adoption, the Spirit of Grace & Truth and they will clothe you with power from on high, transforming you into the image of your Lord and Savior, Jesus Christ. Now you may ask for His gifts that accompany His Spirit.

There is a similar lesson in the Old Testament that mirrors Jesus' command to Seek righteousness and all the things the world is searching after will be added unto you, principle.

> *...the LORD appeared to Solomon in a dream and said, Ask what you will of Me and I shall give it to thee. Solomon answered, ⁶"You have shown great kindness to your servant, my father David, because he was faithful to you and **righteous** and upright in heart... ⁹So give to me an understanding heart to judge Your people to discern between good and evil... ¹⁰Now it pleased the Lord that Solomon had made this request. ¹¹So God replied, "Because you have asked for wisdom in governing my people with justice and have not asked for a long life or wealth or the death of your enemies...¹² I have given you a wise and discerning heart, so that there has been no one like you before you, nor shall one like you arise after you. ¹³ Moreover, I will give you what you have not asked for, both wealth and honor, so that in your lifetime you will have no equal among kings.*
> 1Kings 3:5

Solomon could have asked for material things and God would have given them to him, but because he asked for the wisdom to rule in righteousness, Solomon got both wisdom and all his material needs met, in excess. With the exception of

Jesus, Solomon was the wisest man to ever walk the earth, and his wealth was so vast that He had a mountain of silver which he kept outside the city limits because there wasn't enough room to store it due of all the gold in his kingdom. Hello! Solomon had a mountain of silver thrown out like trash, because he had too much gold? Just exactly how much gold do you have to have to regard silver as trash?

Solomon did exactly what Jesus is instructing us to do when He said, "*...Seek ye first the Kingdom of God and His righteousness....*" Your heavenly Father knows what you have need of before you even ask, if you seek righteousness, all the things the people of the world are searching after, will be provided by your Father for you. As I said earlier, the difference is that our Father is a good Father and He's smart enough, and He loves you enough not to give you anything that will harm you or cause you to return to the world; especially considering how He suffered and the sacrifice He became to get you out of sin in the first place. As I said earlier, the difference is that our Father is a good Father and He's smart enough, and He loves you enough not to give you anything that will harm you or cause you to return to the world, considering how He suffered and the sacrifice He became to get you out of sin in the first place.

Is there a connection between the wisdom of God, the same wisdom that was given to Solomon and the fruit of Righteousness?

> *But **the wisdom of God is** first of all pure, then peaceable, gentle, accommodating, full of mercy and good fruit, impartial, and sincere. **Peacemakers** who sow in peace **reap the fruit of righteousness**....*
> James 3:17

King Solomon

The wisdom of God, the wisdom that God gave to Solomon was the fruit of righteousness Jesus has made available for us by the cross. Solomon was famous for his righteousness as well as his wisdom. Proverbs and Ecclesiastes were written by Solomon and much of their teaching is primarily regarding wisdom & righteousness. One warning, however, let not a greedy heart move you to seek righteousness for the purpose of obtaining wealth, for God knows the heart. Solomon received riches and honor, but only because he sought the wisdom of God with a humble heart. Solomon had no ulterior motive; he wasn't looking to get rich, he just wanted to be a "faithful servant." Little did Solomon know that being a "**faithful servant,**" would contribute to his downfall.

Solomon had Wisdom and Righteousness, but what he lacked was a proper understanding of his Identity as a Son; he lacked the Spirit of Adoption, as well as the Spirit of Grace & Truth.

Even with the Wisdom of God, even with great wealth and peace on his borders, Solomon still fell into sin. The Bible tells us that Solomon had over 400 wives and 700 concubines and he began to worship and serve the false gods of his wives and mistresses. By serving false gods, Solomon proves that he had absolutely no concept of his identity, his Son-ship.

Solomon may have had wisdom and righteousness, but without the Spirit of Adoption he had no understanding of his identity as a child; Solomon always saw himself as a servant. The Spirit of Grace and Truth would not come until after the cross, and their absence left a void that Solomon tried to fill with many worldly things. How many seemingly happy, wealthy, popular people commit suicide each year and no one ever knew they were depressed. The entire book of Ecclesiastes explains the futility of life; in it, Solomon admits that any life absent a relationship with the Father, regardless of how rich, powerful or famous one is, is nothing more than vanity.

A Christian not in right relationship with the Father because of willful sin is left with a void that brings guilt, shame and condemnation. It's a perfect opening for Satan to slide in with a spirit of lust, or greed or any number of demonic spirits to confuse us, distract us, deceive us and attack our identity, and the results are evident in Solomon's life as he rejects the Father and begins worshiping false gods.

The Disciples

The Disciples had Power & Authority but no real understanding of their Identity & Sonship. Neither did they have Righteousness & Wisdom or the Spirit of Grace & Truth.

Even though Jesus constantly referred to God as Father, it was a concept beyond the Jews ability to comprehend, the apostles included.

> *Philip said to Him,* ***"Lord, show us the Father,*** *and that will be enough for us." ⁹Jesus replied, "Philip, I have been with you all this time, and still you do not know Me? Anyone who has seen Me has seen the Father. How can you say, 'Show us the Father'?* John 14:8-9

Remember, the wisdom of God is a mystery to the natural man for it is spiritually discerned. When Jesus asked the disciples,

> *"Who do people say that I am?" They replied, "Some say John the Baptist; others say Elijah; and still others, Jeremiah or one of the prophets." He said to them, "But who do you say that I am?"*
> *¹⁶Simon Peter answered,* ***"You are the Christ, the Son of the living God."*** *¹⁷Jesus replied, "Blessed are you, Simon son of Jonah! Flesh and blood did not reveal this to you by, but by My Father in heaven....* Matthew 16:15-17

The main point here is that Peter didn't figure it out because of his intellect. The Word of God, the wisdom of God is spiritually discerned; it is not meant for your mind, but your heart. It is the Holy Spirit that reveals the scriptures to your heart, because your heart can take you places that your mind cannot go.

Jesus had also been teaching to them about righteousness, but they failed there on many occasions as well. At one point, a foolish argument arose among the disciples as to which of them would be the greatest in the Kingdom. Jesus squelched it immediately when He responded with, *"Whoever is the least among all of you shall be the greatest."* And just like the children they were before the Holy Spirit came upon them; they began arguing about who was the least of them. Without a clear understanding of our identity and righteousness we too are prone to foolishness, immature contentions and arguments. Without identity, Christians really look no different from people of the world, they are easily offended, quick tempered and generally wear their feelings on their sleeve for all to see.

Remember that Jesus gave the disciples power and authority, but when they got it, they wanted to use it to burn up an entire city, forcing Jesus to rebuke them, lest many righteous people suffer with the ungodly.

> *...But the people there refused to welcome Him, because He was heading for Jerusalem. [54]When the disciples James and John saw this, they asked, "Lord, do You want us to call down fire from heaven to consume them?" [55]But Jesus turned and rebuked them,* Luke 9:53-55

Power and authority without a proper understanding of identity, righteousness and wisdom will corrupt anyone; and this kind of power, the awesome power to perform miracles, cast out demons and rain down fire without Godly righteousness and love, corrupts tragically.

Power to heal is an awesome gift, but without righteousness and a sound understanding of your identity as a Child of God in Christ Jesus, pride will begin to rise up and eventually it'll become all about you. It doesn't begin that way, at first you are very careful to give the praise to Jesus, but after awhile people begin to seek you out for what you can do, and before you know it, it becomes all about you, your anointing, your ability, your faith.

Similarly, Solomon was filled with wisdom and righteousness, but he had no understanding whatsoever regarding his identity and son-ship as evidenced by the way Solomon refers to himself in the dream he received of the Lord.

> *And now, O LORD my God, You have made **Your servant king** in my father David's place.* 1 Kings 3:7

Unlike King Solomon, David always saw himself as a Child of God, but Solomon saw himself as a servant. Solomon frequently addressed God as, *"the God of my father David,"* further indicating his lack of a personal relationship with God, choosing rather to ride on the coattails of David's relationship with God. There is a huge difference between the two; children know they have privileges that servants share not. Because Jesus had not yet gone to the cross, Solomon wasn't clothed with the Holy Spirit power from On High, the Spirit of Grace and Truth, nor are there any recorded accounts of him being given authority to do miracles like the disciples. What Solomon did have was the supernatural wisdom & righteousness of Almighty God, and yet he still fell away.

Because the apostles had not been clothed with power from on high before the cross, they had no wisdom, no righteousness and therefore no way of controlling their emotions. They were impulsive, rash, rude at times, petty, argumentative, headstrong, prone to anger, deception, betrayal and even attempted murder.

Without righteousness and wisdom, and without the Spirit of Grace and Truth within the disciples giving them the power not to sin, they really hadn't changed all that much except for the fact that they believed Jesus was who He said He was, and they could heal people, cast out demons and destroy things. The modern, self-proclaimed, spirit-filled, hyper-grace OSAS and prosperity churches look an awful lot like the disciples did before the cross; they too have no understanding of their identity, never learned to die to self, therefore they have no righteousness and no Holy Spirit.

Without a proper understanding of his identity and absent the Holy Spirit power within Solomon, he was eventually corrupted by the world and subject to the lusts of the flesh which ultimately turned him away from his God, the same God that gave him his wisdom, righteousness and wealth beyond measure. If lacking identity and the Holy Spirit could corrupt a man with that much Godly wisdom, why would we think it will be any different for us?

King David

David, unlike Solomon, understood his identity as a Child of God better than just about anyone. He also understood the importance of righteousness as evidenced by the Psalms he wrote. Just like the disciples before the cross, David displayed miracle Power at times when he killed a lion and a bear with his bare hands, not to mention the beheading of Goliath. But the one thing David lacked, the one thing that provided the opening for him to commit adultery and murder was the absence of the Spirit of Grace and Truth that would only become available after the cross.

God referred to David as a man after His own heart. David was:

- **Respectful** - *Be merciful to me, O Lord, for I am in distress; my eyes grow weak with sorrow, my soul and my body with grief.* Psalm 31:9

- **Trusting** - *The LORD is my light and my salvation—whom shall I fear? The LORD is the stronghold of my life, of whom shall I be afraid?* Psalm 27:1

- **Loving** - *I love you, O Lord, my strength.* Psalm 18:1

- **Devoted** - *You have filled my heart with greater joy than when their grain and new wine abound.* Psalm 4:7

- **Faithful** - *Surely goodness and mercy will follow me all the days of my life, and I will dwell in the house of the LORD forever.* Psalm 23:6

- **Obedient** - *Give me understanding, and I will keep your law and obey it with all my heart.* Psalm 119:34

- **Repentant -** *For the sake of your name, O Lord, forgive my iniquity, though it is great.* Psalm 25:11

Yet in all that, David displayed arrogance at times and managed to commit adultery and murder, proving that without the Spirit of Grace and Truth teaching, convicting, correcting and training us to walk in love and righteousness daily, Satan will find a chink in our armor to exploit.

Unless and/or until the Spirit of Adoption comes in and we become sons and daughters who identify as children of the Living God, we are nothing more than spoiled brats who will stop at nothing to get our way. Power and authority without the Spirit of Grace & Truth clothing us and infusing us with *Power from on High*, is dangerous and destructive minus the wisdom and righteousness of God, ultimately leading us back into lawlessness and sin. Therefore, without the Spirit of Adoption revealing to us a proper understanding of our identity and/or absent the Spirit of Grace & Truth, our Fathers inherent ability to walk in love & righteousness evades us so that selfishness and sin is ever present. If even one of the four legs of the altar is missing, the consequences can be devastating.

The 4 Legs of the Altar of Love, Part II

1. **Identity & Son-ship**. Also known as the Spirit of Adoption.
2. **Wisdom & Righteousness**. Also known as the fruit of the Spirit, the fruit of righteousness and walking in love.
3. **Spirit of Grace & Truth**. Being filled with power from on High, baptism in the Holy Spirit. It is Gods supernatural ability within us, empowering us, teaching us, convicting us, correcting us and training us **not** to sin deliberately.
4. **Power & Authority**. Also known as signs, wonders and miracle power. Power & authority is usually accompanied by the Gifts of the Spirit. One who walks in power & authority can cast out demons, heal the sick, prophesy, give and receive words of wisdom & knowledge, discernment

of spirits, speak in tongues, and give the interpretation of tongues spoken by others.

How all 4 Legs of the Altar Fit Together

Within these 4 legs is the fullness of God in us, wherein we properly identity with and begin to take on the likeness of our Lord Jesus. The same power of God that enabled Jesus to walk in righteousness, miracles and authority in a perverse and wicked generation, yet without sin is available to us. It wasn't until the Holy Spirit was poured out on the disciples that they went from dysfunctional, petulant children to Christ-like in an instant; walking out all 4 legs of the Altar just as Jesus did. It was that same Holy Spirit that enabled Paul to go from murderer to Christian martyr.

In Matthew 6 & 7, Jesus outlined the principle for obtaining eternal life hidden within a thinly veiled lesson instructing His followers to Ask, Seek & Knock. The Altar of Love II is a breakdown of this principle; a decoding of the narrow road to eternal life and exposing the false teaching that leads Christians down the wide road to destruction. In studying the life and times of the Old Testament saints as well as the apostles before the cross, this altar representing the life of a Christian, absent any one leg is subject to fall. A 3 legged table cannot stand when pressure is placed upon it; pressure in the form of a trial, a tribulation, a sickness, or a tragic loss. If even one leg of the altar is missing...the ending could be disastrous.

Most Christians filling the seats of the contemporary mega churches likely possess **not even one** of these legs, let alone all of them, but on the rare occasion that they do have an understanding of one or even several of them, the enemy knows what they are missing and exactly how to defeat them. Remember, Satan has been doing this for quite some time now and he is very adept at determining our weaknesses and planning a strategy of attack.

In the illustration below, the plus sign indicates the legs of the altar which are presently working together, but the minus sigh indicates the leg that is missing. The equal sign indicates what the outcome will be as a result of that missing leg.

1) Power & Authority + Wisdom & Righteousness + The Spirit of Grace & Truth – (minus) Identity & Son-ship = **Woe of offense, difficulty in relationships and an inability to control one's emotions causing a fractured love walk and a cycle of sin, condemnation, self-loathing and repentance, leading to a possibility of falling away from the faith.**

2) Identity & Son-ship + Power & Authority + The Spirit of Grace and Truth – (minus) Wisdom & Righteousness = **Grieving Holy Spirit, dysfunction in many areas of life, especially interpersonal relationships with family, friends and on the job; A frequent cycle of sin and repentance. Really bad decisions followed by life altering consequences which can lead to a very real possibility of falling away.**

3) Identity & Son-ship + Power & Authority + Wisdom & Righteousness – (minus) The Spirit of Grace and Truth = **Selfishness causing habitual, deliberate sin giving way to guilt, shame and condemnation which leads to a break in relationship with the Father and may result in a falling away.**

4) Wisdom & Righteousness + Identity & Son-ship + the Spirit of Grace & Truth – (minus) Power & Authority = **Least of all the legs, but it still has its benefits as well as its exposures. Without exercising one's power and authority, there will be a quenching of the Holy Spirit, leaving one vulnerable to the wiles of the devil to kill, steal and destroy. Jesus and the disciples used power & authority to get the attention of and to convince unbelievers of the existence of God and their need for a savior, therefore an absence of Power & Authority will limit the effectiveness of any ministry. Power & authority also prevents the**

devil from wreaking havoc in areas of your life he has no authority over and provides you with powerful miracle evidence of the Living God to those who witness your faith and the results thereof. Lacking Power and Authority authorizes the enemy to do damage to you and those close to you, possibly shipwrecking your faith and providing an opportunity for him to harden your heart towards God in an attempt to drag you back to the world.

Let's not forget, the previous chart was based upon only one missing leg, but most professing Christians likely have only one or two legs, if any at all. Unless all 4 are legs of the altar are present in the life of a Christian, identity & son-ship, wisdom & righteousness, the Spirit of Grace and Truth, and power & authority, we are no better off than the disciples were before the cross. We are selfish, self-centered, petulant children bound in a cycle of sin, condemnation, guilt, shame and repentance. It's a mirror image of the modern church, a house of cards destined to fall. Maybe not today, or tomorrow, but fall it will and great will be that fall.

Frankly, most pastors have no understanding of their identity whatsoever; the sheer size and number of the new mega church's teaching prosperity and OSAS proves the attending flock is ignorant in regards to righteousness and if the pastor is not preaching righteousness, it's because he's not walking in it. It's obvious he's not filled with the Holy Spirit, because if he was, he'd be teaching, correcting, convicting and training them in righteousness, not prosperity and sin covered by grace. Without the Holy Spirit teaching them, the flock is dependent upon their pastor to tell them what to think and how to believe. It's almost as if they have placed themselves under the law again, needing to hear from God through a priest, and thus rejecting the main purpose of the cross which was to enable them to have a personal relationship with their Father.

Without the Holy Spirit, they'll never understand their spiritually discerned authority, and finally, while many of them boast power and miracles as proof and evidence that they are God centered and filled with His Spirit, it really only proves that they are no different than the disciples before the cross; immature little children with dynamite in hand. They are street orphans pretending to be children of the King. Orphans who emulate the behavior of the Kings children; behavior the orphans learned while watching the Kings children play for a few minutes through a window of a building 10 stories up. These orphans have no clue what-so-ever what it truly means to be a child of the Most High God, they are being deceived and deluded playing "make pretend."

> *the Holy Spirit, whom the Father will send in My name,*
> *will teach you all things* John 14:26

Absent the Holy Spirit tutelage, Christians are carnal, who, not being instructed, convicted, corrected and trained in righteousness, have nowhere else to go but back to that which is familiar... the sinful flesh. Paul so eloquently explains this in Ephesians.

> *So I say, walk by the Spirit, and you will not gratify the*
> *desires of the flesh.* Ephesians 5:16

Even if you are adopted into the Kingdom and seek His righteousness, if you are not filled with His Holy Spirit, you cannot **walk in the Spirit**. If you **do not** walk in the Spirit because you **are not** filled with His Spirit, you will return to gratifying the desires of your flesh.

> *"...But if you are led by the Spirit, you are*
> ***not*** *under the law."* Ephesians 5:18

If we are filled with the Spirit of Adoption and the submit to the teaching, the conviction, the correction and training of righteousness, the Spirit of Grace and Truth comes in and covers us, empowering us from the inside-out... **Not To Sin.** We then move out from under the Law of Moses, also referred to as the ministry of condemnation and death, and we are transferred to the law of Grace by the

Spirit of Grace. This Grace, by the Blood of Jesus cleanses us in the event we sin ignorantly and or without premeditation.

Grace is not there to excuse our sin, it literally changes your mind from being **sin conscious** to being **Son Conscious** and when you are Son Conscious the mere thought of sinning against your Father and your Lord Jesus violates your very heart. Now righteousness is there to correct us if we do respond outside love and it convicts our heart in such a way that we have to repent and make it right with the person we offended. Righteousness corrects us and trains us, so we are not caught off-guard in that area again; molding us and forming us into the likeness of Jesus.

Paul goes on to list just a few of the character traits of Christians that are filled with the spirit of the world in verses 19-21 of Galatians, and to warn them of the danger that awaits those who practice such things. WARNING, and at the risk of being redundant, Paul is writing to Christians about Christians. He is addressing his flock, not unbelievers, so read this introspectively, with eyes to perceive, ears to hear and a humble heart.

> *"... sexual immorality, impurity, and debauchery; ²⁰idolatry and sorcery; hatred, discord, jealousy, and rage; rivalries, divisions, factions, ²¹and envy; drunkenness, orgies, and the like. I warn you, as I did before, that **those who practice such things will not inherit the kingdom of God**...."*
> Galatians 5:19-21

You may read that list and say to yourself, "I'm not doing any of those things," but let's not forget what Jesus said, *"If you lust in your heart, it's as if you committed adultery."* If you hate, it's as murder, simple flirting, persuading, encouraging, enticing or seducing someone into doing something they know they should not do or really don't want to do is a form of sorcery. The point is this, without the Holy Spirit, the Spirit of Grace and Truth empowering us, teaching us, convicting us, correcting us and training us to walk in righteousness, we are still under the law and completely unable to live in holiness.

We may want to be righteous, we can strive to behave righteously, but Paul told the Rabbis, the Scribes and the Pharisee's exactly how it would work for anyone without the Spirit of Grace and Truth in Romans 7 when he said, *"I don't really understand myself, for I want to do what is right, but I don't do it. Instead, I do what I hate."*

Remember that Paul was not talking about himself in the present; he was talking to the Jews and referring to the way it was for them all while he was a Pharisee like them. He knew they all had that same propensity to sin without the Holy Spirit empowering them not to.

> *...for it is written: "Be holy, as I am holy."* 1 Peter 1:16

Our Father is not asking us to be Holy as He is Holy, He is commanding it, and He would not give us a commandment to be Holy if He knew we were unable to, as evidenced by The Law. The 613 Laws of Moses and the 10 commandments proved we could not do it in our own strength; we needed Jesus to save us from ourselves and the Holy Spirit to infuse us with His power **not** to sin, the mighty power that comes from receiving the Spirit of Grace and Truth. But even with the Spirit of Grace and Truth, unless we do as Jesus commanded, and ask, seek, knock, we will likely fall back into the world and begin to walk in the flesh again; moving us out from under the umbrella of Grace and back under the law in any attempt to be holy in our own strength.

> **Pursue peace** *with all men, as well as* <u>**holiness**</u>*, without which no one will see the Lord.* **Hebrews 12:14**

The word holiness here is also described as righteousness, therefore it very well could read, **"Without righteousness, nobody will see the Lord,"** and that is why Jesus said, *"Seek ye <u>**first**</u> the Kingdom of God **and His righteousness**,"* and *"unless* *your righteousness exceeds that of the scribes and Pharisees,* **you will never enter the kingdom of heaven."** It cannot be said any more plainly than that.

Even the churches that seem to have an understanding and reject the OSAS and/or the prosperity message are missing the full picture. Son-ship brings Godly wisdom and the pursuit of righteousness by way of the Holy Spirit, but if you take any one Leg of the altar out of the equation, the end result is a life out of balance. It's a life with an appearance of holiness but devoid of the essential power and ability to walk down a path worthy of the King, the path of righteousness. A Christian life out of balance is a life that will eventually fall back to the desires of the flesh, because it doesn't know anything else. People always resort to that which is familiar to them, and Satan's army of familiar spirits are ready, willing and able to assist them in their hapless trek through carnal Christianity followed by their likely descent back to the world.

When the amazing revelation of your identity & son-ship hits your heart, and righteousness comes flooding in, it'll change your attitude, your outlook on everything. Identity & son-ship is not just incorporating Jesus into your life, so you can "have your best life now," and meet all your needs. That's twisted, that's selfish, that's demonic!

You cannot complete this difficult Christian journey by incorporating Jesus, you must become like Jesus, and He didn't give up His divinity, come down off the throne, humble Himself to the point of being born to a human and allow Himself to be tortured beyond recognition just to give you lots of money and a free pass to sin. Jesus paid the highest price that has ever been paid for anything so he could live inside you and enable you to look just like Him. He did it so you could be an imitator of God, to be Holy as He is Holy and to walk in love & righteousness towards all men.

The price that Jesus paid on the cross was not just to get you into heaven either, He paid that price to get Heaven into you, so you could walk like Him, and talk like Him, think like Him and look just like Him. A feat that is utterly impossible unless we get a full and complete understanding of our identity, unless we die to ourselves, unless we seek righteousness like a treasure, unless we ask for, beg for and wait for the Holy Spirit to fill us with power from on High so we can be a reflection of Jesus to everyone we meet.

"But what about power and authority" you say, when does that happen? When you fully understand your identity as a Child of God, when you deny yourself, taking up your cross to follow Him, when you seek righteousness with all your heart and when you are filled with the Holy Spirit; power and authority are natural byproducts. Simply ask your Father for those gifts and He will give them to you as you mature in Him. Power & authority becomes an outward expression of the fullness of the life of a believer with a heart after His Father's own heart.

If God is the same yesterday, today and forever, do we really think it's ok with Him for us to just incorporate Jesus into our lives and live like hell on earth until we get to heaven? That's not ok with Him, that's not His nature at all, and what were we thinking? Simply incorporating Jesus into parts of your life will not enable you to walk in love, it will however, cause you to walk in need and want. It will make you walk with fleshly desires, serving the spirit of the world like the rest of the world.

It will make you walk in works to try to satisfy an idol god you have created from your own twisted thinking that sprang up out of guilt and shame from the sin and stain of sin that so easily ensnares you. Our Father is not satisfied by anything other than perfection which is only made possible by way of the cross and the blood of Jesus that paid the fine and commuted the death sentence of all who seek first the Kingdom of God and his righteousness. And out of a grateful heart, we willingly die to ourselves by laying down our lives, our wants and our desires for the wants and desires of our King.

> *Let us fix our eyes on Jesus, the pioneer and perfecter of our faith,*
> *who **for the joy set before Him endured the cross,***
> Hebrews 12:2

And just what is it that our Father and our Lord Jesus want from us, what is it They desire? They want us to become sons and daughters after their own hearts. They want us to invite the Holy Spirit, the Spirit of Adoption, the Spirit of Grace and the Spirit of Truth into our hearts, so they can come into us and make us Their home. Then They want us to seek righteousness with everything we have so that we are able to imitate Jesus and walk in love everywhere we go, each and every day to a lost and dying world. And just exactly what is the benefit for such a commitment; eternal life! Selfishness and a lust for the things of the world are a very tempting and powerful Alternative, but I believe the Father is making us a fair and generous offer, and I'd also be willing to bet that there isn't a soul in hell that would not trade places with you in an instant for just one more chance to die to self, live in righteousness and walk in love.

The Father loves us, and when He looks at us, He remembers creating us from the dust of the earth and how He breathed life into us, so we became a living, breathing spirit in His image. But we rebelled and took on the very nature of the devil, so that we began to look, talk and think just like Satan. The Father then takes His Son and offers Him up on a tree as payment for our rebellion, and we are once again free to look just like Him. We were spiritually dead because of sin, but when Jesus was crucified and went to be with the Father, God does to us exactly as He did to Adam in the garden, what Jesus did to the disciples immediately after his resurrection; He breathed eternal life into them.

Atheists and agnostics have all kinds of reasons why they reject God, and more than likely a few bad experiences of people that improperly represented the Father and Jesus; experiences that cause them to be angry with God and doubt His love for them, or completely reject Him by denying His vary existence. Maybe it was a priest that molested them in their youth, a pastor that got caught in his own sin and let down the entire congregation, a father, a mother, an aunt or an uncle, a brother or a friend that professed being a Christian but looked just like the world. People are fallible, so please don't let anything they do, or have done keep you from your rightful heritage.

Many Christians get easily offended by people in the church and adopt a very cynical attitude towards it, causing them to stop attending altogether. It happens all the time, maybe they were treated badly; maybe it wasn't that they were treated badly, but that they were just ignored. Sometimes it's because the church didn't notice their so-called "Gift," and didn't put them in a "leadership position," one they thought they were ready for.

So many Christians go from church to church looking for someone to validate them, to notice and approve of them. It's all twisted stuff, demonically inspired thinking that comes because they never learned their identity, they never received the Spirit of Adoption, the Spirit of Grace and Truth and they obviously never sought out righteousness, because if they had...they'd never have gotten offended in the first place. Yet, they did get offended, and now they're hurt, angry and disappointed; they're children behaving as orphans. They never learned their created value to the Father, so they are always looking for and needing the approval of people. The only approval we need is the approval of our Father; anything else is from the wicked one with the sole intention of undermining our identity, assuming our authority and luring us back to the world

Jesus was tempted three times in the desert with the lust of the flesh, the lust of the eyes and the pride of life, but even with that, Satan's first two temptations came by way of Jesus' Identity, His son-ship. In the first temptation Satan said,

> ***"If you are the Son of God*** *tell these stones to become bread."* Luke 4:3

In the second temptation, the scripture says,

> ...⁵*Then the devil took Him to the holy city and set Him on the pinnacle of the temple.* ***"If You are the Son*** *of God," he said, "throw Yourself down. For it is written: 'He will command His angels concerning You,'* Luke 4:4

It is worth noting here that when Satan realized he wasn't able to undermine Jesus' identity, he tempted Him with authority next.

> *...Then the devil led Him up to a high place and showed Him in an instant all the kingdoms of the world.* ⁶*Satan said,* ***"I will give You authority over all these kingdoms*** *and all their glory. For* ***authority has been relinquished to me,*** *and I can give it to anyone I wish.* ⁷*So if You worship me, it will all be Yours."* Luke 4:5-7

There are times when people choose to get serious about God; they're done with it, tired of the rat-race and the mess they made of their life, so they decide to press in. They go after God, but if they press in with the wrong attitude or motives, they'll only come away more confused and filled with more doubt because God is not a Santa Claus God. The kind where kids jump in His lap, dig through His pockets, find a few quarters and go running to the store to buy a snack. Your Father wants to adopt you as His son, fill you with His Spirit and give you all His wonderful attributes and abilities. However, out of desperation and need, most people are just looking for God to solve their problems, fix the aftermath brought about as a result of their own sin and/or give them money and worldly stuff.

If you knock on the door of the Kingdom of God and choose to become a child, if you die to self, seek righteousness and ask for the Holy Spirit you'll never look like the world again, but like a child who is a spitting image of their parent. No matter how you look at this thing, it all begins with your identity as sons and daughters and any imbalances or deficiencies in life can always be traced back to a lack of one's identity. Your ability to properly see yourself as a son or a daughter is paramount to you reaching your potential. This is what I hear the father saying,

"If you knock on the door of My Kingdom, I will open it and My Spirit of Adoption will adopt you as My own. If you deny yourself, become My disciple and follow Me, if you seek Me and My righteousness as one seeks a treasure, I will fill you with perfect love and cast out every worldly spirit that has hindered you. If you diligently ask to be filled with My Spirit of Grace and Truth, and do not relent from this pursuit until I send Him; if that is your desire and not the things of the world, then I will clothe you with Power from on High, and infuse you with a supernatural ability to walk, talk, look, think and act like Jesus. Then Power and Authority will be given to you and boldness to preach My Word will be poured out on you as I extend My hand to perform signs, wonders and miracles through you. All that I have was given to Jesus and all He has is freely given to you if you receive by faith, My generous offer."

The Altar of Love, Part II

Chapter 7

Transformation

Your Father did not put His Son on the cross just to get you into heaven; He did it to get heaven into you.

If you learn who you are in Jesus, His life will begin to flow through you in truth. We cannot depend upon people to notice us, to like us or to validate us. People, even most Christians live their whole life needing to get something from people; some attention, some recognition, anything that makes them feel good about themselves to make it through another day. Most people, believers included, don't even really like who they are, but they desperately need everyone else to like them, so they feel fulfilled, but even that lasts only for the day. They'll need another round of validation from even more people to make it through tomorrow, and on and on it goes.

If someone does not affirm you, you are frustrated, if someone does not encourage you, you are discouraged, and God-forbid someone dislike you, but the Gospel will change all that, if it's taught correctly. We were not created to get up every day and live "the Christian life." That's like waking up and saying, "today, I'm going to have a good day," but then life happens and we lay awake at night wondering how it all went wrong.

The thing is, we were created to look like our Father, but most believers either do not know it or have no idea what that even looks like. To begin with, how about waking up excited to be alive, because:

1. The God of all creation loves you more than you can fathom.
2. He has more thoughts towards you than the grains of sand in the world, and those thoughts are always good and never evil.
3. He wants to have a close personal relationship with you.

4. He is jealous for you, and He wants to be the most important thing in your life; He does not want anything to come between the two of you.
5. He wants you to want Him the same way He wants you.
6. His desire is to live inside you; to give you a part of Him and walk with you daily.
7. He not only wants to give you a piece of Himself, but he wants to lavish many amazing spiritual gifts upon you.
8. He paid the highest price to purchase you that has ever been paid for anything in history; making you the most valuable commodity in the world.
9. He wants you to help Him run the family business; finding other orphans and adopting them as sons and daughters also.
10. He wants you to become a carbon copy of Jesus, and love everybody regardless of their situation.
11. He wants you to dominate everything the enemy brings your way with complete confidence and assurance that you can do what is necessary, because He is faithful to back you up and do what He said He will do.
12. He wants you so full of Jesus that anytime Satan tries to touch you with a trial, Jesus comes pouring out of you like a fire hose and gets all over the devil as well as everyone who witnesses it.
13. He wants you to trust Him in every situation, especially when you don't understand the how's and why's of your circumstance.

Discipleship

Becoming a disciple of Jesus is to have a consistent nature of loving Him so that His love for humanity can be clearly seen in you, and come out of you, every day all the time, not just when the stars align and you feel like it.

It's not about trying to be ok; it's being ok, regardless of your circumstances. It's not being ok if everything goes just right, its being ok even when you had the worst day you've ever had. People have a hard time understanding the fact that their joy is not supposed to be based upon their circumstances, but on the fact that He died for you so you could "become joy" to a lost and dying world. You were not put here to be loved, you were put here to "become love" to everyone you come in contact with. This way of thinking and living is hugely different from the way the world thinks, but I promise you that if you get a hold of this selfless attitude towards others, your life will change for the better, forever.

It's nothing more than a simple change of perspective, because you've been looking at your life from the wrong point of view. Your life was never supposed to be about you, or what makes you feel happy. It's not about what you need or what you can get from other people, and it was never about your best life now or what your Father can bless you with. It's about what you can give now, it's about what you can do for the One who suffered and died for you, who purchased you with His blood; it's about what He needs from you and who He needs you to be love to.

This is your "ah-ha" moment, when you come to terms with the fact that the world no longer revolves around you. Take repentance for instance; repentance does not have to be sorrow and crying, repentance is simply, "Oh wow, now I understand," because you are seeing things from a different perspective. All repentance really means is, "stop thinking like the world, change your mind and begin thinking like your Father."

If you change the way you think, it'll begin to change the way you see things and that will change the way you behave. I can tell you all about how much God loves you, but it's another thing entirely for you to know you are loved by the Father. I can describe to you about how merciful He is, but it's another thing for you to receive His mercy. It's one thing for me to tell you that God is forgiving, but it's another thing for you to know you are forgiven and live a life free of guilt, shame and condemnation.

Sin Conscious vs. Son Conscious

In order to get saved, a person must get a revelation that they need a savior, a come to Jesus moment, an understanding that they are a sinner in need of forgiveness. An honest heartfelt declaration that Jesus is Lord, but your Father does not want you to stay in that place, the devil does. Once true repentance is made, we are supposed to move from being sin conscious to SON conscious. We were orphans, but the Spirit of Adoption comes in and makes us sons and daughters. Unfortunately, most Christians never see themselves as adopted into the beloved and wander through their entire life behaving like orphans still, which was Satan's intended purpose of the OSAS and prosperity message. Think of yourself like an airport runway with God's grace and mercy landing on you all day, every day, but it cannot land on you unless and until you see yourself as a child who has been forgiven. You must see yourself as a child, beloved by a Father who has been waiting all your life for you to wake up, to "come to yourself," and come home. He's not angry at you for the time you spent away, He's just so excited and glad that you are home where He can Father you, because up till now, you've been fathered by the devil and **everything** you have ever learned is a lie.

You need to see yourself as a child whose Father needs a place to land in them so He can be a lamp to this dark and perverted world. You were never created to live for you, you were created to live for Him, and the sooner you come to terms with that, the better. Unfortunately, if you make this choice you most certainly will not have your best life now. How in the world did anyone get that out of what Jesus said or what the apostles went through? Christianity does not guarantee you a new car, a new house, or a great job. Jesus said, *"In this world you will have tribulations, but be of good cheer, for I have overcome the world."* Simply put, you should expect to have many difficulties in life, but in light of them all your Father wants you to have a "good attitude" in every situation, because He died on a cross for you to endure anything and everything the devil throws your way.

Treasures in Heaven

I know it doesn't sound like a fair trade-off or a great deal at first, but think of it as an investment for your retirement, your 401 k. People work their whole lives in difficult jobs because the retirement benefits are so good, so think of this as your retirement investment. Your entire life, your selfless walk of love towards all men is heaping up treasures in heaven for the day you retire from this world.

From the cross until now, Christians have suffered and died horrible, tragic deaths for their faith, but they did it with joy, and an expectation of being with Jesus in heaven. It used to be considered a "badge of honor" to suffer for Christ, and the apostles would brag about how many stripes they took for the sake of Him. Modern Christians have the good fortune to live at a time of peace, prosperity, ingenuity, and comfort, but Satan has skillfully used what should be a blessing to transform us into selfish, spoiled brats while yoking us to sin, and deceiving us into living like orphans again.

Your Father did not put His Son on the cross just to get you into heaven, He put Him there to get heaven into you, so you could walk and talk and think and act like what you were originally created to be...like Him. From as far back as you can remember, you've been trying to make your mark in the world. Trying to become someone you were never created to be, trying to fit in, trying to make it, trying to go along or get along, but nothing ever felt quite right. Even the ever so brief moments of success were followed by disappointments and for many of us, utter despair. But why? Because you were not created for you, you were not created to be used by the devil to kill, steal and destroy through. You were created to be a home for the God of all creation so He could love through you, bless through you, heal through you, and be the light on a hill to a lost and dying world; all through you. He's just so happy and excited at the thought of you waking up and taking your rightful place at His side.

Suddenly, nothing else begins to matter to you, because in your heart, you realize you are a son, a daughter and the same Holy Spirit who raised Jesus from the dead now lives inside you and nothing above the earth, on the earth or below the earth can ever change that. People may criticize you, mock you, insult you, use you, and abuse you, but it doesn't matter anymore, because you are a child whose Father loves and adores them and you live this life like every day is your last and every person you walk past is a potential brother or sister who should be standing beside you in the kingdom.

Knowing you are a Child of God, and that you were created so your Father could live in and through you, you now realize that nobody can take this away from you. Nothing and nobody can separate you from the love your Father has for you. The world may even take our Bibles someday, but they can't stop us from praying, they can't stop us from hearing His voice or keep us from entering into our secret place with Him, because of the intimacy of the relationship the Father provides us.

What can anyone do to you now that you know Him and are known by Him? If you are walking with Him inside you, and someone rejects you when you try to love them, they are not rejecting you, they are rejecting Him who lives inside you. Therefore, don't ever take it personally, not as long as Christ in you is your hope of glory. You don't get hurt or offended any longer, but you hurt for them because they do not know Him who lives in you. The root cause of all conflict is a result of Christ and Him crucified, and the absence of Him in the midst of the conflict. Your Father is trying to get you, or rather, the person you used to be, out of the way so He can come in you and teach you who you are in Him, so your light can shine before all men, that they may see the Father in and through you.

Suddenly you realize that you are a child, not a servant, not just a throw away, and He would never set you up to fail. In fact, the battle has already been won on your behalf; all you have to do is step in the ring so the referee can raise your hand and declare you the winner! You are in Him and He is in you, He will never leave or forsake you because He loves you. He's not sitting on the throne adding up all your failures, because He sees you the way He made you to be, more than a conqueror. He loves you and if He lives in you, all you need to do is get over yourself, get out of the way and let Him do what He does best; loving you and everyone around you through you!

Your Father is excited to live inside you; He's actually tickled pink whenever one of His children decides to come back home. He's not finding fault with you and He doesn't want you focusing on your own faults either. He wants us to stop focusing on sin altogether. Until we stop being sin conscious, and learn to become Son conscious, we'll never know what it truly means to be a son, and I'm here to tell you, it's the most amazing thing in the world. Jesus said, *"If you love me you will obey me,"* but He didn't say it with a tone of accusation. Why, because it's about relationship. It's like the time your 6 year old messed up, but instead of just punishing them out of disappointment and anger, you took the opportunity to talk to him and explain to him the purpose for your rule was to keep him from the hurt he just experienced in his disobedience. Then you give him a big hug to let him know that you still love him just as much as you did before the incident. Oh yea, and he's still grounded for the day.

The 21st Century Christian church has perverted the gospel by making it serve us, benefit us, bless us and provide for us, but so many people are discouraged because they feel like God has failed them, that He has not held up His end of the bargain. They've grown complacent with God or worse yet, they're angry with God because things have not turned out the way they wanted. And why, because we've preached a gospel that's all about what God can do for us, instead of transforming us into His image so He can actually use us wherever He needs us.

Sadly, we've fashioned our own god, an idol god, a Santa Clause god that doles out blessings based upon tithing; a god that grants parking spots, window seats, new cars and houses. We have become adults that behave like selfish, spoiled children who never matured; with our hands out just hoping and praying for another blessing, but that was never the purpose of the cross or the message of the gospel.

This life as a Christian is all about transformation first. Our Father wants to transform us into His image so He can live in and through us. If you miss transformation, you miss the entire point of the gospel. If you miss becoming the express image of Him who loves you, then you've missed the whole purpose of the cross. If we're always trying to find love, then we'll never become love, and we will never understand what Jesus was all about. Jesus did not hang on the cross to get you into heaven; He did it so you could become what he paid for, "love," to a selfish, loveless world. If,

> **The Kingdom of God is** *not a matter of eating and drinking, but*
> *of **righteousness, peace, and joy in the Holy Spirit.***
> Romans 14:17

And,

> *"...the Kingdom of God **is within you.**"* Luke 17:21

Then righteousness, peace and joy should be clearly evident on us and constantly flowing out of us to everyone we meet because of His Holy Spirit within us. Think about it, if the Kingdom of God is truly within us, then why are we still using God like a Genie in a bottle, praying for a bonus, a car, protection and peace? It's like we're using God to get stuff and make it through another day. That's the surest way to get discouraged, yet discouragement isn't even in the New Testament, it's not supposed to be a Christian attribute, because discouragement is of the world. After the resurrection of Jesus, believers didn't walk around discouraged. They walked with gladness while they were being hunted like animals, because they had hope for the joy that was set before them, even though they were being flogged, stoned to death, doused in oil and set on fire to be human torches to light the city streets at night. Yea, that is the way they treated Christians in the 1st century, and yet they were never discouraged. What about us, we're discouraged if our boss doesn't appreciate us, when our spouse isn't treating us the way we feel we deserve, or if our kids aren't behaving right, and we think that's normal.

Wherever there's discouragement there is obviously no conviction for change, because we think it's about us, it's our mentality, our perspective, our view on why we are here. Discouragement and discontent is all just selfishness rooted in the demonic. We let what other people say and do decide what and who we are, but that's a real problem if that person's name isn't Jesus. We wake up each day with all kinds of issues, but issues are not our problem, it's a lack of understanding of our identity that confounds us.

> *Wisdom is the principal thing; therefore, get wisdom. And in all your getting, get understanding.* Proverbs 4:7

It's what you don't know that'll destroy you, yet you grow up hearing things like, "what you don't know won't hurt you," but that's a flat out lie; any lack of understanding regarding God's Word will actually wreak havoc in every area of your life. Not to oversimplify the problem, but we've let so many really unimportant things matter most to us. Why do you think Jesus said, *"...seek ye first the Kingdom of God and His righteousness?"* Because if you seek ye first your needs, your wants, your desires and your well-being, you will grow bitter and resentful towards God when things go wrong.

So many Christians have come to the gospel for the benefit of "gaining things," but if our focus is on acquiring "things," one of those things will likely take the place of Jesus in our heart. We are called, but not to "be saved," we are called to "be disciples" whose sole purpose is to be salt and light unto the world, but how can you do that when you are all wrapped up in yourself and all the stuff you have or desire to accumulate. Jesus said,

> *"It is easier for a camel to go through the eye of a needle than for a rich man to enter the kingdom of God."* Mark 10:25

Now for those that have not read the Altar of Love, Part I, this is simply a metaphor with a very interesting story that is not talking about an actual camel going through the eye of a needle which is quite obviously impossible even if you liquefied it. It just means that it is very difficult for rich people to make it to heaven, because all their hope and faith is in their money, not in the Lord, therefore most wealthy people are unable to do it. Why? They have become so dependent upon their money and possessions that they would not be able to give them up for Jesus, placing them in higher esteem. Jesus said, *"If you love anything more than me, you are not worthy of me."* This is another big problem with the prosperity gospel, it places people in such a state that they would be unable to confess Christ if push came to shove and they were required to do so or face losing everything, even their life.

If the disciples who walked with Jesus for 3 years couldn't do it in the garden, do you think spoiled, spiritually lazy, totally faithless OSAS, hyper-grace Christians will be any different? Not bloody likely! I doubt very many OSAS, prosperity driven Christians would be able to let go of their precious "things," if their "neck" depended upon it. I suppose the OSAS preachers will come up with some grace rationale for taking the mark of the beast and still being saved. They'll probably say something like, "Oh, don't worry, God knows you need to eat, therefore if they tell you to get the mark or you cannot buy food, then just get the mark." Regardless, their faith, their hope and their trust is in the belongings they sought after instead of the Kingdom of God and His righteousness. It's in their wealth, not in the One who gave His life for them. They've taken the light of Jesus which is supposed to be inside them and placed it under a basket of possessions and things that hold them in bondage.

When Jesus said, you are either for me or against me, you either gather or you scatter, He was not talking about unbelievers and believers. You could be born again and see your need for a savior, but have a motive in your life that is contrary to the Kingdom of God and it'll work against everything He desires for you to achieve and become. You cannot name one place in scripture where selfishness and self-centeredness is permissible. With that said, how many sermons are being preached daily about getting blessed and receiving, and how many people get tricked into becoming Christians just for the blessings they're told they will receive and to fulfill their own desires? More than you will ever know.

I wonder how many Christians get up every day and walk by faith and not by need? Faith, like love and righteousness is an intrical part of our survival kit, and a whole new way of looking at things. Getting saved is likened to moving to a new country and learning a new language, the language of faith, love and righteousness. We must learn this new language in order to function as a new creation and as exiles in a world that considers us the aliens.

Don't ever forget this one important fact, this is Satan's domain, and he is the god of this world. Our homeland is heaven; we are sojourners here, exiles and ambassadors for our Father. An ambassador is never tangled up in the affairs of the country he's been assigned to, he never forgets his allegiance to his mother country, his loyalty is not confused and never in question, no matter how long he serves in the foreign land.

This is our new life now, complete with a new way of thinking. In all honesty, you shouldn't even call yourself a Christian unless you are willing to deny yourself, and seek righteousness, so we can look like Him. Everything in life that happen to you is designed to do whatever it takes to get you to the place where you look like the King of your homeland. Your Father loves you so much that He will go to extraordinary measures to mold you into the likeness of Jesus. The more you resist, the greater the struggle, but the sooner you die to yourself, the easier the journey.

Paul said, whether we live or die, we are supposed to do everything like we're doing it for Jesus, because it's all about Him. Leading Israel into the dessert was not so much about getting them out of Egypt, it was mainly about getting Egypt out of them, and just like most Christians, Israel never got it, they never understood that God was trying to purge the world out of them so they could depend upon Him. We, too, will spend some time in our own dessert, it's called our winnowing, and how much time we spend there is dependent upon us, our attitude and our willingness to give up our own self-preservation and die so we can live to love. Then, being filled with the Holy Spirit, love and righteousness can flow through us to everyone around us. Israel spent 40 years, Jesus spent 40 days, how long will it take you to die to yourself, and give up your life for Him?

> *Whatever you do, work at it with all your heart, as though you were working for the Lord and not for people.* Colossians 3:23

This life is not about living the good life and then dying; Christians never really die anyway, we are eternal. Neither is it about the faith to get blessings and special favor; God will do those things for you if are willing to die to yourselves and seek His righteousness, simply because you are His child and He loves you. Faith is a perspective you live by now, a simple confidence in your identity as a child and belief in your authority. There are times faith is described as a tool you can use to move a mountain. If He is in you now, and you finally understand who you are and what you were created for, you live by that truth as a Child of the Father, and you no longer let your past, your color, your parents or your circumstances determine who you are, because none of those things define you. The only thing that should define you is your Father, and what He thinks about you, what He says about you; that is who you are now.

Jesus never let the religious leaders define Him, and he never allowed them to undermine what he knew to be true. Even knowing what evil was in their hearts, He never let their sanctimonious thoughts, rude comments, criticizing statements and their ridiculous questions, which were only put to Him to entrap Him; He never let any of that confuse His identity, or negatively influence his walk of righteousness. Jesus never let any of those things change His attitude, His response or the way He thought about them, because He knew who He was and what His goal was. He knew that none of them had the faintest idea who they were. They were orphans whose Creator loved them enough to send His Son to make a way for them to become children. They had no clue that they were being held captive as slaves to sin in a system designed to kill, steal and destroy them. It was that lack of understanding along with their father, the devil, which fueled their hatred of the very One sent to save them. In their hatred and rejection of Jesus, they also rejected the God of the universe, the God who loved them.

When we come to the understanding of who we are as children of the Living God, as heirs to the throne, seated in heavenly places with our King Jesus; if we get that understanding deep within our hearts, our minds and our souls, we too can walk un-offended, un-insulted, and without need. Neither will we live for the want and desire of worldly things which are only used by the enemy to feed the habit of a sinful nature anyway. When we realize that we are children of our Father, with a purpose and a goal, like Jesus, we no longer desire to walk in the lustful flesh, but we will *walk in the spirit* as we were created to. This is what Paul meant when he said, "Christ in you the hope of glory".

> *I say then:* **Walk in the Spirit, and you shall not fulfill the lust of the flesh.** Galatians 5:6

> *For those who live according to the flesh set their minds on the things of the flesh, but those who live according to the Spirit, set their minds on the things of the Spirit.*
> Romans 8:5

Let me break this down as simply as possible, Jesus was able to walk in the Spirit because He fully understood His identity; He knew who He was and what His mission was. Do you? He did not entangle Himself in the affairs of the world, because He understood the things of the world were only there to distract Him, lure Him away from His calling, and entice Him to sin so it could kill Him and take Him to hell. If we can grasp the concept of our identity as Children of God, it will change our perspective so that we are no longer looking at this thing through eyes of selfishness.

The world is Satan's giant, elaborate death trap, and he spends your entire life trying to figure out exactly what you are susceptible to, what he can use to drag you into sin so he can take you with him to where he will spend eternity, because misery loves company. However, if we can remove ourselves from our own selfish ambitions, rise above our limited point of view, and see it from a better perspective, it will change the way you think about everything. Ultimately, it will change you.

Imagine wandering through a maze with no hope of escape and then suddenly rising up to get a bird's eye view so you could easily see the way out. You were really, really lost, but if you get this you will be really, really found. You were really, really blind but now you can see perfectly. Like Paul, we are adopted children now, called to be bondservants for our Father and our King who died a horrible death to save us from an eternity of torture and hellfire. He died such a horrendous death to infuse us with righteousness, regain our authority and fill us with His Spirit which empowers us with dynamite power to perform signs, wonders and miracles on his behalf. If that doesn't motivate you to get with the program, what will?

> *No soldier in active service entangles himself in the affairs of everyday life, so that he may please the one who enlisted him as a soldier.* 2 Timothy 2:4

I've gotten to where I no longer ask believers how they are doing, because the answers hurt my heart and they almost always give up their authority with their words as they confess two or more trials and ask me to keep them in prayer. Don't misunderstand me, I have no problem with a request for prayer, but it only serves to prove my point that most Christians are just using God to help them out of a difficult situation, and that's exactly where Satan wants them, frustrated, defeated and disgusted.

The alternative is to let His life come into you as you get a revelation of your identity, and begin to seek His righteousness. Then, if you determine in your heart to go after His Holy Spirit with all the tenacity of one who seeks a treasure, He will begin teaching you, changing you, conforming you, correcting you and training you to look like Him so His light can now shine through you so you can walk as He walked, and change the atmosphere of everyplace you go, each and every day.

Whoever claims to abide in Him must walk as Jesus walked. 1 John 2:6

It's as if the entire theme of this book is summed up in the revelation of the verse above, and as powerful and enlightening as it is, how many of us read it a thousand times and never saw it? So, here's the question, are you a Christian, are you a Child of God, is Jesus Lord of all or not Lord at all? If so, it's time to get on board, stop playing Christian and actually become one. This is a call to get Christians saved. It is time to come to terms with the fact that this world is not for you, it belongs to the devil, and it is his domain. You are in hostile territory, behind enemy lines so start behaving like it. In order to do that, you have to see yourself the way your Father sees you; not as a sinner saved by grace, but as a beloved child, walking in love and righteousness, and empowered by the Spirit of Grace to become the person you were created to become; the likeness of Him who died to purchase your freedom from the prison of sin. Romans 8:29 says that Jesus was the firstborn among many brethren.

*For those whom He foreknew, He also predestined **to be conformed into the image of His Son**, that He would be the firstborn among many brothers and sisters."* Romans 8:29

It is time for you to decide whom you will serve, and if it's the Father you choose, then you must jump in completely. You were not chosen before time began to straddle the fence with one foot in the world and one in the kingdom; Satan owns the fence. You were predestined to be conformed to the image of Jesus, so that you could walk in love and righteousness as He did. it's as simple as that. That is what Jesus meant when He said,

"Peace be with you; as the Father has sent Me, I also send you." John 20:21

> *"Truly, truly, I say to you, whoever believes in me will also do the works that I do; and greater works than these will he do, because I am going to the Father."* John 14:12

The Word says, *"... as He is, so are we, in this world."* We need to think about what Jesus and our Father are saying here. When people in the world see us, we must be distinguishable from the world, not a mirror image of it. Let's stop playing pretend Christian and make it our goal to become what He was and what He is saying and stop reading our Bibles like God's Word was written for someone else. But you say, "That's not my thing," well I'm here to tell you, if you're going to call yourself a Christian, it is your thing. God wants to live inside you so He can love and shine through you, but that cannot happen until you die to yourself and seek His righteousness first. And you don't need to try to look for Him, if you are a believer, He's been chasing you this whole time. People...He's right there, He never gave up on you and He never left you. If you would just stop running away from Him and turn towards Him, you're likely to run smack dab into Him.

So many well intentioned Christians cry themselves to sleep every night because of the way they are living. Having knocked on the door of His Kingdom, they received the Truth of Jesus and the purpose of the cross when God revealed it to them. Their heart is spiritually alive now, but they don't look or live like it. Neither do they know how to change from who they used to be. The Father has taken out their heart of stone and given them a new heart of flesh, so for the first time they are convicted by the things that never bothered them before. But now they're tormented all night because they think that the way they are behaving is who they are, when who they are now is found in Christ who died for them. You have to stay in that place where you identify not with any behavior but with the One who gave himself for you, so you can be free from whom you used to be.

But God proves His love for us in this: While we were still sinner's, Christ died for us. Romans 5:8

The Guilt of Sin Or Apathy Towards It

As a believer, your identity as a beloved Child of God is way more important than you will ever know. You will be convicted of habits, of vices, of behavior and attitudes that never used to bother you, but you're not who you used to be so you are seriously conflicted for the first time in your life, and the last thing you need right now is a typical OSAS message that all but encourages you to stay the same and continue in sin. Neither is it a time for you to hear enticing messages about prosperity that will just propel you back into selfishness which only serves to feed sinful behavior. The truth of the matter is that the conviction you are experiencing is a good place to be, because for the first time in your life sin is grieving your heart, but if you are not being taught that, Satan will either heap condemnation and shame upon you, or deceive you with false hyper-grace and harden your heart to accept or even embrace the sin as natural. Most Christians either live on a roller coaster of sin, condemnation, guilt and repentance, or complete apathy to it, but regardless of which way you turn, it all stems from a lack of identity, the need for righteousness and the absence of the Holy Spirit.

If we come to know and understand that we are children of a loving God and not orphans of the world, and if we sincerely go to our Father after a mistake and thank Him that He sent His Son so we could be free from sin, instead of wallowing in regret and self-loathing, the Spirit of Grace will begin to do what He was sent to do, and that is to correct us and teach us how to walk in love and righteousness. Now, instead of crying and grieving about a transgression, thank the Father that you are not that person any longer, for whom the Son sets free is free indeed, and after awhile you will notice that you no longer want to do those worldly things that once brought you pleasure.

At first sin will condemn you, but if you seek His righteousness condemnation will stop as He begins to convict you of sin. If you continue to seek righteousness, sin will begin to prick your heart until it eventually becomes disgusting to you. This is right where He wants you and right where you want to be, because now you ask for Him to give you the one thing He's wanted to give you since you were born, His Holy Spirit. When you do, the Spirit of Grace & Truth will remove your desire for sin while teaching you, convicting you, correcting you and training you how to walk in love and righteousness.

But woe to anyone who has fallen prey to the OSAS lie, and walks about sinning without any remorse or regret, because *the wages of sin is (spiritual) death* and the word "repentance" is not even part of their vocabulary. Their love has grown cold and their hearts are filled with stones from all the unrepentant sin they so capriciously engage in daily as they repeat the lie Satan has masterfully whispered in their ear. "My Father loves me, He's just not happy with me right now." Their false doctrine has convinced them that Paul was talking to the world and not them when he said,

> *...sexual immorality, impurity, and debauchery; ²⁰idolatry and sorcery; hatred, discord, jealousy, and rage; rivalries, divisions, factions, ²¹and envy; drunkenness, orgies, and the like...* **will not** *inherit the kingdom of God.*
> Galatians 5:19-21

But Paul was speaking to Christians and it's proven by his next statement.

> *... I warn you, as I did before,* **whosoever** *practices such things will not inherit the kingdom of God.* Galatians 5:21

The definition of whosoever is anyone, not just unbelievers, and Paul wouldn't say, *whosoever practices such things will not inherit the kingdom of God*, unless it was a very real possibility.

> *Do you not know that the wicked will not inherit the kingdom of God?*
> *...But you were washed, you were sanctified, you were justified, in the name of the Lord Jesus Christ and by the Spirit of our God.*
> 1 Corinthians 6:9-11

Paul is trying to get them to understand that the Father wants to **wash you**, **sanctify you** and **justify you**, so that you no longer want to live in willful, deliberate sin as in the past. When you knock on the Kingdom door, God will open to you His good treasures, He will wash you clean from all your past sins in the blood of Jesus, He will sanctify you by removing your desire for sin thereby justifying you holy in His sight, and He will do all that by His Holy Spirit that makes His home in you. But none of that is even possible for the OSAS who think they have no need to humble themselves, repent and seek righteousness.

Now, for those of you that have a heart of flesh, those that still feel guilt and remorse when they knowingly sin, I say hallelujah, because God loves a contrite heart! Who you are is not what you do for a living, nor is it who you used to be when you were under the law of sin and death while you were in the world. You are not the bad things you did, the things you may currently be doing, and you most certainly are not what someone did to you. Who you are is found in Christ who died for you so He could dwell in you, but that will never happen until conviction of the behavior of the old you occurs first. There are two you's sharing space within your mortal body, the new you that desperately wants to follow Jesus and the old you, the dead man that wants desperately to hang on to the old way of thinking, and the old way of behaving.

Don't freak out, it's a good thing, embrace the conviction, just don't let it condemn you. Thank your Father that you are transforming from who you used to be into who He made you to be; a child of the living God, an heir to the throne, and a new creation in Christ Jesus.

Whatever you do, don't focus on the sin, focus on the relationship, focus on Christ in you and who your Father says you are. Conviction is the Holy Spirit moving you, prodding you, and encouraging you to die to the old you. It's your new man, the Spirit of God that has come to life within you, grieving the old you, the old behavior; stay in that place, live there and little by little you will watch as those old vices and behaviors simply melt away because you are no longer the person you used to be. That man is dead now and the only thing that remains is the experience and knowledge you gained having come through it; experience and knowledge God will use to encourage and sow seeds into others with the same or similar battles. You are now a disciple of your King and you live to die for Him, because He died for you.

I've heard so many believers pour out their hearts before God confessing things that grieved them, and because of their false understanding of grace, they try to excuse themselves saying, "Ugh, I'm such an idiot for doing that again, but I know that God loves me no matter what," and while that is true, God does love them no matter what, that is not the issue. They have fallen into a viscous cycle of sin, guilt, shame and repentance, because "no matter what," now defines them; it has identified them and they never get free from sin, because they think it's just who they are.

Your Father does not want you to stop with "He loves me no matter what," that's a given, but His love is designed to transform you into the likeness of Jesus and get you out of that wrong identity. He wants to empower you to stop practicing the things that are breaking, condemning and tormenting your heart; things that will ultimately cause a separation in the relationship if and when condemnation creeps in.

> *The eye is the lamp of the body. So if your eye is clear,*
> *your whole body will be full of light.* Matthew 6:22

There was a time in your life that you did things and it did not matter, but that was then, now your heart calls you and you see things for what they truly are. Your eye is now clear and your whole body is filling with light. You may do something small now, something that would not have bothered you a week ago, but now your heart is convicted and you think, "oh my goodness, what am I doing?" Eventually, you will catch yourself just thinking a thought that offends you and you will say to yourself, "why would I even think like that?"

Do not despair, but rather rejoice, and thank your Father, because a month ago you would have done that same thing and not thought twice, but now you're offended by the mere thought of it. How far you have come in such a short time, your seed of righteousness has taken root and is doing what it is designed to do. Your clear eye has allowed His light to enter you and you finally understand your new identity. The Holy Spirit is teaching you, convicting you, correcting you and training you in righteousness; His Truth is working in you now. The old you is dead, the Spirit of Grace & Truth are taking over and transformation from the inside out has begun. This is where you live now as your Father gladly, lovingly molds you into His likeness.

While your spirit man is alive now, you have to continue to feed him daily by reading your Word and spending time in prayer. This is war, and there will be a battle raging in your soul for your flesh and the winner will be the one you feed. If you were a king at war and you stopped sending food and supplies to the infantry on the front lines of battle, they will grow weak and weary; afterward discouragement will cause them to begin losing whatever ground they gained previously. Likewise, if you do not read your Word and spend time in prayer, the world will feed your flesh and you will see old habits and old behaviors rise back up and try to take back the ground they lost. But if you feed your newly reborn spirit man with the Word of God and dedicate time to your Father in prayer, your spirit will grow to be a giant and it will overpower your flesh.

Furthermore, this is a lifetime battle, because your enemy will never stop looking for an opportunity to destroy you. Your relationship with your Father must be maintained at all costs by reading and praying for as long as you are alive. If you read your Bible once or twice and think you've got this thing, that you don't need to read it any longer, you will most certainly fall; it's just a matter of time. Never forget what Jesus said, *"Seek ye first the Kingdom of god and His righteousness..."*

> **All Scripture is** *God-breathed* **and is useful** *for instruction, for conviction, for correction, and* **for training in righteousness**, *2 Timothy 3:16*

If we seek His righteousness and all Scripture is for the instruction, conviction, correction and training in righteousness then reading His Word is the way in which you learn how to walk in righteousness. In doing so, we give no place to the enemy; if conviction does reveal an indiscretion immediately confess it to the Father, and begin to speak life over yourself. "I thank you Father that you are teaching me in righteousness, convicting my heart to know and see what it means to live Godly, correcting me in wisdom so that I don't fall back into that behavior again and training me in justice so that I shine like Jesus to those around me. I thank you that I am not that person any longer, that's not who you created me to be, I was made in the image and likeness of Jesus, I am a Child of God, an heir to the throne, adopted into the beloved".

> *From the fruit of his mouth a man's belly is filled; with the harvest from his lips he is satisfied.* [21]*Life and death are in the power of the tongue, and those who love it will eat its fruit.* Proverbs 18:21

This is where you start to take back all the ground the enemy has ever stolen from you because of your worldly upbringing. Do not give one inch to condemnation, this is not entirely your fault, you were born into this system. From the time you were a baby and your mother took your binky, you cried until she gave it back. You didn't learn to be selfish, you were born that way, but God sent His son to destroy the power, the authority and the hold that sin and selfishness has over you; not so you could continue to sin and get away with it, but so you could be free from the desire of it.

> *My little children, I am writing these things to you **so that you may not sin**. But if anyone does sin, we have an advocate with the Father, Jesus Christ the righteous.* 1 John 2:1

You were born into selfishness, you were raised in selfishness and you have lived selfishly your entire life; we all did. Most Christians, if they are being honest, will attest to the fact that they never really changed all that much after their conversion because they never learned this truth. All they ever heard was to "give," because if you give you will receive, therefore if you want to receive more…give more! That, my friend, is a purely selfish motive, it is diametrically opposed to the commandment of love, because love gives, expecting nothing in return.

Without the conviction of righteousness, Satan knows that willful, deliberate sin will give him the authority and power over you that he needs to control you. Among other things, he will introduce condemnation, and within a very short time, condemnation will drag you right back to the person you were before you became enlightened. It happens all the time, so let conviction be your compass, and never, I repeat, NEVER allow yourself to be satisfied with even a little sin, because even a little dog poop ruins the entire chocolate cake.

Seeking righteousness releases conviction on your heart, and conviction produces Godly sorrow. If you make a misstep now that righteousness is what you seek, Godly sorrow is revealed to you by the Spirit of Truth; He's the same Holy Spirit that baptized you when you went into your prayer room, closed the door and begged the Lord for Him; that Holy Spirit.

> *Godly sorrow brings repentance that leads to salvation without regret, but worldly sorrow brings death.* 2 Corinthians 7:10

The Spirit of Truth produces Godly sorrow which brings repentance, not condemnation, but take a moment to notice exactly what the repentance of

Godly sorrow leads to; it leads to salvation, to eternal life, which disproves the OSAS theory and their unrepentant sin.

On the other hand, worldly sorrow produces regret which brings death…Spiritual Death! When you sin without righteousness, you hide your face from God and put on fig leaves and cry about your mistakes. You become sin conscious and regret wraps up your identity in the sinful behavior, obscuring your true identity which is revealed in what He did on the cross.

Some pastors preach that we just need to try harder, we need to discipline ourselves better or else we will misrepresent the cross. They will tell you that every time you behave poorly or sin, it's hypocrisy and you had better just stop. But that's not fair, because all that is doing is making the behavior your identity. They're saying that who you are is what you did or what you are doing, and you had better stop that right now! However, if that was even remotely true, Jesus would not have had to do what He did on the cross.

If it was as easy as will power, there'd be no need for grace or mercy on the earth, only determination, perseverance and fortitude. The Bible says, *"the just shall live by faith,"* not will-power and self-discipline. Now there are components of discipline that are important in your walk with God, but under different circumstances. If you wake up and decide you are too tired to read your Bible or spend time in prayer, that is a time to discipline yourself to do it whether you feel like it or not, because we cannot let our feelings rule us.

Don't ever read your Bible to memorize scripture to impress people with fancy prayers, and don't read out of obligation, but read for one purpose and one purpose only, to get to know your Father. This time of reading, this time of fellowship can be likened to a form of fasting, because sometimes my flesh won't want to, so I need to discipline it and tell it to be quiet because my heart wants to hear… NO, my heart needs to hear from my Father today and every day. We have to learn to stop living by how we feel, because our feelings will deceive us. I have spent countless hours listening to people complain about their feelings, brought on by past experiences and if a minister doesn't understand the power of identity, he'll just try to get them to feel better in the moment, but that's never going to help them, it's nothing more than a band aid on a bullet wound.

Ministering to one's emotions and feelings will just keep sensuality alive in that person. Then, their whole pursuit of counseling hinges upon making them feel better in the moment, but without a true understanding of one's identity and a sincere pursuit of righteousness, their just another bad day away from devastation again. How they are feeling now is based upon how they are doing. When things are going well, they are feeling good, but the moment things don't go their way, they are back to feeling depressed again. The kids aren't acting right, so they're frustrated, their spouse is not treating them the way they feel they deserve, so they feel rejected, their boss just stuck them with the worst job, again, so they're angry. The church didn't recognize their gifting and overlooked them while assigning ministries, now they're offended.

But it's all just a lie, because it's what you know and believe that should be determining how you are doing. It's who Jesus is, what He did for you and who you were adopted to become now that righteousness is your ambition; THAT, is what should be ruling your emotions. Why? Because it's not about you...wait, it is about you; it's about you being transformed to the image of the One who purchased you. And when you finally realize that, you will begin to see and understand that other people behave the way they do for the very same reason you misbehaved; an improper, misunderstood identity, coupled with little or no righteousness, because they do not have the Holy Spirit.

We all have them, a twisted uncle, an alcoholic father, a mother who never knew how to show love because she was never loved; Satan uses these people like pawns to keep us hurt and in bondage, but we cannot allow people who never knew their identity and what they were created for, to rule over us, our emotions, our thoughts and our behavior. A proper identity as an adopted Child of God, along with a seed of righteousness growing in our heart, we begin to understand that people from our past were just selfish orphans without hope too. That does not excuse what they did, but our identity as well as the seed of righteousness within us teaches us, convicts us, corrects us and trains us to forgive because we were forgiven. Since we were shown mercy, we extend mercy, because if we got what we deserved, we'd be destined for hell.

God is love, and the truth is that if God made man in His image, then He made man in the image of love; not just to love, but to be love. God made us to represent love to a lost and dying world. God is amazing, He is fully confident and fulfilled in who He is. He's not lonely, or aggravated or bored or brokenhearted, because He is the epitome of selfless love. Your parents may have meant well when they said, "Oh honey, you just broke Gods heart," but that's not even possible. You couldn't do anything that was capable of breaking His heart for you, and now that you have been adopted, *"...where sin abounds, grace abounds even more."* He's not broken because of what you just did, and He's not asking the angels to minister to Him because you rebelled.

He is Love and He does not seek His own desires, He seeks us. We, on the other hand have been self-driven, self-centered, self-conscious, self-defending, and self-servingly selfish from before we can remember, but the cross is saying, "It's not about you now, in fact, it was never about you, you just didn't know it, therefore die to you so you can live for Him through righteousness."

Let's stop "doing church," it's time to die to ourselves and become the church to everyone we meet. It's time to put selfishness aside, and step into the understanding of your new identity as a child of the Most High God. It's time for all Christians to come to the knowledge of the truth, repent, seek righteousness, get filled with His Spirit and be saved.

The Lord is not slow to fulfill His promise as some understand slowness, but is patient with you, not wanting anyone to perish **but everyone to come to repentance**. 2 Peter 3:9

Remember, Godly sorrow produces repentance and repentance brings salvation. Jesus said, *"If **any man** come after me...."* What an awesome statement, "Any man" that means we're all invited to the wedding, yet not all of us are willing to go, and it's heartbreaking, because only a very few are willing to let go and die to the things of the world so they may live.

People often say stuff like, "life's a grind," or "life's a b*tch," but it's really not, life is a gift and you only have a small window of opportunity to live it with the Spirit of the Living God on the inside of you. His desire is not to fulfill your wants, your needs, or your earthly desires, because those things have no lasting value to Him or you. Those things will not benefit you one bit when your time has ended here and you stand before Him in judgment.

At best, those things will distract you from your true calling, and cause you to forget how to rely on your Father and live by faith. At worst, they will deceive you, desensitizing you and drag you back to old habits and desires. All those things, all the things that the world is seeking after will be burned up in the end and counted as rubbish, so why would He desire to give you anything that not only has no lasting value, but also causes you such harm? His desire for you is to fulfill everything you were created for, to adopt you as His son or daughter and to watch with joy as you die to self and come alive for Him. He longs to see His righteousness blossom in you, to get His Holy Spirit and all His gifts in you and watch adoringly as you flow in them while becoming love to everyone He brings along your path. That is His goal and purpose for your life.

I know I railed against the prosperity message a lot, but the truth of the matter is that you will never out-give God in anything, ever. Giving and receiving has its place in the Kingdom of God, but it's our motive that dictates the outcome. The absolute best attitude towards giving is summed up in this, my favorite proverb:

> *Two things I asked of You, Do not refuse me before I die: Keep*
> *deception and lies far from me, Give me neither poverty nor riches;*
> *Feed me with the food that is my portion, Otherwise, I may have too*

much and deny You, saying, 'Who is the LORD?' Or I may become poor and steal, profaning the name of my God. Proverbs 30:7-9

The End ...is never the End; it's just the beginning of Eternity!

About The Author

Francis J. Santarose, an apostle of God and servant of Jesus Christ, was called to be a teacher of the Gospel by the Holy Spirit. Santarose, an 8th Don, Grand Master Tae Kwon-Do instructor was saved in 1991, and created a Christian children's ministry called, KID FIT, through his martial arts school, United Tae Kwon-Do, in Houston, Texas. Santarose franchised 22 Christian youth sports camps from 1992 to 2014. He is now a lecturer, Bible teacher, and guest speaker at Encourage Christian Academy, Texas Bible Institute, and Believers World Outreach Men's Retreat. He, also, serves as an associate pastor at Christ Over Our Lives Ministries Prison Outreach. In recent years, Santarose has been sought after for his work to remove demons, illnesses, and brokenness from people who are suffering these afflictions, to restore lasting healing in God's Children.

Special thanks to Katerina Rainier for creating the book cover and Christopher Santarose for creating the Altar of Love illustration on the first page.

www.ingramcontent.com/pod-product-compliance
Lightning Source LLC
Chambersburg PA
CBHW080527170426
43195CB00016B/2494